Common UNIX Printing System

MICHAEL R. SWEET

201 West 103rd Street, Indianapolis, Indiana 46290

Common UNIX Printing System

Copyright © 2002 by Sams Publishing

International Standard Book Number: 0-672-32196-3

Library of Congress Catalog Card Number: 2001089505

Printed in the United States of America

First Printing: August 2001

04   03   02   01   4 3 2 1

Trademarks

Warning and Disclaimer

Associate Publisher
Jeff Koch

Acquisitions Editor
Kathryn Purdum

Development Editor
Mark Renfrow

Managing Editor
Matt Purcell

Project Editor
George E. Nedeff

Copy Editors
Cynthia Fields
Margo Catts
Karen A. Gill

Indexer
Larry Sweazy

Proofreader
Teresa Stephens

Technical Editor
Tim Hicks

Team Coordinator
Vicki Harding

Interior Designer
Gary Adair

Cover Designer
Alan Clements

Page Layout
Lizbeth Patterson

Contents at a Glance

Contents

4 Printing with CUPS   **69**

17   Writing Printer Drivers for CUPS   333

18   Writing Backends for CUPS   363

About the Author

Michael Sweet is co-owner of Easy Software Products, a small software firm specializing in Internet and printing technologies. He first started using a computer terminal at the age of 6 and sold his first program at age 12. Michael's obsession with printing and graphics led him to develop image-printing software for dot-matrix and later inkjet printers. After graduating with a bachelor's degree in computer science from the SUNY Institute of Technology in Utica/Rome, he moved to Maryland to pursue a career in real-time computer graphics for the Navy.

The draw of printing was too much. After a few years working for the Navy, Michael again began writing printer drivers. After releasing a freeware program called "topcl," he went on to found Easy Software Products and develop the highly successful ESP Print software. In 1997, Michael began work on the Common UNIX Printing System, and in 1999, his company released CUPS under the GNU GPL license and ESP Print Pro as a commercial product.

Aside from writing printer drivers, Michael is also author or co-author of several books, including the *Serial Programming Guide for POSIX Operating Systems* and the *OpenGL Superbible*. When he has free time, he enjoys cycling, photography, playing the trumpet, and travelling with his wife, Sandra.

About the Technical Editor

Tim Hicks is a Senior Unix Engineer for HomeSide Lending, Inc. He is an HP Certified IT Professional in HP-UX Systems Administration and has been working extensively with HP-UX 10.10–11.00 as well as some work with Solaris 8, AIX 4.1, FreeBSD, and RedHat 6.2. He has an in-depth knowledge and experience with Highly Available Clusters using HP' MC/ServiceGuard, HP-UX 11.00, and Oracle 8.05, as well as Sybase 11. He is currently implementing Storage Area Networks with EMC Fabric Directors and Switches. Tim graduated from Florida State University with a B.S. in both Management Information Systems and Finance.

Dedication

For Sandra, my best friend and love of my life.

Acknowledgments

Writing a book is no easy task, and it takes dedication and sacrifice to make it all happen. None of this would be possible without my wife Sandra at my side. She has given me years of support and encouragement for everything I do, and never once has complained about the sometimes long hours I work on my craft. I can't begin to say how lucky I feel to have her in my life. Every day begins anew, exciting and refreshing and loving with you.

My life as a computer scientist started with my parents. Thanks, Dad, for bringing that first terminal home when I was 6, and Mom, for putting up with the computer books at the dinner table. You always gave me what I needed, whether it was Legos, books, or computers. I feel so very fortunate to have such loving parents.

My friends Andy and Tammy have walked the tricky path of running a computer software company with me; thanks for being a second family. I don't think we'd be as successful as we are without our friendship.

Jim is the person that pointed out that our little printer driver utility was more important than another 3D modeler. Thanks, Jim, for helping us see the forest for the trees.

I'd like to thank Carl Uno Manros, chairperson of the Internet Printing Protocol working group and the man who put the bug in my ear to write a printing book for IPP. His steady hand, even during sometimes heated debate among the IPP working group participants, has helped create a network printing protocol that everyone can be proud of and use.

I'd also like to thank the folks at Sams Publishing for seeing the potential of this book. Katie Purdum has worked with me almost from the beginning, and her support and enthusiasm made writing the book a joy. My project editor George Nedeff as well as editors Margo Catts, Cynthia Fields, Tim Hicks, and Mark Renfrow all contributed greatly to the consistency, accuracy, and readability of the book. Finally, enough can't be said for the production staff who take the final text, images, and figures and turn them into an actual book. The amount of work that is put into each and every book boggles my mind.

CUPS wouldn't be possible without the many contributions from the open source community. L. Peter Deutsch developed the Ghostscript software that CUPS uses to support non-PostScript printers, and Derek Noonburg developed the Xpdf software that is used to print PDF files. Crutcher Dunnavant, Han Holl, Till Kamppeter, Sebastian Krahmer, Robert Krawitz, Johnny Lam, Jeff Licquia, Kurt Pfeifle, Klaus Singvogel, Grant Taylor, and many others have contributed greatly to the success and stability of the CUPS software.

Tell Us What You Think!

As the reader of this book, *you* are our most important critic and commentator. We value your opinion and want to know what we're doing right, what we could do better, what areas you'd like to see us publish in, and any other words of wisdom you're willing to pass our way.

As an Associate Publisher for Sams Publishing, I welcome your comments. You can fax, e-mail, or write me directly to let me know what you did or didn't like about this book—as well as what we can do to make our books stronger.

Please note that I cannot help you with technical problems related to the topic of this book, and that due to the high volume of mail I receive, I might not be able to reply to every message.

When you write, please be sure to include this book's title and author as well as your name and phone or fax number. I will carefully review your comments and share them with the author and editors who worked on the book.

Fax: 317-581-4770

E-mail: feedback@samspublishing.com

Mail: Jeff Koch
            Associate Publisher
            Sams Publishing
            201 West 103rd Street
            Indianapolis, IN 46290 USA

INTRODUCTION

The History of Printing in Unix

In the beginning of human history, knowledge was passed from person to person and generation to generation through direct, spoken communication. Over the millennia this knowledge transfer has changed from drawings on walls of caves, stone tablets, scrolls, and finally flat, printed, paper. Improvements in communication have driven technological and social change.

Throughout the history of computing, printed communication has played a major role in the development and improvements in computers and peripherals. It is not surprising, then, that in the early days of Unix the first killer app was a word processor. With word processing, lawyers, academics, journalists, and scientists were able to better communicate. The line printer daemon ("LPD") was developed to spool and send the print files to the printer. Originally developed for communication with text printers, LPD can send any kind of file to a printer. Later incarnations of Unix added a new line printer system ("LP"), which was incompatible with the old LPD but supported options for print jobs and filtering of the job files. However, very little has changed for Unix printing over the 30 years since Unix was first created—applications produce output suitable for the printer, and the spooler sends this file to the printer.

Printing from Personal Computers

When the IBM Personal Computer appeared in 1981, it duplicated the Unix printing model. Applications came with a certain knowledge of the escape codes and capabilities of popular printers, and users could tell those applications which codes to use for their particular printer. If you wanted to print files in the background, a "print" command was available that would spool jobs to a disk and print them while you worked on something else.

As printers began to support graphics, applications had to support numerous different command sets and capabilities, as well as mixed text and graphics. The complexity of the software used to communicate with printers soon began to rival the applications themselves, and it wasn't long before these "printer drivers" were an industry of their own. Unfortunately, a printer driver for one application rarely worked with another.

Apples' release of the MacIntosh computer changed how printing was done on the personal computer. Designed from the beginning to be a desktop publishing system, the MacIntosh abstracted the printing interface away from the application. Applications only had to tell the printing system where and what to print, and the printing system would translate that request into the desired output on the selected printer. Printer drivers were provided with MacOS or with the printer you purchased for your printer. The same driver supported all MacOS applications, and for a short time the MacIntosh ruled the desktop publishing market.

Microsoft's first Windows operating environment duplicated this paradigm, and to this day printing and displaying information is handled almost identically in Windows and MacOS. Applications for these operating systems and others like NeXT and BeOS are able to produce professional-quality output with a generic printing interface, yet until recently Unix has only had its print file spooling system.

The Evolution of CUPS

In 1993 a new company called Easy Software Products was formed. As one of its founders, my job was to develop a modeling program to build 3D images of aircraft, tanks, ships, and so forth. While developing this program I ran into a problem—how would we support printing of these models?

Applications in Unix almost universally produce Adobe PostScript files for printing. PostScript is a computer language that describes pages mathmatically and is the language of choice for most high-end printers and imagesetters. PostScript is even used for display and was used by the NeWS window environment under the IRIX, NeXT, and Solaris operating systems.

However, PostScript is not generally supported by consumer-level printers and we certainly didn't have a PostScript printer in our office. At the time, Ghostscript (a popular free PostScript interpreter) was not an option, so we had to write our own printer drivers just as thousands of other companies have done before us.

I had written printer drivers before for the Radio Shack Color Computer and later the ill-fated MM/1 computer under the OS-9 operating system, so I took the code from those old programs and created and released to the public a program called *topcl*. Topcl took an RGB image file and converted it to HP Page Control Language (PCL) for a variety of HP and compatible printers. This combined with the tops program supplied with the IRIX operating system were enough to provide the printing support needed for our modeler.

Then one day a friend of mine visited our one-room office and I showed him our modeling program. During my demo he asked *why* we were trying to sell yet another 3D modeling program for IRIX, and why we didn't try selling the printer drivers. "After all," he said, "*you* had to develop drivers, don't you think other people need them, too?"

Not too long after this discussion, Silicon Graphics released a new printing product called Impressario. Impressario did many good things. It introduced the concept of filtering print files to convert them to a printable format. It included a PostScript interpreter to convert PostScript files to a raster format for non-PostScript printers, and it provided a common driver interface that could be used to develop printer drivers for almost any kind of printer. For all these good things, Impressario lacked printer drivers.

We released the first version of ESP Print in 1994, and by 1995 we stopped development of our modeling program to work exclusively on ESP Print. New releases of ESP Print included a modified version of Ghostscript that acted as a drop-in replacement for the Impressario PostScript interpreter, and we continued to add printer drivers as new printers became available. ESP Print was eventually ported to Solaris and HP-UX, and each operating system added a new wrinkle to an already complex software package.

In 1997 we started looking at supporting the Digital Unix and Linux operating systems. Unfortunately, these operating systems used the original LPD for printing so you couldn't pass options to the printer drivers. This alone would cripple any drivers we might develop. To make matters more complicated, at least three versions of LPD were in common use, and they were not 100% compatible with each other. We knew then that we had to take the next step and replace both LPD and LP.

The original design of the Common UNIX Printing System (CUPS) was based around the LPD network protocol (see Figure IN.1). We added support for options and remote administration, and were just finishing the design of the new system when the Internet Printing Protocol (IPP) working group was created. The IPP working group originally was just going to update the LPD network protocol, but quickly changed its direction to create a much more functional and extensible protocol that could evolve as needed to support new technologies.

The switch to IPP probably delayed the release of CUPS by about 18 months, but I think everyone is happier for it. By supporting IPP, CUPS can accept and send print jobs almost anywhere. CUPS also provides the infrastructure needed to support modern printing and printers, something that printer manufacturers need to support their printers under Unix.

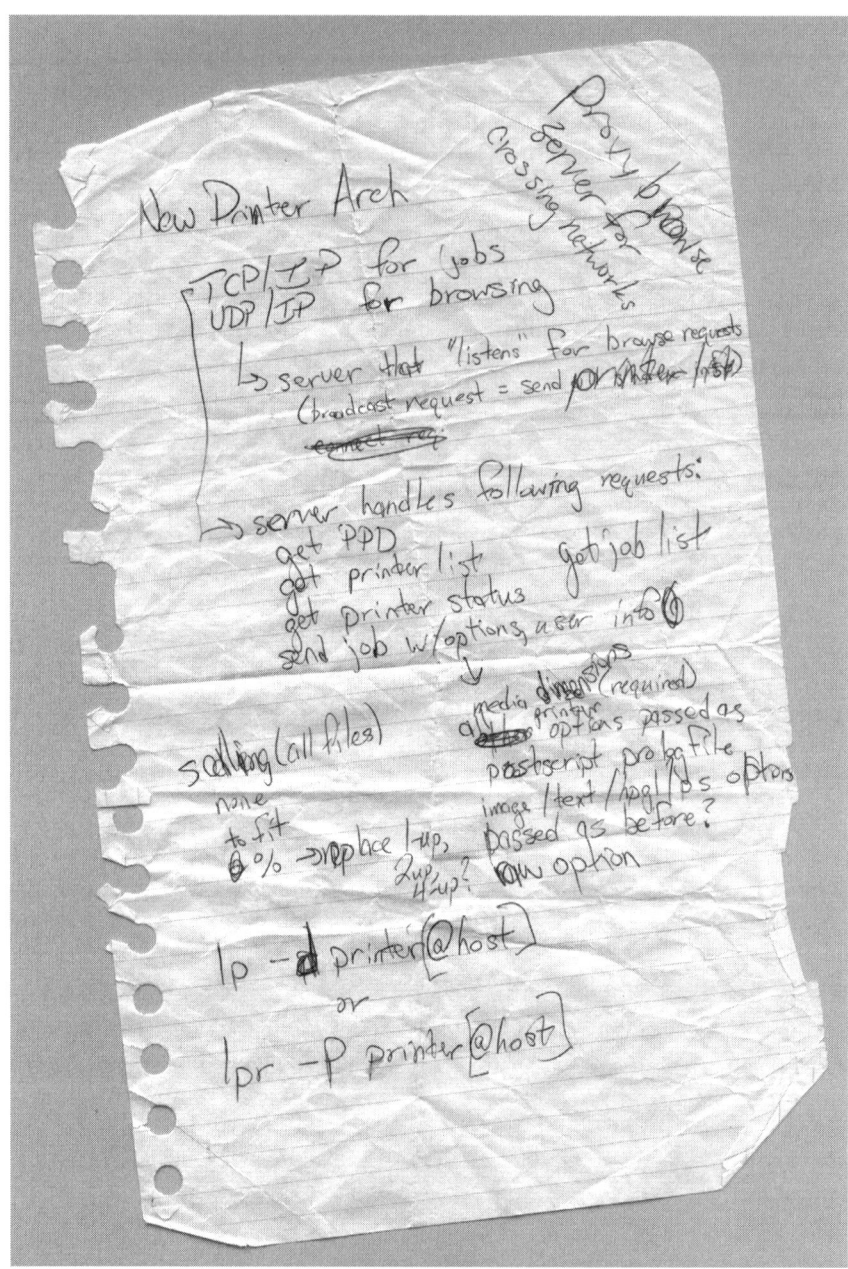

FIGURE IN.1

The first design notes for CUPS.

Today CUPS is included with almost every major Linux distribution and is available freely for all Unix operating systems. Printer drivers for CUPS are available commercially (ESP Print Pro) as well as from several free software projects, with quality often rivaling those under Windows and MacOS. Graphical printing interfaces for endusers and toolkits are also available in great numbers.

Finally, printer manufacturers now provide CUPS printer drivers for Linux, so printing under Unix is no longer a thing of the past.

About This Book

This book covers every facet of the Common UNIX Printing System. There are four sections to the book covering the use of CUPS, the Internet Printing Protocol, programming for CUPS, and reference information on commands, functions, and configuration files.

If you've never used or heard of CUPS before, Chapter 1 "Introduction to CUPS," is the place to start. Here you'll learn how CUPS interacts with you, your printers, and your applications.

If you want to jump in and start using CUPS, use the CD-ROM at the back of this book to get you started. We've included as many of the popular CUPS-based printer drivers and interfaces as we could find!

Welcome to the future of printing under Unix!

PART I

Using CUPS

CHAPTER 1

Introduction to CUPS

This chapter provides an introduction to the Common UNIX Printing System, or CUPS.

The Printing Problem

For years a printing problem has plagued Unix. Unlike Microsoft Windows or Mac OS, Unix has no standard interface or system in place for supporting printers. Among the solutions currently available, the Berkeley and System V printing systems are the most prevalent.

These printing systems support line printers (text only) or PostScript printers (text and graphics), and with some coaxing they can be made to support a full range of printers and file formats. However, because each variant of the Unix operating system uses a different printing system, developing printer drivers for a wide range of printers and operating systems is extremely difficult. That combined with the limited volume of customers for each Unix variant forced most printer vendors to give up supporting Unix entirely.

CUPS is designed to eliminate the printing problem. One common printing system can be used by all Unix variants to support the printing needs of users. Printer vendors can use its modular filter interface to develop a single driver program that supports a wide range of file formats with little or no effort. Because CUPS provides both the System V and Berkeley printing commands, users (and applications) can reap the benefits of this new technology with no changes.

Since its first release in 1999, CUPS has been adopted by many of the Linux distributors and is being used by several printer manufacturers to provide CUPS-based printer drivers for Linux.

The Technology

CUPS is a *printing system* for Unix and Unix-like operating systems. This printing system enables you to print files to just about any printer you can find.

CUPS is based on the Internet Printing Protocol (IPP), a new network printing protocol that enables you to print locally or remotely to networked printers in your office or anywhere in the world. IPP defines a standard protocol for printing as well as managing print jobs and printer options such as media size, resolution, and so forth.

Like all IP-based protocols, IPP can be used locally or over the Internet with printers hundreds or thousands of miles away. Unlike other protocols, however, IPP also supports *authentication*—password protecting your printer and *access control*—only allowing specific machines or people to access your printer. Additionally, IIP supports *encryption*—scrambling the print data so an eavesdropper cannot understand it, making it a much more robust and secure printing solution than the venerable LPD protocol.

IPP is layered on top of the HyperText Transport Protocol (HTTP), which is the basis of Web servers on the Internet. Users can view documentation, check status information on a printer or server, and manage their printers, classes, and jobs using their Web browser (see Figure 1.1).

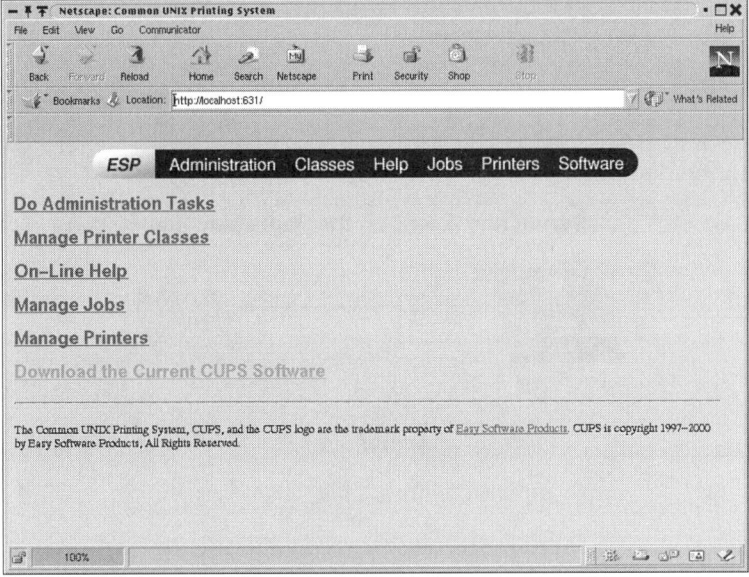

FIGURE 1.1

The CUPS Web interface.

CUPS provides a complete IPP/1.1-based printing system that includes Basic, Digest, and local certificate authentication; user, domain, or IP-based access control; and 128-bit encryption.

CUPS also provides the standard printing commands you've probably been using for years. Both the Berkeley (1pr) and System V (1p) printing commands are included, so applications that use those commands will work without change.

Client and Server

IPP is based on the client/server model. The client and server are often on the same machine. When you print a file, you (or your application) are the client. The server is the CUPS program running in the background that prints this file (see Figure 1.2).

Separate Client and Server

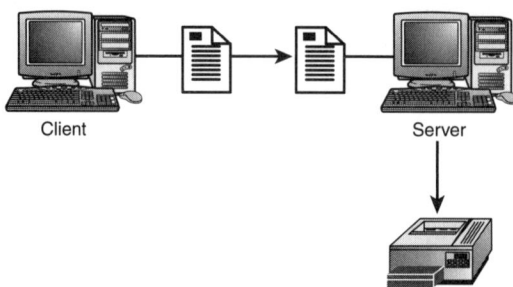

Server and Client on the Same Machine

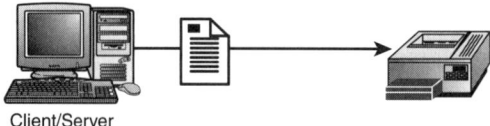

FIGURE 1.2

A client printing a file to a server.

Jobs

Each file or set of files that is submitted for printing is called a *job*. Jobs are identified by a unique number starting at 1 and are assigned to a particular destination, usually a printer. Jobs can also have options associated with them such as media size, number of copies, priority, and so forth.

Classes

CUPS supports collections of printers known as *classes*. Jobs sent to a class are forwarded to the next available printer in the class. This enables you to send your print job to a group of similar (or identical) printers and have it printed on the first one that is idle rather than waiting for someone else's job to finish on the printer you've chosen (see Figure 1.3).

CUPS also supports special *implicit* classes. Implicit classes work just like regular classes but are created automatically when more than one server handles a particular printer. An implicit class routes a print job to the next available server, so if one of your servers goes down your job will still be printed (see Figure 1.4).

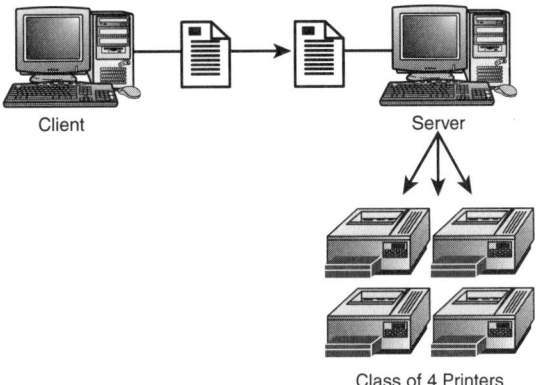

FIGURE 1.3

A diagram of printers in a class.

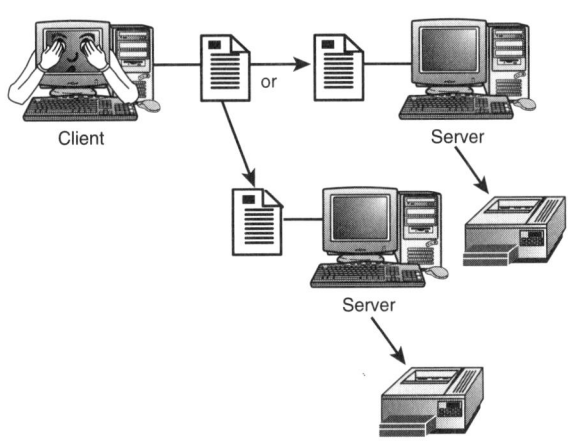

FIGURE 1.4

An illustration of implicit classes.

Filters

Filters enable a user or application to print a file even if the printer doesn't support the file format. Print jobs sent to a CUPS server are filtered before being sent to a printer. Some filters convert job files to different formats that the printer can understand. Others perform page selection and ordering tasks. A third type of filter called a *printer driver* is described in the next section.

CUPS provides filters for printing many types of image files, HP-GL/2 files, PDF files, and text files. CUPS also supplies PostScript and image file raster image processor ("RIP") filters that convert PostScript or image files into bitmaps that can be sent to a raster printer driver (see Figure 1.5).

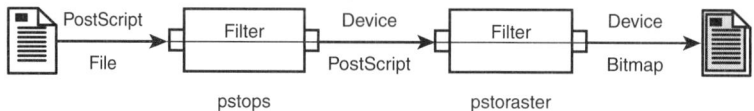

FIGURE 1.5

Filters used to print a file.

Printer Drivers

Printer drivers consist of one or more filters specific to a printer. Each filter converts a general file format such as a bitmap into a printer format such as HP-PCL. In addition to the filter programs, each driver also includes a PostScript printer description (PPD) file that describes the features, options, and capabilities of the printer.

CUPS includes sample printer drivers for EPSON, Hewlett-Packard, and Okidata printers. These drivers support a wide variety of printers from these manufacturers. As a result, they do not generate optimal output for each printer model.

Many commercial and free printer drivers are available for CUPS, as shown in Table 1.1.

TABLE 1.1   Printer Drivers for CUPS

Source	URL	Type	Description
Easy Software Products	`http://www.easysw.com/printpro`	Commercial	Several thousand printer drivers covering most printer manufacturers.
GIMP-print project	`http://gimp-print.sourceforge.net`	Free	Printer drivers for GIMP, Ghostscript, and CUPS. Includes drivers for HP, EPSON, Lexmark, and Canon printers.
CUPS-o-matic	`http://www.linuxprinting.org`	Free	Wrapper drivers for Ghostscript. Provides CUPS interface to Ghostscript printer drivers.
EPSON	`http://www.ercipd.com/isv/linux/index.htm`	Free	EPSON printer drivers for CUPS.
Star Micronics	`http://www.starmicronics.com`	Free	Star Micronics printer drivers for CUPS.

Backends

Backends perform the most important task of all—they send the filtered print data to the printer (see Figure 1.6). Each backend communicates with the printer, copying the filtered print data (or a raw print file) to the printer and relaying any status information from the printer to the CUPS server. Backends generally do not do any filtering or conversion of the print data.

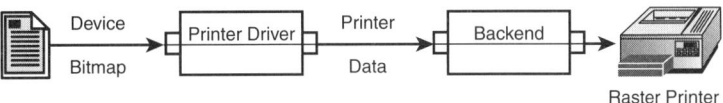

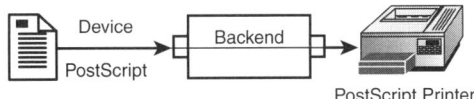

FIGURE 1.6

Printing after filtering files.

CUPS provides backends for printing over parallel, serial, and USB ports, and over the network through the IPP, JetDirect (AppSocket), and line printer daemon (LPD) protocols.

Additional backends are available in network service packages, such as the SMB backend included with the popular SAMBA software.

Backends also provide lists of the available devices. On startup, each backend is asked for a list of devices it supports and for any information that is available. This allows the parallel backend to tell CUPS that an EPSON Stylus Color 600 printer is attached to parallel port 1, for example.

Networking

Printers and classes on the local system can be shared with other systems on the network. This enables users to print through one system set up to be a printer server or spool host for all of the others. Printers are shared by broadcasting the available printer list from the server to the clients (see Figure 1.7).

This broadcast mechanism is also the foundation of the implicit classes that were described earlier. When a client receives information about printers with the same name from more than one server, the client can automatically combine the printers into a single implicit class that can be used for printing.

FIGURE 1.7

A server broadcasting a printer list to clients.

In this way, implicit classes provide an easy way to balance the load on servers and provide fault tolerance if one or more servers fail.

Graphical Interfaces

Although CUPS does not come with a standard GUI interface, many are available. Table 1.2 lists the available interfaces.

TABLE 1.2   GUI Interfaces for CUPS

URL	Software Package
http://www.easysw.com/printpro/	ESP Print Pro
http://www.stud.uni-hannover.de/user/75439/gtklp/	GtkLP
http://cups.sourceforge.net/kups/	KUPS
http://cups.sourceforge.net/qtcups/	QtCUPS
http://cups.sourceforge.net/xpp/	XPP

ESP Print Pro

ESP Print Pro (see Figure 1.8) is a commercial software package. It provides GUIs to manage classes, jobs, and printers; a print panel to set options and to print files; and a screen/window hard-copy program. ESP Print Pro is based on the FLTK toolkit.

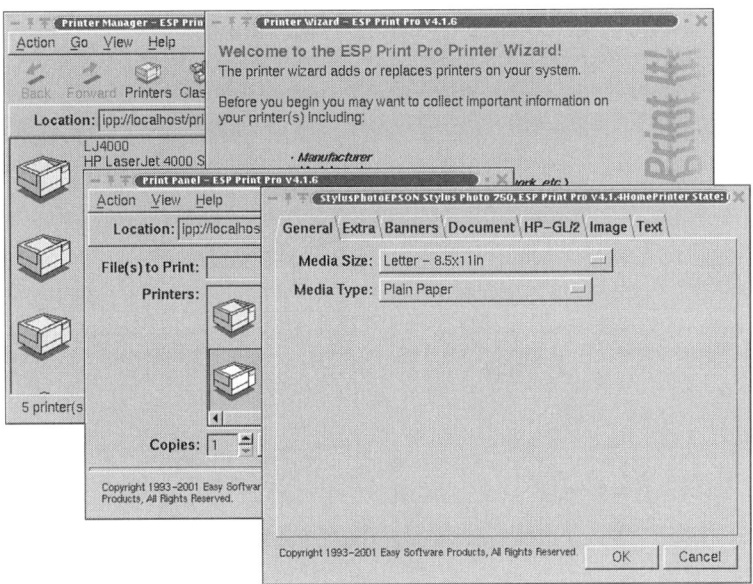

FIGURE 1.8

Managing printers and jobs using the ESP Print Pro Printer manager,
Printer Wizard, Print panel, and Printer Option panel windows.

GtkLP

GtkLP (see Figure 1.9) is a free software program and provides GUI print and option panels to print files. GtkLP is based on the GTK+ toolkit.

KUPS

The KDE management tool for CUPS (KUPS) (see Figure 1.10) is a free software program that provides GUIs to manage classes, jobs, and printers. KUPS is based on the Qt toolkit.

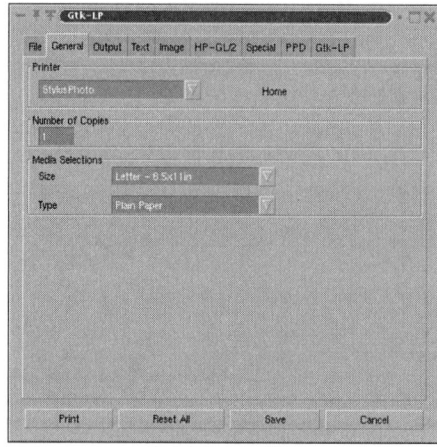

FIGURE 1.9

Printing using the GtkLP Print dialog.

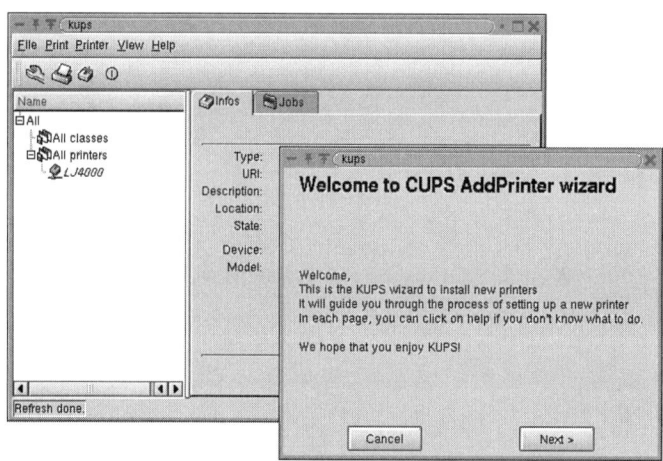

FIGURE 1.10

Adding printers using the KUPS Printer Wizard.

QtCUPS

QtCUPS (see Figure 1.11) is a free software program and provides GUI print and option panels to print files. QtCUPS also provides a library that can be used by Qt programs to support printing directly through CUPS. QtCUPS is based on the Qt toolkit.

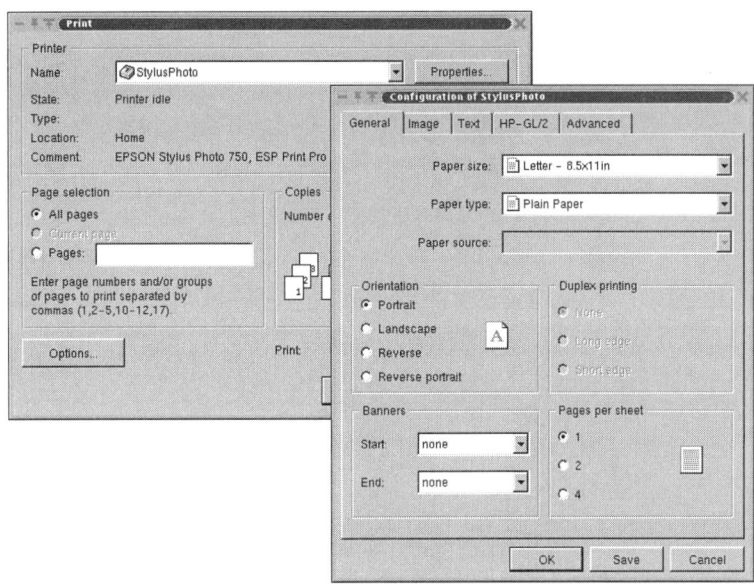

FIGURE 1.11

Printing a file using the QtCUPS Print dialog.

XPP

The X Print Panel (XPP) (see Figure 1.12) is a free software program that provides GUI print and option panels to print files. XPP is based on the FLTK toolkit.

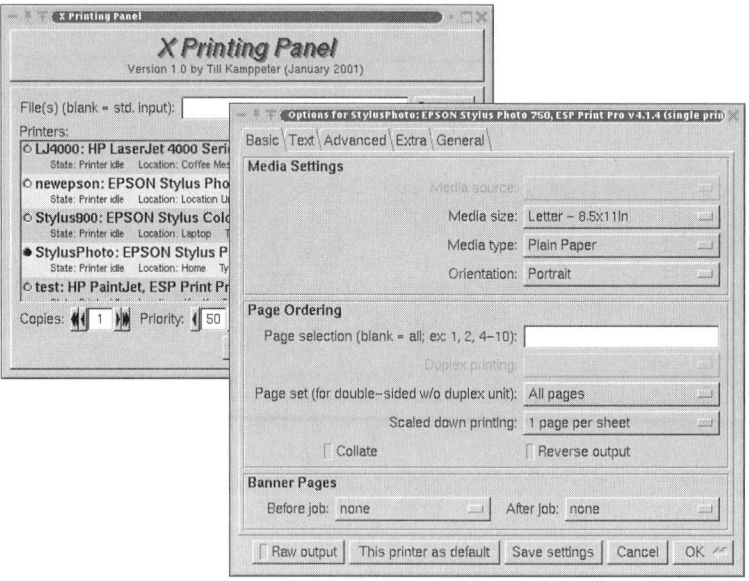

FIGURE 1.12

Printing a file using the XPP Print dialog.

Resources

Many resources are available for CUPS, including an official mailing list, newsgroups hosted by Easy Software Products, and Web pages.

The CUPS Mailing List

The `cups@cups.org` mailing list is available only to subscribers to avoid SPAM problems. Send the following message to `majordomo@cups.org` to subscribe to the list:

```
subscribe cups
```

The list manager will then send a confirming e-mail that you must reply to, and then finally you should receive a message reading:

```
Welcome to the CUPS mailing list!

This mailing list provides a common forum for discussing the Common
Unix Printing System ("CUPS") by Easy Software Products.  The CUPS
```

```
software and documentation is available at:

  http://www.cups.org

To send messages to this list, send E-Mail to "cups@cups.org".
To unsubscribe from the list, send an e-mail to
"majordomo@easysw.com" with the text:

  unsubscribe cups

PLEASE NOTE: You will be automatically unsubscribed from the
list should the list server be unable to send a message to your
e-mail account.  If you suddenly stop receiving messages from the
list, please resubscribe; you'll get an "already subscribed"
message if you are still subscribed.
```

The CUPS mailing list is a public forum for asking questions, discussing problems, and reporting bugs. Please use proper netiquette when posting.

CUPS Newsgroups

Easy Software Products hosts a public news server at:

```
news://news.easysw.com/
```

Unlike the CUPS mailing list, you don't need to subscribe to get access to these resources. Table 1.3 shows the available newsgroups:

TABLE 1.3   CUPS Newsgroups

Name	Description
cups.announce	Announcements of new releases of CUPS and CUPS-related stuff
cups.bugs	Reporting and discussion of bugs in CUPS
cups.cvs	Discussion of problems with the CVS version of CUPS
cups.development	Discussion of developer issues about CUPS
cups.general	Posting of general questions about using CUPS

The cups.general newsgroup is mirrored to and from the CUPS mailing list, so any questions you post to the cups.general newsgroup will be sent to the CUPS mailing list, and vice-versa.

Web Sites

Many Web sites are devoted to CUPS or Linux printing in general. Table 1.4 shows a list of the more popular sites:

TABLE 1.4   CUPS-related Web Sites

URL	Description
http://www.cups.org/	The official CUPS Web site
http://www.linuxprinting.org/	The more-or-less official site for printing under Linux and other open-source operating systems
http://www.stokely.com/unix.sysadm.resources/printing.html	Another great source for Unix printing information
http://www.pwg.org/ipp/	The official IPP Web site
http://www.easysw.com/cups/	Commercial support for CUPS
http://cups.sourceforge.net/	A collection of open-source add-ons for CUPS
http://gimp-print.sourceforge.net/	Printer drivers for CUPS
http://printing.sourceforge.net/	More printing software sponsored by HP and based on code from CUPS
http://www.adobe.com/prodindex/printerdrivers/winppd.html	PPD files that can be used with CUPS
http://www.danka.de/printpro/faq.html	German language CUPS-FAQ
http://kdeprint.sourceforge.net	The new KDE 2.2 printing, which heavily supports CUPS (though not exclusively)

Summary

CUPS is an IPP-based printing solution for Unix. CUPS supports many file formats and the Berkeley and System V printing commands, enabling it to be used with any application.

CUPS provides printer drivers for many popular printers, and both free and commercial printer drivers for CUPS are available for Linux and other operating systems.

CUPS can be extended to support new file formats, printers, and interfaces with the addition of filters, PPD files, and backends.

CUPS provides advanced network printing features including Web-based access to the printing system, printer sharing, implicit classes, authentication, access-control, and encryption.

CHAPTER **2**

Building and Installing CUPS

This chapter shows how to build and install the Common UNIX Printing System. If you are installing a binary distribution from the CD-ROM or CUPS Web site, proceed to the section titled "Installing a Binary Distribution."

Installing a Source Distribution

This section describes how to compile and install CUPS on your system from the source code.

Getting the CUPS Source Code

The CUPS source code is provided on the included CD-ROM. For a typical Linux system you will need to run the following commands to access the source code

```
mount /mnt/cdrom ENTER
tar xvzf /mnt/cdrom/cups/cups-version-source.tar.gz ENTER
```

where *version* is the version of CUPS that is on the CD-ROM.

The most recent version of CUPS is always available online at:

```
http://www.cups.org
```

Click on the *Download* link to access the source code.

Finally, you can download the very latest bleeding-edge CUPS source code using anonymous CVS by running the following commands:

```
cvs -d:pserver:anoncvs@cvs.cups.org:/home/anoncvs login ENTER
Password: anoncvs ENTER
cvs -z3 -d:pserver:anoncvs@cvs.cups.org:/home/anoncvs get cups ENTER
```

Living on the bleeding edge of CUPS development has its dangers—the CVS version of CUPS might not be as stable as an official release because changes are constantly being made. Use the CVS version of CUPS with care.

Requirements

You'll need ANSI-compliant C and C++ compilers to build CUPS on your system. As its name implies, CUPS is designed to run on the Unix operating system; however, the CUPS interface library and most of the filters and backends supplied with CUPS should also compile and run under Microsoft Windows.

Table 2.1 outlines the required libraries and software packages to compile and install CUPS.

TABLE 2.1   Libraries and Software Packages Needed by CUPS

Name	Required?	URL	Description
EPM	No	http://www.easysw.com/epm/	The EPM software is used to create binary distributions on all supported platforms.
GCC	No	http://gcc.gnu.org/	The GCC software provides compilers for Unix, including excellent ANSI-compliant C and C++ compilers.
GROFF	Yes	ftp://ftp.gnu.org/gnu/groff/	The groff software is used to format man pages; you can also use the nroff program if your system has it.
HTMLDOC	No	http://www.easysw.com/htmldoc/	The HTMLDOC software is used to format the CUPS documentation.
JPEG	Yes	http://www.ijg.org/	The JPEG library provides support for JPEG image files, JPEG-compressed image data in PostScript files, and JPEG-compressed image data in TIFF files.
OPENSLP	No	http://www.openslp.org/	The OpenSLP library provides SLPv2 support for CUPS.
OPENSSL	No	http://www.openssl.org/	The OpenSSL library provides 128-bit TLS and SSL encryption support for CUPS.
PNG	Yes	http://www.libpng.org/	The PNG library pub/png/png.html provides support for PNG image files.
TIFF	Yes	http://www.libtiff.org/	The TIFF library provides support for TIFF images.
ZLIB	Yes	http://www.info-zip.org/pub/infozip/zlib/	The ZLIB library provides support for compression in PNG and TIFF image files.

Configuring the CUPS Sources

CUPS uses GNU autoconf to configure the makefiles and source code for your system. Type the following command to configure CUPS for your system:

```
./configure ENTER
```

The configure script accepts multiple options. If you want to configure CUPS with multiple options, include them all on one line, as follows:

```
./configure --prefix=/some/directory --enable-debug --disable-shared ... ENTER
```

Configuring the Installation Directories

The default installation will put the CUPS software in the /etc, /usr, and /var directories on your system, which will overwrite any existing printing commands on your system. Use the --prefix option to install the CUPS software in another location:

```
./configure --prefix=/some/directory ENTER
```

The --prefix option affects the location of all files. Use one or more of the options in Table 2.2 to override the locations assigned by the --prefix option.

TABLE 2.2   Directory Options for the Configure Script

Option	Description	Default Value	Prefixed Value
--datadir	The location of shared data files	/usr/share	${prefix}/share
--exec-prefix	The base directory for executable files	/usr	${prefix}
--includedir	The base directory for include files	/usr/include	${prefix}/include
--libdir	The location of library files	/usr/lib	${prefix}/lib
--libexecdir	The location of server executable files	/usr/lib, /usr/libexec	${prefix}/libexec
--localstatedir	The base directory for local state information	/var	${prefix}/var
--mandir	The base directory for man pages	/usr/man, /usr/share/man, /usr/share/catman/u_man	${prefix}/man
--sysconfdir	The base directory for local configuration files	/etc	${prefix}/etc

A typical local installation might put the CUPS programs, libraries, and data files under /usr/local, the configuration files in /etc, and the state files in /var. The following configure command will provide this configuration:

```
./configure --prefix=/usr/local --sysconfdir=/etc --localstatedir=/var ENTER
```

Locating Header Files and Libraries

The `configure` script normally only looks in the standard system locations for header files and libraries, typically `/usr/include` and `/usr/lib`. To point the `configure` script at other directories, set the `CFLAGS`, `CXXFLAGS`, and `LDFLAGS` environment variables. If you are using the Bourne shell or a derivative the commands are

```
CFLAGS="-I/foo/bar/include -I/bar/foo/include"; export CFLAGS ENTER
CXXFLAGS="-I/foo/bar/include -I/bar/foo/include"; export CXXFLAGS ENTER
LDFLAGS="-L/foo/bar/lib -L/bar/foo/lib"; export LDFLAGS ENTER
```

If you are using C shell or a derivative the commands are

```
setenv CFLAGS "-I/foo/bar/include -I/bar/foo/include" ENTER
setenv CXXFLAGS "-I/foo/bar/include -I/bar/foo/include" ENTER
setenv LDFLAGS "-L/foo/bar/lib -L/bar/foo/lib" ENTER
```

The `-I` options tell the compiler which directories to look in for include files; these options are cumulative and the directories are searched before the standard ones.

The `-L` options tell the linker which directories to look in for library files; these options are cumulative and the directories are searched before the standard ones.

Locating Font Files

CUPS has a complete set of Type1 fonts for the PostScript RIP and text filter. However, many systems already have these fonts installed, and you might have additional Type1 or TrueType fonts that you want to use. The `--fontpath` option enables you to specify where CUPS should look for fonts when printing:

```
./configure --fontpath=/usr/share/cups/fonts:/foo/bar/fonts ENTER
```

As the preceding example shows, the colon (:) character separates directories. The font path can be up to 1024 characters in length.

Compiling with Debug Support

The `--enable-debug` option causes debugging information to be included in the CUPS libraries and programs. Type the following to configure CUPS for debugging:

```
./configure --enable-debug ENTER
```

Enabling Notification Support

The `--enable-notifications` option causes the IPP Notification code to be linked into CUPS. This option enables you to notify yourself and other users when jobs are completed, when the printer runs out of paper, and so forth. Type the following to configure CUPS with notification support:

```
./configure --enable-notifications ENTER
```

Notifications are an optional part of CUPS 1.1.x and standard in CUPS 1.2.x.

Building Static Libraries

The `--disable-shared` option prevents the creation of libraries that can be shared by CUPS programs. The resulting executables and libraries are linked statically to the CUPS API and image libraries, resulting in larger executables. Type the following to configure CUPS with static libraries:

```
./configure --disable-shared ENTER
```

Enabling Server Location Protocol Support

The `--enable-slp` option causes the server location protocol ("SLP") code to be linked into CUPS. This option enables you to use the SLP directory service protocol on your network, which makes discovering network printers and providing network-printing services to non-CUPS systems easier. Type the following to configure CUPS with SLP support:

```
./configure --enable-slp ENTER
```

Enabling Encryption Support

The `--enable-ssl` option causes the encryption code to be linked into CUPS. This option requires the OpenSSL library and enables you to encrypt print jobs and remote commands. Type the following to configure CUPS with encryption support:

```
./configure --enable-ssl ENTER'
```

Enabling All Optional Features

The binary distributions provided for CUPS include all optional features for your convenience. Type the following to configure CUPS with all available features:

```
./configure --enable-notifications --enable-ssl --enable-slp ENTER
```

Summary of Configuration Options

Table 2.3 lists all of the configuration options for the `configure` script.

TABLE 2.3   Configuration Options for CUPS

Option	Description	Default Value
--datadir	The location of shared data files	/usr/share
--disable-debug, --enable-debug	Enables or disables debugging support	Disabled
--disable-notifications, --enable-notifications	Enables or disables IPP notification support	Disabled in CUPS 1.1.x, enabled in CUPS 1.2.x
--disable-shared, --enable-shared	Enables or disables shared libraries	Enabled
--disable-slp, --enable-slp	Enables or disables SLP support	Enabled
--disable-ssl, --enable-ssl	Enables or disables encryption support	Enabled
--exec-prefix	The base directory for executable files	/usr
--fontpath=/dir1:/dir2	The search path for font files	/usr/share/cups/fonts
--includedir	The base directory for include files	/usr/include
--libdir	The location of library files	/usr/lib
--libexecdir	The location of server executable files	/usr/lib, /usr/libexec
--localstatedir	The base directory for local state information	/var
--mandir	The base directory for man pages	/usr/man, /usr/share/man
--sysconfdir	The base directory for local configuration files	/etc

Compiling CUPS

After you have configured the CUPS source code, type the following command to build the software:

make *ENTER*

Depending on the speed of your computer, the compilation process can take 5 minutes to an hour.

Testing the Software

After a successful compilation, it is usually a good idea to test the software before you install it. The "test" target provides an automated test of the CUPS software:

```
make test ENTER
Running CUPS test suite...
Linking ipptest...
Starting scheduler...
Waiting for scheduler to become ready...
Running IPP compliance tests...
Performing 4.1-requests.test...
Performing 4.2-cups-printer-ops.test...
Performing 4.3-job-ops.test...
Running command tests...
Performing 5.1-lpadmin.sh...
Performing 5.2-lpc.sh...
Performing 5.3-lpq.sh...
Performing 5.4-lpstat.sh...
Performing 5.5-lp.sh...
Performing 5.6-lpr.sh...
Performing 5.7-lprm.sh...
Performing 5.8-cancel.sh...
Performing 5.9-lpinfo.sh...
Formatting reports...
htmldoc: Reading cups-str-1.1-2001-03-03-mike.shtml...
htmldoc: Reading cups-str-1.1-2001-03-03-mike.shtml...

All tests passed.

See the following files for details:

    cups-str-1.1-2001-03-03-mike.html
    cups-str-1.1-2001-03-03-mike.pdf
```

If you encounter any errors, use the resources described in Chapter 1, "Introduction to CUPS," to get assistance.

Installing the Software

Use the "install" target to install the software in the directories you chose when configuring the software:

```
make install ENTER
```

WARNING:

Installing CUPS usually overwrites your existing printing system. If you experience difficulties with the CUPS software and need to go back to your old printing system, you will need to reinstall the old printing system from your operating system CDs.

Upgrading the Software

The "install" target preserves any existing configuration files you have for CUPS, so it can also be used to upgrade the software:

```
make install ENTER
```

Running the Software

After you have installed the software you can start the CUPS server by typing:

```
/usr/sbin/cupsd ENTER
```

Congratulations, you have finished the installation of CUPS! You can now proceed to Chapter 3, "Setting Up Printers and Classes."

Installing a Binary Distribution

CUPS comes in a variety of binary distribution formats. Easy Software Products provides binaries in TAR format with installation and removal scripts ("portable" distributions) and in RPM and DPKG formats for Red Hat and Debian-based distributions. Portable distributions are available for all platforms, whereas the RPM and DPKG distributions are only available for Linux.

WARNING:

Installing CUPS will overwrite your existing printing system. If you experience difficulties with the CUPS software and need to go back to your old printing system, you must remove the CUPS software with the provided script and/or reinstall the old printing system from your operating system CDs.

Getting a CUPS Binary Distribution

Binary distributions for CUPS are provided on the included CD-ROM. For a typical Linux system you will need to run the following commands to access the binary distributions:

```
mount /mnt/cdrom ENTER
cd /mnt/cdrom/cups ENTER
```

The most recent version of CUPS is always available online at:

```
http://www.cups.org
```

Click on the *Download* link to access the binary distributions.

Installing or Upgrading a Portable Distribution

To install or upgrade the CUPS software from a portable distribution you will need to be logged in as the root user or do a "su":

```
su ENTER
```

Run the installation script to install or upgrade CUPS:

```
./cups.install ENTER
Copyright 1993-2001 by Easy Software Products, All Rights Reserved.

This installation script will install the Common UNIX Printing System
software version 1.1.7 on your system.

Do you wish to continue? yes ENTER
                Common UNIX Printing System License Agreement

                Copyright 1997-2001 by Easy Software Products
...
Do you agree with the terms of this license? yes ENTER
Backing up old versions of non-shared files to be installed...
Backing up old versions of shared files to be installed...
Creating installation directories...
Installing software...
Checking configuration files...
Setting up init scripts...
cups: scheduler started.
Installation is complete.
```

After answering yes to the two questions, the CUPS software will be installed or upgraded and the scheduler will be started automatically. If you are upgrading the software, your previous configuration files will be used automatically.

You can now proceed to Chapter 3.

Installing an RPM Distribution

To install the CUPS software from a portable distribution you will need to be logged in as the root user or do a "su":

su *ENTER*

If you are installing CUPS for the first time you will first need to remove the existing printing system. Start by removing any Red Hat printing utilities:

rpm -e rhs-printfilters *ENTER*
rpm -e printtool *ENTER*

If you get any conflicts from the removal, remove the conflicting software as well.

Next, remove the lpr or LPRng software. Remove the lpr software with:

rpm -e lpr *ENTER*

If you have the LPRng software installed instead, type:

rpm -e LPRng *ENTER*

Again, if you get any conflicts from the removal, remove the conflicting software as well.

Then install the CUPS rpm using the command

rpm -i cups-*version***-linux-2.2-intel.rpm** *ENTER*

or

rpm -i cups-*version***-linux-2.4-intel.rpm** *ENTER*

where *version* is the CUPS version number. After a short delay the CUPS software will be installed. The only task that remains is to start the CUPS server:

/usr/sbin/cupsd *ENTER*

Congratulations, you have finished the installation of CUPS! You can now proceed to Chapter 3.

Upgrading a Previous Installation of CUPS

The RPM upgrade procedure is very similar to the portable upgrade procedure. Start by upgrading the CUPS rpm using the command

rpm -U cups-*version***-linux-2.2-intel.rpm** *ENTER*

or

```
rpm -U cups-version-linux-2.4-intel.rpm ENTER
```

where *version* is the CUPS version number. After a short delay the CUPS software will be upgraded.

The rpm software will save your old configuration files. Type the following commands to restore them:

```
cd /etc/cups ENTER
mv classes.conf.rpmsave classes.conf ENTER
mv cupsd.conf.rpmsave cupsd.conf ENTER
mv printers.conf.rpmsave printers.conf ENTER
```

Finally, start the CUPS server with:

```
/usr/sbin/cupsd ENTER
```

Congratulations, you have finished the upgrade of CUPS! You can now proceed to Chapter 3.

Installing a Debian Distribution

To install or upgrade the CUPS software from a Debian distribution you will need to be logged in as the root user or do a "su":

```
su ENTER
```

If you are installing CUPS for the first time you will first need to remove the existing printing system. Start by removing the lpr software:

```
dselect remove lpr ENTER
```

If you get any conflicts from the removal, remove the conflicting software as well.

Then install the CUPS package using the command

```
dselect install cups-version-linux-2.2-intel.deb ENTER
```

or

```
dselect install cups-version-linux-2.4-intel.deb ENTER
```

where *version* is the CUPS version number. After a short delay the CUPS software will be installed.

Congratulations, you have finished the installation of CUPS! You can now proceed to Chapter 3.

Upgrading CUPS

The Debian packager automatically handles upgrades using the `install` command. Upgrade the CUPS package using the command

```
dselect install cups-version-linux-2.2-intel.deb ENTER
```

or

```
dselect install cups-version-linux-2.4-intel.deb ENTER
```

where *version* is the CUPS version number. After a short delay the CUPS software will be upgraded.

Congratulations, you have finished the upgrade of CUPS! You can now proceed to Chapter 3.

Summary

CUPS is provided in both source code and binary formats. You can install the CUPS software from the CD-ROM included with this book or by downloading it from the CUPS Web site or anonymous CVS server.

Configuration files are automatically preserved when upgrading the CUPS software. If you upgrade using the RPM package, make sure to restore the backup configuration files that the rpm command creates.

CHAPTER 3

Setting Up Printers and Classes

This chapter describes how to set up and manage printers and classes on your system from the command-line and Web interfaces.

Basics of Printers

Each printer queue has a name associated with it; the printer name must start with a letter and can contain up to 127 letters, numbers, and the underscore (_). Case is not significant, so "PRINTER", "Printer", and "printer" are all considered the same name.

Printer Devices

Printer queues have a device associated with them. The device can be a parallel port, a network interface, or any other interface that is supported by a backend. Devices within CUPS use uniform resource identifiers ("URIs") which are a more general form of the uniform resource locators ("URLs") that are used in your Web browser. For example, the first parallel port in Linux usually uses a device URI of parallel:`/dev/lp0`.

Getting a List of Available Devices

You can see a complete list of supported devices by running the `lpinfo` command:

```
lpinfo -v ENTER
file file
network socket
network http
network ipp
network lpd
direct parallel:/dev/lp0
serial serial:/dev/ttyS0?baud=115200
serial serial:/dev/ttyS1?baud=115200
direct usb:/dev/usb/lp0
network smb
```

The `-v` option specifies that you want a list of available devices. The first word in each line is the type of device (direct, file, network, or serial) and is followed by the device URI or scheme name for that device. File devices have device URIs of the form file:`/directory/filename` whereas network devices use the more familiar scheme:`//server` or scheme:`//server/path` format.

Some backends support options, which are added to the end of the URI starting with a question mark. In the preceding list of devices, the `?baud=115200` option on the serial port URIs specifies the maximum baud rate supported by that port. Other options can be specified such as parity checking, data bits, and flow control.

File Devices

The file device allows you to configure a printer to print to a file for testing, or to blindly send print files to a device or named pipe. The absolute path of the file is appended to the file: scheme name to form the device URI:

```
file:/foo/bar/filename.prn
```

The file device does not support any options.

NOTE:

The file device is currently implemented as an internal device within CUPS. This prevents you from printing raw print files to the printer because no filter is in place to actually copy the print job to the file.

Also, the file device overwrites normal files. Because the scheduler normally runs as root, you should be careful not to configure a printer that points to an important file like /etc/passwd!

HTTP and IPP Devices

The HTTP and IPP devices allow you to send print jobs to a printer or server that supports IPP. The HTTP device handles URIs with a scheme name of "http:" whereas the IPP device handles URIs with a scheme name of "ipp:." These devices do not support any options in the device URI, but print job options are passed to the remote device with little or no change.

You can embed the username and password in the device URI if the remote device requires them:

```
http://username:password@server/path
ipp://username:password@server/path
```

A CUPS server supports printers using the following URIs

```
http://server/printers/name
http://server:port/printers/name
ipp://server/printers/name
ipp://server:port/printers/name
```

where *name* is the name of the printer. Similarly, classes use the following URIs:

```
http://server/classes/name
http://server:port/classes/name
ipp://server/classes/name
ipp://server:port/classes/name
```

Printers with network interfaces and external network print servers use different URIs. Table 3.1 summarizes the common URIs:

TABLE 3.1   Common URIs for Network Printers and Print Servers

Manufacturer	URI
Axis	`ipp://server/LPT1` (Parallel 1)
	`ipp://server/LPT2` (Parallel 2)
	`ipp://server/COM1` (Serial 1)
HP	`ipp://server/ipp` (Internal)
	`ipp://server/ipp/port1` (Parallel 1)
	`ipp://server/ipp/port2` (Parallel 2)
	`ipp://server/ipp/port3` (Parallel 3)
Microsoft	`ipp://server/printers/name`
Tektronix	`ipp://server/ipp`
Xerox	`ipp://server/ipp`

With the Microsoft Windows 2000 IPP server, the *name* in the URI is the share name of the printer.

Consult the documentation that came with your printer or print server if you don't see your manufacturer listed in Table 3.1.

LPD Devices

The LPD device supports the legacy line printer daemon protocol, which is described in RFC 1179. Microsoft implements this protocol in the TCP/IP Printing Service.

The URI used by the LPD device is

`lpd://server/name`

where *name* is the name of the remote printer queue. The queue name for printers on a Windows NT server will be the share name for the printer. For network interfaces and print servers consult Table 3.2.

TABLE 3.2   Common URIs for LPD Printers and Print Servers

Manufacturer	URI
Apple	`lpd://server/PASSTHRU`
Axis	`lpd://server/LPT1` (Parallel 1)
	`lpd://server/LPT2` (Parallel 2)
	`lpd://server/COM1` (Serial 1)
Castelle	`lpd://server/pr1` (Parallel 1)
	`lpd://server/pr2` (Parallel 2)
	`lpd://server/pr3` (Parallel 3)

TABLE 3.2   Continued

Manufacturer	URI
DPI	`lpd://server/pr1` (Parallel 1)
	`lpd://server/pr2` (Parallel 2)
	`lpd://server/pr3` (Parallel 3)
EFI	`lpd://server/print`
Extended System	`lpd://server/pr1` (Parallel 1)
	`lpd://server/pr2` (Parallel 2)
	`lpd://server/pr3` (Parallel 3)
Hewlett Packard	`lpd://server/raw` (Internal)
	`lpd://server/raw1` (Parallel 1)
	`lpd://server/raw2` (Parallel 2)
	`lpd://server/raw3` (Parallel 3)
Intel	`lpd://server/LPT1_PASSTHRU` (Parallel 1)
	`lpd://server/LPT2_PASSTHRU` (Parallel 2)
	`lpd://server/COM1_PASSTHRU` (Serial 1)
Lexmark	`lpd://server/ps`
Linksys	`lpd://server/P1` (Parallel 1)
	`lpd://server/P2` (Parallel 2)
	`lpd://server/P3` (Parallel 3)
Kodak	`lpd://server/ps`
QMS	`lpd://server/ps`
Xerox	`lpd://server/PORT1`
	`lpd://server/PASSTHRU`

The LPD device also supports several options, which are shown in Table 3.3.

TABLE 3.3   LPD Device Options

Option	Description
`banner=no`	Tells the remote printer not to print a banner page (default)
`banner=yes`	Tells the remote printer to print a banner page
`format=c`	Tells the remote printer that the print file is in CalTech intermediate format (CIF)
`format=d`	Tells the remote printer that the print file is in TeX dvi format
`format=f`	Tells the remote printer that the print file is a text file
`format=g`	Tells the remote printer that the print file is a Berkeley plot file
`format=l`	Tells the remote printer that the print file is already formatted for the printer (default)

TABLE 3.3   Continued

Option	Description
format=n	Tells the remote printer that the print file contains the output from the `ditroff` command
format=o	Tells the remote printer that the print file is a PostScript file
format=p	Tells the remote printer that the print file is a text file that should be pretty-printed as with the `pr` command
format=r	Tells the remote printer that the print file is output from a FORTRAN program
format=t	Tells the remote printer that the print file is output from the troff program
format=v	Tells the remote printer that the print file is a Sun raster format file
order=control,data	Sends the control file to the remote printer first
order=data,control	Sends the data file to the remote printer first (default)

Most LPD printers will only need the basic URI:

```
lpd://server/name
```

If print jobs go to the printer but do not print, the banner and order options may correct the situation:

```
lpd://server/name?banner=yes
lpd://server/name?order=control,data
lpd://server/name?banner=yes+order=control,data
```

The output format is normally ignored by most network printers and print servers.

Parallel Devices

The parallel devices support the standard parallel printer ports on the system. The device URI consists of the scheme name followed by the device filename; the following are used in various versions of Linux to refer to the first parallel port:

```
parallel:/dev/lp0
parallel:/dev/par0
parallel:/dev/parallel/0
```

Use the `lpinfo` command described earlier to determine which device filename to use on your system. The parallel device does not support any options.

Serial Devices

The serial devices support the standard RS-232C serial ports on the system. The device URI consists of the scheme name followed by the device filename and any options; the following are used in various versions of Linux to refer to the first serial port:

```
serial:/dev/ttyS0
serial:/dev/serial/0
```

The serial backend supports several options, which are listed in Table 3.4:

TABLE 3.4   Serial Device Options

Option	Description
baud=N	Sets the speed of the serial port in bits per second (baud). The default value is usually 9,600 baud. The maximum value is reported by the lpinfo command.
bits=7	Sets the number of data bits in each character to 7.
bits=8	Sets the number of data bits in each character to 8 (default).
flow=rtscts	Sets the flow control to use the request-to-send (RTS) and clear-to-send (CTS) signal lines.
flow=dtrdsr	Sets the flow control to use the data-terminal-ready (DTR) and data-set-ready (DSR) signal lines.
flow=hard	Sets the flow control to use the request-to-send (RTS) and clear-to-send (CTS) signal lines.
flow=none	Disables flow control completely (default).
flow=soft	Uses the XON and XOFF characters to do flow control; this method is usually not very reliable with printers.
parity=even	Sends a parity check bit with every character; the result of the sum of all bits must be even.
parity=none	Does not send a parity check bit (default).
parity=odd	Sends a parity check bit with every character; the result of the sum of all bits must be odd.

A serial printer on port 1 operating at 19200 baud with 7 data bits, even parity, and DTE-DSR flow control would need the following device URI:

```
serial://dev/ttyS0?baud=19200+bits=7+parity=even+flow=dtedsr
```

Because the serial port is so slow compared to other interfaces, it is generally only used as a last resort or for printing text to dot-matrix printers.

SMB Devices

The SMB device supports printing to Windows printers using the SMB protocol and is provided with the SAMBA software. The device URI for a SMB printer looks like

```
smb://workgroup/server/name
```

where *workgroup* is the name of the workgroup that the server belongs to, *server* is the NetBIOS name of the server, and *name* is the share name of the printer. For a printer named "bar" on server "foo" in workgroup "ESP," the URI would be:

```
smb://ESP/foo/bar
```

If the shared printer requires a username and password, which is usually the case for printers shared from a Windows NT or 2000 server, they can be provided in the URI:

```
smb://username:password@workgroup/server/name
```

NOTE:

Because of the potential security issues that come with including usernames and passwords in the URI, you may want to use the TCP/IP Printing Services supplied with Windows NT or the IPP Printing Services supplied with Windows 2000 instead.

These services have the added benefit of associating the correct username with the print job, because the smb backend can only send the username you provide in the URI.

Socket Devices

The socket device supports direct printing by using TCP/IP sockets, often called AppSocket printing or the JetDirect protocol. The device URI only needs the server name and optionally a port number:

```
socket://server
socket://server:port
```

The default port number is 9100, which is used by all HP JetDirect interfaces and many other network printers. Table 3.5 shows the port numbers to use with various equipment:

TABLE 3.5   URIs for Socket Devices

Manufacturer	URI
Axis	`socket://server:9100` (Parallel 1)
	`socket://server:9101` (Parallel 2)
	`socket://server:9102` (Parallel 3)
EPSON	`socket://server`
Hewlett Packard	`socket://server` (Internal)
	`socket://server:9100` (Parallel 1)
	`socket://server:9101` (Parallel 2)
	`socket://server:9102` (Parallel 3)
Lexmark	`socket://server:5503`

TABLE 3.5   Continued

Manufacturer	URI
Linksys	`socket://server:4010` (Parallel 1)
	`socket://server:4020` (Parallel 2)
	`socket://server:4030` (Parallel 3)
NETGEAR	`socket://server:4010` (Parallel 1)
	`socket://server:4020` (Parallel 2)
	`socket://server:4030` (Parallel 3)
Tektronix	`socket://server`
XEROX	`socket://server:5503`

The socket device is often the best performing and most reliable supported by a network printer or server. The socket device can also stream print data to the printer, whereas other network devices need to store the print data in a temporary file before it can be sent to the printer.

USB Devices

The USB devices support printing over the universal serial bus (USB). USB support is currently available for Linux and the PC BSD operating systems. The device URIs for USB printers vary widely, even among Linux distributions, for example

```
usb:/dev/ulptN
usb:/dev/unlptN
usb:/dev/usblpN
usb:/dev/usb/lpN
usb:/dev/usb/usblpN
```

where N is the USB printer number starting at 0. Like the parallel devices, the USB devices do not support any options.

NOTE:

USB printer numbers are assigned dynamically at boot time and as printers are connected and disconnected. This can cause an existing printer to become associated with the wrong device.

CUPS 1.2 contains a device monitoring daemon that updates the printer device URI as new USB printers are connected and disconnected, and at boot time.

Printer Drivers

Printer queues also usually have a PostScript printer description (PPD) file associated with them. PPD files describe the capabilities of each printer, the page sizes supported, and so forth. CUPS uses PPD files for both PostScript and non-PostScript printers.

You can get PPD files for PostScript printers directly from the printer manufacturer. The PPD files supplied for Windows NT or 2000 are often the best choice for CUPS and are usually available on the driver CD-ROM that comes with the printer. Adobe also maintains an archive of PPD files for licensed printers at:

`http://www.adobe.com/prodindex/printerdrivers/winppd.html`

PPD files for non-PostScript printers are available from a variety of sources. First, CUPS comes with 8 PPD files that provide basic printing services for a large number of EPSON, Hewlett Packard, and Okidata printers. Table 3.6 lists these PPD files and the printers they are used for.

TABLE 3.6   PPD Files for CUPS Sample Printer Drivers

PPD File	Printers
deskjet.ppd	Many Hewlett-Packard OfficeJet products and all Hewlett-Packard DeskJet printers except the Deskjet 710, 712, 720, 722, 820, and 1000
epson9.ppd	All EPSON 9-pin dot-matrix printers and compatibles
epson24.ppd	All EPSON 24-pin dot-matrix printers and compatibles
laserjet.ppd	All Hewlett-Packard LaserJet printers except the LaserJet 3100 and 3150
okidata9.ppd	All Okidata 9-pin dot-matrix printers
okidat24.ppd	All Okidata 24-pin dot-matrix printers
stcolor.ppd	All EPSON Stylus Color printers except the Stylus Color 480 and 580
stphoto.ppd	All EPSON Stylus Photo printers

Because these sample drivers are written to support as wide a range of printers as possible, they only provide basic printing capabilities. In particular, the quality of the inkjet drivers leaves a lot to be desired.

Fortunately, many high-quality printer drivers are available for CUPS. Table 3.7 lists several Web sites that provide CUPS drivers.

TABLE 3.7   Web Sites with CUPS Printer Drivers

URL	Description
http://www.linuxprinting.org/ cups-doc.html	CUPS-o-matic: using Ghostscript printer drivers with CUPS
http://oss.software.ibm.com/ developer/opensource/linux/ projects/omni/	The OMNI printer drivers from IBM
http://gimp-print.sourceforge.net/	Free photo-quality printer drivers for CUPS
http://www.easysw.com/printpro	Commercial printer drivers for CUPS

Adding Your First Printer

CUPS provides two methods for adding printers: a command-line program called lpadmin and a Web interface. The `lpadmin` command allows you to perform most printer administration tasks from the command line and is normally located in /usr/sbin. The Web interface is located at

```
http://localhost:631/admin
```

and provides a wizard that steps you through the printer configuration. If you don't like command-line interfaces, try the Web interface instead.

Adding Your First Printer from the Command-Line

Run the `lpadmin` command with the -p option to add a printer to CUPS:

/usr/sbin/lpadmin -p *name* **-E -v** *device-uri* **-m** *ppd-filename* **_ENTER_**

The -p option specifies the name of the printer. The name can be up to 127 characters long as described earlier in this chapter.

The -E option enables the printer for printing. If you do not provide this option then you will not be able to print to the printer.

The -v option specifies the device URI to use with the printer. Use the `lpinfo` command to find the available devices on your system.

Finally, the -m option specifies an installed PPD file. The `lpinfo` command can be used to list the installed PPD files:

```
lpinfo -m ENTER
epson9.ppd EPSON 9-Pin Series CUPS v1.1
epson24.ppd EPSON 24-Pin Series CUPS v1.1
stcolor.ppd EPSON Stylus Color Series CUPS v1.1
stphoto.ppd EPSON Stylus Photo Series CUPS v1.1
deskjet.ppd HP DeskJet Series CUPS v1.1
laserjet.ppd HP LaserJet Series CUPS v1.1
okidata9.ppd OKIDATA 9-Pin Series CUPS v1.1
okidat24.ppd OKIDATA 24-Pin Series CUPS v1.1
```

For an HP DeskJet printer connected to the parallel port on a Linux system the `lpadmin` command would be:

/usr/sbin/lpadmin -p DeskJet -E -v parallel:/dev/lp0 -m deskjet.ppd _ENTER_

Similarly, an HP LaserJet printer using a JetDirect network interface at IP address 11.22.33.44 would be added with the command:

```
/usr/sbin/lpadmin -p LaserJet -E -v socket://11.22.33.44 -m laserjet.ppd ENTER
```

Configuring Your Printer from the Command-Line

After you have added your printer, you should configure the default options for the printer. The -o option sets a specific option for a printer:

```
lpadmin -p name -o option=value ENTER
```

The *option* name can be any option listed in the PPD file or one of the IPP standard option names described in Chapter 4, "Printing with CUPS."

For now, configure the default media and resolution for your printer with the following:

```
lpadmin -p name -o media=letter -o resolution=600dpi ENTER
```

This sets the default media size to letter (8.5x11 inches) and 600 dots-per-inch (dpi), appropriate for newer Hewlett Packard printers. Table 3.8 lists the supported media and resolution values for each CUPS driver.

TABLE 3.8   Supported Media and Resolution Values

Printer Driver	Supported media	Supported resolutions
EPSON 9-pin Series	letter, legal, a4, fanfoldus	60dpi, 120dpi, 240dpi
EPSON 24-pin Series	letter, legal, a4, fanfoldus	60dpi, 120dpi, 180dpi, 360x180dpi, 360dpi
EPSON Stylus Color	letter, legal, tabloid, a4, a3	180dpi, 360dpi, 720dpi
EPSON Stylus Photo	letter, legal, tabloid, a4, a3	180dpi, 360dpi, 720dpi
HP DeskJet Series	letter, legal, tabloid, a4, a3	150dpi, 300dpi, 600dpi
HP LaserJet Series	letter, legal, tabloid, a4, a3	150dpi, 300dpi, 600dpi
Okidata 9-pin Series	letter, legal, a4, fanfoldus	60dpi, 120dpi, 240dpi
Okidata 24-pin Series	letter, legal, a4, fanfoldus	60dpi, 120dpi, 180dpi, 360x180dpi, 360dpi

The lpoptions command will list the supported options and values for other drivers:

```
lpoptions -p name -l ENTER
```

Finally, the job-sheets-default option specifies the banner page to use when printing files:

```
lpadmin -p name -o job-sheets-default=standard ENTER
```

CUPS includes 7 different banner pages. Table 3.9 lists the standard banner pages.

TABLE 3.9   Banner Pages Supplied with CUPS

Name	Description
none	No banner page (default)
classified	A standard banner page with the word "Classified" at the top and bottom of the page
confidential	A standard banner page with the word "Confidential" at the top and bottom of the page
secret	A standard banner page with the word "Secret" at the top and bottom of the page.
standard	A single page showing the job title, username, and date
topsecret	A standard banner page with the words "Top Secret" at the top and bottom of the page
unclassified	A standard banner page with the word "Unclassified" at the top and bottom of the page

Congratulations, you are now ready to print!

Adding Your First Printer from the Web

The CUPS server provides a user-friendly wizard interface for adding your printers from your Web browser. Rather than figuring out which device URI and PPD file to use, you can click the appropriate listings and fill in some simple information.

Open the following URL in your Web browser to begin:

```
http://localhost:631/admin
```

Click the Add Printer button to display the first page of the Printer Wizard (see Figure 3.1).

Enter the printer name, location, and description in the corresponding text fields. The printer name can be up to 127 characters as described earlier in this chapter. The printer location and description fields can contain any normal text, including spaces.

Click the Continue button to show the next page of the Printer Wizard (see Figure 3.2).

Choose the device from the list and click the Continue button. If you chose a network device, the URI page will appear (see Figure 3.3).

Enter the device URI for your printer and click the Continue button.

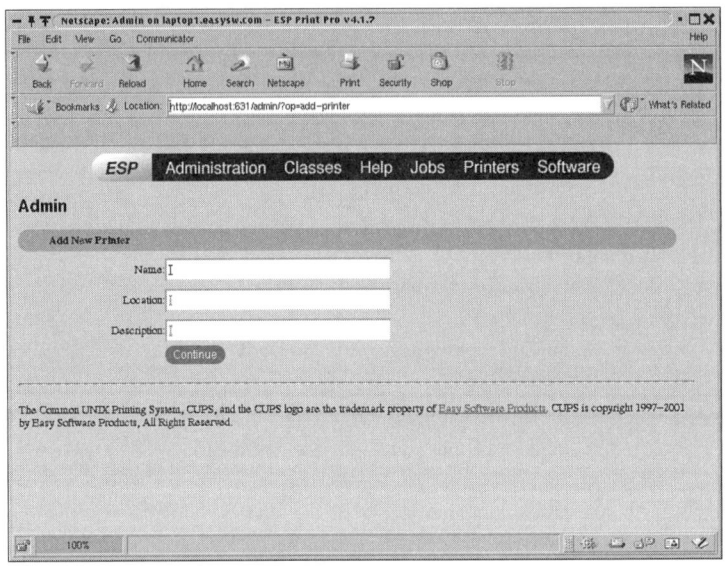

FIGURE 3.1

Opening page of the Printer Wizard.

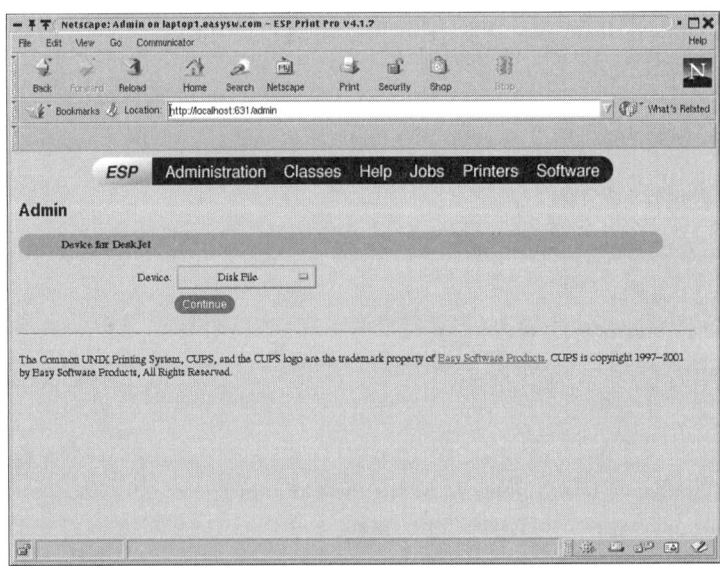

FIGURE 3.2

Device selection page.

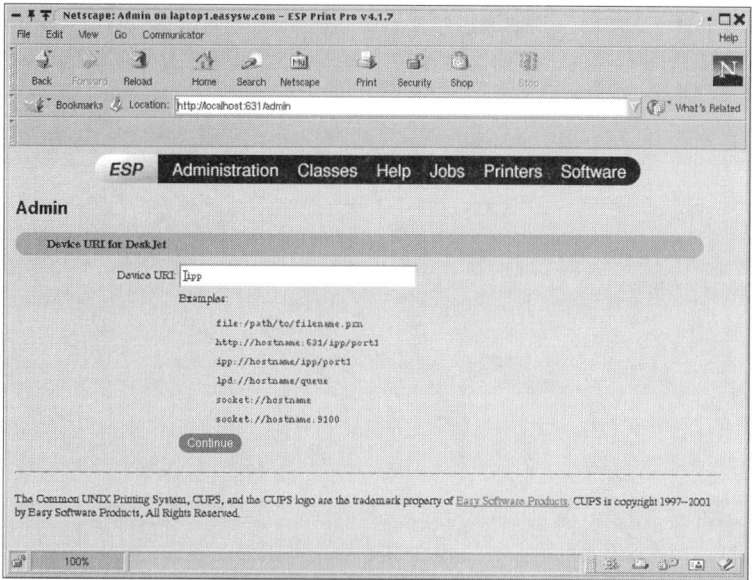

FIGURE 3.3

Network device URI page.

For serial devices the serial configuration page appears instead (see Figure 3.4).

After you have selected and configured the device as needed, the manufacturer selection page appears (see Figure 3.5).

Select the appropriate manufacturer from the list and click the Continue button to show the model selection page (see Figure 3.6).

Select the appropriate model from the list and click the Continue button to add the printer. Click the printer link to view the print queue status (see Figure 3.7).

Configuring Your Printer from the Web Interface

After you have added your printer you should configure the default options for the printer. Click the Configure Printer button to configure your printer (see Figure 3.8).

Review each of the options on the page and make any changes as needed. When you are done making changes, click the Continue button to save your changes.

Congratulations, you are now ready to print!

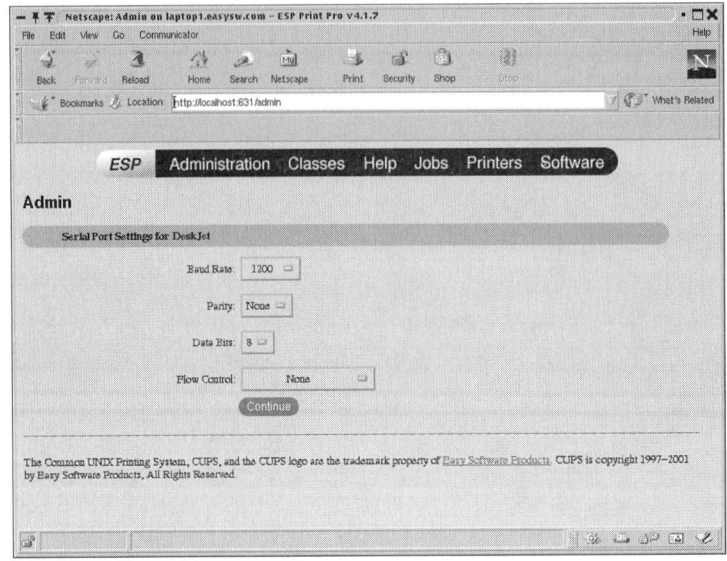

FIGURE 3.4

Serial configuration page.

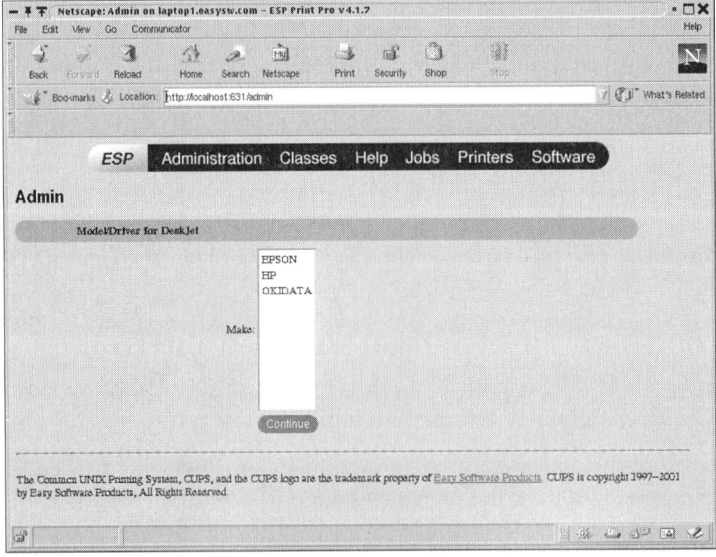

FIGURE 3.5

Manufacturer selection page.

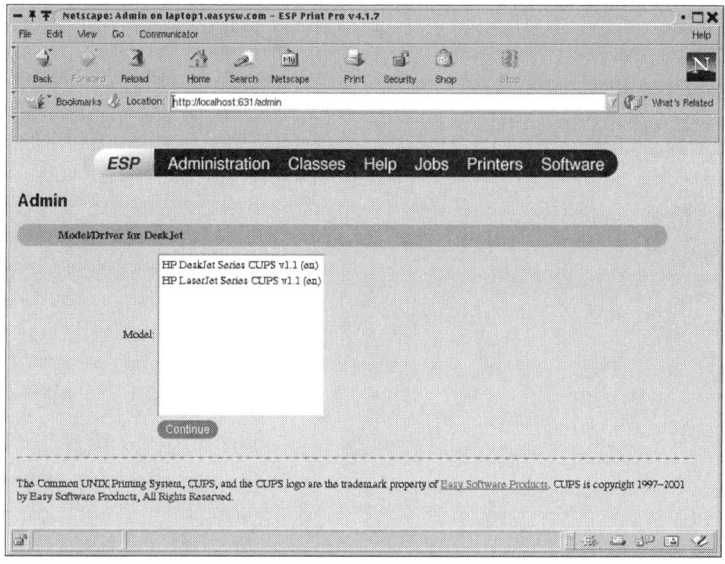

FIGURE 3.6

Model selection page.

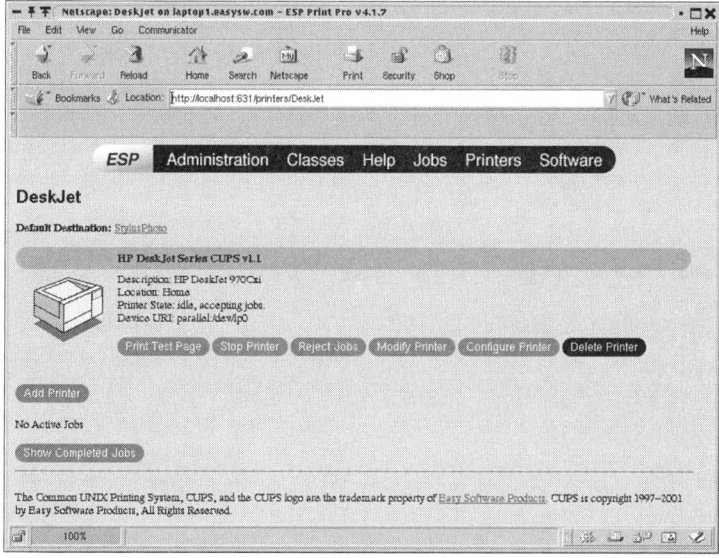

FIGURE 3.7

Print queue status page.

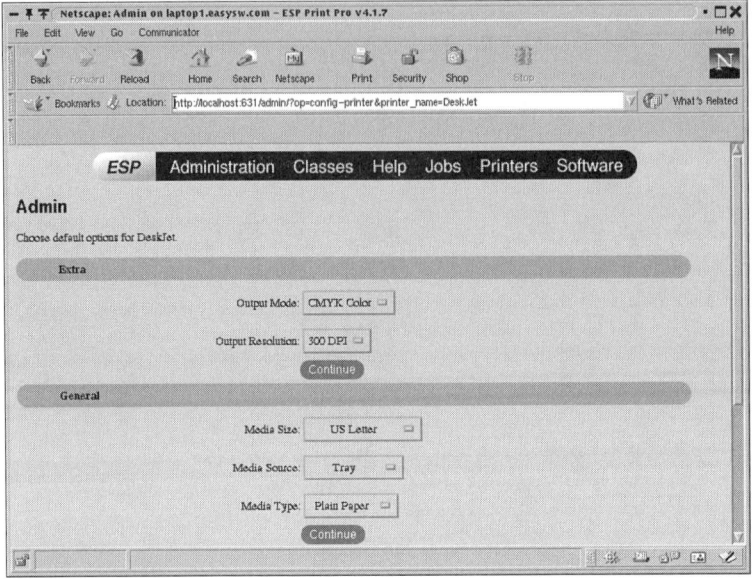

FIGURE 3.8

Printer options page.

Printing a Test Page

After you have added your printer you'll probably want to print a test page. CUPS includes a simple test page file for this purpose. Click the Print Test Page button in the Web interface or run the following command to to print the test page to your new printer:

```
lp -d name /usr/share/cups/data/testprint.ps ENTER
```

The results should look like Figure 3.9.

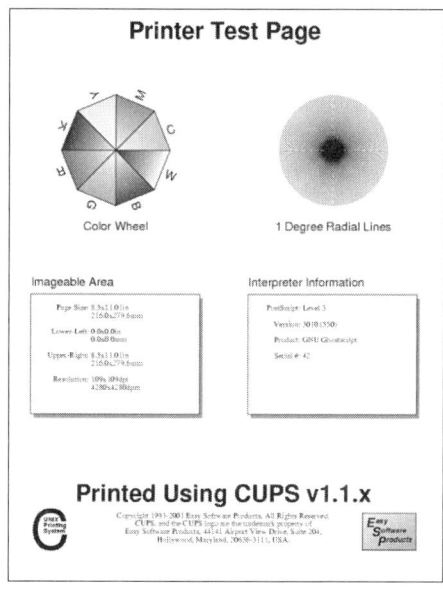

FIGURE 3.9

Printer test page.

Managing Printers from the Command-Line

The lpadmin command allows you to add, modify, and remove printers. You add and modify printers using the -p option:

lpadmin -p *name [options]* **ENTER**

The *name* argument specifies the printer name. The *[options]* parameters specify the device URI, PPD file, and other printer attributes. Table 3.10 summarizes the available options:

TABLE 3.10   The lpadmin Options

Option	Description
-i interface	Copies the named interface script to the printer. Interface scripts are used by System V printer drivers. Because all filtering is disabled when using an interface script, scripts generally should not be used unless there is no other driver for a printer.

TABLE 3.10   Continued

Option	Description
-m model	Specifies a standard printer driver that is usually a PPD file. A list of all available models can be displayed using the lpinfo command with the -m option.
-o option=value	Specifies a printer option to be stored with the printer. The printer option can be any IPP printer attribute or option in the printer's PPD file.
-u allow:all	Allows all users to print to the printer.
-u allow:user1, user2,...,userN	Allows the named users to print to the printer.
-u deny:user1, user2,...,userN	Prevents the named users from printing to the printer.
-v device-uri	Sets the device for communicating with the printer. If a job is currently printing on the named printer, the job is restarted and sent to the new device.
-D info	Provides a textual description of the printer, for example, "John's Personal Printer."
-E	Enables the printer and accepts job. This option is equivalent to running the enable and accept commands on the printer.
-L location	Provides a textual location for the printer, for example, "Computer Lab 5."
-P ppd-file	Specifies a local PPD file for the printer driver.

Setting the Printer Description

The -D option sets the printer description:

lpadmin -p *name* **-D "John\'s Personal Printer"** *ENTER*

The description can contain any text up to 255 characters, including spaces.

Setting the Printer Location

The -L option sets the printer location:

lpadmin -p *name* **-L "Computer Lab 5"** *ENTER*

The location can contain any text up to 255 characters, including spaces.

Changing the Printer Device

The -v option sets the printer device URI:

lpadmin -p *name* **-v** *device-uri* *ENTER*

The device URI is as described earlier in this chapter.

Changing the Printer Driver

The `-i`, `-m`, and `-P` options set the printer driver file to use:

lpadmin -p *name* **-i** *script-filename* ***ENTER***

lpadmin -p *name* **-m** *ppd-filename* ***ENTER***

lpadmin -p *name* **-P** *ppd-filename* ***ENTER***

The `-m` option copies the file from the `/usr/share/cups/model` directory. The other options copy the file from the current directory unless you specify an absolute path.

NOTE:

You can get a list of the available printer drivers using the `lpinfo -m` command.

Changing the Printer Configuration

The `-o` option sets printer options:

lpadmin -p *name* **--o** *option=value* ***ENTER***

The option can be any option from the printer's PPD file or from Table 3.11:

TABLE 3.11   Printer Options That Can Be Set Using `lpadmin`

Option	Description
job-k-limit=value	Sets a per-user limit on the number of kilobytes of print files that a user can print. Set value to 0 to disable kilobyte limits.
job-page-limit=value	Sets a per-user limit on the number of pages that a user can print. Set value to 0 to disable page limits.
job-quota-period=value	Sets the period in seconds for quota calculations. Set the period to 0 seconds to disable quotas.
job-sheets-default= value[,value]	Sets the default banner page to print with each job. If a second value is specified, adds a trailer page to each job as well, which is useful for printing banners on printers that produce face-up prints.
media=value [,value,...]	Sets a media option for the size, type, or source of the printed media.
output-bin=value	Sets the output bin for the printer.
resolution=value	Sets the resolution of printed jobs.
sides=value	Sets single or double-sided printing. The allowed values are one-sided, two-sided-long-edge (portrait), and two-sided-short-edge (landscape).

Setting Quotas on a Printer

CUPS supports page and size-based quotas for each printer. The quotas are tracked individually for each user, but a single set of limits applies to all users for a particular printer. For example, you can limit every user to 5 pages per day on an expensive printer, but you cannot limit every user except Johnny.

The job-k-limit, job-page-limit, and job-quota-period options determine whether and how quotas are enforced for a printer.

The job-quota-period option determines the time interval for quota tracking. The interval is expressed in seconds, so a day is 86,400, a week is 604,800, and a month is 2,592,000 seconds.

For quotas to be enforced, the period and at least one of the limits must be set to a non-zero value. The following options will enable quotas

```
lpadmin -p name -o job-quota-period=604800 -o job-k-limit=1024 ENTER
lpadmin -p name -o job-quota-period=604800 -o job-page-limit=100 ENTER
lpadmin -p name -o job-quota-period=604800 -o job-k-limit=1024 -o job-page-
➥limit=100 ENTER
```

while these options by themselves will not:

```
lpadmin -p name -o job-quota-period=604800 ENTER
lpadmin -p name -o job-page-limit=100 ENTER
lpadmin -p name -o job-k-limit=1024 ENTER
```

Restricting Access to a Printer

The -u option controls which users can print to a printer. The default configuration allows all users to print to a printer:

```
lpadmin -p name -u allow:all ENTER
```

CUPS supports allow and deny lists—you can specify a list of users who are allowed to print or not allowed to print. Along with your list of users you can specify whether they are allowed or not allowed to use the printer:

```
lpadmin -p name -u allow:peter,paul,mary ENTER
```

This command allows peter, paul, and mary to print to the named printer, but all other users cannot print. The command:

```
lpadmin -p name -u deny:peter,paul,mary ENTER
```

has the opposite effect. All users *except* peter, paul, and mary will be able to print to the named printer.

NOTE:

The `allow` and `deny` options are not cummulative. That is, you must provide the complete list of users to allow or deny each time.

Also, CUPS only maintains one list of users—the list can allow or deny users from printing. If you specify an allow list and then specify a deny list, the deny list will replace the allow list—only one list is active at any time.

Deleting Printers

The `-x` option deletes a printer:

`/usr/sbin/lpadmin -x` *name* **ENTER**

When a printer is deleted, all printer data, job history, and quota information is lost. There is no `undo` command.

Setting the Default Printer

Every server has a default printer. The default printer is used when the user does not specify a printer when printing. The `-d` option sets the server default printer:

`/usr/sbin/lpadmin -d` *name* **ENTER**

In addition to the server default, the local printing commands support a client default printer that overrides the server default. This client default printer can be set for the whole computer or an individual user. The `lpoptions` command sets the client default:

`/usr/bin/lpoptions -d` *name* **ENTER**

If you run this command as the root user, the default is set for the entire system; otherwise it sets the default for that account only.

Starting and Stopping Printers

The `enable` and `disable` commands start and stop printer queues, respectively:

`/usr/bin/enable` *name* **ENTER**
`/usr/bin/disable` *name* **ENTER**

Printers that are disabled can still accept jobs for printing, but won't actually print any files until they are started. This is useful if the printer malfunctions and you need time to correct the problem. Any queued jobs are printed after the printer is enabled (started).

Accepting and Rejecting Print Jobs

The `accept` and `reject` commands accept and reject print jobs for the named printer, respectively:

/usr/sbin/accept *name* ***ENTER***
/usr/sbin/reject *name* ***ENTER***

As noted, a printer can be stopped but still accept new print jobs. A printer can also be rejecting new print jobs while it finishes those that have been queued. This is useful when you must perform maintenance on the printer and will not have it available to users for a long period of time.

Managing Printers from the Web Interface

The Web printer management interface is located at:

`http://localhost:631/printers`

From there you can perform all printer management tasks with a few simple mouse clicks. Figure 3.10 shows the printer management page.

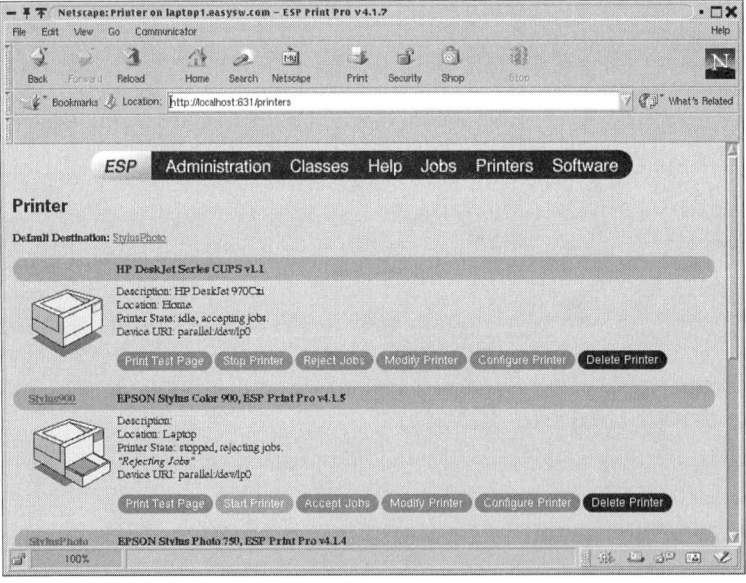

FIGURE 3.10

Web printer management page.

Configuring Printers from the Web Interface

The Configure Printer button displays the printer configuration page. Choose the options you want and then click the Continue button to save them.

Modifying Printers

The Modify Printer button starts the Printer Wizard, showing the original configuration values as you go. This is useful for updating a printer to the latest version of a printer driver, or for updating the device URI when a printer's IP address changes.

Deleting Printers

The Delete Printer button displays a confirmation page (see Figure 3.11). When you click the Continue button the printer will be deleted.

After a printer is deleted, all printer data, job history, and quota information is lost. There is no undo command.

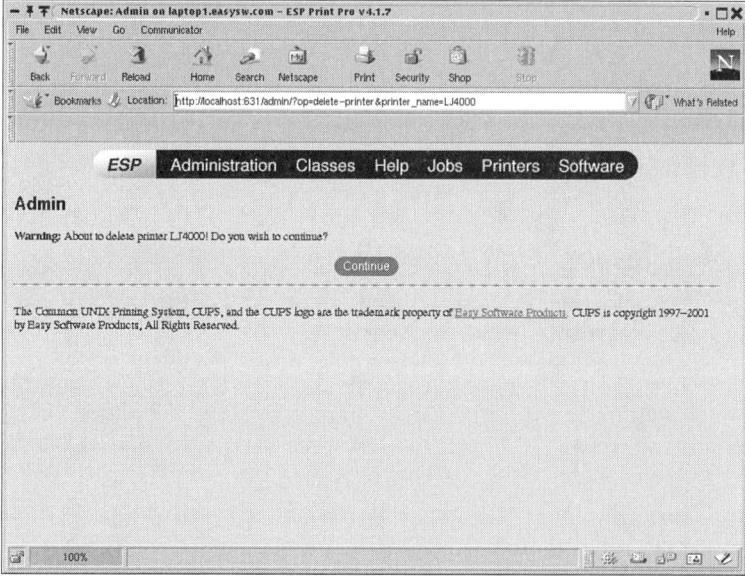

FIGURE 3.11

Printer deletion confirmation page.

Starting Printers

Click the Start Printer button to start a stopped printer. Any pending jobs for that printer will begin printing immediately.

Stopping Printers

Click the Stop Printer button to stop a running printer. Any active jobs for that printer will be paused immediately.

Accepting Print Jobs

Click the Accept Jobs button to accept new jobs on a printer. Users will immediately be able to submit print jobs to that printer.

Rejecting Print Jobs

Click the Reject Jobs button to reject new jobs on a printer. Users will no longer be able to submit print jobs to that printer.

Printing a Test Page

Click the Print Test Page button to print a test page to the printer. Refer to Figure 3.9 to see the test page.

Basics of Classes

CUPS provides collections of printers called printer classes. Jobs sent to a class are forwarded to the first available printer in the class.

Like printers, each class queue has a name associated with it. The class name must start with a letter and can contain up to 127 letters, numbers, and the underscore (_). Case is not significant, so "CLASS", "Class", and "class" are all considered to be the same name.

NOTE:

Classes can themselves be members of other classes, so it is possible for you to define very large, distributed printer classes for high-availability printing.

Managing Printer Classes from the Command-Line

The `lpadmin` command provides options to manage classes on your system. The `-p` and `-c` options are used to add a printer to a class:

```
/usr/sbin/lpadmin -p name -c class ENTER
```

The class is automatically created if it does not exist already. The named printer is then added to the class. Run the `lpadmin` command multiple times to construct a class with multiple printers. For example, running the following commands

```
/usr/sbin/lpadmin -p LaserJet1 -c AllLaserJets ENTER
/usr/sbin/lpadmin -p LaserJet2 -c AllLaserJets ENTER
/usr/sbin/lpadmin -p LaserJet3 -c AllLaserJets ENTER
/usr/sbin/lpadmin -p LaserJet4 -c AllLaserJets ENTER
```

will create a class named `AllLaserJets`, which contains the printers LaserJet1, LaserJet2, LaserJet3, and LaserJet4.

Removing Printers from a Class

The `-r` option removes the named printer from a class:

```
/usr/sbin/lpadmin -p name -r class ENTER
```

The class is automatically deleted if you remove all printers from a class.

Removing a Class Completely

The `-x` option allows you to remove a class without first removing all of the printers from it:

```
/usr/sbin/lpadmin -x class ENTER
```

The printers that are part of the class are unaffected by the removal of the class.

Adding Classes from the Web Interface

The Web interface for classes is located at:

```
http://localhost:631/admin
```

The Add Class button displays the first page of the Class Wizard (see Figure 3.12).

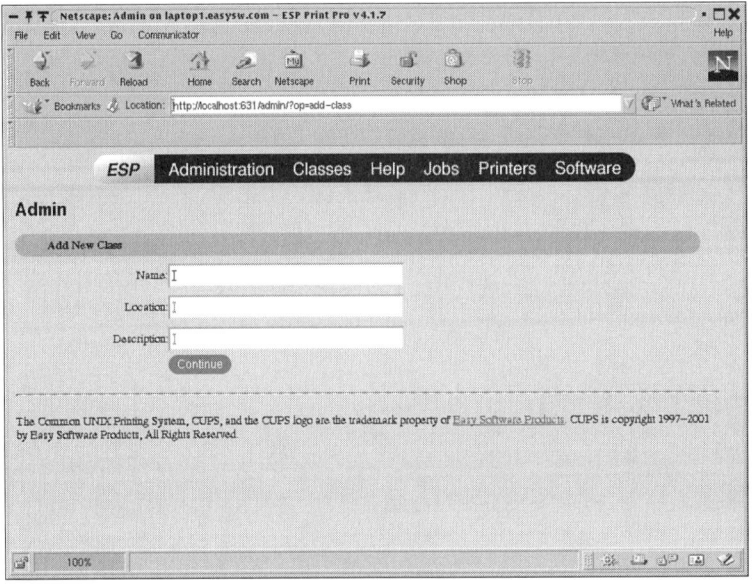

FIGURE 3.12

The opening page of the Class Wizard.

The first thing you'll need to provide is the name, location, and description of the class. The location and description can be any normal text you like. Click the Continue button to choose which printers will be part of the class (see Figure 3.13).

Select each printer that should be a part of your class and click the Continue button to add the class to the system.

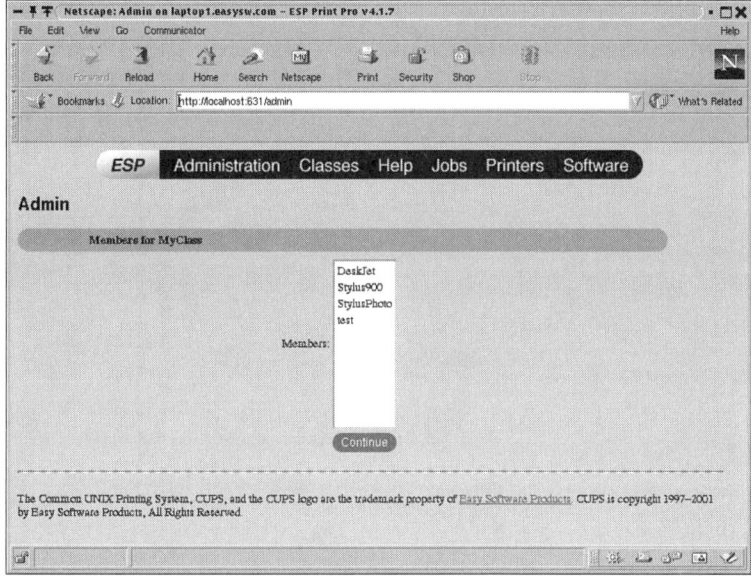

FIGURE 3.13

The class membership page.

Managing Classes from the Web Interface

After you have added your classes, they can be accessed from the following URL:

```
http://localhost:631/classes
```

Each class is shown with buttons to perform administration functions (see Figure 3.14).

Modifying Classes

The Modify Class button starts the Class Wizard, showing the original information and member printers as you go. This is most useful for adding and removing printers from a class.

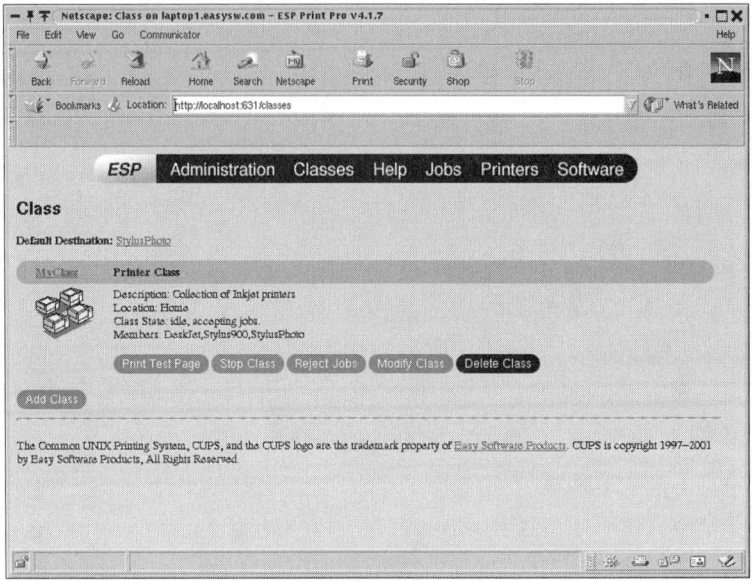

FIGURE 3.14

The class management page.

Deleting Classes

The Delete Class button displays a confirmation page (see Figure 3.15). When you click the Continue button the class will be deleted.

After a class is deleted, all class data, job history, and quota information is lost. There is no undo command. This does not affect the individual printers in the class.

Starting Classes

Click the Start Class button to start a stopped class. Any pending jobs for that class will begin printing immediately on the next available printer in the class.

NOTE:

Starting a class does not affect the individual printers in the class

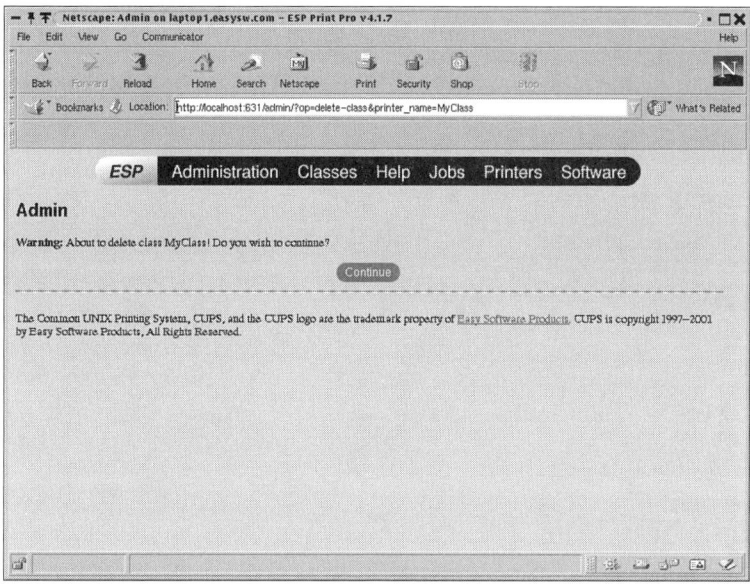

FIGURE 3.15

Class deletion confirmation page.

Stopping Classes

Click the Stop Class button to stop a running class. Any active jobs for that class will be paused immediately. The printers that were active will be able to print other jobs while the class is stopped.

NOTE:

Stopping a class does not affect the individual printers in the class.

Accepting Print Jobs

Click the Accept Jobs button to accept new jobs on a class. Users will immediately be able to submit print jobs to that class.

NOTE:

Accepting jobs for a class does not affect the individual printers in the class.

Rejecting Print Jobs

Click the Reject Jobs button to reject new jobs on a class. Users will no longer be able to submit print jobs to that class.

NOTE:

Rejecting jobs for a class does not affect the individual printers in the class.

Printing a Test Page

Click the Print Test Page button to print a test page to the class. Refer to Figure 3.9 to see the test page.

Implicit Classes

CUPS also supports implicit classes. Implicit classes work like regular classes but are created automatically by the client based on the available printers on the network.

Implicit classes allow you to set up multiple print servers with identical printer configurations and have the client machines send their print jobs to the first available server. If one or more servers go down, the jobs are automatically redirected to the servers that are running, providing fail-safe printing. When all the servers are running, the effect is a general load balancing.

Summary

CUPS supports printers, classes, and implicit classes. The `lpadmin` command provides most of the printer and class management functions on the command-line, whereas the Web interface provides wizards and configuration pages for more user-friendly administration.

CHAPTER 4

Printing with CUPS

This chapter shows how to submit, query, and cancel print jobs to different printers. It also shows how to configure popular applications to print through CUPS.

Printing Files

Unlike legacy printing systems, CUPS supports printing many different types of files directly out of the box. For example, without CUPS you might have to load a PDF file into Acrobat Reader or Xpdf to print it. With CUPS you just print the PDF file directly!

CUPS provides both the System V (lp) and Berkeley (lpr) printing commands. Type one of the following commands to print a file to the default (or only) printer on the system:

```
lp filename ENTER
lpr filename ENTER
```

Choosing a Printer

Many systems will have more than one printer available to the user. These printers can be attached to the local system through a parallel, serial, or USB port or available over the network.

Use the lpstat command to see a list of the available printers:

```
lpstat -p -d ENTER
printer CLJ4550 is idle.
printer LJ4000 is idle.
printer StylusColor600 is idle.
system default destination: LJ4000
```

The -p option asks for a list of printers and the -d option asks for the current default printer or class.

After you know the name of the printer you want, use the -d option with lp command or the -P option with the lpr command to print to that printer:

```
lp -d name filename ENTER
lpr -P name filename ENTER
```

The name is the name reported by the lpstat command. Printers on remote servers can be accessed using name@server.

Printing Multiple Copies

Both the lp and lpr commands have options for printing more than one copy of a file:

```
lp -n num-copies filename ENTER
lpr -#num-copies filename ENTER
```

By default, copies are uncollated for speed. If you need to print collated copies, see the section titled "Printing Collated Copies."

Encrypting Your Print Jobs

Some documents that you print may contain sensitive information, such as contracts and other legal documents. If you are printing to a printer on another machine, an unscrupulous person could eavesdrop on your print job and collect that information.

All of the printer commands support the -E option to encrypt (scramble) the communications between you and the print server, making it very difficult for someone to eavesdrop on your communications. For example, to encrypt a print job you could use the following command:

```
lp -E -d name@server filename ENTER
```

Setting Printer Options

For many types of files, the default printer options may be sufficient for your needs. However, at times you may need to change the options for a particular file you are printing.

The lp and lpr commands allow you to pass printer options using the -o option:

```
lp -o landscape -o scaling=75 -o media=A4 filename.jpg ENTER
lpr -o landscape -o scaling=75 -o media=A4 filename.jpg ENTER
```

The available printer options vary depending on the printer. All printers support a common set of options as well.

Printing Collated Copies

Copies are normally not collated for you. Use the collate option to produce collated copies:

```
lp -n num-copies -o collate=True filename ENTER
lpr -#num-copies -o collate=True filename ENTER
```

Printer-Specific Options

Each printer has its own options that are based on the options in the PPD (driver) file. The lpoptions command provides a way to see a list of the available options:

```
lpoptions -p LaserJet4000 -l ENTER
HPCollate/Collate: *False True
HPPaperPolicy/Fit to Page: NearestSizeNoAdjust NearestSizeAdjust *PromptUser
```

```
HPHalftone/Levels of Gray: Enhanced *PrinterDefault Standard
HPNup/Pages per Sheet: OneUpL *OneUp TwoUpL TwoUp FourUpL FourUp SixUpL
➥SixUp NineUpL NineUp SixteenUpL SixteenUp
HPwmLocation/Print Watermark: *True False
Smoothing/Resolution Enhancement: False *True
HPScalePatterns/Scale Patterns: Off *Scale
HPwmText/Watermark: CompanyConfidential CompanyPrivate CompanyProprietary
➥ Confidential Copy Copyright Draft FileCopy Final ForInternalUse
➥*None Preliminary Proof ReviewCopy Sample TopSecret Urgent
HPwmTextAngle/Watermark Angle: DegN15 DegN30 DegN45 DegN60 DegN75 DegN90 Deg0
➥Deg15 Deg30 *Deg45 Deg60 Deg75 Deg90
HPwmFont/Watermark Font: CourierB *HelveticaB TimesB
HPwmFontSize/Watermark Size: pt24 pt30 pt36 pt42 *pt48 pt54 pt60 pt66
➥pt72 pt78 pt84 pt90
HPwmTextStyle/Watermark Style: *Medium Narrow Halo Wide
Duplex/Duplex: DuplexNoTumble DuplexTumble *None
PageSize/Media Size: A4 A5 B5 Custom Env10 EnvISOB5 EnvC5 EnvDL EnvMonarch
➥Executive Legal *Letter
InputSlot/Media Source: Envelope Upper ManualFeed Middle Lower *LargeCapacity
MediaType/Media Type: Bond Cardstock Color Labels Letterhead *None Plain
➥Preprinted Prepunched Recycled Rough Transparency
PageRegion/PageRegion: A4 A5 B5 Env10 EnvISOB5 EnvC5 EnvDL EnvMonarch
➥Executive Legal Letter
Option3/Duplex Unit: *True False
Option5/Envelope Feeder: *True False
Option4/Printer Hard Disk: True *False
InstalledMemory/Total Printer Memory: 4MB 8MB 12MB 20MB 28MB *36MB
Option1/Tray 3: *True False
Option2/Tray 4: *True False
JCLEconomode/EconoMode: *False True
JCLResolution/Resolution: 300dpi 600dpi *1200dpi
```

Each option starts with the option name, a slash, the human readable text for that option, and a colon. The options themselves follow the colon:

```
JCLResolution/Resolution: 300dpi 600dpi *1200dpi
```

This option controls the resolution on an HP LaserJet 4000. The option name is JCLResolution. It supports values of 300dpi, 600dpi, and 1200dpi. The asterisk (*) in front of the 1200dpi value indicates that the default resolution is 1200 DPI.

The -o option can be used to specify a different resolution when printing. For example, the following commands print a job at 600 DPI:

```
lp -o JCLResolution=600dpi filename ENTER
lpr -o JCLResolution=600dpi filename ENTER
```

Standard Printer Options

This section describes the standard printer options that are available when printing with the lp and lpr commands.

General Options

Table 4.1 lists the general options that apply when printing all types of files.

TABLE 4.1   General Printing Options for CUPS

Name	Description
brightness	Sets the overall brightness of the output
gamma	Sets the overall gamma correction (contrast) of the output
job-sheets	Chooses the banner pages to use for the job
landscape	Prints in landscape orientation
media	Sets the media size, source, and/or type
number-up	Sets the number of document pages to print on each sheet of paper
page-ranges	Prints the selected pages in the document
page-set	Prints all, even, or odd pages in the document
sides	Prints single- or double-sided

Setting the Orientation

The landscape option will rotate the page 90 degrees to print in landscape orientation:

```
lp -o landscape filename ENTER
lpr -o landscape filename ENTER
```

Selecting the Media Size, Type, and Source

The media option sets the media size, type, and/or source:

```
lp -o media=Letter filename ENTER
lp -o media=Letter,MultiPurpose filename ENTER
lpr -o media=Letter,Transparency filename ENTER
lpr -o media=Letter,MultiPurpose,Transparency filename ENTER
```

You can specify multiple media values by separating the values with commas.

The available media sizes, types, and sources depend on the printer, but most support the options shown in Table 4.2.

TABLE 4.2   Common Media Options

Value	Description
Letter	U.S. Letter (8.5×11 inches, or 216×279mm)
Legal	U.S. Legal (8.5×14 inches, or 216×356mm)
A4	ISO A4 (8.27×11.69 inches, or 210×297mm)
COM10	US #10 Envelope (9.5×4.125 inches, or 241×105mm)
DL	ISO DL Envelope (8.66×4.33 inches, or 220×110mm)
Transparency	Transparency media type or source
Upper	Upper paper tray
Lower	Lower paper tray
MultiPurpose	Multipurpose paper tray
LargeCapacity	Large capacity paper tray

The actual media options are derived from the `PageSize`, `InputSlot`, and `MediaType` options in the printer's PPD file. You can view these options by filtering the output from `lpoptions` using egrep:

```
lpoptions -p name -l | egrep 'PageSize|MediaType|InputSlot' ENTER
PageSize/Media Size: A4 A5 B5 Custom Env10 EnvISOB5 EnvC5 EnvDL EnvMonarch
➥Executive Legal *Letter
InputSlot/Media Source: Envelope Upper ManualFeed Middle Lower *LargeCapacity
MediaType/Media Type: Bond Cardstock Color Labels Letterhead
➥*None Plain Preprinted Prepunched Recycled Rough Transparency
```

Printing On Both Sides of the Paper

The `sides` option turns double-sided printing on or off. Table 4.3 shows the valid values for the `sides` option:

TABLE 4.3   Valid `sides` Option Values

Option	Description
-o sides=one-sided	Prints single-sided
-o sides=two-sided-long-edge	Prints double-sided for portrait orientation documents
-o sides=two-sided-short-edge	Prints double-sided for landscape orientation documents

The most commonly used value is two-sided-long-edge, as shown in the following:

```
lp -o sides=two-sided-long-edge filename ENTER
lpr -o sides=two-sided-long-edge filename ENTER
```

Banner Options

The job-sheets option applies when printing all types of files. and sets the banner page(s) to use for a job:

```
lp -o job-sheets=none filename ENTER
lp -o job-sheets=standard filename ENTER
lpr -o job-sheets=classified,classified filename ENTER
```

If only one banner file is specified it will be printed before the files in the job and no banner will be printed after the job. If two banner files are specified, the first is printed before and the second after the files in the job.

The available banner pages depend on the local system configuration. The standard CUPS banner files are listed in Table 4.4.

TABLE 4.4   Standard Banner Files

Name	Description
none	Do not produce a banner page.
classified	A banner page with a "classified" label at the top and bottom.
confidential	A banner page with a "confidential" label at the top and bottom.
secret	A banner page with a "secret" label at the top and bottom.
standard	A banner page with no label at the top and bottom.
topsecret	A banner page with a "top secret" label at the top and bottom.
unclassified	A banner page with an "unclassified" label at the top and bottom.

Document Options

The document options shown in Table 4.5 apply when printing all types of files.

TABLE 4.5   Common Document Printing Options

Name	Description
brightness	Adjusts the brightness for the printed output
gamma	Adjusts the gamma (contrast) for the printed output
number-up	Prints multiple document pages on a single page
page-ranges	Chooses ranges of pages for printing

Selecting a Range of Pages

The page-ranges option selects a range of pages for printing:

```
lp -o page-ranges=1 filename ENTER
lp -o page-ranges=1-4 filename ENTER
lp -o page-ranges=1-4,7,9-12 filename ENTER
lpr -o page-ranges=1-4,7,9-12 filename ENTER
```

As shown previously, the pages value can be a single page, a range of pages, or a collection of page numbers and ranges separated by commas. The pages will always be printed in ascending order, regardless of the order of the pages in the page-ranges option.

The default is to print all pages.

Selecting Even or Odd Pages

Use the page-set option to select the even or odd pages:

```
lp -o page-set=odd filename ENTER
lp -o page-set=even filename ENTER
lpr -o page-set=all filename ENTER
```

The legal values for the page-set option are shown in Table 4.6.

TABLE 4.6   page-set Option Legal Values

Name	Description
all	Prints all pages (default)
even	Prints only even-numbered pages
odd	Prints only odd-numbered pages

N-Up Printing

The number-up option selects N-Up printing. N-Up printing places multiple document pages on a single printed page.

CUPS supports 1-Up, 2-Up, and 4-Up formats:

```
lp -o number-up=1 filename ENTER
lp -o number-up=2 filename ENTER
lp -o number-up=4 filename ENTER
lpr -o number-up=4 filename ENTER
```

The default format is 1-Up.

Setting the Brightness

You can control the overall brightness of the printed output using the brightness option:

```
lp -o brightness=120 filename ENTER
lpr -o brightness=80 filename ENTER
```

Values greater than 100 lighten the print, whereas values less than 100 darken it.

Setting the Gamma Correction

You can control the overall gamma correction of the printed output using the gamma option:

```
lp -o gamma=1700 filename ENTER
lpr -o gamma=455 filename ENTER
```

Values greater than 1000 lighten the print, whereas values less than 1000 darken it. The default gamma is 1000.

Text Options

The following options apply only when printing text files. Table 4.7 lists the text printing options.

TABLE 4.7   Options for Printing Text Files

Name	Description
columns	Sets the number of columns of text
cpi	Sets the number of characters per inch
lpi	Sets the number of lines per inch
page-bottom	Sets the bottom margin
page-left	Sets the left margin.
page-right	Sets the right margin
page-top	Sets the top margin
prettyprint	Prints a header at the top and highlights syntax

Setting the Number of Characters Per Inch

The cpi option sets the number of characters per inch:

```
lp -o cpi=10 filename ENTER
lp -o cpi=12 filename ENTER
lpr -o cpi=17 filename ENTER
```

The default characters per inch is 10.

Setting the Number of Lines Per Inch

The lpi option sets the number of lines per inch:

```
lp -o lpi=6 filename ENTER
lpr -o lpi=8 filename ENTER
```

The default lines per inch is 6.

Setting the Number of Columns

The `columns` option sets the number of text columns:

```
lp -o columns=2 filename ENTER
lpr -o columns=3 filename ENTER
```

The default number of columns is 1.

Setting the Page Margins

Normally the page margins are set to the hard limits of the printer. Use the `page-left`, `page-right`, `page-top`, and `page-bottom` options to adjust the page margins:

```
lp -o page-left=72 -o page-right=36 filename ENTER
lp -o page-top=36 page-bottom=36 filename ENTER
lpr -o page-left=72 -o page-right=36 -o page-top=36 page-bottom=36 filename ENTER
```

The value argument is the margin in points; 72 points are in each inch and 28 points are in each centimeter.

Pretty Printing

The `prettyprint` option puts a header at the top of each page with the page number, job title (usually the filename), and the date. Also, script, perl, C, and C++ keywords are bold-face, comment lines are italicized, and preprocessor lines and strings are highlighted. The `prettyprint` option has no value associated with it:

```
lp -o prettyprint filename ENTER
lpr -o prettyprint filename ENTER
```

Image Options

The following options apply only when printing image files. Table 4.8 lists the valid image printing options.

TABLE 4.8   Options for Printing Images

Name	Description
hue	Adjusts the hue of an image
position	Sets the position of the image on the page
ppi	Sets the resolution of the image in pixels per inch
saturation	Adjusts the color saturation of an image
scaling	Sets the size of the image in percent of the page

Positioning the Image

The `position` option specifies where to position the image on the page. Table 4.9 lists the valid positions:

TABLE 4.9   Image Positions

Option	Description
-o position=center	Center the image on the page (default).
-o position=top	Print the image centered at the top of the page.
-o position=left	Print the image centered on the left of page.
-o position=right	Print the image centered on the right of the page.
-o position=top-left	Print the image at the top left corner of the page.
-o position=top-right	Print the image at the top right corner of the page.
-o position=bottom	Print the image centered at the bottom of the page.
-o position=bottom-left	Print the image at the bottom left corner of the page.
-o position=bottom-right	Print the image at the bottom right corner of the page.

Scaling the Image

Normally images are scaled using resolution information in the image file itself. If no information is present, a default resolution of 128 pixels per inch is used.

The `scaling` and `ppi` options change the size of the printed image:

```
lp -o scaling=100 filename ENTER
lp -o ppi=128 filename ENTER
lpr -o ppi=300 filename ENTER
```

The `scaling` value is a percentage from 1 to 800. The percentage is based on the page size and not the image size, so a scaling of 100% will fill the page as completely as possible. A scaling of 200% will print on up to 4 pages, and a scaling of 50% will make the image occupy approximately one-half of the page.

The `ppi` value is a number from 1 to 1200 specifying the resolution of the image in pixels per inch. An image that is 3000×2400 pixels will print 10×8 inches at 300 pixels per inch, for example. If the specified resolution makes the image larger than the page allows, multiple pages will be printed to satisfy the request.

Adjusting the Hue (Tint) of an Image

The `hue` option adjusts the color hue of the printed image, much like the tint control on your television:

```
lp -o hue=0 filename ENTER
lp -o hue=45 filename ENTER
lpr -o hue=-45 filename ENTER
```

The value is a number from −360 to 360 and represents the color hue rotation in degrees. Table 4.10 summarizes the change you'll see with different colors:

TABLE 4.10   Color Hue Adjustments

Original	hue=−45	hue=45
Red	Purple	Yellow-orange
Green	Yellow-green	Blue-green
Yellow	Orange	Green-yellow
Blue	Sky-blue	Purple
Magenta	Indigo	Crimson
Cyan	Blue-green	Light-navy-blue

The default hue adjustment is 0.

Adjusting the Saturation (Color) of an Image

The saturation option adjusts the saturation of the colors in an image, much like the color knob on your television:

```
lp -o saturation=100 filename ENTER
lp -o saturation=0 filename ENTER
lpr -o saturation=200 filename ENTER
```

The value specifies the color saturation from 0 to 200. A normal color saturation is 100 percent. A color saturation of 0 produces a black-and-white print, whereas a value of 200 will make the colors extremely intense.

The default saturation is 100.

HP-GL/2 Options

The following options apply only to HP-GL/2 files. Table 4.11 lists the HP-GL/2 printing options.

TABLE 4.11   Options for Printing HP-GL/2 Files

Name	Description
blackplot	Draws the plot in black ink
fitplot	Fits the plot to the page
penwidth	Sets the default pen width

Printing in Black

The `blackplot` option specifies that all pens should plot in black:

```
lp -o blackplot filename ENTER
lpr -o blackplot filename ENTER
```

The default is to use the colors defined in the plot file or the standard pen colors defined in the HP-GL/2 reference manual from Hewlett Packard.

Fitting the Plot on the Page

The `fitplot` option specifies that the plot should be scaled to fit on the page:

```
lp -o fitplot filename ENTER
lpr -o fitplot filename ENTER
```

The default is to use the absolute distances specified in the plot file.

NOTE:

This feature depends on an accurate plot size (PS) command in the HP-GL/2 file. If no plot size is given in the file then no scaling will be performed.

Setting the Default Pen Width

The `penwidth` option specifies the default pen width for HP-GL/2 files:

```
lp -o penwidth=1000 filename ENTER
lpr -o penwidth=0 filename ENTER
```

The `penwidth` value specifies the pen width in micrometers. The default value of 1000 produces lines that are 1 millimeter in width. Specifying a pen width of 0 produces lines that are exactly 1 pixel wide.

NOTE:

This option is ignored when the pen widths are set in the plot file.

Raw or Unfiltered Output

The `raw` option allows you to send files directly to a printer without filtering. This is sometimes required when printing from applications that provide their own printer drivers for your printer:

```
lp -o raw filename ENTER
lpr -o raw filename ENTER
```

The -l option can also be used with the lpr command to send files directly to a printer:

```
lpr -l filename ENTER
```

Saving Printer Options

Each printer supports a large number of options. Rather than specifying these options each time you print a file, CUPS allows you to save them as default options for the printer.

The lpoptions command saves the options for your printers. Like the lp and lpr commands, it accepts printer options using the -o option:

```
lpoptions -o media=A4 -o sides=two-sided-long-edge ENTER
lpoptions -o media=Legal -o scaling=100 ENTER
```

After these are saved, any lp or lpr command will use them when you print.

Setting Options for a Specific Printer

The previous example shows how to set the options for the default printer. The -p printer option specifies the options are for a specific printer:

```
lpoptions -p name -o media=A4 -o sides=two-sided-long-edge ENTER
lpoptions -p name -o media=Legal -o scaling=100 ENTER
```

Viewing the Current Saved Options

The lpoptions command can also be used to show the current options by not specifying any new options on the command line:

```
lpoptions ENTER
media=A4 sides=two-sided-long-edge


lpoptions -p deskjet ENTER
media=Legal scaling=100
```

Setting the Default Printer

The administrator normally will set a server default printer that is used as the default printer by everyone. Use the -d printer option to set your own default printer:

```
lpoptions -d name ENTER
```

Printer Instances

In addition to setting options for each print queue, CUPS supports printer instances which allow you to define several different sets of options for each printer. You specify a printer instance using the slash (/) character:

```
lpoptions -p laserjet/duplex -o sides=two-sided-long-edge ENTER
lpoptions -p laserjet/legal -o media=Legal ENTER
```

The `lp` and `lpr` commands also understand this notation:

```
lp -d laserjet/duplex filename ENTER
lpr -P laserjet/legal filename ENTER
```

NOTE:

The `lpoptions` command is used to create printer instances as well as set the default options. The instance is created the first time you use an instance name with lpoptions. For example, running this command

```
lpoptions -p deskjet/photo -o resolution=600dpi -o media=photo ENTER
```

will create a new instance named "photo" for the printer "deskjet."

Removing Options and Instances

Use the `-x` option to remove all options for a printer or instance that you no longer need:

```
lpoptions -x deskjet ENTER
lpoptions -x laserjet/duplex ENTER
lpoptions -x laserjet/legal ENTER
```

The `-x` option only removes the options for that printer or instance; the original printer and system defaults remain.

Checking the Printer Status from the Command Line

The `lpstat` command can be used to check for jobs that you have submitted for printing:

```
lpstat ENTER
Printer-1 johndoe 4427776
Printer-2 johndoe 15786
Printer-3 johndoe 372842
```

The jobs are listed in the order they will be printed. Use the `-p` option to see which files and printers are active:

```
lpstat -p ENTER
printer DeskJet now printing DeskJet-1.
```

Use the -o and -p options together to show the jobs and the printers:

```
lpstat -o -p ENTER
DeskJet-1 johndoe 4427776
DeskJet-2 johndoe 15786
DeskJet-3 johndoe 372842
printer DeskJet now printing DeskJet-1.
```

Checking the Printer Status from the Web

Open the following URL to monitor the status of printers and jobs from your Web browser:

```
http://localhost:631
```

From there you can view the status of classes, jobs, and printers with the click of a button!

Canceling a Print Job from the Command-Line

The cancel and lprm commands cancel a print job:

```
cancel job-id ENTER
lprm job-id ENTER
```

The *job-id* is the number that was reported to you by the lp or lpstat commands.

Canceling a Print Job from the Web Interface

You can also cancel print jobs from the Web interface. Start by opening the following URL in your Web browser:

```
http://localhost:631/jobs
```

Then click the Cancel Job button for the job you want to cancel.

Configuring Applications for CUPS

Although most applications will work with CUPS without changes, some applications require a small amount of configuration to use the correct printer drivers and so forth. Other applications can be enhanced to take advantage of the features of CUPS.

GIMP

The GIMP is probably the best-known Unix imaging application these days. GIMP includes a print plug-in that handles printing to many different kinds of printers—in fact, you can get CUPS versions of these drivers on the GIMP-print home page!

The print plug-in shipped with GIMP 1.2.x will work properly out of the box for any of the printers that GIMP-print supports. To use GIMP with other printer drivers you'll need to do some configuration of the plug-in.

To configure the print plug-in for CUPS, open an image file in GIMP and then choose Print from the File menu. This will display the print plug-in window (see Figure 4.1).

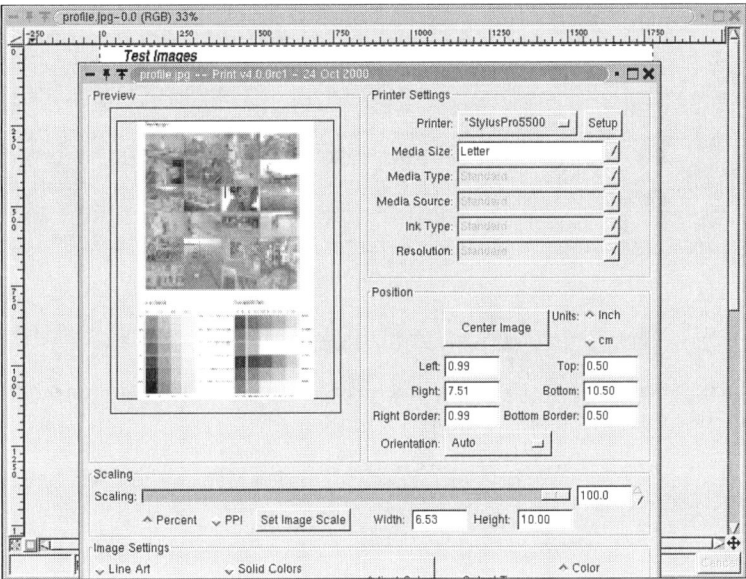

FIGURE 4.1

The GIMP print plug-in window.

Choose the printer you want to configure and click the Setup button. This will display the Print Setup dialog (see Figure 4.2).

Choose PostScript Level 2 for the printer driver.

Next, enter the name of the PPD file for the printer or click the Browse button to locate it. Local printers store the PPD files in /etc/cups; for remote printers, copy the PPD file from that directory on the server, or load the PPD file in your browser and do a Save As; the PPD file is available on any server at the URL:

```
http://server:631/printers/name.ppd
```

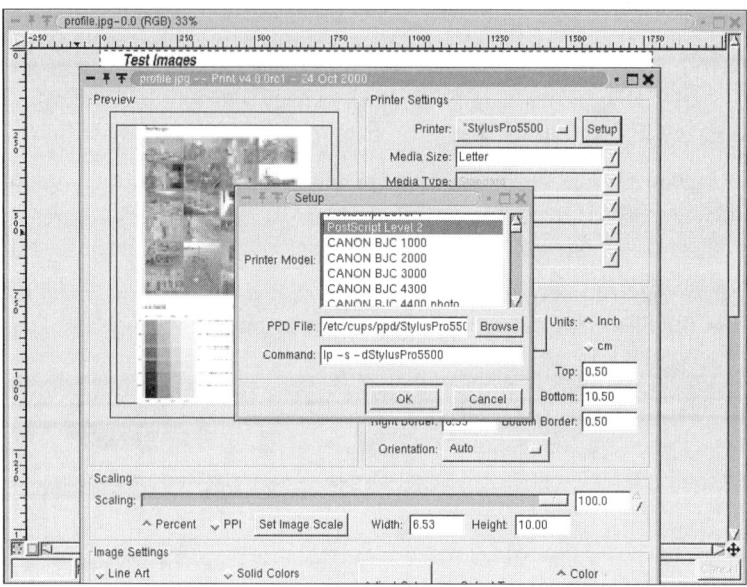

FIGURE 4.2

The GIMP Print Setup window.

Finally, remove the -oraw option from the print command—you won't need it for CUPS drivers. Click OK to complete the printer setup.

Netscape

Netscape requires very little configuration. The Netscape Print dialog (see Figure 4.3) shows the print command along with various other options.

The default print command will send the page to the default printer; you can use the -d or -P options with the lp and lpr commands to direct the page to another printer.

There are also several add-on GUI print commands you can use. These GUIs are discussed in Chapter 1, "Introduction to CUPS."

Star Office

Star Office provides fairly good printer support using the Generic printer driver or through PPD files, and printer configuration is fairly simple. Start by running the spadmin command included with Star Office to show the window in Figure 4.4. For Star Office 5.1 the command is the following:

```
~/Office51/bin/spadmin ENTER
```

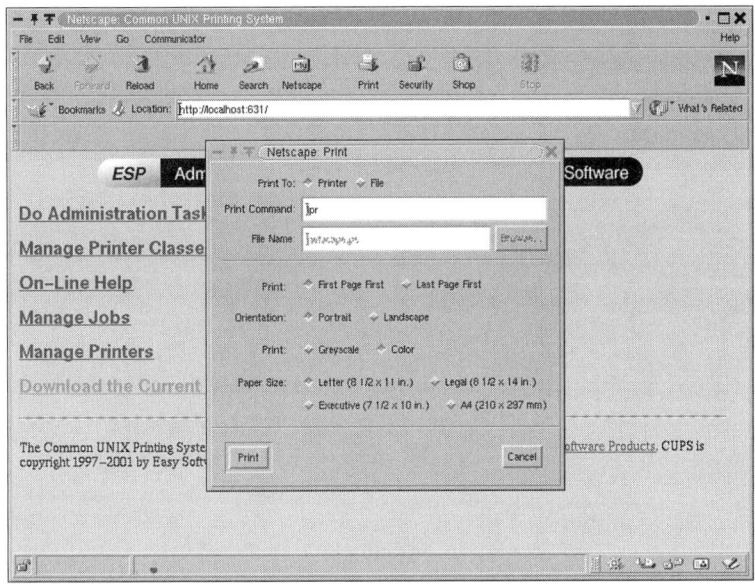

FIGURE 4.3

The Netscape Print dialog.

The Star Office 5.2 program is in a different directory:

`~/office52/program/spadmin ENTER`

First click the Install New Driver. . .button to display the Driver Installation dialog (see Figure 4.5). Click the Browse button and go to the `/etc/cups/ppd` or `/usr/share/cups/model` directories. Select the printer drivers you are interested in (you can select more than one) and click the OK button.

After adding the printer drivers, scroll through the list of available printer drivers and select the driver for your printer. Click the Add New Printer button to add the driver to the list of available printers at the top.

Now that the printer driver is added, click the Configure button to configure the driver (see Figure 4.6).

When the dialog appears, click the Additional Settings tab and then click the Default Values button to set the default margins for that printer. Make any other changes to the default options that you like and click the OK button to close the Configuration dialog.

Finally, click the Connect button to connect the printer driver to a print queue. The Connect dialog appears, as shown in Figure 4.7.

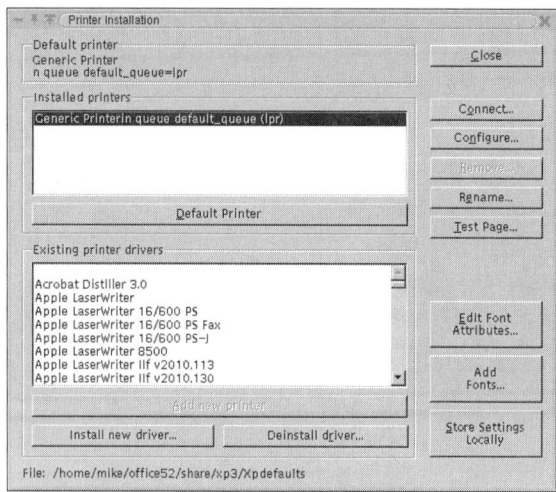

FIGURE 4.4

The spadmin window.

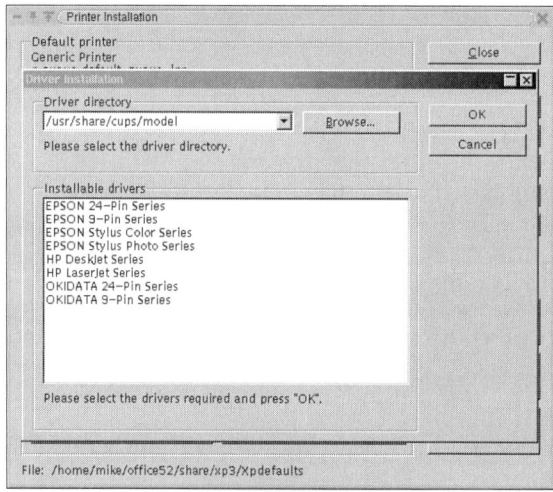

FIGURE 4.5

The Driver Installation dialog.

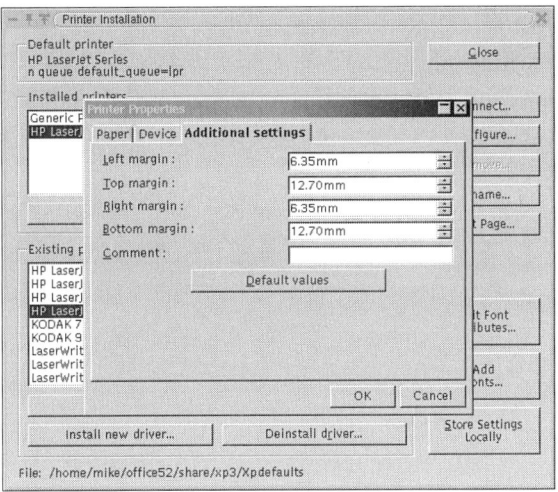

FIGURE 4.6

The Printer Properties dialog.

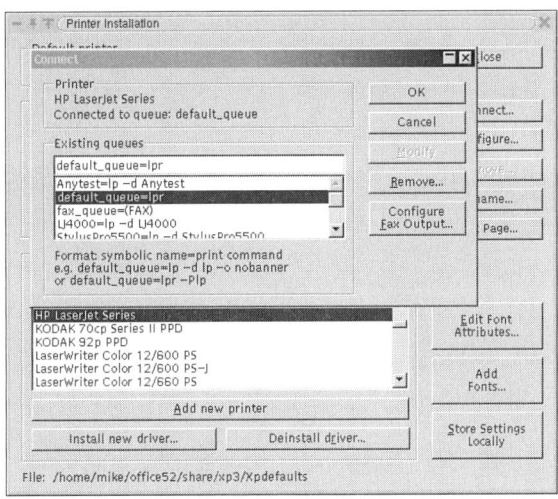

FIGURE 4.7

The Printer Connection dialog.

Select the printer you want to print to and click the OK button to complete the printer setup.

Summary

CUPS provides both the Berkeley and System V printing commands. Printer options allow you to control the appearance of your printed output, and these options can be saved for individual printers and printer instances. Jobs can be listed and canceled from the command-line or Web interfaces.

Most applications will work with CUPS without change; however some applications can be customized to provide enhanced printing capabilities through CUPS.

CHAPTER 5

Server Configuration

This chapter shows how to configure the CUPS server and includes several examples of typical server configurations.

The Basics

The CUPS scheduler consists of an IPP server (cupsd), a polling daemon (cups-polld), and a line printer daemon gateway (cups-lpd). These programs all work together to provide printing services to the client.

Configuration Files

The CUPS server (cupsd) reads several configuration files when it starts up. Normally these files are located under the /etc/cups directory. Table 5.1 lists the configuration files and their purpose:

TABLE 5.1   Server Configuration Files

File	Purpose
classes.conf	Contains information on each printer class. Normally you manipulate this file using the lpadmin command or the Web interface.
client.conf	Provides the default server name for client machines. See Chapter 6, "Client Configuration," for more information.
cupsd.conf	Controls how the CUPS server (cupsd) operates and is normally edited by hand.
mime.convs	Contains a list of standard file conversion filters and their costs. You normally do not edit this file.
mime.types	Contains a list of standard file formats and how to recognize them. You normally do not edit this file.
printers.conf	Contains information on each printer. Normally you manipulate this file using the lpadmin command or the Web Interface.
ssl/server.crt	SSL/TLS certificate file.
ssl/server.key	SSL/TLS private key file.

Changing the Server Configuration

The cupsd.conf file contains configuration directives that control how the server functions. The format is purposely similar to the popular Apache Web server configuration files.

Each line is either blank, contains a configuration directive, or contains a comment. Each directive is listed on a line by itself followed by its value. Comments are introduced using the number sign (#) character at the beginning of a line.

Because the server configuration file consists of plain text, you can use your favorite text editor to make changes to it.

NOTE:

Several configuration file editors are available for CUPS that eliminate the need to hand-edit configuration files.

The KUPS software includes a KDE-based editor that allows you to edit the configuration file on the local server.

ESP Print Pro 4.2 and higher includes a GUI editor that can edit configuration files locally or remotely.

Finally, CUPS 1.2 includes a Web-based configuration editor.

Server Directives

CUPS supports most of the standard Apache configuration directives as well as some new ones specific to CUPS. You'll find a complete reference to the directives in Appendix A, "Configuration File Directives."

Restarting the CUPS Server

After you have made a change to a configuration file you need to restart the CUPS server by sending it a HUP signal or using the supplied initialization script. The CUPS distributions install the script in the init.d directory with the name cups. The location varies based on the operating system:

```
/etc/init.d/cups restart ENTER
/etc/rc.d/init.d/cups restart ENTER
/sbin/init.d/cups restart ENTER
```

Basic Configuration Options

The sample configuration file included with CUPS is suitable for a standalone system. The next few sections will show how to make common modifications to the basic configuration to support server operation, easy Web browser integration, enhanced security, and encryption.

Configuring CUPS as a Server

The default CUPS configuration does not enable connections from client systems. To enable connections from client systems, edit the cupsd.conf file and locate the section reading:

```
<Location />
Order deny,allow
```

```
Deny from all
Allow from 127.0.0.1
</Location>
```

Assuming that your local network has an address of 192.168.0.0 and a netmask of 255.255.0.0, the following change will enable remote printing from clients:

```
<Location />
Order deny,allow
Deny from all
Allow from 127.0.0.1
Allow from 192.168.0.0/255.255.0.0
</Location>
```

> **NOTE:**
>
> Early versions of CUPS allowed connections from all hosts by default.
>
> Unless you will be providing an Internet-wide printing service, **do not** allow connections from all hosts. Although adding an "Allow from all" line would seem to be the easiest way to configure your server, it will needlessly open your print server to unwanted print jobs and other denial-of-service attacks from outside systems.

Next you need to enable broadcasting from your server by specifying the network broadcast address for your local network. Add the following directive to set the broadcast address to 192.168.255.255:

```
BrowseAddress 192.168.255.255
```

After saving the changes to cupsd.conf, restart the server. All of your CUPS clients will now see the printers on the server and be able to print to them.

> **NOTE:**
>
> CUPS provides printer-browsing support to clients using UDP broadcasting. The BrowseAddress directive is so-named to allow for other types of browsing in the future such as multicasting, SLP, and LDAP.

Easy Web Browsing

Normally CUPS listens for HTTP requests on the IPP port, port 631. Users access the CUPS server with the following URL:

```
http://server:631
```

To make it easier for clients to access the CUPS server, add a second port directive to the `cupsd.conf` file to make the CUPS server listen on the normal HTTP port (80):

```
Port 631
Port 80
```

Now your users will also be able to access the CUPS server with the following (simpler) URL:

```
http://server
```

Enhanced Security

The default configuration of CUPS runs the CUPS server as the root user, but runs all external programs as an unprivileged user. Although this provides excellent security against unpriviledged access to system resources, because the server is running as root it may be possible to exploit an undiscovered bug to gain root access.

CUPS provides a `RunAsUser` directive to run the server as an unpriviledged user after setting up the network services. Add the following line to `cupsd.conf` to enable this mode:

```
RunAsUser Yes
```

NOTE:

When running the server as an unpriviledged user, the SIGHUP reconfigure mechanism is disabled. Any files under /etc/cups (and the /etc/cups directory itself) must be owned by the unpriviledged user as well.

Also, any local devices (parallel, serial, and USB ports) must be accessible to the unpriviledged user, otherwise a "permission denied" message will result when you print.

Finally, some networked LPD printers may not work in unpriviledged mode because the LPD backend will be unable to reserve a privileged port as required by RFC 1179.

Encryption

CUPS supports 128-bit encryption of any request or response sent to the server. Encryption scrambles the data sent between the client and server so that an eavesdropper is unable to understand it. The most common use of encryption is to scramble passwords that are sent when doing administration tasks from a remote machine. It is also often used to print sensitive documents over the Internet.

Before you can enable encryption on your server, you must get an encryption certificate. This can be one purchased from one of the many Certificate Authorities (see Table 5.2) or an unsigned one you create by using the tools provided with the OpenSSL library.

NOTE:

Encryption certificates can be signed by a Certificate Authority or unsigned. A signed certificate includes information that identifies it as coming from an official source, whereas an unsigned certificate does not.

Because unsigned encryption certificates are not generated by an official Certificate Authority, most browsers will generate a warning message when you access your server for the first time. The user must approve the new certificate before it can be used, so make sure your users are aware of this.

Unsigned certificates are just as secure as signed certificates in most circumstances. However, it is more likely that successful man-in-the-middle attacks can be carried out with the unsigned certificate because your users are expecting the warning dialog and won't know whether the certificate is valid. For this reason, don't use unsigned certificates to provide encryption beyond your LAN.

TABLE 5.2   Commercial Certificate Authorities

Company	URL
128i Ltd.(New Zealand)	http://www.128i.com
BelSign NV/SA	http://www.belsign.be
CertiSign Certificadora Digital Ltda.	http://www.certisign.com.br
Certplus SA (France)	http://www.certplus.com
Deutsches Forschungsnetz	http://www.pca.dfn.de/dfnpca/certify/ssl/
Entrust.net Ltd.	http://www.entrust.net/products/index.htm
Equifax Inc.	http://www.equifaxsecure.com/ebusinessid/
GlobalSign NV/SA	http://www.GlobalSign.net
IKS GmbH	http://www.iks-jena.de/produkte/ca/
NetLock Kft.(Hungary)	http://www.netlock.net
NLsign B.V.	http://www.nlsign.nl
TC TrustCenter (Germany)	http://www.trustcenter.de/html/Produkte/
Thawte Consulting	http://www.thawte.com/certs/server/TC_Server/855.htmrequest.html
Verisign, Inc.	http://www.verisign.com/guide/apache

Generating an Unsigned Encryption Certificate

If you decide to use the OpenSSL library to generate your own unsigned certificate, run the following commands:

```
openssl req -new -x509 -keyout /etc/cups/ssl/server.key \
    -out /etc/cups/ssl/server.crt -days 365 -nodes ENTER
Using configuration from /usr/ssl/openssl.cnf
Generating a 1024 bit RSA private key
.......++++++
...................++++++
writing new private key to '/etc/cups/ssl/server.key'
-----
You are about to be asked to enter information that will be incorporated
into your certificate request.
What you are about to enter is what is called a Distinguished Name or a DN.
There are quite a few fields but you can leave some blank
For some fields there will be a default value,
If you enter '.', the field will be left blank.
-----
Country Name (2 letter code) ?: US ENTER
State or Province Name (full name) [Some-State]: Maryland ENTER
Locality Name (eg, city) []:Hollywood ENTER
Organization Name (eg, company) [Internet Widgits Pty Ltd]:Easy Software Products
ENTER
Organizational Unit Name (eg, section) []: ENTER
Common Name (eg, YOUR name) []:host.easysw.com ENTER
Email Address []:mike@host.easysw.com ENTER
chmod 600 /etc/cups/ssl/server.* ENTER
```

The openssl command creates the server key and certificate files in the /etc/cups/ssl directory. The chmod command makes sure that only the root user can read them.

Getting a Signed Certificate

If you decide to get a signed certificate, request a certificate to be used with the Apache or Stronghold Web servers—these certificates will be in the correct format for CUPS.

Requesting a certificate involves some more openssl commands to generate the server key and certificate request. Start by generating the server key:

```
openssl genrsa -des3 -out /etc/cups/ssl/server.key 1024 ENTER
Generating RSA private key, 1024 bit long modulus
........................++++++
...++++++
e is 65537 (0x10001)
Enter PEM pass phrase:password ENTER
Verifying password - Enter PEM pass phrase:password ENTER
```

The password you use is not important—you will be removing it in the last step of this process.

Next, generate your certificate request file with the following:

```
openssl req -new -key /etc/cups/ssl/server.key -out /etc/cups/server.csr ENTER
Using configuration from /usr/ssl/openssl.cnf
Enter PEM pass phrase: password ENTER
You are about to be asked to enter information that will be incorporated
into your certificate request.
What you are about to enter is what is called a Distinguished Name or a DN.
There are quite a few fields but you can leave some blank
For some fields there will be a default value,
If you enter '.', the field will be left blank.
-----
Country Name (2 letter code) ?:US ENTER
State or Province Name (full name) [Some-State]:Maryland ENTER
Locality Name (eg, city) []:Hollywood ENTER
Organization Name (eg, company) [Internet Widgits Pty Ltd]:Easy Software Products
ENTER
Organizational Unit Name (eg, section) []:ENTER
Common Name (eg, YOUR name) []:host.easysw.com ENTER
Email Address []:mike@host.easysw.com ENTER

Please enter the following 'extra' attributes
to be sent with your certificate request
A challenge password []:ENTER
An optional company name []:ENTER
```

Send the file /etc/cups/ssl/server.csr to your Certificate Authority. They will provide you with a signed certificate that can be used with your CUPS server. The certificate should be copied to the file /etc/cups/ssl/server.crt.

Finally, remove the password from your server key with these commands

```
cd /etc/cups/ssl ENTER
mv server.key server.old ENTER
openssl rsa -in server.old -out server.key ENTER
rm server.old ENTER
```

and then make sure that the files can be read only by the server

```
chmod 600 server.* ENTER
```

That's it! You now have an official, signed certificate for your server!

Enabling Encryption in Your Server

Now that your server certificate and key are installed, you need to tell CUPS to use them. CUPS provides two encryption methods—the dedicated https-type of service as well as the newer HTTP Upgrade method. The `https` service encrypts the connection to the server immediately, while the HTTP Update method upgrades the connection only when the client or server requests it. Figure 5.1 shows how the two methods work.

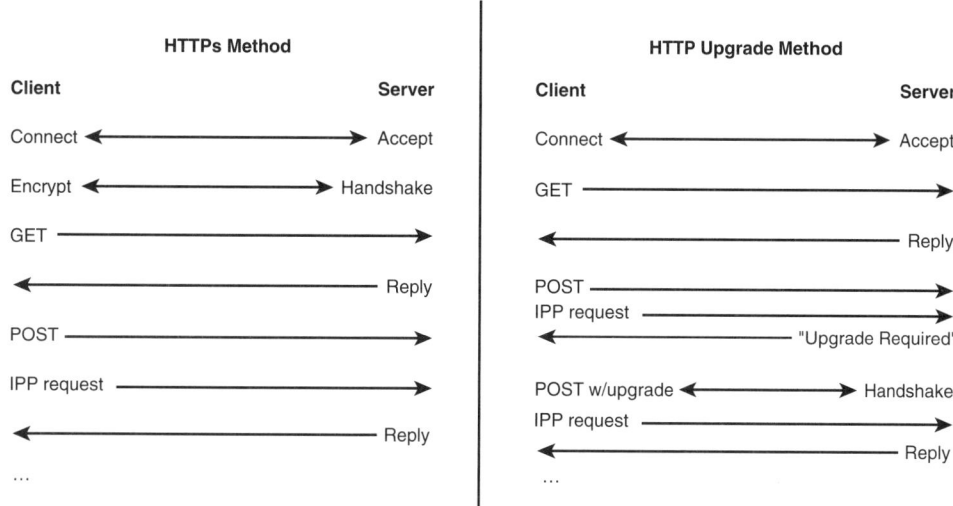

FIGURE 5.1

CUPS encryption methods.

If you will be doing remote administration using a Web browser, you'll want to enable the `https` service. The `SSLPort` directive tells CUPS to use `https` on the specified port number:

SSLPort 443

Port 443 is the standard port for `https` URLs. If you already have a secure Web server running on your system on port 443 you can generally use any other port number in addition to 80 and 631.

The `Encryption` directive is another you'll want to use. It specifies the level of encryption that is required for various resources. For remote administration you'll need to update the following section reading:

```
<Location /admin>
#
# You definitely will want to limit access to the administration functions.
# The default configuration requires a local connection from a user who
# is a member of the system group to do any admin tasks.  You can change
# the group name using the SystemGroup directive.
#
```

```
AuthType Basic
AuthClass System

## Restrict access to local domain
Order Deny,Allow
Deny From All
Allow From 127.0.0.1

#Encryption Required
</Location>
```

Assuming that your local network has an address of 192.168.0.0 and a netmask of 255.255.0.0, the following changes will enable remote administration with encryption:

```
<Location /admin>
#
# You definitely will want to limit access to the administration functions.
# The default configuration requires a local connection from a user who
# is a member of the system group to do any admin tasks.  You can change
# the group name using the SystemGroup directive.
#

AuthType Basic
AuthClass System

## Restrict access to local domain
Order Deny,Allow
Deny From All
Allow From 127.0.0.1
Allow from 192.168.0.0/255.255.0.0

Encryption Required
</Location>
```

Advanced Access Control

CUPS supports access control based on the client address, the user certificate or username and password, and encryption.

Address-based access control enables you to limit access to specific systems, networks, or domains. Although this does not provide authentication, it does enable you to limit the potential users of your system efficiently.

Certificates, usernames, and passwords provide ways to limit access to individual people or groups.

Finally, you can require encryption on specific resources; this is often used to provide secure remote administration access, as described in the previous section titled "Enabling Encryption in Your Server."

Basics of Access Control

CUPS maintains a list of locations that have access control, authentication, and encryption enabled. Locations are specified using the `Location` directive:

```
<Location /resource>
AuthClass ...
AuthGroupName ...
AuthType ...
Encryption ...

Order ...
Allow from ...
Deny from ...
</Location>
```

Locations generally follow the directory structure of the `DocumentRoot` directory; however, CUPS does have several virtual locations for administration, classes, jobs, and printers. Table 5.3 lists the virtual locations that CUPS provides.

TABLE 5.3   CUPS Virtual Locations

Resource	Description
/admin	The resource for all administration operations
/classes	The resource for all classes
/classes/*name*	The resource for class *name*
/jobs	The resource for all jobs
/jobs/*id*	The resource for job *id*
/printers	The resource for all printers
/printers/*name*	The resource for printer *name*
/printers/*name*.ppd	The PPD file for printer *name*

Authentication of Users

CUPS supports user authentication through HTTP Basic and Digest authentication. Basic authentication uses Unix accounts and passwords, whereas Digest authentication uses a special MD5 password file just for CUPS.

NOTE:

Basic authentication sends the username and password Base64-encoded from the client to the server, so it offers no protection against eavesdropping unless you are using encryption on the connection. This means that a malicious user can monitor network packets and discover valid users and passwords that could result in a serious compromise in network security. Use Basic authentication only in conjunction with encryption.

Unlike Basic authentication, Digest passes the MD5 sum (basically a complicated checksum) of the username and password instead of the strings themselves. Also, Digest authentication does not use the Unix password file, so if an attacker does discover the original password it is less likely to result in a serious security problem as long as you use a different Digest password from the corresponding Unix password.

Because most Web browsers do not support Digest authentication, your best choice is Basic authentication with Encryption enabled.

CUPS also supports a local certificate-based authentication scheme that can be used in place of Basic or Digest authentication by clients connecting on the local machine. Certificate authentication is not supported or enabled from remote clients.

Authentication is enabled using the following `AuthType` directive inside a location section:

```
<Location /printer/DeskJet>
AuthType Basic
Encryption Required
</Location>
```

This example requires a Unix password when a user prints a file to a printer queue named DeskJet. To use Digest passwords instead, use the following:

```
<Location /printer/DeskJet>
AuthType Digest
Encryption Required
</Location>
```

Digest authentication works with users and passwords defined in the `/etc/cups/passwd.md5` file. The `lppasswd` command is used to add, change, or remove accounts from the `passwd.md5` file. To add a user to the default system group, type the following:

```
lppasswd -a user ENTER
Password: password ENTER
Password again: password ENTER
```

After this is added, a user can change his/her password by typing

```
lppasswd ENTER
Old password: password ENTER
Password: password ENTER
Password again: password ENTER
```

To remove a user from the password file, type the following:

```
lppasswd -x user ENTER
```

Authentication of Groups

Group authentication adds an extra requirement that the user is part of a Unix or Digest group. The default CUPS configuration uses group authentication to require that administration requests be performed by valid administrative users in the "root," "sys," or "system" group, depending on your OS.

The `AuthClass` directive specifies the type of group authentication to perform. Table 5.4 lists the authentication classes:

TABLE 5.4   Authentication Classes

Class	Description
None	No group membership is required.
System	Membership in the system group is required.
Group	Membership in the named group is required.

For System authentication, the user must be a member of the system group, which by default is set to the "root," "sys," or "system" group on your system. This group can be explicitly set using the `SystemGroup` directive:

```
SystemGroup administrators

<Location /admin>
AuthType Basic
AuthClass System
Encryption Required
</Location>
```

For Group authentication, the `AuthGroupName` directive is used instead:

```
<Location /admin>
AuthType Basic
AuthClass Group
AuthGroupName administrators
Encryption Required
</Location>
```

NOTE:

The root user is considered by CUPS to be a member of every group.

Address-Based Access Control

Address-based access control restricts access based on the IP address of the client. The `Allow` and `Deny` directives specify hosts or networks that are allowed or not allowed to access the resource:

```
<Location /printer/DeskJet>
Deny from all
Allow from 192.168.0.1
Allow from 192.168.0.2
Allow from 192.168.1.0/255.255.255.0
</Location>
```

This would allow clients at IP addresses 192.168.0.1, 192.168.0.2, and 192.168.1.0 to access the printer named DeskJet. The last line for the 192.168.1 network could also be written as

```
Allow from 192.168.1
```

or:

```
Allow from 192.168.1.0/24
```

The /24 indicates that the top 24 bits of the network address are significant.

Name-Based Access Control

Name-based access control restricts access based on the host or domain name. The hostname is resolved from the client's IP address. For name-based access control to work, you must first enable hostname resolution:

```
HostNameLookups on
```

NOTE:

Hostname lookups can add a large performance penalty because of the time it takes to do the reverse-lookup on the IP address. Use name-based access control only if you absolutely must.

After that, use the name in the `Allow` or `Deny` lines:

```
<Location /printer/DeskJet>
Deny from all
Allow from host.foo.bar.com
Allow from *.easysw.com
Allow from .bar.net
</Location>
```

Log Files

CUPS maintains three log files for the accesses, errors, and pages that are processed by the server. The log files are normally located in the `/var/log/cups` directory.

The log files are normally rotated when they reach 1MB. The `MaxLogSize` directive controls when they are rotated:

```
MaxLogSize 0
MaxLogSize 65536
MaxLogSize 64k
MaxLogSize 1024k
MaxLogSize 1m
```

A max size of 0 disables log rotation.

The Access Log File

The access log file contains a log of all HTTP requests processed by the CUPS server. It is a text file in the so-called "common log format" and can be analyzed using most Web server log analysis tools.

Each line looks like this:

```
host group user date-time \"method resource version\" status bytes
```

```
127.0.0.1 - - [20/May/1999:19:20:29 +0000] "POST /admin/ HTTP/1.1" 401 0
127.0.0.1 - mike [20/May/1999:19:20:31 +0000] "POST /admin/ HTTP/1.1" 200 0
```

The *host* field is normally only an IP address unless you have enabled the `HostNameLookups` directive in the `cupsd.conf` file.

The *group* field always contains "-" in CUPS.

The *user* field is the authenticated username of the requesting user. If no username and password are supplied for the request then this field contains "-".

The *date-time* field is the date and time of the request in local time and is in the format

```
[DD/MON/YYYY:HH:MM:SS +ZZZZ]
```

where *zzzz* is the timezone offset in hours and minutes from Greenwich Mean Time (also known as GMT also known as ZULU).

The *method* field is the HTTP method used (for example, GET, PUT, or POST).

The *resource* field is the filename of the requested resource.

The *version* field is the HTTP specification version used by the client. For CUPS clients this will always be HTTP/1.1.

The *status* field contains the HTTP result status of the request. Usually it is 200, but other HTTP status codes are possible. For example, 401 is the "unauthorized access" status in the preceding example.

The *bytes* field contains the number of bytes in the request. For POST requests the bytes field contains the number of bytes that was received from the client.

The Error Log File

The error log file lists messages from the scheduler (errors, warnings, and so forth):

```
level date-time message
```

```
I [20/May/1999:19:18:28 +0000] Job 1 queued on 'DeskJet' by 'mike'.
I [20/May/1999:19:21:02 +0000] Job 2 queued on 'DeskJet' by 'mike'.
I [20/May/1999:19:22:24 +0000] Job 2 was cancelled by 'mike'.
```

The *level* field contains the type of message, as shown in Table 5.5:

TABLE 5.5   Message Levels

Level	Description
X	An emergency condition exists.
A	An alert occurred.
C	A critical error occurred.
E	An error occurred.
W	The server was unable to perform some action.
N	Notice message.
I	Informational message.
D	Debugging message.
d	Detailed debugging message.

The *date-time* field contains the date and time that the error occurred. The format of this field is identical to the data-time field in the access_log file.

The *message* field contains a free-form textual message.

The Page Log File

The page log file lists each page that is sent to a printer. Each line contains the following information:

```
printer user job-id date-time page-number num-copies job-billing
DeskJet root 2 [20/May/1999:19:21:05 +0000] 1 0 acme-123
```

The *printer* field contains the name of the printer that printed the page. If you send a job to a printer class, this field will contain the name of the printer that was assigned the job.

The *user* field contains the name of the user (the IPP requesting-user-name attribute) that submitted this file for printing.

The *job-id* field contains the job number of the page being printed.

The *date-time* field contains the date and time that the page started printing. The format of this field is identical to the data-time field in the access_log file.

The *page-number* and *num-pages* fields contain the page number and number of copies being printed of that page. For printers that cannot produce copies on their own, the num-pages field will always be 1.

The *job-billing* field contains a copy of the job-billing attribute provided with the IPP create-job or print-job requests or "–" if none was provided.

Summary

CUPS uses several text configuration files that determine how the server operates and what services are provided to remote machines. CUPS supports access control and authentication to restrict access to the server and encryption to protect the privacy of the data or print that files you send.

The log files are plain text files that are automatically rotated by the CUPS server. The access log file is stored in common log format so it can be analyzed easily using most Web server tools.

CHAPTER 6

Client Configuration

This chapter discusses several ways to configure CUPS clients for printing.

The Basics

A client is any machine that sends print jobs to another machine for final printing. Clients can also be servers if they communicate directly with printers of their own.

Each client can have a local server that spools jobs before sending them to the remove server, or the client can run without a local server and send jobs directly to the server.

CUPS supports the following methods of configuring client machines:

1. Manual configuration of print queues
2. Specifying a single server for printing
3. Automatic configuration of print queues
4. Specifying multiple servers for printing
5. Relaying printers to other clients

WHICH CONFIGURATION SHOULD I USE?

The choice of client configuration depends a great deal on your network and client machines.

Running a local CUPS server on a client provides the best overall functionality, but does use a small amount of system resources to print the files in the background and monitor the network for available printers.

If you have many servers or printers, consider tuning the BrowseInterval and BrowseTimeout settings on both the server and client machines to minimize network congestion. For very busy networks, the hardwired remote printer approach may be necessary, but often a combination of BrowsePoll and BrowseRelay on selected client machines will be a better solution that involves less maintenance.

If you choose to disable the local server and print files directly to a remote server, your clients will require less memory and disk space but will be exposed to a single point of failure—the remote server. In a large network, this can often be catastrophic to both the users and network administrator.

Manual Configuration of Print Queues

The most tedious method of configuring client machines is to configure each remote queue by hand using the lpadmin command:

lpadmin -p *name* **-E -v ipp:**//*server*/**printers**/*name* ***ENTER***

The *name* is the name of the printer on the server machine. The *server* is the hostname or IP address of the server machine. Repeat the lpadmin command for each remote printer you want to use.

NOTE:

Manual configuration of print queues is not recommended for large numbers of client machines because of the administration nightmare it creates. For busy networks, consider subnetting groups of clients and polling and relaying printer information instead.

Specifying a Single Server for Printing

CUPS can be configured to run without a local spooler and send all jobs to a single server. However, if that server goes down then all printing will be disabled. Use this configuration only as absolutely needed.

The default server is normally "localhost". To override the default server, create a file named /etc/cups/client.conf and add a line reading:

ServerName *server*

to the file. The *server* name can be the hostname or IP address of the default server.

The default server can also be customized on a per-user basis. To set a user-specific server, create a file named ~/.cupsrc and add a line reading

ServerName *server*

to the file. The *server* name can be the hostname or IP address of the default server.

Automatic Configuration of Print Queues

CUPS supports automatic client configuration of printers on the same subnet. To configure printers on the same subnet, set the BrowseAddress on the server and do nothing on the clients. Each client should see the available printers within 30 seconds automatically. The printer and class lists are updated automatically as printers and servers are added or removed.

If you want to see printers on other subnets as well, use the BrowsePoll directive as described next.

NOTE:

The BrowseAddress directive enables broadcast traffic from your server. The default configuration broadcasts printer information every 30 seconds. Although this printer information does not use much bandwidth, typically about 80 bytes per printer, it can add up with large numbers of servers and printers.

Use the `BrowseInterval` and `BrowseTimeOut` directives to tune the amount of data that is added to your network load. In addition, subnets can be used to minimize the amount of traffic that is carried by the "backbone" of your large network.

Specifying Multiple Servers for Printing

If you have CUPS servers on different subnets then you should configure CUPS to poll those servers. Polling provides the benefits of automatic configuration without significant configuration on the clients, and multiple clients on the same subnet can share the same configuration information.

Polling is enabled by specifying one or more `BrowsePoll` directives in the `/etc/cups/` `cupsd.conf` file. Each `BrowsePoll` line shows the hostname or IP address of the server:

BrowsePoll *server*

Multiple `BrowsePoll` lines can be used to poll multiple CUPS servers. To limit the amount of polling you do from client machines, you can have only one of the clients do the polling and relay that information to the others on the same subnet (described next).

Relaying Printers to Other Clients

When you have clients and servers spread across multiple subnets, the polling method is inefficient. CUPS provides a `BrowseRelay` directive that enables a single client to relay (broadcast) the polled printer information to the local subnet. Figure 6.1 shows a typical corporate network with multiple subnets.

Server A and Server B are on subnet 1 and subnet 2, while the clients are on subnet 3. To provide printers to all of the clients in subnet 3, client C will be configured with the following directives in `/etc/cups/cupsd.conf`:

```
# Poll the two servers
BrowsePoll ServerA
BrowsePoll ServerB

# Relay the printers to the local subnet
BrowseRelay 127.0.0.1 192.168.3.255
```

The `BrowseRelay` line specifies a source address and mask. Any browse packets coming from a matching address will be sent to the given broadcast address. In this case, we want the packets from the local machine (127.0.0.1) relayed to the other clients.

As printers are found using polling, they are relayed from client C to the rest of the clients through a broadcast on subnet 3. The rest of the clients can use the standard `cupsd.conf` configuration.

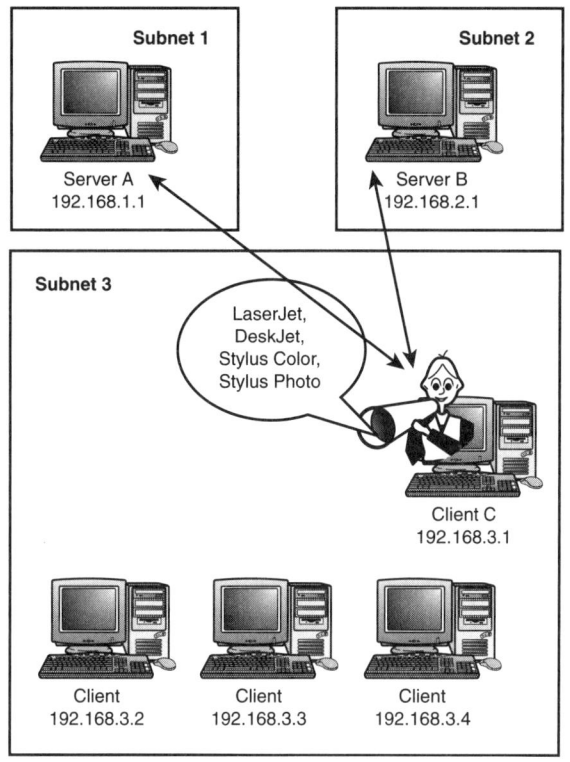

FIGURE 6.1

A typical corporate network with multiple subnets.

NOTE:

The BrowseRelay directive can also be used to relay browsing packets from one network interface to another. For example, if client C in the previous example had network interfaces attached to both subnet 1 and subnet 2, it could use the BrowseRelay directive exclusively:

```
# Relay the printers from subnet 1 and 2 to subnet 3
BrowseRelay 192.168.1 192.168.3.255
BrowseRelay 192.168.2 192.168.3.255
```

Load Balancing and Failsafe Operation

When using server polling or broadcasting, CUPS clients can automatically merge identical printers on multiple servers into a single implicit class queue. Clients assume that printers with the same name on multiple servers are in fact the same printer or type of printer being served by multiple machines.

If you have two printers, LaserJet@ServerA and LaserJet@ServerB, a third implicit class called `LaserJet` will be created automatically on the client that refers to both printers. If the client also has a local printer with the name LaserJet then an implicit class named `AnyLaserJet` will be created instead.

The client will alternate between servers and automatically stop sending jobs to a server if it goes down, providing a load-balancing effect and fail-safe operation with automatic switchover.

Add the following line to the `/etc/cups/cupsd.conf` file to disable implicit classes:

```
ImplicitClasses off
```

NOTE:

Implicit classes are enabled by default. If you want to provide classes for some printers, but not all, you should set up printer classes by hand on the client machines using the `lpadmin` command or the Web interface.

Printing from LPD Clients

CUPS supports limited functionality for LPD-based clients. With LPD you can print files to specific printers, list the queue status, and so forth. However, the automatic client configuration and printer options are not supported by the LPD protocol, so you must manually configure each client for the printers it needs to access.

The cups-lpd program provides support for LPD clients and is used as a "inetd" type of daemon. If you are using the `inetd` super-daemon (most versions of Unix), edit the `/etc/inetd.conf` file and add a line reading:

```
printer stream tcp nowait lp /usr/lib/cups/daemon/cups-lpd cups-lpd
```

After you have added this line, send the `inetd` process a HUP signal or reboot the system. In IRIX and some servers of Linux, the command will be the following:

```
killall -HUP inetd ENTER
```

For other Unix systems, use the `kill` command after finding the ID for the inetd process:

```
kill -HUP pid ENTER
```

Many Linux systems use the newer xinetd daemon, which stores this information in /etc/xinetd.conf or /etc/xinetd.d/cups:

```
service printer
{
    socket_type = stream
    protocol = tcp
    wait = no
    user = lp
    server = /usr/lib/cups/daemon/cups-lpd
}
```

The xinetd daemon checks the configuration files for changes and automatically reads them as needed.

Printing from Mac OS Clients

CUPS does not provide Mac OS support directly. However, several free and commercial software packages do.

Columbia Appletalk Package (CAP)

CAP is probably the oldest EtherTalk server around. It is probably the most portable of the solutions available, but also the slowest.

Because the CAP LaserWriter server (lwsrv) does not support specification of PPD files, we do not recommend that you use CAP with CUPS. However, you can run the lpsrv program for limited printing with the command

```
lwsrv -n "Share Name" -p name -a /usr/lib/adicts -f /usr/lib/LW+Fonts ENTER
```

where "Share Name" is the name you want to use when sharing the printer, and name is the name of the CUPS print queue.

XINET KA/Spool

KA/Spool is a commercial solution that is popular on high-end Unix boxes. To use your system as a print server for Mac OS clients, configure each printer using a papserver in the /usr/adm/appletalk/services file, specifying the corresponding PPD file in the /etc/cups/ppd directory for each printer. For a printer named MyPrinter the entry would look like the following:

```
/usr/etc/appletalk/papserver -I -L -P /etc/cups/ppd/MyPrinter.ppd
➥"Printer Description" MyPrinter
```

NetATalk

NetATalk is a popular free EtherTalk package for Linux and Solaris. To use your system as a print server for Mac OS clients, configure each printer in the `papd.conf` file, specifying the corresponding PPD file in the `/etc/cups/ppd` directory for each printer. For a printer named MyPrinter the entry would look like

```
Printer Description:MyPrinter@MyServer:\
        :pr=|/usr/bin/lp -d MyPrinter:\
        :op=daemon:\
        :pd=/etc/cups/ppd/MyPrinter.ppd
```

Printing from Windows Clients

Although CUPS does not provide Windows support directly, the free SAMBA software package does. SAMBA version 2.0.6 is the first release of SAMBA that supports CUPS. You can download SAMBA from the following Web site:

```
http://www.samba.org
```

Windows 98, Me, and 2000 also support the Internet Printing Protocol for printing.

Configuring SAMBA 2.0.x

To configure SAMBA 2.0.0–2.0.5 for CUPS, edit the `smb.conf` file and replace the existing printing commands and options with the lines:

```
printing = sysv
printcap = lpstat
print command = lp -d%p -oraw %s; rm -f %s
```

To configure SAMBA 2.0.6 and 2.0.7 for CUPS, edit the `smb.conf` file and replace the existing printing commands and options with the lines:

```
printing = cups
printcap = lpstat
```

That's all there is to it! Remote users will now be able to browse and print to printers on your system.

Configuring SAMBA 2.2.x

SAMBA 2.2.0 and later include support for downloading printer drivers from Windows clients. Start by editing the `smb.conf` file and replacing the existing printing commands and options with the following lines:

```
printing = cups
printcap = cups
```

Then run the `cupsaddsmb` program to add the printers you want to share

cupsaddsmb *name* **ENTER**

where *name* is the name of the printer you want to share. To share all printers, type:

cupsaddsmb -a **ENTER**

Configuring Windows Clients with IPP

If you are using Windows 98, Me, or 2000, you can add a printer as a network printer using the IPP URI for the printer:

`ipp://server/printers/name`

The *server* is the hostname or IP address of the server. The *name* is the name of the printer on the server.

Summary

CUPS supports many types of client configurations, including non-CUPS clients. The basic CUPS client configuration offers automatic load-balancing and fail-safe operation of remote printer when two or more servers are set up with the same printers. When clients and servers are on different subnets, polling and relaying can be used to join the subnets and propagate the printers to clients.

LPD clients can submit jobs, but lack the capability to send job options or participate in auto-configuration.

MacOS clients are supported by a variety of third-party programs and can usually provide PPD files to clients and support job options.

Windows clients are supported through SAMBA or IPP. SAMBA 2.2.x supports printer driver downloads using the `cupsaddsmb` command. Older versions of SAMBA and IPP require a local Windows printer driver to be used.

PART II

The Internet Printing Protocol

CHAPTER 7

Introduction to the Internet Printing Protocol

This chapter provides background information on the Internet Printing Protocol, the network printing protocol from the Internet Engineering Task Force. IPP forms the basis of the Common UNIX Printing System.

History of IPP

The IPP working group was created in 1997 by the Internet Engineering Task Force (IETF) and Printer Working Group (PWG) to develop a standard network printing protocol that addressed the needs of the Internet community and current technologies.

The Line Printer Daemon Protocol

The first thing the IPP working group did was to throw away the previous standard line-printer daemon (LPD) protocol described in RFC 1179. The LPD protocol was based on a sample implementation developed for Unix in the early 1970s to support printing to line printers, and it has remained largely unchanged since that time.

Figure 7.1 shows a typical LPD session. LPD clients connect to the server and send a `print file` command to the server. The server then responds with an OK or FAIL status, and then the client sends a control file and one or more data files containing the data to be printed. The server replies with an OK or FAIL for each file, and then a final OK or FAIL for the print command as a whole. Only one command can be processed per connection.

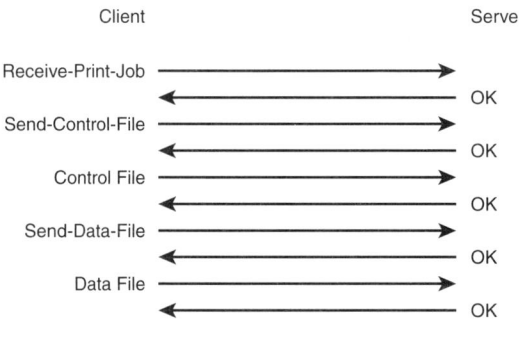

FIGURE 7.1

A typical LPD protocol session.

As you can see from Figure 7.1, there is no authentication step in the session—the original implementations relied on a reserved source port number (721–731) to ensure that the client (user) was printing from a trusted system. Because only the root user (or an application that runs as root) can reserve a port under 1024, this was considered to be adequate security at the time.

As computing matured, however, the limitations of this method became apparent—personal computers became increasingly prevalent, and with them came many valid root users that could masquerade as any user on the network. When Windows started supporting TCP/IP, the number of users that could do this increased a thousand-fold overnight.

To combat this problem, most implementations added support for host-based access control. Some implementations of LPD also added support for Kerberos authentication, but this is rarely implemented and not documented.

Aside from authentication, there is no way to initiate a secure (encrypted) session with LPD unless proprietary extensions are used. Encryption support is essential for printing confidential documents over a WAN or the Internet. It also helps to make password-based authentication more secure.

A third problem with LPD is that it does not provide generic support for various print file formats. For example, the current LPD implementations provide a format switch for PostScript files but not for PDF files.

Finally, LPD generally does not support job options such as media size or duplexing, and those variants of LPD that do support job options use different and incompatible commands in the LPD protocol. This means that applications that send print files must either embed the printer control commands or rely on the defaults.

In the end, it was universally agreed that the new Internet Printing Protocol should not be based on the LPD protocol.

Making a New Protocol

When the decision to drop the LPD protocol was made, the group started working on a replacement based on the document printing application (DPA) standard (ISO 10175). The DPA standard is a rather broad document that covers everything from printing to administration. It defines attributes for pages, jobs, and printers, and also covers standard values that should be supported. What DPA doesn't cover is the actual low-level protocol used to communicate this information among an application, printing system, and printer.

The low-level protocol developed for IPP consists of a header followed by tags, names, and values. Had IPP been started a few years later, an XML-based text format would probably have been used, but instead a binary encoding was chosen for its compact size and ease of parsing. The new low-level protocol addresses the flaws in the LPD protocol by adding support for document formats and options such as DPA attributes. It also can be extended to support new attributes and values without affecting the core protocol, enabling it to grow with the technology.

To send the IPP data over the network, Hypertext Transport Protocol (HTTP) was chosen as the transport protocol. This, too, was the source of much debate (and is even to this day), but in the end the extensibility and flexibility of HTTP won out. HTTP provides several methods of authentication and supports encryption, making it much more secure than LPD. It also enables existing HTTP servers to be extended to support IPP, or new IPP servers to support HTTP clients (Web browsers) with human-readable content. Figure 7.2 shows a typical IPP session.

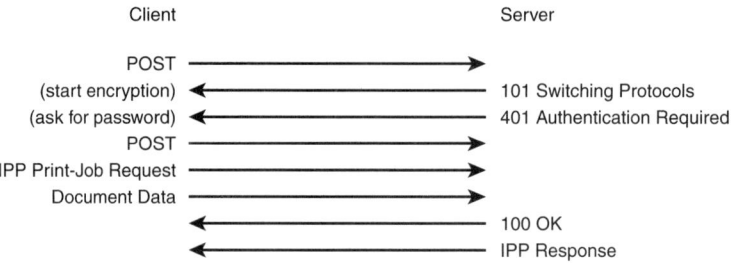

FIGURE 7.2

A typical IPP session.

All IPP requests are sent to the server using a HTTP POST request with a content type of application/ipp. The HTTP server can then challenge the request (ask for a username and password) and/or require encryption using the HTTP Upgrade mechanism described in RFC 2817. After the POST has been accepted, an IPP request and the document to be printed are sent to the server, which responds with an IPP response message.

Unlike LPD, the HTTP connection can be persistent, offering better efficiency when polling the status of printers or jobs. IPP also offers a broader range of commands and information for the client, making it better suited as a complete printing interface.

Object Model

The IPP object model defines several types of objects; these objects interact with each other to support printing and notification. Figure 7.3 shows the relationships among each of the objects.

Printer objects encapsulate a printer device, providing a generic picture of the printer to the application. Most operations are directed at printer objects.

Job objects encapsulate a print job, which can consist of one or more files. The typical IPP printer supports a single set of options for all files in the job, although extensions are available on some printers to set the options for each file or even each page of output.

Subscription objects encapsulate a notification mechanism that is triggered by state changes in a job or printer object. Notifications can be made through e-mail, instant messaging services, or direct application interfaces.

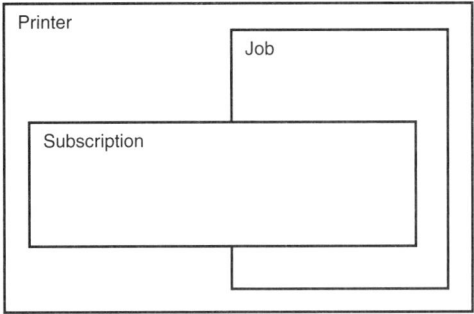

FIGURE 7.3

The relationships of IPP Objects.

The relationship and operation of each of these objects can be driven by a finite state machine, making IPP extremely easy to implement on a wide range of hardware.

Extensions

IPP supports a flexible extension mechanism from the HTTP transport layer to the low-level IPP protocol itself. Extensions can be added for attributes, authentication, encryption, document formats, notification, operations, and value types without breaking compatibility with the IPP standard. This extension mechanism allows IPP to be a living, growing standard without sacrificing compatibility with older implementations, making it a better long-term network printing solution than the venerable LPD.

References

IPP is described by several Request for Comment (RFC) papers for the IETF standards as well as several standards papers from the PWG. Table 7.1 describes the current IETF specifications:

TABLE 7.1   IETF IPP Specifications

Document	Description
RFC 2568 Rationale for the Structure of the Model and Protocol for the Internet Printing Protocol	Describes why the IPP was designed the way it was
RFC 2567 Design Goals for an Internet Printing Protocol	Describes the ultimate goals of the Internet Printing Protocol

TABLE 7.1   Continued

Document	Description
RFC 2569 Mapping between LPD and IPP Protocols	Describes how to map IPP to LPD and vice versa
RFC 2911 IPP/1.1: Model and Semantics	Describes all printer and job object operations and attributes for IPP
RFC 2910 IPP/1.1: Encoding and Transport	Describes the low-level IPP protocol
IPP/1.1: Implementer's Guide	Describes how to develop a compliant IPP implementation
IPP: IPP Job and Printer Administrative Operations	Describes extensions to IPP for printer and job administration
IPP: Job and Printer Set Operations	Describes extensions to IPP for controlling printers and jobs
IPP: Job Progress Attributes	Describes new job attributes useful for detailed monitoring of job status
IPP: The `collection` attribute syntax	Describes a new collection value type that is used by certain extensions
IPP: IPP Event Notification Specification	Describes the IPP notification mechanism and subscription objects
The `indp` Delivery Method for Event Notifications and Protocol/1.0	Describes the `indp` (broadcast) notification scheme
IPP: The `ippget` Event Notifications Delivery Method	Describes the `ippget` (polled) notification scheme
IPP: The `mailto:` Notification Delivery Method	Describes the `mailto` (E-mail) notification scheme

The PWG has several additional standards that have been endorsed by the PWG members, as well as some experimental documents on using IPP with wireless devices using the Bluetooth protocol.

You can find the current IPP documentation at the following Web site:

```
http://www.pwg.org/ipp/
```

Summary

IPP is a replacement for the LPD protocol described in RFC 1179. IPP was designed to be a reasonably simple protocol to implement while providing many advanced printing capabilities. The IPP extension mechanism enables IPP to grow to support new technologies while maintaining compatibility with existing IPP implementations.

CHAPTER 8

Anatomy of an IPP Request

This chapter describes the low-level format of the Internet Printing Protocol, including how each value in a request or response is encoded and how the data is exchanged between the client and server.

Dissecting an IPP Request

Every IPP request is composed of the following parts:

- A HTTP request
- An IPP request message
- Optional additional (document) data
- A HTTP response
- An IPP response message

The following sections describe each of these parts.

The HTTP Request

The HTTP request is a POST request containing data of type application/ipp. Each POST contains a single IPP request message and potentially the document data for a Print-Job or Send-Document request. Figure 8.1 shows the data flow.

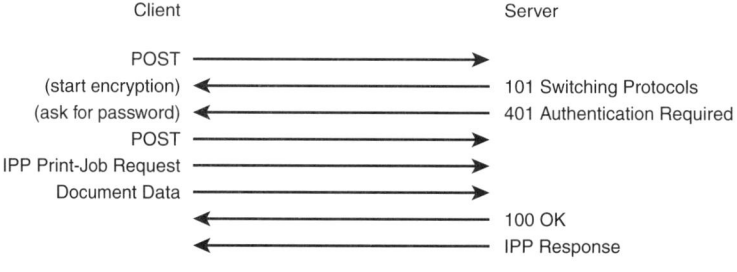

FIGURE 8.1

Sending an IPP request using a HTTP POST.

Because IPP requires full HTTP/1.1 compliance, the IPP request can be sent all at once using the Content-Length field or incrementally using chunking. The result of the POST is also data of type application/ipp and consists of the IPP response message.

Both the request and response use a common format beginning with a fixed-length header followed by a series of attributes. The data in IPP messages is byte-aligned, so it usually must be read into and written from properly aligned data structures in your programs.

The Request Header

The request header consists of 8 bytes of binary data as shown in Figure 8.2.

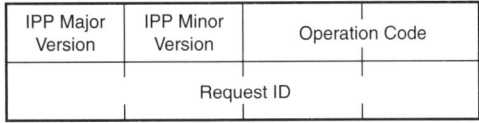

FIGURE 8.2

The IPP request header consists of 8 bytes of binary data.

The first two bytes contain the IPP version number, either 01 00 for IPP/1.0 or 01 01 for IPP/1.1. You should normally send an IPP/1.1 request unless the server responds with a `server-error- version-not-supported` error.

Bytes 3–4 contain the operation code, a 16-bit integer in network (big-endian) byte order. Table 8.1 lists the currently defined operation codes.

TABLE 8.1   IPP Operation Codes

Code	Name	Description
0×0002	Print-Job	Prints a single file
0×0003	Print-URI	Prints a single URI
0×0004	Validate-Job	Validates print job options
0×0005	Create-Job	Creates an empty print job
0×0006	Send-Document	Adds a single file to an existing print job
0×0007	Send-URI	Adds a single URI to an existing print job
0×0008	Cancel-Job	Cancels a print job
0×0009	Get-Job-Attributes	Gets the attributes for a print job
0×000A	Get-Jobs	Gets a list of print jobs
0×000B	Get-Printer-Attributes	Gets the attributes for a printer
0×000C	Hold-Job	Holds a print job
0×000D	Release-Job	Releases a print job for printing
0×000E	Restart-Job	Restarts the printing of a print job
0×0010	Pause-Printer	Temporarily stops a printer
0×0011	Resume-Printer	Resumes printing on a printer
0×0012	Purge-Jobs	Cancels all jobs on a printer
0×0013	Set-Printer-Attributes	Changes printer attributes
0×0014	Set-Job-Attributes	Changes print job attributes
0×0015	Get-Printer-Supported-Values	Gets supported printer attributes for the specified document format

TABLE 8.1   Continued

Code	Name	Description
0×0016	Create-Printer-Subscription	Creates a subscription for printer state changes
0×0017	Create-Job-Subscription	Creates a subscription for print job state changes
0×0018	Get-Subscription-Attributes	Gets the attributes for a subscription
0×0019	Get-Subscriptions	Gets a list of subscriptions
0×001A	Renew-Subscription	Renews an existing (unexpired) subscription
0×001B	Cancel-Subscription	Cancels a subscription
0×001C	Get-Notifications	Gets pending notifications using the ipp-get method
0×001D	Send-Notifications	Gets pending notifications using the indp method
0×0021	Get-Print-Support-Files	Gets required support (driver) files for a printer
0×0022	Enable-Printer	Allows new print jobs to be submitted to a printer
0×0023	Disable-Printer	Prevents new print jobs from being submitted to a printer
0×0024	Pause-Printer-After-Current-Job	Stops a printer after printing the current job
0×0025	Hold-New-Jobs	Holds all new print jobs
0×0026	Release-Held-New-Jobs	Releases (start printing) any held jobs
0×0027	Deactivate-Printer	Stops a printer and disallows changes to it
0×0028	Activate-Printer	Starts a printer and allows changes to it
0×0029	Restart-Printer	Starts a printer, restarting any jobs that were stopped by a Deactivate-Printer request
0×002A	Shutdown-Printer	Powers the printer off
0×002B	Startup-Printer	Powers the printer on
0×002C	Reprocess-Job	Copies a completed job and prints it again
0×002D	Cancel-Current-Job	Cancel the current print job on a printer
0×002E	Suspend-Current-Job	Pauses the current print job on a printer
0×002F	Resume-Job	Restarts the current print job on a printer
0×0030	Promote-Job	Prints a job before any others in the line
0×0031	Schedule-Job-After	Prints a job after another job
0×4001	CUPS-Get-Default	Gets the default printer
0×4002	CUPS-Get-Printers	Gets the list of printers
0×4003	CUPS-Add-Printer	Adds or modifies a printer on the server
0×4004	CUPS-Delete-Printer	Deletes a printer from the server
0×4005	CUPS-Get-Classes	Gets the list of printer classes
0×4006	CUPS-Add-Class	Adds or modifies a printer class on the server
0×4007	CUPS-Delete-Class	Deletes a printer class from the server
0×4008	CUPS-Accept-Jobs	Allows new print jobs on a printer or printer class (similar to new Enable-Printer operation)

TABLE 8.1   Continued

Code	Name	Description
0×4009	CUPS-Reject-Jobs	Rejects new print jobs on a printer or printer class (similar to new Disable-Printer operation)
0×400A	CUPS-Set-Default	Sets the default printer
0×400B	CUPS-Get-Devices	Gets a list of available printer devices
0×400C	CUPS-Get-PPDs	Gets a list of available printer drivers
0×400D	CUPS-Move-Job	Moves a print job to another printer or printer class

Bytes 5–8 contain the request ID, a 32-bit integer in network (big-endian) byte order. The request ID is generated by the client and returned by the server so that a client can determine which response message goes with which request.

WHAT ARE LITTLE- AND BIG-ENDIAN?

Big- and little-endian refer to the order of the bytes in a number or pointer value that is larger than a byte. Multibyte numbers sent over most network protocols are stored in big-endian order, thus the term "network byte order" is equivalent to big-endian.

Big-endian numbers are stored with the most-significant byte (high bits) first: a 32-bit integer whose value is 1234 would be stored in memory as the bytes 0, 0, 4, and 210.

Little-endian numbers are stored with the least-significant byte (low bits) first: a 32-bit integer whose value is 1234 would be stored in memory as the bytes 210, 4, 0, and 0.

The terms big-endian and little-endian come from Swift's "Gulliver's Travels" by way of the famous paper "On Holy Wars and a Plea for Peace" by Danny Cohen.

Groups and Attributes

IPP groups and attributes follow the request header. Each group or attribute begins with a one-byte value tag. Some value tags introduce attribute groups whereas others indicate the beginning of an attribute value. Attribute tags are followed by the name of the attribute and the value itself (see Figure 8.3).

The request in the figure starts with the standard 8-byte header for a Get-Jobs request. This is followed by a group tag (01) that starts the operation attributes and a charset tag (47) that starts a charset value. The charset tag is followed by the length of the attribute name (18) and the name string ("attributes-charset"). After the name, the value length (5) and value string ("utf-8") follow, completing the attribute. This is repeated for all of the attributes in the request and is finished using the end-of-attributes tag (03).

01 01	IPP/1.1 version number
00 0A	Get-Jobs
00 00 00 01	Request ID #1
01	operation-group-tag
47	charset
00 12	name length = 18
"attributes-charset"	
00 05	value length = 5
"utf-8"	
48	naturalLanguage
00 1B	name length = 27
"attributes-natural-language"	
00 02	value length = 2
"en"	
45	uri
00 0B	name length = 11
"printer-uri"	
00 0D	value length = 13
"ipp://foo/bar"	
03	end-of-attributes-tag

FIGURE 8.3

IPP Attribute Data in a Request.

Groups

IPP currently defines the seven group tags shown in Table 8.2. Each group tag is used once before the first attribute of that group; if no attributes are provided in that group then the group tag is omitted. The end-of-attributes tag is a special group tag that is used as the last tag in an IPP message.

Except for the end-of-attributes tag, all group tags in an IPP request must be sent in ascending order (the same order as shown in Table 8.2).

TABLE 8.2   IPP Group Tags

Tag	Name	Description
0×01	operation-attributes-tag	The operation attributes group
0×02	job-attributes-tag	The job attributes group
0×03	end-of-attributes-tag	The end tag for an IPP message
0×04	printer-attributes-tag	The printer attributes group
0×05	unsupported-attributes-tag	The group for unsupported attributes returned by an IPP server

TABLE 8.2   Continued

Tag	Name	Description
0×06	subscription-attributes-tag	The subscription attributes group (used when creating subscriptions)
0×07	event-notification-attributes-tag	The event attributes group (used when reporting events from a subscription)

Attributes

Within each attribute group are the attributes themselves. Each attribute starts with a one-byte tag (see Table 8.3), followed by a 16-bit name length in network (big-endian) byte order, the characters in the name, a 16-bit value length in network (big-endian) byte order, and the value data.

TABLE 8.3   IPP Value Tags

Code	Name	Description
0×16	delete-attribute	Deletes the named attribute (IPP requests only).
0×21	integer	A 32-bit signed integer in network (big-endian) byte order.
0×22	boolean	A one-byte integer with 0 representing a false value and 1 representing a true value.
0×23	enum	A 32-bit signed integer enumeration in network (big-endian) byte order.
0×30	octetString	An arbitrary string of up to 32767 bytes.
0×31	dateTime	A date and time in the 11-byte RFC 1903 format.
0×32	resolution	A 9-byte resolution value consisting of two 32-bit signed integers in network (big-endian) byte order representing the horizontal and vertical resolutions followed by a one-byte unit value. A unit value of 3 means that the resolution values are per inch, whereas a value of 4 means that the resolution values are per centimeter.
0×33	rangeOfInteger	Two 32-bit signed integers in network (big-endian) byte order. The first integer is the lower bound of the range, whereas the second integer is the upper bound.
0×34	begCollection	Marks the beginning of a collection value.
0×35	textWithLanguage	A text string with an associated language string. The value consists of a 16-bit text length in network (big-endian) byte order, the text string, a 16-bit language length in network (big-endian) byte order, and the language string.
0×36	nameWithLanguage	A name string with an associated language string. The value consists of a 16-bit name length in network (big-endian) byte order, the name string, a 16-bit language length in network (big-endian) byte order, and the language string.

TABLE 8.3   Continued

Code	Name	Description
0×37	endCollection	Marks the end of a collection value.
0×41	textWithoutLanguage	A text string in the default language and character set.
0×42	nameWithoutLanguage	A name string in the default language and character set.
0×44	keyword	A keyword string.
0×45	uri	A URI string.
0×46	uriScheme	A URI scheme name string.
0×47	charset	A character set name string.
0×48	naturalLanguage	A language name string.
0×49	mimeMediaType	A MIME type string.
0×4A	memberAttrName	The name of a collection value.

Array (1setof) Values

IPP supports unordered arrays of values for some attributes; arrays are represented in an IPP message by using a name length of 0 for each of the values following the first value in the array. Figure 8.4 shows a `document-format-supported` attribute consisting of three MIME types: "`application/octet-stream`," "`application/postscript`," and "`application/vnd.hp-pcl`."

49	mimeMediaType
00 19	name length = 25
"document-format-supported"	
00 16	value length = 22
"application/postscript"	
49	mimeMediaType
00 00	name length = 0
00 18	value length = 24
"application/octet-stream"	
49	mimeMediaType
00 00	name length = 0
00 16	value length = 22
"application/vnd.hp-pcl"	

FIGURE 8.4

IPP array values.

The Response

An IPP response uses exactly the same format as an IPP request, except that the operation code in the header is replaced by a status code of the same size.

Status Codes

The status code is a 16–bit integer in network (big-endian) byte order that defines the general success or failure of a request. Most errors include additional attributes that define the specific error condition (for example a `printer-state-reasons` attribute with the value `media-jam-error`). Table 8.4 shows the possible status codes.

TABLE 8.4   IPP Status Codes

Code	Name	Description
0x0000	successful-ok	Everything went okay with no errors.
0x0001	successful-ok-ignored-or-substituted-attributes	Everything went okay but the server ignored or substituted some attributes.
0x0002	successful-ok-conflicting-attributes	Everything went okay, but some of the attributes conflicted with each other.
0x0003	successful-ok-ignored-subscriptions	Everything went okay, but the subscriptions could not be created.
0x0004	successful-ok-ignored-notifications	Everything went okay, but the recipient of the notifications was unable to consume all of the events.
0x0005	successful-ok-too-many-events	Everything went okay, but there were more events than the printer could send.
0x0006	successful-ok-but-cancel-subscription	Everything went okay, but the recipient of the notifications wants the subscription cancelled.
0x0300	redirection-other-site	Redirects a get-notifications operation to a different server.
0x0400	client-error-bad-request	The client's request contained invalid data.
0x0401	client-error-forbidden	The client is forbidden from performing the operation.
0x0402	client-error-not-authenticated	The client is not authenticated and needs to do so before the operation can be allowed.
0x0403	client-error-not-authorized	The client is not authorized to perform the operation.
0x0404	client-error-not-possible	The operation cannot be successful.
0x0405	client-error-timeout	The client request was not received in a timely fashion.
0x0406	client-error-not-found	The client request referred to an object that does not exist.
0x0407	client-error-gone	The requested object is no longer available.
0x0408	client-error-request-entity-too-large	The client request contains additional data that is too large to process.
0x0409	client-error-request-value-too-large	The client request contains an attribute value that is too large.

TABLE 8.4   Continued

Code	Name	Description
0×040A	client-error-document-format-not-supported	The document format is not supported.
0×040B	client-error-attributes-or-values-not-supported	The request contains attributes or values that are not supported.
0×040C	client-error-uri-scheme-not-supported	The URI scheme in a URI attribute is not supported.
0×040D	client-error-charset-not-supported	The client request uses an unsupported character set.
0×040E	client-error-conflicting-attributes	The client request contains conflicting attributes.
0×040F	client-error-compression-not-supported	The client request uses a compression type that is not supported.
0×0410	client-error-compression-error	The compressed data contains an error.
0×0411	client-error-document-format-error	The document data contains an error.
0×0412	client-error-document-access-error	The remote document cannot be accessed.
0×0413	client-error-attributes-not-settable	The attributes specified in a client set request cannot be changed.
0×0414	client-error-ignored-all-subscriptions	The server could not create the subscriptions in a Create-Job, Print-Job, Print-URI, or Reprocess-Job operation.
0×0415	client-error-too-many-subscriptions	The server cannot create another subscription.
0×0416	client-error-ignored-all-notifications	The notification recipient was unable to collect any of the events.
0×0417	client-error-print-support-file-not-found	The printer support file (driver) could not be found.
0×0500	server-error-internal-error	A permanent internal error has occurred on the server.
0×0501	server-error-operation-not-supported	The requested operation is not supported by the server.
0×0502	server-error-service-unavailable	The requested operation could not be performed due to a temporary condition.
0×0503	server-error-version-not-supported	The IPP version number in the request header is not supported.
0×0504	server-error-device-error	The printer object is unable to print a job.
0×0505	server-error-temporary-error	The requested operation could not be performed due to a temporary server error.

TABLE 8.4   Continued

Code	Name	Description
0×0506	server-error-not-accepting-jobs	The printer object is not accepting jobs at this time.
0×0507	server-error-busy	The server is temporarily unavailable due to high load.
0×0508	server-error-job-canceled	The print job was cancelled before all of the document data was received from the client.
0×0509	server-error-multiple-document-jobs-not-supported	The server does not support more than one document in a print job.
0×050A	server-error-printer-is-deactivated	The printer is currently off-line or powered down.

Value Tags

When an attribute in an IPP request cannot be used by a server, the response will contain those attributes using a special value tag. These attributes are found in the unsupported attributes group (unsupported-attributes-tag) and the different value tags help indicate why an attribute was rejected. Table 8.5 shows the additional value tags that are used in responses.

TABLE 8.5   IPP Value Tags in Responses

Code	Name	Description
0×10	unsupported	The attribute name was unsupported.
0×12	unknown	The value of the named attribute is currently unknown.
0×13	no-value	There is no value associated with the named attribute.
0×15	not-settable	The value of the named attribute cannot be set.
0×17	admin-define	The value is defined by the administrator and cannot be changed.

Responses Containing Multiple Objects

The IPP responses for the Get-Jobs, Get-Notifications, Get-Subscriptions, CUPS-Get-Classes, and CUPS-Get-Printers operations can contain attributes for multiple objects that introduce the same group tag multiple times. However, the group tags within the object's attributes are still sent in ascending order. See Figure 8.5 for an example of this with the Get-Jobs operation.

01 01	IPP/1.1 version number
00 00	successful-ok
00 00 00 01	Request ID #1
01	operation-group-tag
47	charset
00 12	name length = 18
"attributes-charset"	
00 05	value length = 5
"utf-8"	
48	naturalLanguage
00 1B	name length = 27
"attributes-natural-language"	
00 02	value length = 2
"en"	
02	job-attributes-tag
45	uri
00 07	name length = 7
"job-uri"	
00 14	value length = 20
"ipp://foo/bar/jobs/1"	
21	integer
00 06	name length = 6
"job-id"	
00 04	value length = 4
00 00 00 01	value = 1
23	enum
00 09	name length = 9
"job-state"	
00 04	value length = 4
00 00 00 05	value = 5 (processing)
…	
02	job-attributes-tag
45	uri
00 07	name length = 7
"job-uri"	
00 14	value length = 20
"ipp://foo/bar/jobs/2"	
21	integer
00 06	name length = 6
"job-id"	
00 04	value length = 4
00 00 00 02	value = 2

23	enum
00 09	name length = 9
"job-state"	
00 04	value length = 4
00 00 00 03	value = 3 (pending)
...	
02	job-attributes-tag
45	uri
00 07	name length = 7
"job-uri"	
00 14	value length = 20
"ipp://foo/bar/jobs/3	
21	integer
00 06	name length = 6
"job-id"	
00 04	value length = 4
00 00 00 03	value = 3
23	enum
00 09	name length = 9
"job-state"	
00 04	value length = 4
00 00 00 03	value = 3 (pending)
...	
03	end-of-attributes-tag

FIGURE 8.5

Get-Jobs Response.

Summary

IPP requests are sent using the HTTP POST method with a content type of application/ipp. Each HTTP POST contains a single IPP request. The IPP request and response use a common binary format that consists of a fixed-length header followed by attributes and groups. All multibyte integer values are in network (big-endian) byte order. Each group of attributes must appear together and in a specific order for the server to accept the request.

Each request has an operation code. Some operations also take additional data (such as print files) after the IPP request message data.

Each response has a status code and potentially other attributes that fully describe any error condition.

CHAPTER 9

Printer Objects

This chapter describes the attributes and operations provided for IPP printer objects.

What Is a Printer Object?

A printer object represents a single printer that accepts and prints job objects. The printer object can also have subscription objects associated with it.

Each printer object is always in one of three states: idle, processing, or stopped. An idle printer object is doing nothing because it has no job objects to print. When a new job object becomes available for printing, the printer object will start printing it.

A printer object in the processing state is currently printing at least one job object. Printer objects that print multiple jobs at a time are typically large-format plotters or printers that can output document pages along the width of the media for faster printing. Most IPP implementations, including CUPS, only print one job at a time.

Finally, a stopped printer object is not printing job objects and will not start printing a pending job object if one becomes available. Typically a printer object is stopped if a physical error has occurred (out of toner or paper, for example) and the administrator has decided to take the printer offline while work is done on it.

Required Attributes

Printer objects have several required attributes associated with them. These attributes are always available from an IPP server, although they can have empty values if they are undefined or not used by the implementation. Table 9.1 lists the required attributes for printer objects.

TABLE 9.1   Required Attributes for Printer Objects

Name	Type	Description
charset-configured	charset	The default character set for text attributes
charset-supported	1setOf charset	The supported character sets
compression-supported	1setOf type3 keyword	The type of compression that is supported by the server
copies-default	integer (1:MAX)	The default number of copies that are produced
copies-supported	rangeOfInteger (1:MAX)	The minimum and maximum number of copies that are supported
document-format-default	mimeMediaType	The default document format for print jobs
document-format-supported	1setOf mimeMediaType	The supported document formats

TABLE 9.1   Continued

Name	Type	Description
finishings-default	1setOf type2 enum	The default finishings to apply to document pages
finishings-supported	1setOf type2 enum	The available finishings for document pages
generated-natural-language-supported	1setOf naturalLanguage	The supported languages
ipp-versions-supported	1setOf type2 keyword	The version numbers supported by the printer object
job-hold-until-default	type3 keyword | name	The default hold time for new jobs
job-hold-until-supported	1setOf (type3 keyword | name)	The supported hold times for new jobs
job-priority-default	integer (1:100)	The default print job priority
job-priority-supported	integer (1:100)	The maximum job priority values that are supported
job-sheets-default	type3 keyword | name	The default job sheets to print with a job
job-sheets-supported	1setOf (type3 keyword | name)	The supported job sheets
media-default	type3 keyword | name	The default media to use when printing a job
media-ready	1setOf type3 keyword | name	Which media types are ready for printing
media-supported	1setOf tpye3 keyword | name	The supported media types
multiple-document-handling-default	type2 keyword	The default document handling when printing multiple copies
multiple-document-handling-supported	1setOf type2 keyword	The supported document handling types
natural-language-configured	naturalLanguage	The configured language for returned text attributes
number-up-default	integer(1:MAX)	The number of document pages to print on each output page
number-up-supported	1setOf integer(1:MAX) | rangeOfInteger(1:MAX)	The supported number-up values
operations-supported	1setOf type2 enum	The operations supported by the printer object
orientation-requested-default	type2 enum	The default orientation of pages in the document
orientation-requested-supported	1setOf type2 enum	The orientations that are supported

TABLE 9.1   Continued

Name	Type	Description
pages-ranges-supported	boolean	Whether page number filtering is supported when printing documents
pdl-override-supported	type2 keyword	Whether IPP attributes will override commands in print files
printer-is-accepting-jobs	boolean	Whether the printer object is accepting new jobs
printer-name	name(127)	An identifying name for the printer object, for example, LaserJet
printer-state	type1 enum	The current printer state
printer-state-reasons	1setOf type2 keyword	The reasons for the current printer state
printer-up-time	integer (1:MAX)	The number of seconds that the printer has been operating
printer-uri-supported	1setOf uri	The URIs that can be used to access the printer object
queued-job-count	integer (0:MAX)	The number of jobs in the queue for this printer object
sides-default	type2 keyword	The default duplex setting for jobs
sides-supported	1setOf type2 keyword	The available duplex settings
uri-authentication-supported	1setOf type2 keyword	The type of authentication that is supported by the corresponding URI
uri-security-supported	1setOf type2 keyword	The type of security that is supported by the corresponding URI

The charset-configured Attribute

The charset-configured attribute contains the default character set for text attributes on the server. For CUPS this is usually iso-8859-1.

The charset-supported Attribute

The charset-supported attribute lists the supported character sets. For CUPS this will contain the following:

iso-8859-1

iso-8859-2

iso-8859-3

iso-8859-4

iso-8859-5

```
iso-8859-6
iso-8859-7
iso-8859-8
iso-8859-9
iso-8859-10
iso-8859-13
iso-8859-14
iso-8859-15
us-ascii
utf-8
windows-874
windows-1250
windows-1251
windows-1252
windows-1253
windows-1254
windows-1255
windows-1256
windows-1257
windows-1258
```

The `compression-supported` Attribute

The `compression-supported` attribute lists the supported document compression methods. For CUPS 1.1.x, this attribute will contain the single keyword string `none`. For CUPS 1.2.x, this attribute will contain the following strings:

```
none
deflate
gzip
```

The `copies-default` Attribute

The `copies-default` attribute specifies the default number of copies that are produced for each job. For CUPS this value will always be 1.

The `copies-supported` Attribute

The `copies-supported` attribute specifies the minimum and maximum number of copies that can be produced by the printer. For CUPS the minimum is always 1 and the maximum is always 65535.

The `document-format-default` Attribute

The `document-format-default` attribute contains the default document type. For CUPS this will always be the string `application/octet-stream`, which indicates that the document will be "auto-typed" from the file contents.

The document-format-supported Attribute

The document-format-supported attribute lists the supported document types. For CUPS this attribute will contain the following values:

```
application/pdf
application/postscript
application/vnd.hp-HPGL
image/gif
image/png
image/jpeg
image/tiff
image/x-photocd
image/x-portable-anymap
image/x-portable-bitmap
image/x-portable-graymap
image/x-portable-pixmap
image/x-sgi-rgb
image/x-xbitmap
image/x-xpixmap
image/x-xwindowdump
image/x-sun-raster
image/x-alias
image/x-bitmap
text/html
application/x-cshell
application/x-perl
application/x-shell
text/plain
application/vnd.cups-postscript
application/vnd.cups-raster
application/vnd.cups-raw
application/octet-stream
```

The finishings-default Attribute

The finishings-default attribute specifies the default finishings that are applied to document pages. The finishings values are shown in Table 9.2. The default value in CUPS is always 3 for "none."

TABLE 9.2   Finishing Values

Value	Description
3	No finishing.
4	Staple the output in a corner.
5	Punch holes in the output for binding.
6	Put a cover on the output.
7	Bind the output together.
8	Staple the output along the middle of the page so the output can be folded.
9	Staple the output along an edge.
20	Staple the output in the top-left corner.
21	Staple the output in the bottom-left corner.
22	Staple the output in the top-right corner.
23	Staple the output in the bottom-right corner.
24	Staple the output along the left edge.
25	Staple the output along the top edge.
26	Staple the output along the right edge.
27	Staple the output along the bottom edge.
28	Staple the output along the left edge with two staples.
29	Staple the output along the top edge with two staples.
30	Staple the output along the right edge with two staples.
31	Staple the output along the bottom edge with two staples.
50	Bind the output along the left edge.
51	Bind the output along the top edge.
52	Bind the output along the right edge.
53	Bind the output along the bottom edge.

The `finishings-supported` Attribute

The `finishings-supported` attribute lists the available finishings for document pages. For CUPS this attribute is derived from the `StapleLocation` and `BindEdge` options.

The `generated-natural-language-supported` Attribute

The `generated-natural-language-supported` attribute lists the supported languages. For CUPS this attribute will contain the following languages:

de

en

es

fr

it

The `ipp-versions-supported` Attribute

The `ipp-versions-supported` attribute lists the supported IPP versions. For CUPS this attribute will contain the following strings:

```
1.0
1.1
```

The `job-hold-until-default` Attribute

The `job-hold-until-default` attribute specifies the default hold time for new print jobs. Table 9.3 shows the standard keyword names. For CUPS the default is `no-hold`, but can be overridden by the user or administrator. CUPS also supports name values of the form `HH:MM:SS` in Greenwich Mean Time.

TABLE 9.3   Job Hold Keywords

Keyword	Description
no-hold	Do not hold the job—print as soon as possible.
indefinite	Hold the job until is it manually released.
day-time	Print the job between 6 a.m. and 6 p.m. local time.
evening	Print the job between 6 p.m. and 6 a.m. local time.
night	Print the job between 6 p.m. and 6 a.m. local time.
weekend	Print the job on the weekend.
second-shift	Print the job between 4 p.m. and 12 a.m. (midnight).
third-shift	Print the job between 12 a.m. (midnight) and 8 a.m.

The `job-hold-until-supported` Attribute

The `job-hold-until-supported` attribute lists the supported hold time keywords. For CUPS this includes all of the keywords in Table 9.3.

The `job-priority-default` Attribute

The `job-priority-default` attribute specifies the default print job priority from 1 to 100, where 1 is the lowest priority and 100 is the highest priority. In CUPS the default priority is 50.

The `job-priority-supported` Attribute

The `job-priority-supported` attribute specifies the maximum number of priority values that are supported. That is, if the printer internally maps the IPP values to numbers between 0–39, the `job-priority-supported` attribute will have a value of 40. For CUPS this attribute is always 100.

The `job-sheets-default` Attribute

The `job-sheets-default` attribute specifies the default job sheets to print with a job. For CUPS, job sheets are treated as banner and trailer pages and are treated as a `1setOf` array of names. The default value is normally `none` but can be overridden by the administrator. Table 9.4 lists the standard job sheets that come with CUPS.

TABLE 9.4   Job Sheets

Name	Description
none	Print no job sheet pages.
classified	Print a job sheet with the word "Classified" in boldface at the top and bottom.
confidential	Print a job sheet with the word "Confidential" in boldface at the top and bottom.
secret	Print a job sheet with the word "Secret" in boldface at the top and bottom.
standard	Print a job sheet with no special markings.
topsecret	Print a job sheet with the word "Top Secret" in boldface at the top and bottom.
unclassified	Print a job sheet with the word "Unclassified" in boldface at the top and bottom.

The `job-sheets-supported` Attribute

The `job-sheets-supported` attribute lists the available job sheets. For CUPS this value is derived from the files in the `/usr/share/cups/banners` directory.

The `media-default` Attribute

The `media-default` attribute specifies the media to use when printing. It is a catchall for the media size, type, and source fields. In CUPS this attribute mirrors the value of the `DefaultPageSize` attribute in the printer's PPD file.

The `media-ready` Attribute

The `media-ready` attribute lists which media sizes, types, and sources are ready for printing. CUPS does not use this attribute.

The `media-supported` Attribute

The `media-supported` attribute lists the media sizes, types, and sources that the printer supports. In CUPS this attribute contains a list of the `InputSlot`, `MediaType`, and `PageSize` attributes from the printer's PPD file.

The `multiple-document-handling-default` Attribute

The `multiple-document-handling-default` attribute specifies the default document handling when printing multiple copies. Table 9.5 lists the keyword values that can be used. In CUPS the default is `separate-documents-uncollated-copies`.

TABLE 9.5   Multiple Document Handling Keywords

Keyword Values	Description
`single-document`	Produces collated copies (for example, 1, 2, 1, 2, 1, 2). Each document and copy is treated as a single output stream, so the second document and/or copy will continue where the last one left off.
`separate-documents-uncollated-copies`	Produces uncollated copies (for example, 1, 1, 1, 2, 2, 2).
`separate-documents-collated-copies`	Produces collated copies (for example, 1, 2, 1, 2, 1, 2). All documents in a job start on a new sheet.
`single-document-new-sheet`	Produces collated copies but starts each copy on a new sheet. This is similar to the `single-document` keyword but results in whole documents that can be bound individually rather than N copies of a document that would have to be bound together.

The `multiple-document-handling-supported` Attribute

The `multiple-document-handling-supported` attribute lists the supported document handling types. For CUPS this consists of the keywords `separate-documents-uncollated-copies` and `separate-documents-collated-copies`.

The `natural-language-configured` Attribute

The `natural-language-configured` attribute contains the default language the server uses for text messages. For CUPS this attribute is usually set to the string en, although this can be changed in the `cupsd.conf` file.

The `number-up-default` Attribute

The `number-up-default` attribute specifies the number of document pages to print on each output page. For CUPS this will always be 1.

The `number-up-supported` Attribute

The `number-up-supported` attribute specifies the supported number-up values. For CUPS this will always be the numbers 1, 2, and 4.

The operations-supported Attribute

The operations-supported attribute lists the supported operation codes. CUPS 1.1.x lists all of the standard IPP operation codes except for the Print-URI and Send-URI operations. CUPS 1.2.x lists all of the IPP operation codes.

The orientation-requested-default Attribute

The orientation-requested-default attribute specifies the default orientation of pages in the document. Table 9.6 lists the supported values. For CUPS this attribute is always the value 3 (portrait).

TABLE 9.6   Orientation Values

Value	Description
3	Print in portrait orientation (no rotation).
4	Print in landscape orientation (90 degrees counterclockwise rotation).
5	Print in reverse-landscape orientation (90 degrees clockwise rotation).
6	Print in reverse-portrait orientation (180 degrees rotation).

The orientation-requested-supported Attribute

The orientation-requested-supported attribute lists the available orientations. For CUPS this consists of all 4 orientation values (3, 4, 5, and 6).

The pages-ranges-supported Attribute

The pages-ranges-supported attribute specifies whether page number filtering is supported when printing documents. For CUPS this attribute is always true.

The pdl-override-supported Attribute

The pdl-override-supported attribute specifies whether the server can override options in document data. For CUPS this will always be false.

The printer-is-accepting-jobs Attribute

The printer-is-accepting-jobs attribute specifies whether the printer is accepting new print jobs. For CUPS this value will be true or false depending on the current state of the printer.

The printer-name Attribute

The printer-name attribute provides an identifying name for the printer. In CUPS the printer name can only contain letters, numbers, and the underscore to ensure compatibility with the command-line interfaces.

The `printer-state` Attribute

The `printer-state` attribute specifies the current state of a printer and can be one of the three values listed in Table 9.7.

TABLE 9.7   Printer State Values

Value	Description
3	The printer is idle.
4	The printer is processing a job.
5	The printer is stopped and requires intervention.

The `printer-state-reasons` Attribute

The `printer-state-reasons` attribute is an array of reason keywords that describes a detailed reason for the current printer state. Except for the "none" reason, all reasons can have the strings `-report`, `-warning`, or `-error` appended to them to indicate whether the reason is informational, a warning, or an error condition. Table 9.8 lists the supported reason strings.

TABLE 9.8   Printer State Reason Strings

String	Description
`connecting-to-device`	The server is connecting to the printer device.
`cover-open`	A cover is open on the printer.
`developer-empty`	The printer is out of developer.
`developer-low`	The printer is low on developer.
`door-open`	A door is open on the printer.
`fuser-over-temp`	The printer's fuser temperature is high.
`fuser-under-temp`	The printer's fuser temperature is low.
`input-tray-missing`	The selected input tray is missing.
`interlock-open`	An interlock is open on the printer.
`interpreter-resource-unavailable`	The printer cannot find a required font or form.
`mark-waste-almost-full`	An ink waster task is nearly full.
`mark-waste-full`	An ink waste tank is full.
`marker-supply-empty`	An ink cartridge is empty.
`marker-supply-low`	An ink cartridge is almost empty.
`media-empty`	The selected input tray is empty.
`media-jam`	There is a media/paper jam in the printer.
`media-low`	The selected input tray is almost empty.
`media-needed`	The printer needs more media/paper.
`moving-to-paused`	The printer is about to be paused.

TABLE 9.8   Continued

String	Description
none	The printer has no reason for the current condition.
opc-life-over	The printer's optical photo conductor is no longer operative.
opc-near-eol	The printer's optical photo conductor is near its end of life.
other	The printer has a condition that is not described by any other reason.
output-area-almost-full	The output bin or mailbox is almost full.
output-area-full	The output bin or mailbox is full.
output-tray-missing	An output tray is missing.
paused	The printer is paused.
shutdown	The printer is powered off and cannot produce any output.
spool-area-full	The spool directory is out of disk space.
stopping	The printer is stopping.
stopped-partly	The printer has partially stopped.
timed-out	Communications with the printer have timed out.
toner-low	A toner cartridge is almost empty.
toner-empty	A toner cartridge is empty.

The printer-up-time Attribute

The printer-up-time attribute specifies the number of seconds that the printer has been operating. For CUPS this is the Unix time value (seconds since January 1, 1970).

The printer-uri-supported Attribute

The printer-uri-supported attribute lists the supported URIs for the printer. For CUPS the list will consist of one or two URIs that look like

```
ipp://ServerName/printers/PrinterName
```

for printers and

```
ipp://ServerName/classes/ClassName
```

for printer classes, where ServerName is the fully-qualified hostname of the server (for example, foo.bar.com) and ClassName and PrinterName are the values of the printer-name attribute.

If the CUPS server has been configured to support encryption then there will be two identical URIs in the list. Otherwise only a single URI will be provided.

The queued-job-count Attribute

The queued-job-count attribute specifies the number of uncompleted jobs in the printer queue.

The `sides-default` Attribute

The `sides-default` attribute specifies the default duplex setting for jobs. Table 9.9 lists the available keywords. For CUPS the default value mirrors the `Duplex` option in the printer's PPD file.

TABLE 9.9   Sides Keywords

Keyword	Description
one-sided	Print on one side of the media.
two-sided-long-edge	Print on both sides of the media with no rotation (duplex printing for portrait pages).
two-sided-short-edge	Print on both sides of the media, rotating the back side by 180 degrees (duplex printing for landscape pages).

The `sides-supported` Attribute

The `sides-supported` attribute lists the available duplex settings. For CUPS this mirrors the `Duplex` option in the printer's PPD file.

The `uri-authentication-supported` Attribute

The `uri-authentication-supported` attribute lists the type of authentication that is supported on each URI listed in the `printer-uri-supported` attribute. Each method can be one of the keyword strings listed in Table 9.10.

TABLE 9.10   Authentication Keyword Strings

Keyword	Description
none	No authentication is supported or required.
requesting-user-name	Identifies the owner of a request.
basic	Identifies the owner of a request using Basic authentication.
digest	Identifies the owner of a request using Digest authentication.
certificate	Identifies the owner of a request using a certificate.

For CUPS the strings will be `requesting-user-name`, `basic`, or `digest`. A different certificate-based authentication mechanism is also supported but is used in conjunction with `basic` and `digest` authentication rather than as a separate method.

The `uri-security-supported` Attribute

The `uri-security-supported` attribute specifies the type of encryption that is supported by each of the URIs listed in the `printer-uri-supported` attribute. Table 9.11 lists the available security methods.

TABLE 9.11   Security Keyword Strings

Keyword	Description
none	The printer does not support any type of encryption.
ssl3	The printer supports SSL v3.0 encryption on a dedicated port.
tls	The printer supports TLS v1.0 encryption using the HTTP Upgrade protocol.

CUPS will normally return `tls` for all URIs unless the server has been otherwise configured.

Optional Attributes

In addition to the required attributes, printer objects include a number of optional attributes that vary from printer to printer. Table 9.12 lists the optional attributes.

TABLE 9.12   Optional Printer Attributes

Name	Type	Description
color-supported	boolean	Whether the printer supports color printing.
job-impressions-supported	rangeOfInteger (0:MAX)	The minimum and maximum number of printed pages that are supported per job.
job-k-octets-supported	rangeOfInteger(0:MAX)	The minimum and maximum document sizes.
job-media-sheets-supported	rangeOfInteger (0:MAX)	The minimum and maximum number of job sheets that are supported.
multiple-document-jobs-supported	boolean	Whether the printer supports print jobs with multiple files.
multiple-operation-time-out	integer (1:MAX)	The number of seconds allowed between Create-Job, Send-Document, and Send-URI operations before the job will be started.
pages-per-minute	integer (0:MAX)	The average number of pages that the printer can produce per minute.
pages-per-minute-color	integer (0:MAX)	The average number of color pages that the printer can produce per minute.
print-quality-default	type2 enum	Specifies the default print quality.
print-quality-supported	1setOf type2 enum	Lists the supported qualities.
printer-current-time	dateTime	The current time and date as known to the printer.
printer-driver-installer	uri	The location of a printer driver installation page.

TABLE 9.12   Continued

Name	Type	Description
printer-info	text(127)	Additional descriptive information about the printer.
printer-location	text(127)	The location of the printer.
printer-make-and-model	text(127)	The printer make and model name.
printer-message-from-operator	text(127)	A human-readable message from the printer operator.
printer-more-info	uri	A Web page with more information on the printer.
printer-more-info-manufacturer	uri	The location of the printer manufacturer's Web page for the product.
printer-resolution-default	resolution	Specifies the default output resolution.
printer-resolution-supported	1setOf resolution	Lists the supported output resolutions.
printer-state-message	text(MAX)	A human-readable state message for the printer.
reference-uri-schemes-supported	1setOf uriScheme	The list of schemes that Print-URI and Send-URI operations can use.

The color-supported Attribute

The color-supported attribute specifies whether the printer can print in color. For CUPS this attribute mirrors the PPD ColorDevice attribute.

The job-impressions-supported Attribute

The job-impressions-supported attribute specifies the minimum and maximum number of printed pages that are supported per job. CUPS does not use this attribute.

The job-k-octets-supported Attribute

The job-k-octets-supported attribute specifies the minimum and maximum size of each document file in a print job in kilobytes. CUPS does not use this attribute.

The job-media-sheets-supported Attribute

The job-media-sheets-supported attribute specifies the minimum and maximum number of job sheets that are supported in each print job. CUPS does not use this attribute.

The `multiple-document-jobs-supported` Attribute

The `multiple-document-jobs-supported` attribute specifies whether print jobs can contain more than one file. For CUPS this attribute will always be `true`.

The `multiple-operation-time-out` Attribute

The `multiple-operation-time-out` attribute specifies the number of seconds that are allowed between files in a job. Once the time interval has expired the job will be "closed" and started as necessary. For CUPS this attribute mirrors the value of the TimeOut configuration directive in the `cupsd.conf` file.

The `pages-per-minute` Attribute

The `pages-per-minute` attribute specifies the number of pages that the printer can produce per minute. For CUPS this attribute mirrors the value of the Throughput attribute in the printer's PPD file.

The `pages-per-minute-color` Attribute

The `pages-per-minute-color` attribute specifies the number of color pages that the printer can produce per minute. For color printers in CUPS this attribute mirrors the value of the Throughput attribute in the printer's PPD file. For B&W printers this attribute is not supplied.

The `print-quality-default` Attribute

The `print-quality-default` attribute specifies the default print quality. Table 9.13 lists the available print qualities. CUPS does not use this attribute.

TABLE 9.13   Print Quality Values

Value	Description
3	Draft quality
4	Normal quality
5	High quality

The `print-quality-supported` Attribute

The `print-quality-supported` attribute lists the supported output qualities. CUPS does not supply this attribute.

The `printer-current-time` Attribute

The `printer-current-time` attribute specifies the local time and date in the 11-byte format defined in RFC 1903. CUPS currently does not supply this attribute.

The `printer-driver-installer` Attribute

The `printer-driver-installer` attribute defines the location of a printer driver installation page. CUPS does not use this attribute.

The `printer-info` Attribute

The `printer-info` attribute provides additional human-readable descriptive information about the printer. In CUPS the administrator defines the value of this attribute when the printer or class is added.

The `printer-location` Attribute

The `printer-location` attribute provides a human-readable location of the printer. In CUPS the administrator defines the value of this attribute when the printer or class is added.

The `printer-make-and-model` Attribute

The `printer-make-and-model` attribute describes the make and model of the printer. In CUPS this attribute is mirrored from the `NickName` attribute in the printer's PPD file.

The `printer-message-from-operator` Attribute

The `printer-message-from-operator` attribute provides a human-readable message from the printer operator. CUPS does not use this attribute.

The `printer-more-info` Attribute

The `printer-more-info` attribute provides a URL for a Web page containing more information about the printer. In CUPS this attribute will have the same value as the first URI in the `printer-uri-supported` attribute.

The `printer-more-info-manufacturer` Attribute

The `printer-more-info-manufacturer` attribute provides a URL for a manufacturer's Web page on the printer model. CUPS does not use this attribute.

The `printer-resolution-default` Attribute

The `printer-resolution-default` attribute specifies the default output resolution. CUPS does not use this attribute.

The `printer-resolution-supported` Attribute

The `printer-resolution-supported` attribute lists the supported output resolutions. CUPS does not supply this attribute.

The `printer-state-message` Attribute

The `printer-state-message` attribute provides a human-readable text message from the printer. In CUPS this attribute contains the last message from a filter or back end during a print job, or a message provided in a Pause-Printer operation.

The `reference-uri-schemes-supported` Attribute

The `reference-uri-schemes-supported` attribute lists the supported URI schemes for the `Print-URI` and `Send-URI` operations. The list must at least include the `ftp` scheme. CUPS 1.1.x does not support this attribute or the Print-URI or Send-URI operations. CUPS 1.2.x lists the schemes `ftp`, `http`, and `https`, and supports both the `Print-URI` and `Send-URI` operations.

CUPS Attributes

In addition to the standard IPP attributes, CUPS adds several new attributes that describe the printer or class type, the device used for printer queues, and the members in class queues. Table 9.14 lists the new attributes.

TABLE 9.14 CUPS Attributes for Printers and Classes

Name	Type	Description
device-uri	uri	The device the printer is connected through.
job-k-limit	integer	The maximum size of a user's print jobs for the given job-quota-period.
job-page-limit	integer	The maximum number of pages for a user's print jobs for the given job-quota-period.
job-quota-period	integer	The number of seconds to use per-user page/size accounting information.
member-names	1setOf name(127)	A list of member printer names in a class.
member-uris	1setOf uri	A list of member printer URIs in a class.

TABLE 9.14   Continued

Name	Type	Description
printer-type	type2 enum	Printer/class capability bits.
requesting-user-name-allowed	1setOf name(127)	A list of users that are allowed to print.
requesting-user-name-denied	1setOf name(127)	A list of users that are not allowed to print.

The `device-uri` Attribute

The `device-uri` attribute specifies a unique identifier for the device in the form of a URI. URIs containing a username and password for authentication have the information automatically filtered when the device URI is reported to a client. That is, if you set the device-uri to `ipp://user:pass@foo.bar.com/ipp`, the returned value will be `ipp://foo.bar.com/ipp`.

The `job-k-limit` Attribute

The `job-k-limit` attribute specifies the maximum size (in kilobytes) of a user's print jobs for the given `job-quota-period`. A limit of 0 disables this quota check.

The `job-page-limit` Attribute

The `job-page-limit` attribute specifies the maximum number of pages for a user's print jobs for the given `job-quota-period`. A limit of 0 disables this quota check.

The `job-quota-period` Attribute

The `job-quota-period` attribute specifies the number of seconds to use per-user page/size accounting information. A value of 0 disables quotas for the printer, whereas a value of 86,400 provides daily quotas, 604,800 provides weekly quotas, and so on.

The `member-names` Attribute

The `member-names` attribute lists the member printer names in a class. Each name corresponds to the same URI in the `member-uris` attribute.

The `member-uris` Attribute

The `member-uris` attribute lists the member printer URIs in a class. Each URI corresponds to the same name in the `member-names` attribute.

The `printer-type` Attribute

The `printer-type` attribute defines the printer/class type and its capabilities. For printer classes the capability bits reflect the common subset of capabilities shared by each of the member printers. Table 9.15 lists the type bits, which are bitwise ORed to form the printer type value.

TABLE 9.15   Printer Type Bits

Bit	Description
0	Is a printer class
1	Is a remote destination
2	Can print in black
3	Can print in color
4	Can print on both sides of the page in hardware
5	Can staple output
6	Can do fast uncollated copies in hardware
7	Can do fast collated copies in hardware
8	Can punch output
9	Can cover output
10	Can bind output
11	Can sort output
12	Can handle media up to US-Legal/A4
13	Can handle media from US-Legal/A4 to ISO-C/A2
14	Can handle media larger than ISO-C/A2
15	Can handle user-defined media sizes
16	Is an implicit class

The `requesting-user-name-allowed` Attribute

The `requesting-user-name-allowed` attribute lists the users that are allowed to print. Only one of the `requesting-user-name-allowed` and `requesting-user-name-denied` attributes will be defined.

The `requesting-user-name-denied` Attribute

The `requesting-user-name-denied` attribute lists the users that are not allowed to print. Only one of the `requesting-user-name-allowed` and `requesting-user-name-denied` attributes will be defined.

Printer Operations

IPP provides several operations that act on printer objects exclusively. Table 9.16 lists them.

TABLE 9.16   Printer Operation Codes

Code	Name	Description
0×000A	Get-Jobs	Get a list of print jobs.
0×000B	Get-Printer-Attributes	Get the attributes for a printer.
0×0010	Pause-Printer	Temporarily stop a printer.
0×0011	Resume-Printer	Resume printing on a printer.
0×0012	Purge-Jobs	Cancel all jobs on a printer.
0×0013	Set-Printer-Attributes	Change printer attributes.
0×0015	Get-Printer-Supported-Values	Get supported printer attributes for the specified document format.
0×0022	Enable-Printer	Allow new print jobs to be submitted to a printer.
0×0023	Disable-Printer	Prevent new print jobs from being submitted to a printer.

The Get-Jobs Operation

The Get-Jobs operation returns a list of print jobs for the printer. Each request must contain at least the following attributes in the operation group:

```
attributes-charset (charset)
attributes-natural-language (naturalLanguage)
printer-uri (uri)
```

The requested-attributes (1setOf type2 keyword) attribute can also be included to potentially limit the number of attributes returned, where each keyword represents an attribute name or group. The requesting-user-name (name(127)) attribute can be used to limit the list to those jobs submitted by that username. The limit (integer (1:MAX)) attribute can limit the maximum number of jobs that are returned. Finally, the which-jobs (type2 keyword) attribute specifies which jobs you are interested in. A value of completed means that you want information on completed print jobs, whereas a value of not-completed means that you want information on jobs that are pending, pending-held, processing, or processing-stopped.

CUPS also supports a printer-uri value of ipp://ServerName/, which will return jobs for all printers and classes.

The Get-Printer-Attributes Operation

The Get-Printer-Attributes operation returns the current printer attributes. Each request must contain at least the following attributes in the operation group:

attributes-charset (charset)

attributes-natural-language (naturalLanguage)

printer-uri (uri)

The requested-attributes (1setOf type2 keyword) attribute can also be included to potentially limit the number of attributes returned, where each keyword represents an attribute name or group.

The Pause-Printer Operation

The Pause-Printer operation puts the specified printer object in the stopped state. Each request must contain at least the following attributes in the operation group:

attributes-charset (charset)

attributes-natural-language (naturalLanguage)

printer-uri (uri)

For CUPS this operation must be initiated by a POST to the /admin resource, which will normally also require administrative authentication.

The Resume-Printer Operation

The Resume-Printer operation puts the specified printer object in the idle or processing states, depending on the existence of pending print jobs. Each request must contain at least the following attributes in the operation group:

attributes-charset (charset)

attributes-natural-language (naturalLanguage)

printer-uri (uri)

For CUPS this operation must be initiated by a POST to the /admin resource, which will normally also require administrative authentication.

The Purge-Jobs Operation

The Purge-Jobs operation cancels all print jobs on the specified printer object. Each request must contain at least the following attributes in the operation group:

attributes-charset (charset)

attributes-natural-language (naturalLanguage)

printer-uri (uri)

For CUPS this operation must be initiated by a POST to the /admin resource, which will normally also require administrative authentication. CUPS will also purge the job history when using this operation.

The Set-Printer-Attributes Operation

The Set-Printer-Attributes operation sets the values of any read/write attribute on the specified printer object. Each request must contain at least the following attributes in the operation group:

```
attributes-charset (charset)
attributes-natural-language (naturalLanguage)
printer-uri (uri)
```

Printer attributes that should be set must follow in the printer attribute group.

CUPS does not currently support this operation.

The Get-Printer-Supported-Values Operation

The Get-Printer-Supported-Values operation returns the supported printer attribute values. Each request must contain at least the following attributes in the operation group:

```
attributes-charset (charset)
attributes-natural-language (naturalLanguage)
printer-uri (uri)
```

CUPS does not support this operation.

The Enable-Printer Operation

The Enable-Printer operation sets the printer-is-accepting attribute for the specified printer object to true. Each request must contain at least the following attributes in the operation group:

```
attributes-charset (charset)
attributes-natural-language (naturalLanguage)
printer-uri (uri)
```

For CUPS this operation must be initiated by a POST to the /admin resource, which will normally also require administrative authentication. Also see the identical (but earlier) operation CUPS-Accept-Jobs.

The `Disable-Printer` Operation

The `Disable-Printer` operation sets the `printer-is-accepting` attribute for the specified printer object to `false`. Each request must contain at least the following attributes in the operation group:

```
attributes-charset (charset)
attributes-natural-language (naturalLanguage)
printer-uri (uri)
```

For CUPS this operation must be initiated by a POST to the /admin resource, which will normally also require administrative authentication. Also see the identical (but earlier) operation CUPS-Reject-Jobs.

Summary

IPP printer objects manage a single printer or class of printers. Each object has an associated state and collection of print jobs destined for that printer.

Every printer object has a common set of required attributes as well as several optional printer-specific attributes. Printers that are served by CUPS have several additional extension attributes that define how the printer object is connected to the device or other printers.

IPP provides many operations to control printer objects. These operations control the state of the printer object as well as default values for some printer attributes.

## CHAPTER 10

Job Objects

This chapter describes the attributes and operations provided for IPP job objects.

What Is a Job Object?

A job object represents one or more documents that are queued for printing on a printer object. A job object can also have subscription objects associated with it.

Each job object is always in one of the seven states shown in Table 10.1. Pending jobs are printed using the priority values and the order they were submitted.

TABLE 10.1   Job States

Value	Name	Description
3	pending	The job is waiting to be printed.
4	pending-held	The job is waiting to be printed once the hold condition is satisfied.
5	processing	The job is currently being processed or printed.
6	processing-stopped	The job was stopped while it was being processed or printed.
7	canceled	The job was cancelled by a user or administrator.
8	aborted	The job was aborted by the system due to a processing error. This is different than the processing-stopped state because a stopped job can always be restarted.
9	completed	The job was completely processed and printed successfully.

Jobs are also associated with a username, which can be authenticated. This allows the enduser to list and cancel their own jobs, or an administrator to list and cancel all jobs.

Required Attributes

Each job includes several required attributes, which are listed in Table 10.2.

TABLE 10.2   Required Job Attributes

Name	Type	Description
attributes-charset	charset	The character set used for the job
attributes-natural-language	naturalLanguage	The language used for the job
job-id	integer (1:MAX)	The job object number
job-name	name(MAX)	The name or title of the job
job-originating-user-name	name(MAX)	The owner of the job
job-printer-up-time	integer(1:MAX)	The current printer-up-time value for the printer

TABLE 10.2   Continued

Name	Type	Description
job-printer-uri	uri	The URI for the printer object to which this job belongs
job-state	type1 enum	The current job state
job-state-reasons	1setOf type2 keyword	Detailed reason codes for the job
job-uri	uri	The URI for the job object
time-at-completed	integer(MIN:MAX)	The printer-up-time when the job was completed, aborted, or cancelled
time-at-creation	integer(MIN:MAX)	The printer-up-time when the job was created
time-at-processing	integer(MIN:MAX)	The printer-up-time when the job was processed

The attributes-charset Attribute

The attributes-charset attribute specifies the character set to use for the job and request.

The attributes-natural-language Attribute

The attributes-natural-language attribute specifies the language to use for the job and request.

The job-id Attribute

The job-id attribute is used to identify a print job.

The job-name Attribute

The job-name attribute specifies the name or title of the job.

The job-originating-user-name Attribute

The job-originating-user-name attribute specifies the owner of the job. This is a mirror of the requesting-user-name attribute provided in the original Create-Job, Print-Job, or Print-URI operations.

The job-printer-up-time Attribute

The job-printer-up-time attribute provides the current printer-up-time value for the printer associated with the job.

The `job-printer-uri` Attribute

The `job-printer-uri` attribute provides the URI for the printer object associated with the job.

The `job-state` Attribute

The `job-state` attribute specifies the current job state, which can be one of the values listed in Table 10-1.

The `job-state-reasons` Attribute

The `job-state-reasons` attribute is an array of reason keywords that describes a detailed reason for the current job state. Table 10.3 lists the supported reason strings.

TABLE 10.3   Job State Reason Strings

String	Description
none	There is no reason for the current state.
aborted-by-system	The job was aborted by the system and placed in the aborted state.
compression-error	One or more documents contain an error in the compressed data.
document-access-error	The specified URI cannot be accessed.
document-format-error	One or more documents contain errors that prevent them from being printed.
job-canceled-at-device	The job was cancelled at the device.
job-canceled-by-operator	The job was cancelled by the printer operator.
job-canceled-by-user	The job was cancelled by the user.
job-completed-successfully	The job was completed successfully.
job-completed-with-errors	The job completed with some errors.
job-completed-with-warnings	The job completed with some warnings.
job-data-insufficient	No document data has been received.
job-hold-until-specified	The job is currently held due to a job-hold-until attribute.
job-incoming	The document files are currently being received from the client.
job-interpreting	The job is currently being interpreted/RIPd.
job-outgoing	The job is currently being sent to the printer.
job-printing	The job is currently printing.
job-queued	The job has been queued for printing.
job-queued-for-marker	The job is ready to print but the printer needs ink/marker/toner.
job-restartable	The job can be restarted.
job-transforming	The job is being transformed into a different format.

TABLE 10.3 Continued

String	Description
printer-stopped	The printer is stopped.
printer-stopped-partly	The printer-state-reasons attribute contains the stopped-partly reason.
processing-to-stop-point	The job has been cancelled but is printing any remaining pages on the printer that have already been processed.
queued-in-device	The job has been queued on the output device.
resources-are-not-ready	One or more resources (media, fonts, and so forth) are not available to print the job.
service-off-line	The job is being held because the printer is offline.
submission-interrupted	One or more document files were not received in full.
unsupported-compression	One or more documents in the job are compressed using an unknown algorithm.
unsupported-document-format	One or more documents are in an unsupported format.

The job-uri Attribute

The job-uri attribute provides the URI for the job object.

For CUPS the job-uri will look like

ipp://ServerName/jobs/JobID

where ServerName is the name of the server and JobID is the value of the job-id attribute.

The time-at-completed Attribute

The time-at-completed attribute specifies the printer-up-time when the job was completed, aborted, or cancelled.

For CUPS the time-at-completed value is the Unix time value in seconds since January 1, 1970.

The time-at-creation Attribute

The time-at-creation attribute specifies the printer-up-time when the job was created.

For CUPS the time-at-completed value is the Unix time value in seconds since January 1, 1970.

The `time-at-processing` Attribute

The `time-at-processing` attribute specifies the `printer-up-time` when the job entered the processing state.

For CUPS the `time-at-completed` value is the Unix time value in seconds since January 1, 1970.

Optional Attributes

Most of the optional attributes are job template attributes used when submitting print jobs. Table 10.4 lists the optional job attributes.

TABLE 10.4   Optional Job Attributes

Name	Type	Description
copies	integer (1:MAX)	The number of copies for this job
date-time-at-completed	dateTime	The date and time when the job was completed, cancelled, or aborted
date-time-at-creation	dateTime	The date and time when the job was created
date-time-at-processing	dateTime	The date and time when the job was processed
finishings	1setOf type2 enum	Finishing actions for this job
job-detailed-status-messages	1setOf text(MAX)	A log of human-readable status messages
job-document-access-errors	1setOf text(MAX)	A log of human-readable document access error messages
job-hold-until	type3 keyword | name	The job hold condition, if any
job-impressions	integer (0:MAX)	The number of printed sides in the print job
job-impressions-completed	integer (0:MAX)	The number of sides that have been printed
job-k-octets	integer (0:MAX)	The number of kilobytes in the document files
job-k-octets-processed	integer (0:MAX)	The number of kilobytes that have been processed
job-media-sheets	integer (0:MAX)	The number of media sheets in the print job
job-media-sheets-completed	integer (0:MAX)	The number of media sheets that have been printed
job-message-from-operator	text (127)	A human-readable text message from the printer operator

TABLE 10.4   Continued

Name	Type	Description
job-more-info	uri	A URL for more information through a Web browser
job-priority	integer (1:100)	The priority of the print job
job-sheets	type3 keyword | name	The job sheets
job-state-message	text (MAX)	A human-readable status message
media	type3 keyword | name	The media size, type, or source
multiple-document-handling	type2 keyword	How to handle copies of documents
number-of-documents	integer (0:MAX)	The number of document files in the job
number-of-intervening-jobs	integer (0:MAX)	The number of jobs that are scheduled to print before this one
number-up	integer (1:MAX)	The number of document pages to place on each output page
orientation-requested	type2 enum	The orientation of the output
output-device-assigned	name(127)	The name of the output device that was assigned for the job
page-ranges	1setOf rangeOfInteger	Which pages in the job to print
print-quality	type2 enum	The output quality
printer-resolution	resolution	The output resolution
sides	type2 keyword	Whether to print single or double-sided

The copies Attribute

The copies attribute specifies the number of copies that will be produced for the job. The copies only apply to the document files, not to any job sheets that are associated with the job. The value of the copies attribute must lie inside the range defined by the printer's copies-supported attribute.

The date-time-at-completed Attribute

The date-time-at-completed attribute provides the date and time when the job was completed, cancelled, or aborted.

CUPS does not supply this attribute.

The date-time-at-creation Attribute

The date-time-at-creation attribute provides the date and time when the job was created.

CUPS does not supply this attribute.

The `date-time-at-processing` Attribute

The `date-time-at-processing` attribute provides the date and time when the job was processed.

CUPS does not supply this attribute.

The `finishings` Attribute

The `finishings` attribute specifies the finishing actions for this job. The available keyword values are defined by the printer's `finishings-supported` attribute.

The `job-detailed-status-messages` Attribute

The `job-detailed-status-messages` attribute provides a list of human-readable text messages concerning the current status of the job.

CUPS does not provide this attribute.

The `job-document-access-errors` Attribute

The `job-document-access-errors` attribute provides a list of human-readable text message concerning any access errors that were encountered when retrieving a remote document submitted using the `Print-URI` or `Send-URI` operations.

CUPS 1.1 does not provide this attribute.

CUPS 1.2 provides the text from HTTP and FTP access errors.

The `job-hold-until` Attribute

The `job-hold-until` attribute specifies a hold condition for the job. The list of acceptable values is shown in Chapter 9, "Printer Objects."

The `job-impressions` Attribute

The `job-impressions` attribute provides the number of printed sides in the print job. This differs from the `job-media-sheets` attribute because the `job-media-sheets` attribute counts the number of sheets that are printed.

CUPS does not support this attribute.

The `job-impressions-completed` Attribute

The `job-impressions-completed` attribute provides the number of sides that have been printed in the job. This differs from the `job-media-sheets-completed` attribute because the `job-media-sheets-completed` attribute counts the number of sheets that have been printed.

CUPS updates this number as PAGE comments are received from job filters.

The `job-k-octets` Attribute

The `job-k-octets` attribute provides the number of kilobytes in the document files.

CUPS automatically updates this value as additional documents are added to the job.

The `job-k-octets-processed` Attribute

The `job-k-octets-processed` attribute provides the number of kilobytes that have been processed.

CUPS does not support this attribute.

The `job-media-sheets` Attribute

The `job-media-sheets` attribute provides the number of media sheets in the print job. This differs from the job-impressions attribute because the `job-impressions` attribute counts the number of sides that are printed. For example, a typical double-sided print job with 20 pages will have a `job-media-sheets` value of 10 and a `job-impressions` value of 20.

CUPS does not support this attribute.

The `job-media-sheets-completed` Attribute

The `job-media-sheets-completed` attribute provides the number of media sheets that have been printed. This differs from the `job-impressions-completed` attribute because the `job-impressions-completed` attribute counts the number of sides that have been printed.

CUPS does not support this attribute.

The `job-message-from-operator` Attribute

The `job-message-from-operator` attribute provides a human-readable text message from the printer operator. This might contain a message such as "Job is being held until we get another roll of glossy photo paper."

CUPS does not support this attribute.

The `job-more-info` Attribute

The `job-more-info` attribute provides a URL for more information through a Web browser.

For CUPS, the `job-more-info` attribute is the same as the `job-uri` attribute.

The `job-priority` Attribute

The `job-priority` attribute specifies the priority of the print job. Job priorities are used to control the order of printed jobs in the queue; higher priorities are printed first.

CUPS uses the job priority to position the job in the queue but will not stop a lower priority job that is already in the queue.

The `job-sheets` Attribute

The `job-sheets` attribute specifies the banner pages to use when printing the job.

CUPS supports 1 or 2 job sheets. The first job sheet is printed before the documents in the job, and the second job sheet is printed after the documents in the job. Because of the way job sheets are implemented in CUPS, the `job-sheets` attribute cannot be changed after the job has been created.

The `job-state-message` Attribute

The `job-state-message` attribute provides a human–readable status message for the job.

CUPS currently does not support this attribute.

The `media` Attribute

The `media` attribute specifies the media size, type, or source for the job.

CUPS accepts 1 or more `media` attribute values for each job to allow for specification of all three media values.

The `multiple-document-handling` Attribute

The `multiple-document-handling` attribute specifies how to handle copies of documents. Essentially this attribute controls whether copies are collated.

CUPS supports the `multiple-documents-collated-copies` and `multiple-documents-uncollated-copies` values.

The `number-of-documents` Attribute

The `number-of-documents` attribute provides the total number of document files in the job.

CUPS includes the job sheets in the count.

The `number-of-intervening-jobs` Attribute

The `number-of-intervening-jobs` attribute provides the number of jobs that are scheduled to print before this one.

CUPS does not support this attribute.

The `number-up` Attribute

The `number-up` attribute specifies the number of document pages to place on each output page.

CUPS supports printing 1, 2, or 4 pages per side or sheet.

The `orientation-requested` Attribute

The `orientation-requested` attribute specifies the orientation of the output. The value must be one of the values in the printer's `orientation-supported` attribute.

The `output-device-assigned` Attribute

The `output-device-assigned` attribute provides the name of the output device that was assigned for the job.

CUPS does not provide this attribute.

The `page-ranges` Attribute

The `page-ranges` attribute specifies which pages in the job to print. The page ranges in the set must be unique and apply to all documents in the job. For example, if you specify a `page-ranges` attribute with a value of 1–4, pages 1–4 will be printed in each document and not just the first 4 pages of the first document.

CUPS prints page ranges in ascending order, so specifying a `page-ranges` attribute with the values 7–8 and 1–2 will print pages 1, 2, 7, and 8.

The `print-quality` Attribute

The `print-quality` attribute specifies the output quality. The value must be one of the values in the printer's `print-quality-supported` attribute.

CUPS does not support this attribute.

The `printer-resolution` Attribute

The `printer-resolution` attribute specifies the output resolution of the print job. The value must be one of the values in the printer's `printer-resolution-supported` attribute.

The `sides` Attribute

The `sides` attribute specifies whether to print single or double-sided output. The value must be one of the values in the printer's `sides-supported` attribute.

CUPS Attributes

CUPS defines several new job template attributes that are used by the CUPS file filters. Table 10.5 defines the CUPS attributes.

TABLE 10.5   CUPS Job Attributes

Name	Type	Description
blackplot	boolean	Whether to print HP-GL/2 plot files in black ink only
brightness	integer (0:200)	The overall brightness of the print job
columns	integer (1:4)	The number of columns for text files
cpi	type2 enum	The number of characters per inch when printing text files
fitplot	boolean	Whether to scale HP-GL/2 plot files to the media size
gamma	integer (1:10000)	The overall gamma correction for the print job
hue	integer (-180:180)	The color rotation to apply to image files
job-billing	text(MAX)	Job billing information
job-originating-host-name	name(MAX)	The hostname or IP address of the client that created the job
lpi	type2 enum	The number of lines per inch when printing text files
page-bottom	integer (0:MAX)	The bottom margin in points when printing text files
page-label	text(MAX)	A label to show at the top and bottom of each printed page
page-left	integer (0:MAX)	The left margin in points when printing text files
page-right	integer (0:MAX)	The right margin in points when printing text files
page-set	type2 keyword	The pages to print in each document

TABLE 10.5   Continued

Name	Type	Description
page-top	integer (0:MAX)	The top margin in points when printing text files
penwidth	integer (0:MAX)	The default pen width in HP-GL/2 plot files
position	type2 keyword	The position of image files on the page
ppi	integer (1:MAX)	The pixel resolution per inch of image files
prettyprint	boolean	Whether or not to apply special formatting to text files
saturation	integer (0:200)	The color saturation for image files
scaling	integer (1:1000)	The scaling to apply to image files
wrap	boolean	Whether to wrap long lines in text files

The `blackplot` Attribute

The `blackplot` attribute specifies whether HP-GL/2 plot files should be rendered entirely in black ink (`blackplot=true`) or using the colors and shades specified in the file (`blackplot=false`). This attribute is ignored for all other types of files. The default value is `false`.

The `brightness` Attribute

The `brightness` attribute specifies the overall brightness of the printed output in percent. A brightness of 100 is normal, whereas 200 is twice as bright and 50 is half as bright. The default value is 100.

Brightness is applied equally to the Cyan, Magenta, Yellow, and Black values using the function:

```
f(x) = brightness / 100 * x
```

The `columns` Attribute

The `columns` attribute specifies the number of columns to generate when printing text files. This attribute is ignored for all other types of files. The default value is 1.

The `cpi` Attribute

The `cpi` attribute specifies the number of characters per inch when printing text files. This attribute is ignored for all other types of files. Only the values 10, 12, and 17 are currently supported. The default value is 10.

The `fitplot` Attribute

The `fitplot` attribute specifies whether to scale HP-GL/2 plot files to fit on the selected media (`fitplot=true`) or use the physical scale specified in the plot file (`fitplot=false`). This attribute is ignored for all other types of files. The default value is `false`.

Scaling only works if the HP-GL/2 file contains a `PS` (Plot Size) command.

The `gamma` Attribute

The `gamma` attribute specifies the luminance correction for the output. A value of 1000 specifies no correction, whereas values of 2000 and 500 will generate lighter and darker output, respectively. The default value is `1000`.

Gamma is applied to the Red, Green, and Blue values (or luminance for grayscale output) equally using the function:

`f(x) = x`$^{(1000/gamma)}$

The `hue` Attribute

The `hue` attribute specifies a color hue rotation when printing image files. The `hue` attribute is ignored for all other types of files. The default value is `0`. Table 10.6 shows the effect of different hue values on the primary colors.

TABLE 10.6   The Effect of Color Hue on Colors

Color	hue=-45	hue=45
Red	Purple	Yellow-orange
Green	Yellow-green	Blue-green
Yellow	Orange	Green-yellow
Blue	Sky-blue	Purple
Magenta	Indigo	Crimson
Cyan	Blue-green	Light-navy-blue

The `job-billing` Attribute

The `job-billing` attribute provides a text value to associate with a job for billing purposes, such as `Customer #12345`.

The `job-originating-host-name` Attribute

The `job-originating-host-name` attribute specifies the host from which the job was queued. The value will be the hostname or IP address of the client depending on whether hostname resolution is enabled. The localhost address (127.0.0.1) is always resolved to the name "localhost".

This attribute is read-only.

The `lpi` Attribute

The `lpi` attribute specifies the number of lines per inch when printing text files. This attribute is ignored for all other types of files. Only the values 6 and 8 are currently supported. The default value is `6`.

The `page-bottom` Attribute

The `page-bottom` attribute specifies the bottom margin in points (72 points equals 1 inch). The default value is the device physical margin as defined in the printer's PPD file.

The `page-label` Attribute

The `page-label` attribute provides a text value to place in the header and footer on each page. If a classification level is set on the server, this classification is printed before the page label and the page label serves to hold the caveats associated with the job classification. The default is to have no page label.

The `page-left` Attribute

The `page-left` attribute specifies the left margin in points (72 points equals 1 inch). The default value is the device physical margin as defined in the printer's PPD file.

The `page-right` Attribute

The `page-right` attribute specifies the right margin in points (72 points equals 1 inch). The default value is the device physical margin as defined in the printer's PPD file.

The `page-set` Attribute

The `page-set` attribute specifies which pages to print in a file. The supported keywords are shown in Table 10.7. The default value is `all`.

TABLE 10.7   Page Set Keywords

Keyword	Description
all	Print all pages
even	Print only the even-numbered pages
odd	Print only the odd-numbered pages

The `page-top` Attribute

The `page-top` attribute specifies the top margin in points (72 points equals 1 inch). The default value is the device physical margin as defined in the printer's PPD file.

The `penwidth` Attribute

The `penwidth` attribute specifies the default pen width in micrometers when printing HP-GL/2 plot files (1000 micrometers = 1 millimeter). This attribute is ignored for all other types of files and is overridden in HP-GL/2 files that use the PW (Pen Width) command. The default value is 1000 (1 millimeter).

The `position` Attribute

The `position` attribute specifies the location of image files on the media. This attribute is ignored for all other types of files. Table 10.8 lists the supported keyword values. The default value is `center`.

TABLE 10.8   Position Keyword Values

Keyword	Description
center	Center the image on the page
top	Print the image centered at the top of the page
left	Print the image centered on the left of the page
right	Print the image centered on the right of the page
top-left	Print the image at the top left corner of the page
top-right	Print the image at the top right corner of the page
bottom	Print the image centered at the bottom of the page
bottom-left	Print the image at the bottom left corner of the page
bottom-right	Print the image at the bottom right corner of the page

The `ppi` Attribute

The `ppi` attribute specifies the resolution of an image file in pixels per inch. This attribute is ignored for all other types of files. The default value is the resolution included with the file or 128 if no resolution information is available.

The `prettyprint` Attribute

The `prettyprint` attribute specifies whether text files should be printed with a shaded header and keyword highlighting (`prettyprint=true`) or without additional formatting (`prettyprint=false`). The default value is false.

The keyword highlighting is content-sensitive, so Bourne shell scripts are highlighted differently than C source code.

The `saturation` Attribute

The `saturation` attribute specifies the color saturation when printing image files. This attribute is ignored for all other types of files. A saturation of 100 is normal, while values of 50 and 200 will be half and twice as colorful, respectively. The default value is 100.

The `scaling` Attribute

The `scaling` attribute specifies the scaling of image files with respect to the selected media. This attribute is ignored for all other types of files. A value of 100 specifies that the image file should fit on exactly one page, filling as much as possible given the image dimensions. The default value is unspecified.

The `scaling` attribute overrides the `ppi` attribute if specified.

The `wrap` Attribute

The `wrap` attribute specifies whether long lines should be wrapped (`wrap=true`) or not (`wrap=false`) when printing text files. This attribute is ignored for all other types of files. The default value is true.

Job Operations

IPP provides several operations, listed in Table 10.9, to create and manage job objects.

TABLE 10.9   IPP Job Operations

Code	Name	Description
0x0002	Print-Job	Print a single file.
0x0003	Print-URI	Print a single URI.
0x0004	Validate-Job	Validate print job options.
0x0005	Create-Job	Create an empty print job.
0x0006	Send-Document	Add a single file to an existing print job.
0x0007	Send-URI	Add a single URI to an existing print job.
0x0008	Cancel-Job	Cancel a print job.
0x0009	Get-Job-Attributes	Get the attributes for a print job.
0x000C	Hold-Job	Hold a print job.
0x000D	Release-Job	Release a print job for printing.
0x000E	Restart-Job	Restart the printing of a print job.
0x0014	Set-Job-Attributes	Change print job attributes.

The `Print-Job` Operation

The `Print-Job` operation prints a single file. Each request must contain at least the following attributes in the operation group:

```
attributes-charset (charset)
attributes-natural-language (naturalLanguage)
printer-uri (uri)
requesting-user-name (name)
```

The document file immediately follows the IPP request data in the HTTP POST. If the print job is accepted, the IPP response will contain `job-uri`, `job-printer-uri`, and `job-id` attributes for the newly created job object.

The `Print-URI` Operation

The `Print-URI` operation prints a single remote file. Each request must contain at least the following attributes in the operation group:

```
attributes-charset (charset)
attributes-natural-language (naturalLanguage)
printer-uri (uri)
requesting-user-name (name)
document-uri (uri)
```

The `document-uri` attribute provides the location of the document file. If the print job is accepted, the IPP response will contain `job-uri`, `job-printer-uri`, and `job-id` attributes for the newly created job object.

Versions of CUPS prior to 1.2 do not support the Print–URI operation.

The `Validate-Job` Operation

The `Validate-Job` operation validates the attributes that will be used for a later `Create-Job`, `Print-Job`, or `Print-URI` operation. Each request must contain at least the following attributes in the operation group:

```
attributes-charset (charset)
attributes-natural-language (naturalLanguage)
printer-uri (uri)
requesting-user-name (name)
```

The IPP response will contain a success or failure code, along with any unsupported attributes or values.

The Create-Job Operation

The Create-Job operation creates an empty print job. Each request must contain at least the following attributes in the operation group:

```
attributes-charset (charset)
attributes-natural-language (naturalLanguage)
printer-uri (uri)
requesting-user-name (name)
```

The document files are sent later using the Send-Document or Send-URI operations. If the print job is accepted, the IPP response will contain job-uri, job-printer-uri, and job-id attributes for the newly created job object.

The Send-Document Operation

The Send-Document operation adds a single file to an existing print job. Each request must contain at least the following attributes in the operation group:

```
attributes-charset (charset)
attributes-natural-language (naturalLanguage)
printer-uri (uri) and job-id (integer) or job-uri (uri)
requesting-user-name (name)
last-document (boolean)
```

The document file immediately follows the IPP request data in the HTTP POST. The IPP response will contain a success or failure code for the document. The last-document attribute specifies whether this document file is the last document in the job.

The Send-URI Operation

The Send-URI operation adds a single remote file to an existing print job. Each request must contain at least the following attributes in the operation group:

```
attributes-charset (charset)
attributes-natural-language (naturalLanguage)
printer-uri (uri) and job-id (integer) or job-uri (uri)
requesting-user-name (name)
last-document (boolean)
document-uri (uri)
```

The document-uri attribute specifies the URL for the remote document file. The IPP response will contain a success or failure code for the document. The last-document attribute specifies whether this document file is the last document in the job.

The Cancel-Job Operation

The Cancel-Job operation cancels an existing print job. Each request must contain at least the following attributes in the operation group:

```
attributes-charset (charset)
attributes-natural-language (naturalLanguage)
printer-uri (uri) and job-id (integer) or job-uri (uri)
requesting-user-name (name)
```

The job must belong to the user named in the requesting-user-name attribute or the request must come from an administrative user. For CUPS any user in the system group can delete any job on the server.

The IPP response will contain a success or failure code.

The Get-Job-Attributes Operation

The Get-Job-Attributes operation gets the attributes for an existing print job. Each request must contain at least the following attributes in the operation group:

```
attributes-charset (charset)
attributes-natural-language (naturalLanguage)
printer-uri (uri) and job-id (integer) or job-uri (uri)
```

The IPP response will contain a success or failure code along with the attributes for the job object. The requested-attributes attribute can be supplied in the IPP request to select which attributes are returned (otherwise all job attributes are returned.)

The Hold-Job Operation

The Hold-Job operation holds an existing print job from printing. Each request must contain at least the following attributes in the operation group:

```
attributes-charset (charset)
attributes-natural-language (naturalLanguage)
printer-uri (uri) and job-id (integer) or job-uri (uri)
requesting-user-name (name)
job-hold-until (keyword | name)
```

The job-hold-until attribute specifies the new hold condition or time. The job must belong to the user named in the requesting-user-name attribute or the request must come from an administrative user. For CUPS any user in the system group can hold any job on the server.

The IPP response will contain a success or failure code.

The `Release-Job` Operation

The `Release-Job` operation releases an existing print job for printing. Each request must contain at least the following attributes in the operation group:

```
attributes-charset (charset)
attributes-natural-language (naturalLanguage)
printer-uri (uri) and job-id (integer) or job-uri (uri)
requesting-user-name (name)
```

The job must belong to the user named in the `requesting-user-name` attribute or the request must come from an administrative user. For CUPS any user in the system group can release any job on the server.

The IPP response will contain a success or failure code.

The `Restart-Job` Operation

The `Restart-Job` operation restarts an existing print job. Each request must contain at least the following attributes in the operation group:

```
attributes-charset (charset)
attributes-natural-language (naturalLanguage)
printer-uri (uri) and job-id (integer) or job-uri (uri)
requesting-user-name (name)
```

Jobs can only be restarted if the job file history (`PreserveJobFiles`) is enabled in the server.

The job must also belong to the user named in the `requesting-user-name` attribute or the request must come from an administrative user. For CUPS any user in the system group can restart any job on the server.

The IPP response will contain a success or failure code. Restart the printing of a print job.

The `Set-Job-Attributes` Operation

The `Set-Job-Attributes` operation changes the job template attributes for an existing print job. Each request must contain at least the following attributes in the operation group:

```
attributes-charset (charset)
attributes-natural-language (naturalLanguage)
printer-uri (uri) and job-id (integer) or job-uri (uri)
requesting-user-name (name)
```

The job must belong to the user named in the `requesting-user-name` attribute or the request must come from an administrative user. For CUPS any user in the system group can change any job on the server.

CUPS also does not allow changing of the `job-sheets` attribute.

The IPP response will contain a success or failure code.

Summary

Job objects hold the print files and options for each job sent to a printer. Each job object is associated with one printer or class and can be associated with multiple subscription objects. Job objects contain state attributes as well as job template attributes that define how the printed output is produced. The IPP job operations enable you to create and manage print jobs on the print server.

CHAPTER 11

IPP Subscription Objects

This chapter describes the attributes and operations provided for IPP subscription objects. IPP subscription objects provide the basis for event notification in IPP. The `mailto`, `indp`, and `ippget` notification schemes are discussed.

What Is a Subscription Object?

A subscription object is an event notification service. Each subscription object contains the address (URI) of a notification recipient, a subscription scheme or method, and a list of events in which the subscriber is interested.

IPP subscription objects are associated with printer or job objects. Job subscriptions can be created when you send a print job or to monitor the status of an existing job. For example, you might want to receive an e-mail when a long print job has completed. Job subscriptions last only as long as the job exists.

Printer subscriptions are created when they reference an existing printer object. These subscriptions are generally long-lived and allow third parties, such as the administrator, to monitor printer events such as out-of-paper conditions. Each printer subscription has a *lease time,* which specifies the duration of the subscription in seconds. Lease times are used so that server resources can be recovered after long periods of inactivity without contact with the client. Printer subscriptions can be renewed periodically by the client to continue monitoring the events, or cancelled at any time to discontinue monitoring.

CUPS extends the IPP subscription mechanism by supporting server subscriptions. Server subscriptions use the existing printer subscription mechanism but a different `printer-uri` value and event list. Server subscriptions allow you to monitor when printers and classes are added or deleted and when other server conditions change.

Notifications are only available in CUPS 1.2 and higher.

Standard Notification Attributes

The IPP notification specification adds many attributes for subscription objects. Table 11.1 lists the subscription object attributes.

TABLE 11.1   Subscription Object Attributes

Name	Type	Description
notify-attributes	1setOf type2 keyword	The list of attributes to send in a machine-readable notification
notify-attributes-supported	1setOf type2 keyword	The list of supported notification attributes
notify-charset	charset	The character set to use for notifications

TABLE 11.1 Continued

Name	Type	Description
notify-events	1setOf type2 keyword	The list of events to monitor
notify-events-default	1setOf type2 keyword	The default list of events to monitor
notify-events-supported	1setOf type2 keyword	The list of supported events that can be monitored
notify-job-id	integer (1:MAX)	The ID of the associated job object
notify-lease-duration	integer (0:67108863)	The duration of the subscription in seconds
notify-lease-duration-default	integer (0:67108863)	The default duration of the subscription in seconds
notify-lease-duration-supported	1setOf integer (0:67108863) | rangeOfInteger (0:67108863)	The supported durations of the subscription objects in seconds
notify-lease-expiration-time	integer (0:MAX)	The expiration time of the subscription in seconds
notify-max-events-supported	integer (2:MAX)	The maximum number of events that can be monitored
notify-natural-language	naturalLanguage	The language to use for notifications
notify-printer-up-time	integer (1:MAX)	The current time on the printer object
notify-printer-uri	uri	The URI of the associated printer object
notify-recipient-uri	uri	The URI of the recipient of notifications
notify-schemes-supported	1setOf uriScheme	The notification schemes that are supported
notify-sequence-number	integer (0:MAX)	A unique sequence number for the event
notify-subscribed-event	type2 keyword	The event that triggered the notification
notify-subscriber-user-name	name(MAX)	The username of the subscriber
notify-subscription-id	integer (1:MAX)	The ID number for this subscription object
notify-text	text(MAX)	A human-readable notification message
notify-time-interval	integer (0:MAX)	The minimum time between notifications

TABLE 11.1   Continued

Name	Type	Description
notify-user-data	octetString(63)	Opaque data that is sent as-is to the subscriber in notifications
printer-state-change-date-time	dateTime	The date and time of the last state change
printer-state-change-time	integer (1:MAX)	The printer object time of the last state change

notify-attributes

The `notify-attributes` attribute lists the attributes that should be sent in a machine-readable notification. It is not used for human-readable notifications, such as provided by the `mailto` notification scheme.

notify-attributes-supported

The `notification-attributes-supported` attribute lists the available notification attributes. It normally contains the name of each job and printer attribute supported by the server.

notify-charset

The `notify-charset` attribute specifies the character set to use when sending a notification. The character set of the original subscription request is used by default.

notify-events

The `notify-events` attribute lists the events to monitor for this subscription. The events can be any of the keywords listed in Table 11.2. Any IPP server that supports notifications must support at least two events per subscription.

CUPS places no limit on the number of events that can be monitored.

notify-events-default

The `notify-events-default` attribute lists the default events that will be monitored if no `notify-events` attribute is provided in the subscription creation request. For CUPS, the default events are "none".

notify-events-supported

The `notify-events-supported` attribute provides the supported events that can be monitored. Table 11-2 lists the event keywords that can be used.

TABLE 11.2   Notification Event Keywords

Keyword	Description
"none"	No events for notifications.
"job-completed"	A job was completed.
"job-config-changed"	The configuration (attributes) of a job changed, or the job-message-from-operator attribute changed.
"job-created"	A job was created.
"job-progress"	The printer has completed printing a page in the job.
"job-state-changed"	The job-state or job-state-reasons attribute has changed.
"job-stopped"	A job was stopped.
"printer-config-changed"	The printer configuration attributes have changed or the printer-message-from-operator attribute changed.
"printer-finishings-changed"	The finishings-ready attribute has changed.
"printer-media-changed"	The media-ready attribute has changed.
"printer-queue-order-changed"	The order of jobs in the printer's queue has changed.
"printer-restarted"	The printer was powered on.
"printer-shutdown"	The printer was powered off.
"printer-state-changed"	The printer-state, printer-state-reasons, or printer-is-accepting-jobs attributes changed.
"printer-stopped"	The printer-state attribute changed to "stopped".

CUPS defines several additional keywords for server subscriptions. Table 11.3 lists the CUPS server event keywords.

TABLE 11.3   CUPS Notification Event Keywords

Keyword	Description
"cups-add-class"	A printer class was added to the server.
"cups-add-device"	A device was added to the server.
"cups-add-printer"	A printer was added to the server.
"cups-delete-class"	A printer class was removed from the server.
"cups-delete-device"	A device was removed from the server.
"cups-delete-printer"	A printer was removed from the server.
"cups-modify-class"	A printer class was modified on the server.
"cups-modify-device"	A device was modified on the server.
"cups-modify-printer"	A printer was modified on the server.
"cups-server-restart"	The scheduler was restarted.
"cups-server-start"	The scheduler was started.
"cups-server-stop"	The scheduler was stopped.

notify-job-id

The `notify-job-id` attribute provides the job ID of the associated job object. This attribute is used when creating or querying a job subscription.

notify-lease-duration

The `notify-lease-duration` attribute specifies the life of the subscription object in seconds. If the lease duration is 0 seconds, the subscription object never expires.

Leases are available only for printer subscriptions. For CUPS, leases are also available for server subscriptions.

notify-lease-duration-default

The `notify-lease-duration-default` attribute specifies the default life of subscription objects in seconds.

notify-lease-duration-supported

The `notify-lease-duration-supported` attribute lists the supported lifespans of subscription objects in seconds. The lease durations can be discrete (0, 60, 120, 180) or ranges of values.

notify-lease-expiration-time

The `notify-lease-expiration-time` attribute provides the expiration time of the subscription in seconds. If the expiration time is 0, the subscription does not expire.

For CUPS, the value will be the Unix time in seconds since January 1, 1970.

notify-max-events-supported

The `notify-max-events-supported` attribute specifies the maximum number of events that can be monitored by a subscription object. The IPP specification requires a minimum of two events per subscription.

CUPS subscriptions can monitor all events simultaneously in a single subscription; therefore, the value of this attribute will be the number of supported events minus one for the `"none"` keyword.

notify-natural-language

The `notify-natural-language` attribute specifies the language to use when sending event notifications. This language is used for all text (human-readable) data.

This attribute must be one of the languages listed in the printer's `generated-natural-language-supported` attribute.

notify-printer-up-time

The `notify-printer-up-time` attribute mirrors the `printer-up-time` attribute and provides the current up time in seconds on the printer object.

CUPS uses the Unix time value in seconds since January 1, 1970.

notify-printer-uri

The `notify-printer-uri` attribute provides the URI of the associated printer object.

For CUPS, this attribute can be any valid printer or class URI, or the root URI for the server:

```
ipp://ServerName/
ipp://ServerName/classes/ClassName
ipp://ServerName/printers/PrinterName
```

notify-recipient-uri

The `notify-recipient-uri` attribute specifies the URI of the recipient of the notifications. The URI must use one of the schemes listed in the `notify-schemes-supported` attribute.

An e-mail notification would use the familiar `mailto` URI:

```
mailto:foo@bar.com
```

Other notification schemes are described later in this chapter.

notify-schemes-supported

The `notify-schemes-supported` attribute lists the notification schemes that are supported. The scheme is the word before the : in the URI, such as `"mailto"`.

notify-sequence-number

The `notify-sequence-number` attribute provides a unique sequence number for the event in an event notification. It is incremented with each notification that is sent to the client and is unique for each subscription.

notify-subscribed-event

The `notify-subscribed-event` attribute is sent in machine-readable notifications and provides the keyword for the event that triggered the notification.

notify-subscriber-user-name

The `notify-subscriber-user-name` provides the name of the user that created the subscription and is usually the same as the `requesting-user-name` attribute that is passed in the creation request.

notify-subscription-id

The `notify-subscription-id` provides the ID number for this subscription object. This number is used along with the `printer-uri` attribute to identify individual subscription objects on a server.

notify-text

The `notify-text` attribute is sent in notifications and contains a human-readable notification message such as `"paper is out"`.

notify-time-interval

The `notify-time-interval` attribute specifies the minimum number of seconds between job-progress event notifications. This attribute allows a client to reduce the frequency of event notifications so that fast printers do not bog down the client.

notify-user-data

The `notify-user-data` attribute provides so-called "opaque data" that is sent as-is to the subscriber in notifications. This can be used to identify a particular subscription to a client.

printer-state-change-date-time

The `printer-state-change-date-time` attribute contains the time and date (printer-date-time) of the previous state change for the associated printer object for any printer event.

printer-state-change-time

The `printer-state-change-time` attribute contains the time of the previous state change in seconds for the associated printer object for any printer event.

Subscription Operations

IPP defines several new operations to support notifications. Most operations apply to subscription objects in general, whereas a few are used by the various notification schemes to deliver events to the client. Table 11.4 lists the subscription object operations.

TABLE 11.4   Subscription Operations

Code	Name	Description
0x0016	Create-Printer-Subscription	Create a subscription for printer state changes.
0x0017	Create-Job-Subscription	Create a subscription for print job state changes.
0x0018	Get-Subscription-Attributes	Get the attributes for a subscription.
0x0019	Get-Subscriptions	Get a list of subscriptions.
0x001A	Renew-Subscription	Renew an existing (unexpired) subscription.
0x001B	Cancel-Subscription	Cancel a subscription.
0x001C	Get-Notifications	Get pending notifications using the ipp-get method.
0x001D	Send-Notifications	Send pending notifications using the indp method.

Create-Printer-Subscription

The Create-Printer-Subscription operation creates one or more printer subscriptions that track state changes in a printer object. A typical Create-Printer-Subscription operation will contain the following attributes in the operation group:

```
attributes-charset (charset)
attributes-natural-language (naturalLanguage)
printer-uri (uri)
requesting-user-name (name)
```

Following the operation group are one or more subscription groups containing the subscription creation attributes:

```
notify-recipient-uri (uri)
notify-lease-time (integer)
notify-events (1setOf type2 keyword)
```

If the subscriptions are created, the IPP response will contain the notify-subscription-id attributes for each subscription group in the request. If the server was unable to create all of the subscriptions you specified, the server will return the "client-error-too-many-subscriptions" status code.

Create-Job-Subscription

The Create-Job-Subscription operation creates one or more job subscriptions that track state changes in a job object. A typical Create-Job-Subscription operation will contain the following attributes in the operation group:

```
attributes-charset (charset)
attributes-natural-language (naturalLanguage)
printer-uri (uri) and job-id (integer), or job-uri (uri)
requesting-user-name (name)
```

Following the operation group are one or more subscription groups containing the subscription creation attributes:

```
notify-recipient-uri (uri)
notify-events (1setOf type2 keyword)
```

If the subscriptions are created, the IPP response will contain the notify-subscription-id attributes for each subscription group in the request. If the server was unable to create all of the subscriptions you specified, the server will return the "client-error-too-many-subscriptions" status code.

Get-Subscription-Attributes

The Get-Subscription-Attributes operation gets the attributes for a subscription object. A typical Get-Subscription-Attributes operation will contain the following attributes in the operation group:

```
attributes-charset (charset)
attributes-natural-language (naturalLanguage)
printer-uri (uri)
notify-subscription-id (integer)
requesting-user-name (name)
```

The IPP response will contain the attributes for the requested subscription object.

Get-Subscriptions

The Get-Subscriptions operation gets the list of subscription objects for a job or printer object. A typical Get-Subscription operation will contain the following attributes in the operation group:

```
attributes-charset (charset)
attributes-natural-language (naturalLanguage)
printer-uri (uri)
job-id (integer) [only for job subscriptions]
my-subscriptions (boolean)
limit (integer)
requesting-user-name (name)
```

The IPP response will contain the attributes for the requested subscription objects, each in its own subscription group. If the `job-id` attribute is provided in the IPP request, only those subscriptions destined for that job ID will be returned. Otherwise, all job and printer subscriptions related to the printer object are returned.

If the `my-subscriptions` attribute is provided with a value of `true`, only those subscriptions that have a `notify-subscriber-user-name` equal to the `requesting-user-name` will be returned. Finally, the `limit` attribute will limit the maximum number of subscriptions that are returned.

For CUPS, specifying a printer-uri of

```
ipp://ServerName
```

will return job, printer, and server subscriptions.

Renew-Subscription

The `Renew-Subscription` operation renews an existing printer subscription. Only the owner of a subscription or the administrator can renew a subscription. A typical `Renew-Subscription` operation will contain the following attributes in the operation group:

```
attributes-charset (charset)
attributes-natural-language (naturalLanguage)
printer-uri (uri)
notify-subscription-id (integer)
requesting-user-name (name)
```

Following the operation group is an optional subscription group containing the subscription creation attribute:

```
notify-lease-time (integer)
```

The IPP response will either return an error because the subscription has already expired or will return the new `notify-lease-time` for the subscription.

Cancel-Subscription

The `Cancel-Subscription` operation cancels an existing subscription. Only the owner of the subscription or the administrator can cancel a subscription. A typical `Cancel-Subscription` operation will contain the following attributes in the operation group:

```
attributes-charset (charset)
attributes-natural-language (naturalLanguage)
printer-uri (uri)
notify-subscription-id (integer)
requesting-user-name (name)
```

Get-Notifications

The Get-Notifications operation gets any pending events for the specified recipient. A typical Get-Notifications operation will contain the following attributes in the operation group:

```
attributes-charset (charset)
attributes-natural-language (naturalLanguage)
notify-recipient-uri (uri)
notify-no-wait (boolean)
```

The notify-no-wait attribute specifies whether the client wants to wait for more events. If false, the connection to the client will remain open until all subscriptions for the recipient expire or the client closes the connection. If true, the server will send all pending events and end the response. The default is false.

The IPP response will contain the notifications in event notification groups. Each notification will contain at least the following attributes:

```
notify-subscription-id (integer)
notify-printer-uri (uri)
notify-subscribed-event (type2 keyword)
printer-up-time (integer)
printer-current-time (integer)
notify-sequence-number (integer)
notify-charset (charset)
notify-natural-language (charset)
notify-user-data (octetString)
notify-text (text)
```

The event data might also contain printer or job state information depending on the type of subscription and event.

The events reported by the Get-Notifications operation are removed from the server, so each new request will only return the new events. Only one client can be active at any time for the specified recipient.

Send-Notifications

The Send-Notifications operation is used by the indp notification scheme to send notifications to another IPP server or client. A client does not normally send it to a server.

A typical Send-Notifications operation will contain the following attributes in the operation group:

```
attributes-charset (charset)
attributes-natural-language (naturalLanguage)
notify-recipient-uri (uri)
```

Following the operation group are one or more notification event groups containing the events to be reported. Each event group contains at least the following attributes:

```
notify-subscription-id (integer)
notify-printer-uri (uri)
notify-subscribed-event (type2 keyword)
printer-up-time (integer)
printer-current-time (integer)
notify-sequence-number (integer)
notify-charset (charset)
notify-natural-language (charset)
notify-user-data (octetString)
notify-text (text)
```

The event data might also contain printer or job state information depending on the type of subscription and event.

The IPP server or client will then respond with a `successful-ok`, `successful-ok-ignored-notifications`, or `client-error-ignored-all-notifications` status, depending on whether the receiver was able to process all, some, or none of the events in the request.

Creating Subscriptions in Print Jobs

Besides the `Create-Printer-Subscription` and `Create-Job-Subscription` operations, you can also create subscriptions in `Create-Job`, `Print-Job`, and `Print-URI` operations using the same attributes.

A typical `Print-Job` operation will contain the following attributes in the operation group:

```
attributes-charset (charset)
attributes-natural-language (naturalLanguage)
printer-uri (uri)
requesting-user-name (name)
```

Following the operation group is the job group containing any job options:

```
copies (integer)
media (type2 keyword | name)
```

After the job group are one or more subscription groups containing the subscription creation attributes:

```
notify-recipient-uri (uri)
notify-events (1setOf type2 keyword)
```

Finally, the document file will immediately follow the IPP request data in the HTTP POST. If the print job is accepted, the IPP response will contain the `notify-subscription-id` attributes for each subscription group in the request. If the server was unable to create all of the subscriptions you specified, the server will return the `"client-error-too-many-subscriptions"` status code.

Notification Schemes

The current IPP specifications define three separate notification schemes. Figure 11.1 shows these schemes.

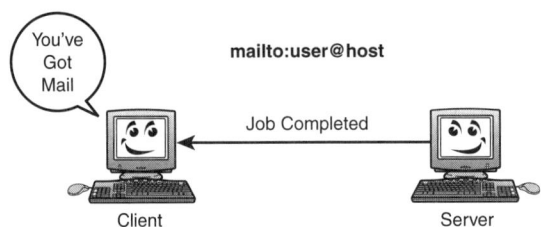

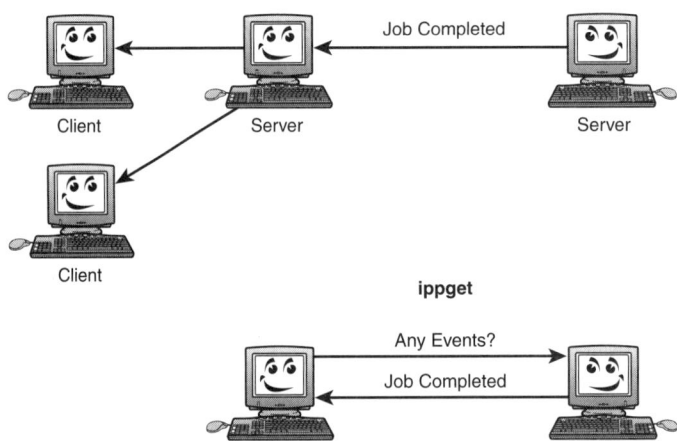

FIGURE 11.1

IPP notification schemes.

The `mailto` scheme defines an immediate notification scheme that sends an e-mail when certain conditions occur. The `indp` scheme provides a similar mechanism using IPP as the transport to the recipient. Finally, the `ippget` scheme provides a polling interface that allows a client to collect a list of events that have occurred since the previous check.

As you might expect, the `mailto` scheme is the most popular, but as more applications become IPP-aware, you will likely see the other machine-readable formats gain in popularity. Future schemes will also likely include support for specific instant-messaging protocols such as AOL's AIM.

Before using any of these notification schemes, be sure to send a `Get-Printer-Attributes` request to get the `notify-schemes-supported` attribute.

The `mailto` Notification Scheme

The `mailto` notification scheme uses e-mail to send notifications. E-mail notifications are not available for `job impressions` events; that would generate an e-mail for every page that is printed.

E-mail notifications are human-readable text messages that specify the reason for the notification and current condition of the subscribed object. For example, an administrator could request an e-mail whenever the printer runs out of paper by requesting notification for the `"printer-state-change"` event.

The `notify-recipient-uri` attribute contains the e-mail address of the recipient using the `mailto` scheme:

```
mailto:joe@foo.bar.com
```

In CUPS, the `mailto` notifier program is responsible for sending e-mail notifications.

The `ippget` Notification Scheme

The `ippget` notification scheme stores notification events on the server until the recipient requests them using the `Get-Notifications` operation. This scheme is often called the "polling" scheme because the server normally queues the pending events in memory for the recipient. However, the `ippget` scheme also supports a "streaming" mode, which keeps the HTTP connection open between the server and client until all subscriptions are exhausted or the client closes the connection.

The `notify-recipient-uri` attribute contains a URI for the recipient using the `ippget` scheme:

```
ippget://foo.bar.com/me
```

Because an IPP server will send all events for a particular recipient in response to a `Get-Notifications` request, you will probably want to generate a unique identifier of some type for your application. Under Unix, the `gethostname()` and `getpid()` functions can be used to generate a reasonably unique URI:

```
char hostname[1024];
int pid;
char uri[1024];

gethostname(hostname, sizeof(hostname));
pid = getpid();

snprintf(uri, sizeof(uri), "ippget://%s/%d", hostname, pid);
```

The indp Notification Scheme

The indp notification scheme provides an indirect notification scheme, such that a client can request that notifications for particular events be sent to another IPP server that supports the Send-Notifications operation. This third-party scheme can be useful for propagating event information or notifying an IPP print server that a forwarded job has been completed.

The notify-recipient-uri attribute contains a URI for the recipient using the indp scheme:

```
indp://foo.bar.com/resource
```

This attribute is passed to the remote IPP server in the Send-Notifications operation along with the events in the notification.

Summary

IPP notifications provide the means for getting asynchronous event notifications from the server when the state of a job or printer object changes. Printer subscriptions are valid for a specified amount of time, whereas job subscriptions are valid only for the life of the job. The current specifications provide three methods of delivering notifications: mailto, ippget, and indp.

CUPS adds server subscriptions to monitor the status of the server and its printer and job objects. Notifications are supported in CUPS starting with version 1.2.

## CHAPTER 12

CUPS Extensions to IPP

This chapter describes the attributes, operations, and browsing protocol enhancements provided by CUPS. Use this information in conjunction with Chapters 7–11 when writing IPP client applications for CUPS.

CUPS Attributes

CUPS defines several additional attributes that are used solely for the CUPS operations. Table 12.1 lists these attributes.

TABLE 12.1   Additional CUPS Attributes

Name	Type	Description
device-class	type2 keyword	The class of device
device-info	text(127)	A description of the device
device-make-and-model	text(127)	The make and model of the printer connected to the device
ppd-natural-language	naturalLanguage	The language for the PPD file
ppd-make	text(127)	The manufacturer of the PPD file
ppd-make-and-model	text(127)	The make and model of the PPD file
ppd-name	name(255)	The name of the PPD file
printer-type-mask	type2 enum	A mask for the printer-type attribute

device-class

The `device-class` attribute defines the type of device, which can be one of the values listed in Table 12.2.

TABLE 12.2   Device Class Keywords

Keyword	Description
"file"	A disk file
"direct"	A parallel or fixed-rate serial data port, such as USB or IRDA
"serial"	A variable-rate serial data port
"network"	A network connection of any kind

device-info

The device-info attribute provides a description of the device. For example, the first parallel port might have a value of "Parallel Port #1".

device-make-and-model

The device-make-and-model attribute provides the make and model of the printer connected to the device. If the device is unknown, this attribute will contain the string "Unknown".

ppd-natural-language

The ppd-natural-language attribute mirrors the LanguageVersion attribute in the PPD file. The language name is converted to the standard two-letter string, such as "en" for English, "es" for Spanish, and so on.

ppd-make

The ppd-make attribute mirrors the Manufacturer attribute in the PPD file. If the PPD file does not provide this attribute, the first word from the ModelName attribute is used instead.

ppd-make-and-model

The ppd-make-and-model attribute mirrors the NickName attribute in the PPD file. If the PPD file does not provide this attribute, the ModelName attribute is used instead.

ppd-name

The ppd-name attribute provides the filename of the PPD file relative to the model directory (usually /usr/share/cups/model).

printer-type-mask

The printer-type-mask attribute specifies the significant bits in the printer-type attribute when processing a CUPS-Get-Classes or CUPS-Get-Printers request. The value of the printer-type-mask attribute is used to mask the printer's printer-type attribute using a bitwise AND operation and then is compared to the request printer-type attribute value.

CUPS Operations

CUPS defines 14 new operations for IPP. Table 12.3 lists them.

TABLE 12.3   CUPS Extension Operations

Code	Name	Description
0x4001	CUPS-Get-Default	Get the default printer.
0x4002	CUPS-Get-Printers	Get the list of printers.
0x4003	CUPS-Add-Printer	Add or modify a printer on the server.
0x4004	CUPS-Delete-Printer	Delete a printer from the server.
0x4005	CUPS-Get-Classes	Get the list of printer classes.
0x4006	CUPS-Add-Class	Add or modify a printer class on the server.
0x4007	CUPS-Delete-Class	Delete a printer class from the server.
0x4008	CUPS-Accept-Jobs	Allow new print jobs on a printer or printer class (similar to new Enable-Printer operation).
0x4009	CUPS-Reject-Jobs	Reject new print jobs on a printer or printer class (similar to new Disable-Printer operation).
0x400A	CUPS-Set-Default	Set the default printer.
0x400B	CUPS-Get-Devices	Get a list of available printer devices.
0x400C	CUPS-Get-PPDs	Get a list of available printer drivers.
0x400D	CUPS-Move-Job	Move a print job to another printer or printer class.
0x400E	CUPS-Add-Device	Add or modify a device to the device list.
0x400F	CUPS-Delete-Device	Remove a device from the device list.

CUPS-Get-Default

The CUPS-Get-Default operation returns the printer attributes for the default printer object. A CUPS-Get-Default operation contains the following attributes in the operation group:

```
attributes-charset (charset)
attributes-natural-language (naturalLanguage)
```

If no default destination exists, a client-error-not-found error is returned. Otherwise, the attributes in the default printer object are returned.

CUPS-Get-Printers

The CUPS-Get-Printers operation gets the list of available printer objects. A typical CUPS-Get-Printers operation contains the following attributes in the operation group:

```
attributes-charset (charset)
attributes-natural-language (naturalLanguage)
printer-type (type2 enum)
printer-type-mask (type2 enum)
requested-attributes (1setOf type2 keyword)
limit (integer)
```

The IPP response will contain the printer attributes for each printer in separate printer groups. The printer-type, printer-type-mask, requested-attributes, and limit attributes will limit the attributes and printers that are returned by the request.

CUPS-Add-Printer

The CUPS-Add-Printer operation adds or modifies a printer on the server. A typical CUPS-Add-Printer operation contains the following attributes in the operation group:

```
attributes-charset (charset)
attributes-natural-language (naturalLanguage)
printer-uri (uri)
requesting-user-name (name)
ppd-name (name)
device-uri (uri)
printer-is-accepting-jobs (boolean)
printer-state (type2 enum)
```

The printer-uri attribute specifies the new printer name and must be of the following format:

```
ipp://ServerName/printers/PrinterName
```

The ppd-name attribute is optional and specifies the PPD file to use for the printer. The PPD file can also be sent from the client following the IPP request data.

The device-uri attribute specifies the device to which to connect when printing.

The printer-is-accepting-jobs and printer-state attributes specify the state of the printer object that is created. If not specified, the printer will default to stopped and reject jobs.

The IPP response will return the status of the request.

The POST resource path must be /admin. The requesting-user-name or authenticated user must be a member of the system group.

CUPS-Delete-Printer

The CUPS-Delete-Printer operation removes a printer from the server. A typical CUPS-Delete-Printer operation contains the following attributes in the operation group:

```
attributes-charset (charset)
attributes-natural-language (naturalLanguage)
printer-uri (uri)
requesting-user-name (name)
```

The IPP response will return the status of the request.

The POST resource path must be /admin. The requesting-user-name or authenticated user must be a member of the system group.

CUPS-Get-Classes

The CUPS-Get-Classes operation gets the list of available printer class objects. A typical CUPS-Get-Classes operation contains the following attributes in the operation group:

```
attributes-charset (charset)
attributes-natural-language (naturalLanguage)
printer-type (type2 enum)
printer-type-mask (type2 enum)
requested-attributes (1setOf type2 keyword)
limit (integer)
```

The IPP response will contain the printer attributes for each printer class in separate printer groups. The printer-type, printer-type-mask, requested-attributes, and limit attributes will limit the attributes and printers that are returned by the request.

CUPS-Add-Class

The CUPS-Add-Class operation adds or modifies a printer class on the server. A typical CUPS-Add-Class operation contains the following attributes in the operation group:

```
attributes-charset (charset)
attributes-natural-language (naturalLanguage)
printer-uri (uri)
requesting-user-name (name)
member-uris (1setOf uri)
printer-is-accepting-jobs (boolean)
printer-state (type2 enum)
```

The printer-uri attribute specifies the new printer name and must be of the following format:

```
ipp://ServerName/printers/PrinterName
```

The member-uris attribute lists the printer objects that are part of the printer class. These URIs must be known to the server (that is, the URIs must be reported in a CUPS-Get-Printers or CUPS-Get-Classes request).

The printer-is-accepting-jobs and printer-state attributes specify the state of the printer object that is created. If these attributes are not specified, the printer will default to stopped and reject jobs.

The IPP response will return the status of the request.

The POST resource path must be /admin. The requesting-user-name or authenticated user must be a member of the system group.

CUPS-Delete-Class

The CUPS-Delete-Class operation removes a printer class from the server. A typical CUPS-Delete-Class operation contains the following attributes in the operation group:

```
attributes-charset (charset)
attributes-natural-language (naturalLanguage)
printer-uri (uri)
requesting-user-name (name)
```

The IPP response will return the status of the request.

The POST resource path must be /admin. The requesting-user-name or authenticated user must be a member of the system group.

CUPS-Accept-Jobs

The CUPS-Accept-Jobs operation changes the printer-is-accepting-jobs attribute to true and is similar to the new IPP Enable-Printer operation. A typical CUPS-Accept-Jobs operation contains the following attributes in the operation group:

```
attributes-charset (charset)
attributes-natural-language (naturalLanguage)
printer-uri (uri)
requesting-user-name (name)
```

The IPP response will return the status of the request.

The POST resource path must be /admin. The requesting-user-name or authenticated user must be a member of the system group.

CUPS-Reject-Jobs

The CUPS-Reject-Jobs operation changes the printer-is-accepting-jobs attribute to false and is similar to the new IPP Enable-Printer operation. A typical CUPS-Reject-Jobs operation contains the following attributes in the operation group:

```
attributes-charset (charset)
attributes-natural-language (naturalLanguage)
printer-uri (uri)
requesting-user-name (name)
```

The IPP response will return the status of the request.

The POST resource path must be /admin. The requesting-user-name or authenticated user must be a member of the system group.

CUPS-Set-Default

The CUPS-Set-Default operation sets the default printer object on the server. A typical CUPS-Set-Default operation contains the following attributes in the operation group:

```
attributes-charset (charset)
attributes-natural-language (naturalLanguage)
printer-uri (uri)
requesting-user-name (name)
```

The IPP response will return the status of the request.

The POST resource path must be /admin. The requesting-user-name or authenticated user must be a member of the system group.

CUPS-Get-Devices

The CUPS-Get-Devices operation gets a list of available printer devices. A typical CUPS-Get-Devices operation contains the following attributes in the operation group:

```
attributes-charset (charset)
attributes-natural-language (naturalLanguage)
device-class (keyword)
limit (integer)
```

The IPP response will return a list of devices. Each device will contain the following attributes in their own printer group:

```
device-class
device-info
device-make
device-make-and-model
device-uri
```

The device-class and limit attributes can be specified to restrict the type and number of devices that are reported.

If the device represents a whole class of devices, the device-uri attribute will contain only the scheme name. For example, the AppSocket device appears in the list of devices as "socket" because you can use the same scheme with many addresses.

CUPS-Get-PPDs

The CUPS-Get-PPDs operation gets a list of available printer drivers. A typical CUPS-Get-PPDs operation contains the following attributes in the operation group:

```
attributes-charset (charset)
attributes-natural-language (naturalLanguage)
ppd-make (name)
limit (integer)
```

The IPP response will return a list of PPDs. Each PPD will contain the following attributes in their own printer group:

```
ppd-make
ppd-make-and-model
ppd-name
ppd-natural-language
```

The ppd-make and limit attributes can be specified to restrict the make and number of PPDs that are reported.

CUPS-Move-Job

The CUPS-Move-Job operation moves a print job to another printer or printer class object. Only the job owner or an administrator can move jobs. A typical CUPS-Move-Job operation contains the following attributes in the operation group:

```
attributes-charset (charset)
attributes-natural-language (naturalLanguage)
printer-uri (uri) and job-id (integer) or job-uri (uri)
job-printer-uri (uri)
requesting-user-name (name)
```

The print job will be moved to the printer or class specified by the job-printer-uri attribute. This printer or class must exist on the local server.

The IPP response will return the updated job-uri, printer-uri, and job-id for the job.

CUPS-Add-Device

The CUPS-Add-Device operation adds or modifies a printer device on the server. A typical CUPS-Add-Device operation contains the following attributes in the operation group:

```
attributes-charset (charset)
attributes-natural-language (naturalLanguage)
device-uri (uri)
requesting-user-name (name)
device-class (keyword)
device-info (text)
device-make-and-model (text)
```

The device-uri attribute specifies the device to be added or modified. The other attributes specify the information and state for the device.

The IPP response will return the status of the request.

The POST resource path must be /admin. The requesting-user-name or authenticated user must be a member of the system group.

CUPS-Delete-Device

The CUPS-Delete-Device operation removes a printer device from the server. A typical CUPS-Delete-Device operation contains the following attributes in the operation group:

```
attributes-charset (charset)
attributes-natural-language (naturalLanguage)
device-uri (uri)
requesting-user-name (name)
```

The IPP response will return the status of the request.

The POST resource path must be /admin. The requesting-user-name or authenticated user must be a member of the system group.

CUPS Browsing Protocol

The CUPS browsing protocol consists of a line of up to 1450 bytes that is broadcast on UDP port 631. Servers send UDP packets on the LAN for all local printers and classes, but not for implicit classes. Clients receive and add local printers and classes and then create or update implicit classes as necessary based on the available network printers and classes.

Each UDP packet contains exactly one line of browse data. Each line consists of the following space-delimited data describing one printer:

```
type SP state SP uri SP "location" SP "info" SP "make-and-model" NL
```

where SP is the ASCII space character (decimal 32) and NL is the ASCII newline character (decimal 10).

The type field is the value of the printer-type attribute in hexadecimal.

The state field is the value of the printer-state attribute in decimal.

The uri field is the value of the first URI in the printer-uri-supported attribute.

The location field is the value of the printer-location attribute inside double quotes.

The info field is the value of the printer-info attribute inside double quotes.

The make-and-model field is the value of the printer-make-and-model attribute inside double quotes.

Summary

CUPS supports many new operations to manage multiple printer objects, printer classes, devices, and PPD files for printer drivers. The POST resource path must be /admin for CUPS operations that change the server state, while the query operations can use any resource path.

The CUPS browsing protocol provides a simple UDP-based protocol for passing printer information to other hosts on the network. Each packet that is sent on the network describes a single printer or class on the server.

PART III

Programming with CUPS

CHAPTER 13

Overview of CUPS Programming

This chapter covers the basics of CUPS programming from header files to libraries. It also discusses the licenses that are used and how they may affect your software.

The Basics

CUPS provides two libraries that can be used by applications and other programs to communicate with CUPS servers and manage CUPS data. You normally access these libraries from C or C++ code; however, they are also accessible from other languages such as Java, Perl, PHP, and Python by using the appropriate hooks.

The CUPS libraries are accessed in your source code by including certain header files. The final program is then linked with the CUPS library files to form a working program.

Header Files

CUPS provides many header files that define the constants, data structures, and functions in the CUPS libraries. CUPS header files are located in the cups subdirectory and are usually accessed using the #include directive:

```
#include <cups/cups.h>
```

The <cups/cups.h> header file defines the basic data structures and interfaces that most CUPS programs will use. Table 13.1 lists the CUPS header files.

TABLE 13.1   CUPS Header Files

Filename	Description
<cups/cups.h>	Defines the common CUPS constants, structures, and functions
<cups/http.h>	Defines the Hypertext Transfer Protocol (HTTP) interfaces
<cups/image.h>	Defines the CUPS imaging interfaces
<cups/ipp.h>	Defines the Internet Printing Protocol (IPP) interfaces
<cups/language.h>	Defines the internationalization (I18N) message catalog and interfaces
<cups/md5.h>	Defines the message digest 5 (MD5) interfaces
<cups/ppd.h>	Defines the PostScript printer description (PPD) file interfaces
<cups/raster.h>	Defines the CUPS raster file interfaces

The <cups/http.h>, <cups/ipp.h>, <cups/md5.h>, and <cups/ppd.h> header files are automatically included when you include the <cups/cups.h> header file.

Libraries

CUPS provides two libraries that you can use in your program. The first is the cups library, which provides all of the CUPS functions *except* for the functions defined in the <cups/image.h> and <cups/raster.h> header files. You include this library in your program using the -lcups option:

```
cc -o myprogram myprogram.c -lcups -lnsl -lsocket ENTER
```

The -lnsl and -lsocket options include extra networking libraries that are not required on all systems.

NOTE:

The nsl and socket libraries are needed on some systems to include networking support. In general, if your system has these libraries then you should use them. The only exception to this rule is the IRIX operating system, which provides the networking support in both the standard C library and the nsl and socket libraries. The standard C library provides the faster implementation.

The cups library provides all of the basic CUPS interfaces for printing files, managing destinations and options, and localizing messages for the user. It also contains functions to send HTTP requests and receive responses, manage IPP attributes, requests, and responses, and manipulate PPD files. All of the CUPS programs use the cups library.

The second CUPS library is cupsimage, which provides all of the CUPS imaging functions that are defined in the <cups/image.h> and <cups/raster.h> header files. This library is usually only used by raster filters like printer drivers. You include this library in your program using the -lcupsimage option:

```
cc -o myprogram myprogram.c -lcupsimage ENTER
```

The cupsimage library also includes functions for loading image files, doing colorspace conversions, managing large amounts of raster data, and scaling raster data on-the-fly. All of the CUPS printer drivers and raster image processor (RIP) filters use the cupsimage library.

Your First CUPS Program

For your first CUPS program we will list the default and available printers on the system. To do this we will use the cupsGetDefault() and cupsGetPrinters() functions. Listing 13.1 shows the complete program.

LISTING 13.1   The `firstcups.c` Source File

```c
/* Include the CUPS header file. */
#include <cups/cups.h>


int                             /* O - Exit status */
main(void)
{
  int        i;                 /* Looping var */
  int        num_printers;      /* Number of printers */
  char       **printers;        /* List of printers */
  const char *default_printer;  /* Default printer */


  /* Get the default printer */
  default_printer = cupsGetDefault();

  /* Show the default printer */
  if (default_printer != NULL)
    printf("The default printer is %s\n", default_printer);
  else
    puts("There is no default printer.");

  /* Get the list of printers */
  num_printers = cupsGetPrinters(&printers);

  /* Show the available printers */
  if (num_printers > 0)
  {
    puts("The available printers are:");

    for (i = 0; i < num_printers; i ++)
      printf("    %s\n", printers[i]);

    /* Free the printer list */
    for (i = 0; i < num_printers; i ++)
      free(printers[i]);

    free(printers);
  }
  else
    puts("There are no printers on this system.");
```

LISTING 13.1   Continued

```
  /* Return with no error */
  return (0);
}
```

The `cupsGetDefault()` function returns a string containing the default printer. If no default printer is defined then a NULL pointer is returned instead:

```
/* Get the default printer */
default_printer = cupsGetDefault();
```

```
/* Show the default printer */
if (default_printer != NULL)
  printf("The default printer is %s\n", default_printer);
else
  puts("There is no default printer.");
```

The `cupsGetPrinters()` function returns the number of printers that are available and a pointer to an array of strings:

```
/* Get the list of printers */
num_printers = cupsGetPrinters(&printers);
```

```
/* Show the available printers */
if (num_printers > 0)
{
  puts("The available printers are:");

  for (i = 0; i < num_printers; i ++)
    printf("    %s\n", printers[i]);
```

This array of strings has been allocated using the `malloc()` and `strdup()` functions, so you must call `free()` on each string and the entire array after you are done with them:

```
  /* Free the printer list */
  for (i = 0; i < num_printers; i ++)
    free(printers[i]);

  free(printers);
```

To compile this program type the following:

cc -o firstcups firstcups.c -lcups *ENTER*

On some systems you may also need the ns1 and socket libraries:

cc -o firstcups firstcups.c -lcups -lnsl *ENTER*
cc -o firstcups firstcups.c -lcups -lnsl -lsocket *ENTER*

After the program is compiled you can run it to get the default and available printers. The output should look something like this:

```
./firstcups ENTER
The default printer is DeskJet
The available printers are:
    DeskJet
    LaserJet
    StylusColor
    StylusPhoto
```

Detecting the CUPS API Library with GNU Autoconf

Now that you have developed the software that uses CUPS, you will probably want to release it to the world. If you distribute source code, you'll want to provide a way to detect the CUPS header files and libraries. For most free software, this means creating a configure script.

The GNU autoconf software is a popular free development tool that produces configuration scripts for software packages. If your software needs to run on multiple platforms, autoconf is probably the best solution. You can find the autoconf software online at:

```
http://www.gnu.org/software/autoconf/autoconf.html
```

If you are developing your software on the Linux operating system, chances are that you already have autoconf loaded.

Autoconf Basics

Autoconf builds a configuration script from a source file called configure.in. This configuration script can then be used to create header files, makefiles, and just about any other type of text file you can think of.

The configure.in file contains a series of tests that look for programs, libraries, and header files. You can also write your own custom tests using normal shell commands. A configure script for the CUPS program in the previous section would look like Listing 13.2.

LISTING 13.2   The configure.in Source File for autoconf

```
dnl Look for a source file that should be in the distribution.
AC_INIT(firstcups.c)

dnl Generate a config.h file.
AC_CONFIG_HEADER(config.h)
```

LISTING 13.2   Continued

```
dnl Find the C compiler.
AC_PROG_CC
dnl Get the operating system name.
uname=`uname`
if test $uname = IRIX64; then
    uname=IRIX
fi

dnl Get the networking libraries if needed.
AC_CHECK_LIB(socket,socket,
if test "$uname" != "IRIX"; then
    LIBS="-lsocket $LIBS"
else
    echo "Not using -lsocket since you are running IRIX."
fi)

AC_CHECK_LIB(nsl,gethostbyaddr,
if test "$uname" != "IRIX"; then
    LIBS="-lnsl $LIBS"
else
    echo "Not using -lnsl since you are running IRIX."
fi)

dnl Find the cups library and header file.
AC_CHECK_LIB(cups,cupsPrintFiles)
AC_CHECK_HEADER(cups/cups.h, AC_DEFINE(HAVE_CUPS_H))

dnl Stop if we don't have CUPS.
if test $ac_cv_lib_cups_cupsPrintFiles = no -o $ac_cv_header_cups_cups_h = no;
then
    AC_MSG_ERROR(Could not find CUPS.)
fi

dnl Generate the Makefile
AC_OUTPUT(Makefile)
```

The first thing you might notice is that comments start with the characters dnl, which stand for the words do not load. You can also use the pound sign (#) for comments, just as in a regular shell script.

Every configure.in file must include an AC_INIT command that specifies a source file in the distribution that must be present for the configure script to work. This can be a C source file in your program or any other file you expect to be included in the distribution.

```
dnl Look for a source file that should be in the distribution.
AC_INIT(firstcups.c)
```

Another common command is AC_CONFIG_HEADER, which specifies the name of a header file to generate, and that contains all of the definitions from the configure script.

```
dnl Generate a config.h file.
AC_CONFIG_HEADER(config.h)
```

The AC_PROG_CC command follows and is required before you can check for any of the libraries or header files you need. It basically determines which C compiler to use and where it is located on the system. If your system has both a vendor-supplied C compiler (cc) and the GNU C compiler (gcc), the AC_PROG_CC command will choose the GNU C compiler.

```
dnl Find the C compiler.
AC_PROG_CC
```

After the AC_PROG_CC command has been issued, we can check for libraries using the AC_CHECK_LIB and headers with the AC_CHECK_HEADER commands. For CUPS we must first determine whether we need the socket and nsl libraries:

```
dnl Get the networking libraries if needed.
AC_CHECK_LIB(socket,socket,
if test "$uname" != "IRIX"; then
    LIBS="-lsocket $LIBS"
else
    echo "Not using -lsocket since you are running IRIX."
fi)

AC_CHECK_LIB(nsl,gethostbyaddr,
if test "$uname" != "IRIX"; then
    LIBS="-lnsl $LIBS"
else
    echo "Not using -lnsl since you are running IRIX."
fi)
```

Then we can check for the cups library and header file:

```
dnl Find the cups library and header file.
AC_CHECK_LIB(cups,cupsPrintFiles)
AC_CHECK_HEADER(cups/cups.h, AC_DEFINE(HAVE_CUPS_H))

dnl Stop if we don't have CUPS.
if test $ac_cv_lib_cups_cupsPrintFiles = no -o $ac_cv_header_cups_cups_h = no;
then
    AC_MSG_ERROR(Could not find CUPS.)
fi
```

The AC_DEFINE command defines a C constant in your program. It usually will appear in the config.h header file.

The AC_MSG_ERROR command displays an error message and stops the configuration script. This will prevent users from compiling your program until they install the required files.

Finally, the AC_OUTPUT command generates the Makefile for your program:

```
dnl Generate the Makefile
AC_OUTPUT(Makefile)
```

The config.h Header File

Although the config.h header file is an optional part of the configuration process, all but the simplest software programs use it. This is because every library and header file check creates a definition for source files; without the config.h header file to hold them, these definitions are added to the compiler options in the Makefile. For some programs these definitions could make each compile command several thousand bytes long!

The config.h header file is built from a source file called config.h.in. Listing 13.3 shows the config.h.in file for our sample CUPS application.

LISTING 13.3   The config.h.in Source File

```
/* This file is automatically generated. Do not edit by hand! */
#undef HAVE_LIBCUPS
#undef HAVE_CUPS_H
```

As you can see, there is not much to the config.h.in file. Any AC_DEFINE definitions are included using the preprocessor's #undef command. If the corresponding name is defined in the configure script, the #undef will be replaced by a #define.

The Makefile

The last piece of the puzzle is the Makefile. This file is used by the make program to compile the various source files together into one or more programs. The configure script can generate the Makefile for you from a file called Makefile.in. Listing 13.4 shows the Makefile.in file for our sample application.

LISTING 13.4   The Makefile.in Source File

```
# C compiler options
CC      = @CC@
CFLAGS  = @CFLAGS@
LIBS    = @LIBS@
```

LISTING 13.4   Continued

```
# Source files
SRCS    = firstcups.c

# Object files
OBJS    = $(SRCS:.c=.o)

# Make the firstcups application
firstcups: $(OBJS)
        $(CC) $(CFLAGS) -o firstcups $(OBJS) $(LIBS)

# Dependencies
$(OBJS): config.h Makefile
```

Each value from the configure script is inserted in the Makefile using the @NAME@ nota-tion. The beginning of the Makefile sets the C compiler (CC), C compiler options (CFLAGS), and libraries to use (LIBS):

```
# C compiler options
CC      = @CC@
CFLAGS  = @CFLAGS@
LIBS    = @LIBS@
```

The rest of the Makefile is static and associates the firstcups program with the firstcups.c source file.

Putting It All Together

After you have created the configure.in, config.h.in, and Makefile.in source files, run the autoconf command to generate the configure script:

autoconf *ENTER*

Then run the configure script with the following:

./configure *ENTER*

```
creating cache ./config.cache
checking for gcc... gcc
checking whether the C compiler (gcc  ) works... yes
checking whether the C compiler (gcc  ) is a cross-compiler... no
checking whether we are using GNU C... yes
checking whether gcc accepts -g... yes
checking for socket in -lsocket... no
checking for gethostbyaddr in -lnsl... yes
checking for cupsPrintFiles in -lcups... yes
```

```
checking how to run the C preprocessor... gcc -E
checking for cups/cups.h... yes
updating cache ./config.cache
creating ./config.status
creating Makefile
creating config.h
```

This will generate the `config.h` and `Makefile` files. Finally, run the `make` command

make *ENTER*

```
gcc -g -02   -c -o firstcups.o firstcups.c
gcc -g -02 -o firstcups firstcups.o -lcups -lnsl
```

to build the `firstcups` program.

Licensing Issues

The two CUPS libraries are licensed under different terms. If you are writing software for internal use only or will be releasing your software to the public in source code form, these licenses probably won't affect you. However, it is important to understand the differences between these licenses if you distribute your software.

The `cups` library is licensed under the terms of the GNU Library General Public License (LGPL). This license allows you to link your programs against the `cups` library without providing source code or using a GNU software license. The LGPL is also the license that the GNU C and other publicly available libraries use to allow programmers to develop software under whatever terms they feel are appropriate.

The `cupsimage` library is licensed under the terms of the GNU General Public License (GPL). Unlike the LGPL, this license requires that all programs that use the `cupsimage` library be provided under the terms of the GPL. Among other things, the GPL requires the distribution of the source code for your software.

The complete text of these licenses is available in Appendix F, "Common Unix Printing System License Agreement." As always, if you are unsure of how to apply these licenses to your software you should consult a lawyer. You can also contact Easy Software Products for advice or to negotiate different licensing conditions for your software.

Summary

CUPS has two libraries and eight header files that provide all of the interfaces to CUPS. The `cups` library provides the basic client functions and is used by all CUPS programs. The `cupsimage` library provides the imaging functions and is used by raster filters and printer drivers.

Because of operating system differences, you may or may not need to use additional networking libraries with CUPS. The easiest way to manage these differences is to use the GNU autoconf software to locate the necessary libraries and configure your source code.

The CUPS libraries are provided under two licenses. The cups library is provided under the LGPL to provide the most flexibility when developing and distributing software. The cupsimage library is provided under the GPL and requires software using that library to be distributed under the GPL as well.

## CHAPTER 14

Using CUPS API Functions

This chapter will show you how to use the CUPS API functions to get the list of available printers and classes, submit print jobs, and manage print jobs from your application. You'll also learn how to access PostScript Printer Description (PPD) files from your application and use them to display printer-specific options and customize your output for a particular printer.

Printing Services

CUPS provides many functions to manage printers, classes, jobs, and options.

Managing Printers and Classes

CUPS supports both printers and classes of printers. The first CUPS program in Chapter 13, "Overview of CUPS Programming," introduced two CUPS functions, cupsGetDefault() cupsGetPrinters(), which retrieved the current default printer and list of printers, respectively. A third function, cupsGetClasses(), is also available to retrieve the list of printer classes from the server.

The cupsGetDefault() function takes no arguments and returns the name of the current default printer or class. If no default printer or class is defined, a NULL pointer is returned instead:

```
const char *defdest;

defdest = cupsGetDefault();
if (defdest != NULL)
  printf("Default destination is %s.\n", defdest);
else
  puts("No default destination available.");
```

The string that cupsGetDefault() returns is stored in a static buffer that is overwritten with each call.

The cupsGetClasses() function retrieves the list of printer classes and takes a single argument, a pointer to a char ** variable. It returns the number of classes:

```
int    i;
int    num_classes;
char **classes;

num_classes = cupsGetClasses(&classes);
if (num_classes == 0)
  puts("No printer classes found.");
else
{
  printf("%d printer class(es) were found:\n", num_classes);
```

```
  for (i = 0; i < num_classes; i ++)
    printf("    %s\n", classes[i]);
}
```

Similarly, the `cupsGetPrinters()` function retrieves the list of printers:

```
int   i;
int   num_printers;
char **printers;

num_printers = cupsGetPrinters(&printers);
if (num_printers == 0)
  puts("No printers found.");
else
{
  printf("%d printer(s) were found:\n", num_printers);
  for (i = 0; i < num_printers; i ++)
    printf("    %s\n", printers[i]);
}
```

Both `cupsGetClasses()` and `cupsGetPrinters()` return an array of strings that have been allocated using the `malloc()` function. To free the memory used by the strings you must free each of the printer or class name strings, and then free the array pointer. Do not attempt to free the array if the number of printers or classes is 0:

```
if (num_classes > 0)
{
  for (i = 0; i < num_classes; i ++)
    free(classes[i]);
  free(classes);
}

if (num_printers > 0)
{
  for (i = 0; i < num_printers; i ++)
    free(printers[i]);
  free(printers);
}
```

Listing 14.1 shows how to combine these functions to show the default printer or class along with the available printers and classes.

LISTING 14.1   The "showdests.c" Source File

```
/* Include the CUPS header file. */
#include <cups/cups.h>
```

LISTING 14.1 Continued

```c
int                         /* 0 - Exit status */
main(void)
{
  int        i;             /* Looping var */
  int        num_classes;   /* Number of classes */
  char       **classes;     /* List of classes */
  int        num_printers;  /* Number of printers */
  char       **printers;    /* List of printers */
  const char *defdest;      /* Default destination */


  /* Get the default destination */
  defdest = cupsGetDefault();

  /* Show the user the default printer */
  if (defdest != NULL)
    printf("Default destination is %s.\n", defdest);
  else
    puts("No default destination.");

  /* Get the list of classes */
  num_classes = cupsGetClasses(&classes);

  /* Show the user the available classes */
  if (num_classes > 0)
  {
    printf("%d class(es) were found:\n", num_classes);

    for (i = 0; i < num_classes; i ++)
      printf("    %s\n", classes[i]);

    /* Free the class list */
    for (i = 0; i < num_classes; i ++)
      free(classes[i]);

    free(classes);
  }
  else
    puts("No classes found.");

  /* Get the list of printers */
  num_printers = cupsGetPrinters(&printers);
```

LISTING 14.1   Continued

```
  /* Show the user the available printers */
  if (num_printers > 0)
  {
    printf("%d printer(s) were found:\n", num_printers);

    for (i = 0; i < num_printers; i ++)
      printf("    %s\n", printers[i]);

    /* Free the printer list */
    for (i = 0; i < num_printers; i ++)
      free(printers[i]);

    free(printers);
  }
  else
    puts("No printers found.");

  /* Return with no error */
  return (0);
}
```

After compiling the showdests.c file you can run it to get something like this:

```
./showdests ENTER
Default destination is DeskJet
2 class(es) were found:
    EPSON
    HP
4 printer(s) were found:
    DeskJet
    LaserJet
    StylusColor
    StylusPhoto
```

Printing Files

Now that you have a list of available printers and classes, you can send a print job. The CUPS API provides two functions for printing files. The first is cupsPrintFile(), which prints a single named file:

```
#include <cups/cups.h>
...
int jobid;
...
jobid = cupsPrintFile("destination", "filename", "title", 0, NULL);
```

The `destination` string is the name of the printer or class to which to print. The `filename` string is the name of the file to print. The `title` string is the name of the print job, such as Acme Word Document. The `0` and `NULL` values are the printer options; they are explained later in this chapter.

The `cupsPrintFile()` function returns a job ID > 0 on success or 0 if there was an error.

The second printing function is `cupsPrintFiles()`, which prints one or more files:

```
#include <cups/cups.h>
...
int        jobid;
int        num_files;
const char *files[100];
...
jobid = cupsPrintFiles("destination", num_files, files, "title", 0, NULL);
```

Instead of passing a filename string as with `cupsPrintFile()`, you pass a file count (`num_files`) and an array of filenames (`files`) with a `const char *` for each file that you want to print. As with `cupsPrintFile()`, `cupsPrintFiles()` returns a job ID > 0, or 0 if there was an error.

Managing Print Jobs

CUPS provides three functions to manage print jobs. The `cupsCancelJob()` function cancels an existing print job and accepts the printer or class name and a job ID number. It returns 1 if the job was successfully cancelled or 0 otherwise:

```
#include <cups/cups.h>
...
int jobid;
int status;
...
status = cupsCancelJob("destination", jobid);
```

The `destination` string specifies the destination and is used to determine the server to which to send the request. The `jobid` value is the integer returned from a previous `cupsPrintFile()` or `cupsPrintFiles()` call.

The other two functions are `cupsGetJobs()` and `cupsFreeJobs()`. The `cupsGetJobs()` function gets a list of jobs from the server and returns the number of jobs:

```
#include <cups/cups.h>
...
int        num_jobs;
cups_job_t *jobs;
...
num_jobs = cupsGetJobs(&jobs, "destination", myjobs, completed);
```

The `jobs` argument is a pointer to a `cups_job_t *` variable that holds the address of the job list. The `destination` string specifies a printer in which you are interested, or `NULL` if you want the list of jobs on every printer. The `myjobs` argument specifies whether you are interested only in your own jobs; if the value is 0, all jobs for all users will be returned. The `completed` argument specifies if you are interested in the list of completed jobs.

The `cups_job_t` structure contains several informational fields for each job. Table 14.1 lists the members of this structure.

TABLE 14.1   The Members of the `cups_job_t` Structure

Name	Type	Description
completed_time	time_t	The date and time the job was completed, cancelled, stopped, or aborted
creation_time	time_t	The date and time the job was created
dest	const char *	The destination printer or class
format	const char *	The format of the print file
id	int	The job ID value
impressions	int	The number of pages that have been printed in the job
kbytes	int	The size of the job in kilobytes
priority	int	The priority of the job
processing_time	time_t	The date and time the job was first processed
state	ipp_jstate_t	The current state of the job
title	const char *	The job name or title
user	const char *	The user who printed the file

The `cupsFreeJobs()` function frees the memory associated with a job list:

```
cupsFreeJobs(num_jobs, jobs);
```

The second example program, `showjobs`, lists all active print jobs using the `cupsGetJobs()` function. Listing 14.2 shows the source for this program.

LISTING 14.2   The `showjobs.c` Source File

```
/* Include the CUPS header file */
#include <cups/cups.h>


int                     /* O - Exit status */
main(void)
```

LISTING 14.2   Continued

```
{
  int        i;         /* Looping var */
  int        num_jobs;  /* Number of jobs */
  cups_job_t *jobs;     /* Jobs */


  /* Get the current jobs */
  num_jobs = cupsGetJobs(&jobs, NULL, 0, 0);

  if (num_jobs > 0)
  {
    /* Show the job list */
    printf("%d job(s) found:\n", num_jobs);
    puts("");
    puts("    Job ID  Destination      Title       User        Size");
    puts("    ------  ---------------  ----------  ----------  ------");

    for (i = 0; i < num_jobs; i ++)
      printf("    %-6d  %-15.15s  %-10.10s  %-10.10s  %dk",
             jobs[i].id, jobs[i].dest, jobs[i].title, jobs[i].user,
             jobs[i].size);

    cupsFreeJobs(num_jobs, jobs);
  }
  else
    puts("No jobs found.");

  /* Return with no error */
  return (0);
}
```

After calling `cupsGetJobs()` to get the active print jobs, we display the job list in a loop. The output looks something like this:

```
./showjobs ENTER
4 job(s) found:
    Job ID  Destination      Title       User        Size
    ------  ---------------  ----------  ----------  ------
    42      LaserJet         Test Page   mike        12k
    43      DeskJet          showdests.c mike        2k
    44      StylusColor      Test Page   mike        12k
    45      StylusPhoto      showjobs.c  mike        1k
```

Exploring Printer Options

Printer options are one of the things that set CUPS apart from the venerable LPD software. The CUPS API exposes options as an array of cups_option_t structures. The cups_option_t structure consists of a name and value string that are converted by the API functions into the appropriate IPP attribute types as needed.

Adding Options

CUPS provides several functions for managing printer options. The first is called cupsAddOption(). It adds a single option to the array of options:

```
#include <cups/cups.h>
...
int          num_options;
cups_option_t *options;
...
num_options = 0;
options      = NULL;
...
num_options = cupsAddOption("name", "value", num_options, &options);
num_options = cupsAddOption("name", "value", num_options, &options);
num_options = cupsAddOption("name", "value", num_options, &options);
num_options = cupsAddOption("name", "value", num_options, &options);
```

The name string is the name of the option and is not case sensitive; that is, "name," "Name," and "NAME" are identical.

The value string is the value for that option. Arrays of values are separated by the comma (,) character, and ranges use the minus (–) character.

The num_options and options parameters are the current number of options and a reference to a cups_option_t * variable, respectively.

Each call to cupsAddOption() returns the new number of options as an integer. The options pointer is also updated as necessary to point to the updated array.

Adding multiple options with the same name will only create a single copy of that option with the previous value. Do not assume that calling cupsAddOptions() 20 times will result in an array of 20 options.

Adding Multiple Options

Whereas cupsAddOption() adds a single option to the array, the cupsParseOptions() function will add zero or more options passed in a string:

```
#include <cups/cups.h>
...
int          num_options;
```

```
cups_option_t *options;
...
num_options = 0;
options     = NULL;
...
num_options = cupsParseOptions("name=value name2=value2", num_options, &options);
```

Options in the string are separated by spaces. The values in the string can be surrounded by single (') or double ("") quotes or use the backslash (\) to include spaces in the value. The lp and lpr commands, and many of the CUPS filters and printer drivers, often use the cupsParseOptions() function.

Retrieving Option Values

After you have built the option array, you can retrieve the current value of a named option using the cupsGetOption() function:

```
#include <cups/cups.h>
...
int           num_options;
cups_option_t *options;
const char    *value;
...
value = cupsGetOption("name", num_options, options);
```

The name string is the name of the option. The num_options and options arguments are the number of options and a pointer to a cups_option_t structure, respectively.

The cupsGetOption() function returns the current option value if the option is defined, or NULL if the option is not defined.

Releasing the Memory Used by Options

After you are finished using an option array, call the cupsFreeOptions() function to free the memory used:

```
#include <cups/cups.h>
...
int             num_options;
cups_option_t *options;
...
cupsFreeOptions(num_options, options);
```

The num_options and options arguments are the number of options and a pointer to a cups_option_t structure, respectively.

Managing Destinations

CUPS 1.1 introduced the notion of a destination instead of just a printer or a class. A *destination* is a printer or class with a set of associated printer options that are normally sent with each job.

A destination is identified using the printer or class name and an optional instance name:

```
DeskJet
DeskJet/Photo
LaserJet
LaserJet/Duplex
```

Each instance name can contain up to 127 letters, numbers, and the underscore character. As with printer names, instance names are not case sensitive, meaning that "instance," "Instance," and "INSTANCE" are all the same. Options defined for the primary instance (DeskJet, LaserJet, and so on) are not automatically included in the options for a secondary instance (DeskJet/Photo, LaserJet/Duplex, and so on).

Obtaining the List of Available Destinations

Destinations are stored in the system lpoptions file (usually /etc/cups/lpoptions) and in the user lpoptions file (~/.lpoptions). The cupsGetDests() function can be used to get a list of the available printers, classes, and instances that are defined by the system and user:

```
#include <cups/cups.h>
...
int         num_dests;
cups_dest_t *dests;
...
num_dests = cupsGetDests(&dests);
```

Each destination is stored in a cups_dest_t structure, which defines the printer or class name, the instance name (if any), whether it is the default destination, and the default options the user has defined for the destination. The destinations are sorted alphabetically by name and instance for your convenience. Table 14.2 lists the members of the cups_dest_t structure.

TABLE 14.2   The cups_dest_t Structure

Name	Type	Description
name	char *	The name of the printer or class
instance	char *	The name of the instance (NULL for the primary instance)
is_default	int	Non-zero if this is the default destination
num_options	int	Number of options for this destination
options	cups_option_t *	Options for this destination

Finding the Destination You Need

After you have the list of available destinations, you can look up a specific destination using the cupsGetDest() function:

```
#include <cups/cups.h>
...
int        num_dests;
cups_dest_t *dests;
cups_dest_t *mydest;
...
mydest = cupsGetDest("name", "instance", num_dests, dests);
```

The name string is the printer or class name. You can pass a value of NULL to get the default destination.

The instance string is the user-defined instance name. Pass NULL to select the primary instance, such as "name" instead of "name/instance."

The return value will be a pointer to the cups_dest_t structure for that destination, or NULL if the destination does not exist.

Adding New Destinations

Adding an instance is similar to adding an option to an option array. Start by calling the cupsAddDest() function to add an instance to the destination array:

```
#include <cups/cups.h>
...
int        num_dests;
cups_dest_t *dests;
cups_dest_t *mydest;
...
num_dests = cupsAddDest("name", "instance", num_dests, &dests);
mydest    = cupsGetDest("name", "instance", num_dests, dests);
```

Then call cupsAddOption() or cupsParseOptions() as needed to add the options for the new instance:

```
mydest->num_options = cupsAddOption("name", "value", mydest->num_options,
                                    &(mydest->options));
mydest->num_options = cupsParseOptions("name=value name1=value1",
                                       mydest->num_options, &(mydest->options));
```

Saving Destinations to Disk

If you have added or changed the list of destinations, you can save the destinations using the cupsSetDests() function:

```
#include <cups/cups.h>
...
int          num_dests;
cups_dest_t *dests;
...
cupsSetDests(num_dests, dests);
```

When run as the root user, the destinations are saved to the system lpoptions file. For any other user, the destinations are stored in the user's .lpoptions file.

Releasing the Memory Used by Destinations

When you are finished with the destination array, call the cupsFreeDests() function to free the memory used by it:

```
#include <cups/cups.h>
...
int          num_dests;
cups_dest_t *dests;
...
cupsFreeDests(num_dests, dests);
```

Printing with Options

All of the previous printing examples have passed 0 and NULL for the last two arguments to the cupsPrintFile() and cupsPrintFiles() functions. These last two arguments are the number of options and a pointer to the option array.

The simplest way of handling options is to use the num_options and options members of the cups_dest_t structure described earlier:

```
#include <cups/cups.h>
...
int          jobid;
int          num_dests;
cups_dest_t *dests;
cups_dest_t *mydest;
...
mydest = cupsGetDest("name", "instance", num_dests, dests);
jobid  = cupsPrintFile(mydest->name, "filename", "title",
                       mydest->num_options, mydest->options);
```

This effectively uses the options a user has previously selected without adding much code.

You can also use options defined by the `cupsAddOption()` and `cupsParseOptions()` functions, or a combination of the destination and user options.

The third example uses all of the option, destination, and printing functions described so far. Start by getting the list of available destinations and options:

```
int num_dests;
cups_dest_t *dests;

num_dests = cupsGetDests(&dests);
```

Then get the current default destination:

```
cups_dest_t *dest;

dest = cupsGetDests(NULL, NULL, num_dests, dests);
```

Next, collect the command-line arguments. On some systems, you can use the `getopt()` function to handle this. However, many systems do not provide this function and it is fairly easy to parse options by hand. Support "-d" and "-P" options to specify the printer, and the "-o" option to specify printer options.

For the "-d" and "-P" options, grab the destination name, separate the instance name if it was specified, and look up the destination with the `cupsGetDest()` function:

```
char *name;
char *instance;

if ((instance = strrchr(name, '/')) != NULL)
  *instance++ = '\0';

dest = cupsGetDest(name, instance, num_dests, dests);
```

For the "-o" option, use the `cupsParseOptions()` function to add the options on the command line:

```
num_options = cupsParseOptions(argv[i], num_options, &options);
```

Then add any filenames to an array of const char *'s for the `cupsPrintFiles()` function:

```
int         num_files;
const char *files[100];
...
else if (num_files < 100)
{
  files[num_files] = argv[i];
  num_files ++;
}
```

Before you print the files, merge the user options with the destination options. To do this, loop through the destination options and add them to the print options array if they are not already defined:

```
for (i = 0; i < dest->num_options; i ++)
  if (cupsGetOption(dest->options[i].name, num_options, options) == NULL)
    num_options = cupsAddOption(dest->options[i].name,
                                dest->options[i].value,
                                num_options, &options);
```

Finally, print the file using the cupsPrintFiles() function:

```
int id;
...
id = cupsPrintFiles(dest->name, num_files, files, files[0],
                    num_options, options);
```

The final program is shown in Listing 14.3. After building the program you should be able to pretty-print the source file with the following:

./print -o prettyprint print.c _ENTER_
Job ID is 123.

LISTING 14.3   The print.c Source File

```
/* Include the CUPS header file */
#include <cups/cups.h>


int             /* O - Exit status */
main(int  argc,     /* I - Number of command-line arguments */
     char *argv[]) /* I - Command-line arguments */
{
  int           i;          /* Looping var */
  int           id;         /* Job ID */
  int           num_files;  /* Number of files */
  const char    *files[100]; /* Files to print */
  char          *name;      /* Destination name */
  char          *instance;  /* Instance name */
  int           num_dests;  /* Number of destinations */
  cups_dest_t   *dests;     /* Destinations */
  cups_dest_t   *dest;      /* Current destination */
  int           num_options; /* Number of options */
  cups_option_t *options;   /* Options */
```

LISTING 14.3   Continued

```c
/* Get the list of destinations */
num_dests = cupsGetDests(&dests);

/* Get the default destination */
dest = cupsGetDest(NULL, NULL, num_dests, dests);

/* Parse the command-line */
num_files   = 0;
num_options = 0;
options     = NULL;

for (i = 1; i < argc; i ++)
  if (strncmp(argv[i], "-d", 2) == 0 ||
      strncmp(argv[i], "-P", 2) == 0)
  {
    if (argv[i][2])
      name = argv[i] + 2;
    else
    {
      i ++;

      if (i >= argc)
      {
        puts("ERROR: Expected destination name!");
        cupsFreeDests(num_dests, dests);
        cupsFreeOptions(num_options, options);
        return (1);
      }
      else
        name = argv[i];
    }

    if ((instance = strrchr(name, '/')) != NULL)
      *instance++ = '\0';

    if ((dest = cupsGetDest(name, instance, num_dests, dests)) == NULL)
    {
      if (instance != NULL))
        printf("ERROR: %s/%s does not exist!\n", name, instance);
      else
        printf("ERROR: %s does not exist!\n", name);
```

LISTING 14.3   Continued

```c
        cupsFreeDests(num_dests, dests);
        cupsFreeOptions(num_options, options);
        return (1);
      }
    }
    else if (strncmp(argv[i], "-o", 2) == 0)
    {
      /* Add one or more options */
      if (argv[i][2])
        num_options = cupsParseOptions(argv[i] + 2, num_options, &options);
      else
      {
        i ++;

        if (i >= argc)
        {
          puts("ERROR: Expected option=value!");
          cupsFreeDests(num_dests, dests);
          cupsFreeOptions(num_options, options);
          return (1);
        }

        num_options = cupsParseOptions(argv[i], num_options, &options);
      }
    }
    else if (num_files < 100)
    {
      /* Add a file to print */
      files[num_files] = argv[i];
      num_files ++;
    }

  /* See if we have any files to print... */
  if (num_files == 0)
  {
    puts("ERROR: Expected print files!");
    cupsFreeDests(num_dests, dests);
    cupsFreeOptions(num_options, options);
    return (1);
  }

  /* Merge the printer options */
```

LISTING 14.3   Continued

```
  for (i = 0; i < dest->num_options; i ++)
    if (cupsGetOption(dest->options[i].name, num_options, options) == NULL)
      num_options = cupsAddOption(dest->options[i].name,
                                  dest->options[i].value,
                                  num_options, &options);

  /* Print the file */
  id = cupsPrintFiles(dest->name, num_files, files, files[0],
                      num_options, options);

  /* Show the job ID or error */
  if (id > 0)
    printf("Job ID is %d.\n", id);
  else
    printf("ERROR: Unable to print file - %s\n",
           ippErrorString(cupsLastError()));

  /* Return 1 on error or 0 on success */
  return (id < 1);
}
```

PPD Files

CUPS includes functions to access and manipulate PostScript Printer Description (PPD) files that are used with the printer drivers in CUPS. Each PPD file enumerates the available features provided by a printer and includes conflict information, such as the inability to duplex output on envelopes.

Include the <cups/ppd.h> header file to use the PPD functions:

```
#include <cups/ppd.h>
```

The <cups/cups.h> header file accessalso includes this header file.

Getting a PPD File for a Printer

The cupsGetPPD() function access retrieves the PPD file for the named printer or class:

```
#include <cups/cups.h>
...
const char *filename;

filename = cupsGetPPD("name");
```

The name string is the name of the printer or class, including the remote server name as appropriate, such as "printer@server".

The return value is a pointer to a filename in static storage; this value is overwritten with each call to cupsGetPPD(). If the printer or class does not exist, a NULL pointer will be returned. This filename is also a temporary file; therefore, call unlink() to remove the file when you are finished using it:

```
unlink(filename);
```

Loading a PPD File

The ppdOpenFile() function "opens" a PPD file and loads it into memory:

```
#include <cups/ppd.h>
...
ppd_file_t *ppd;

ppd = ppdOpenFile("filename");
```

The filename string is the name of the file to load, such as the value returned by the cupsGetPPD() function.

The return value is a pointer to a structure describing the contents of the PPD file, or NULL if the PPD file could not be read.

Releasing the Memory Used by a PPD File

When you are finished using a PPD file, call the ppdClose() function to free all memory that has been used:

```
#include <cups/ppd.h>
...
ppd_file_t *ppd;
...
ppdClose(ppd);
```

Examining the PPD File Structures

Each PPD file contains a number of capability attributes, printer options, and conflict definitions. The page size options also include the physical margins and the minimum and maximum sizes for the printer. All of this information is stored in the ppd_file_t structure. The members of the ppd_file_t structure are shown in Table 14.3.

TABLE 14.3   PPD Capability Values

Name	Type	Description
accurate_screens	int	An indication of whether the printer supports accurate screens
color_device	int	An indication of whether the printer supports color
colorspace	ppd_cs_t	The default colorspace
num_consts	int	The number of constraints
consts	ppd_const_t *	Constraints
contone_only	int	An indication of whether the printer is continuous tone only
custom_margins	float [4]	The left, bottom, right, and top margins for custom page sizes
custom_max	float [2]	The maximum dimensions supported for custom page sizes
custom_min	float [2]	The minimum dimensions supported for custom page sizes
num_emulations	int	The number of emulations the printer supports
emulations	ppd_emul_t *	The emulations supported by the printer
num_filters	int	The number of filters for this printer
filters	char **	The filters for this printer
flip_duplex	int	An indication of whether the printer needs the back pages to be flipped when duplexing
num_fonts	int	The number of fonts the printer has
fonts	char **	The fonts available on the printer
num_groups	int	The number of option groups
groups	ppd_group_t *	Option groups
jcl_begin	char *	The Job Control Language (JCL) string to send before each job
jcl_ps	char *	The JCL string to send to put the printer in PostScript mode
jcl_end	char *	The JCL string to send to end each job
landscape	int	The orientation of landscape pages
lang_encoding	char *	The character set used for the option text
lang_version	char *	The language used for the option strings, such as English, French, or Spanish
language_level	int	The PostScript language level, from 1 to 3
manual_copies	int	An indication of whether copies need to be done manually
manufacturer	char *	The name of the printer manufacturer
model_number	int	The driver-specific model number
modelname	char *	The model name of the printer

TABLE 14.3   Continued

Name	Type	Description
nickname	char *	The nickname for the printer; this is usually the name shown to a user
patches	char *	The patch commands to send to the printer before each job
product	char *	The product name for the printer
num_profiles	int	The number of color profiles
profiles	ppd_profile_t *	Color profiles
shortnickname	char *	The short nickname for the printer
num_sizes	int	The number of sizes
sizes	ppd_size_t *	Sizes
throughput	int	The print speed in pages per minute
ttrasterizer	char *	The TrueType font rasterizer provided, usually "Type42"
variable_sizes	int	An indication of whether the printer supports custom page sizes

Most of the string values can be NULL if the corresponding PPD file attribute is not included in the file. In particular, be cautious about displaying the value of the manufacturer field, which is not present in all PPD files despite being required by the PPD specification.

Options and Groups

PPD files support multiple options, which the PPD functions store in ppd_option_t and ppd_choice_t structures.

Each option in turn is associated with a group stored in the ppd_group_t structure. Groups can be specified in the PPD file; if an option is not associated with a group, it is put in a "General" or "Extra" group depending on the option.

The group list for the PPD file is stored in the num_groups and groups members. Each group has a human-readable name, such as "General" or "Installable Options," and contains an array of options.

The options in a group are in the num_options and options members of the ppd_group_t structure. Each option has an option name ("PageSize"), a human-readable name ("Media Size"), command ordering information, an option type (boolean, single choice, or multiple choice), the default choice for this option, and an array of choices. The option name is not case sensitive.

The choices in an option are in the num_choices and choices members of the ppd_option_t structure. Each choice has a choice value ("Letter"), a human-readable name

("Letter - 8.5x11 inches"), a boolean value indicating whether the choice has been marked, and the PostScript command(s) to send to the printer when the option is chosen. The choice value is not case sensitive.

Showing the Contents of a PPD File

The CUPS sources include a program called testppd that loads a PPD file and displays the groups, options, and choices. Listing 14.4 shows the testppd source code. After you build the testppd program, you should be able to run the following:

```
./testppd /usr/share/cups/model/deskjet.ppd ENTER
FILE: /usr/share/cups/model/deskjet.ppd
    language_level = 3
    color_device = TRUE
    variable_sizes = FALSE
    landscape = 90
    colorspace = PPD_CS_RGB
    num_emulations = 0
    lang_encoding = ISOLatin1
    lang_version = English
    modelname = HP DeskJet Series
    ttrasterizer = Type42
    manufacturer = ESP
    product = (CUPS v1.1)
    nickname = HP DeskJet Series CUPS v1.1
    shortnickname = HP DeskJet Series
    patches = 0 bytes
    num_groups = 2
        group[0] = Extra
            options[0] = ColorModel (Output Mode) PICKONE ANY 10
                RGB (CMY Color)
                CMYK (CMYK Color) *
                Gray (Grayscale)
            options[1] = Resolution (Output Resolution) PICKONE ANY 20
                150dpi (150 DPI)
                300dpi (300 DPI) *
                600dpi (600 DPI)
        group[1] = General
            options[0] = PageSize (Media Size) PICKONE ANY 10
                A3 (A3) = 11.69x16.54in (0.2,0.5,11.4,16.0)
                A4 (A4) = 8.26x11.69in (0.2,0.5,8.0,11.2)
                ...
                Legal (US Legal) = 8.50x14.00in (0.2,0.5,8.2,13.5)
                Letter (US Letter) = 8.50x11.00in (0.2,0.5,8.2,10.5) *
                Tabloid (US Tabloid) = 11.00x17.00in (0.2,0.5,10.8,16.5)
```

```
            options[1] = InputSlot (Media Source) PICKONE ANY 10
                Envelope (Envelope Feed)
                Manual (Manual Feed)
                Tray (Tray) *
            options[2] = MediaType (Media Type) PICKONE ANY 10
                Bond (Bond Paper)
                Glossy (Glossy Paper)
                Plain (Plain Paper) *
                Special (Special Paper)
                Transparency (Transparency)
            options[3] = PageRegion (PageRegion) PICKONE ANY 10
                A3 (A3) = 11.69x16.54in (0.2,0.5,11.4,16.0)
                A4 (A4) = 8.26x11.69in (0.2,0.5,8.0,11.2)
                ...
                Letter (US Letter) = 8.50x11.00in (0.2,0.5,8.2,10.5) *
                Tabloid (US Tabloid) = 11.00x17.00in (0.2,0.5,10.8,16.5)
    num_profiles = 0
    num_fonts = 35
        fonts[0] = AvantGarde-Book
        fonts[1] = AvantGarde-BookOblique
        fonts[2] = AvantGarde-Demi
        ...
        fonts[32] = Times-Roman
        fonts[33] = ZapfChancery-MediumItalic
        fonts[34] = ZapfDingbats
```

LISTING 14.4   The testppd.c Source File

```c
/* Include the CUPS header file. */
#include <cups/cups.h>
/* Include the string function definitions */
#include <string.h>

int                     /* O - Exit status */
main(int  argc,         /* I - Number of command-line arguments */
    char *argv[])       /* I - Command-line arguments */
{
  int        i, j, k, m; /* Looping vars */
  const char  *filename; /* File to load */
  ppd_file_t  *ppd;      /* PPD file record */
  ppd_size_t  *size;     /* Size record */
  ppd_group_t *group;    /* UI group */
  ppd_option_t *option;  /* Standard UI option */
```

LISTING 14.4   Continued

```c
ppd_choice_t *choice;     /* Standard UI option choice */
static char  *uis[] = { "BOOLEAN", "PICKONE", "PICKMANY" };
static char  *sections[] = { "ANY", "DOCUMENT", "EXIT",
                             "JCL", "PAGE", "PROLOG" };


/* Display PPD files for each file listed on the command-line... */
if (argc == 1)
{
  fputs("Usage: ppdtest filename1.ppd [... filenameN.ppd]\n", stderr);
  return (1);
}

for (i = 1; i < argc; i ++)
{
  if (strstr(argv[i], ".ppd"))
    filename = argv[i];
  else
    filename = cupsGetPPD(argv[i]);

  if ((ppd = ppdOpenFile(filename)) == NULL)
  {
    fprintf(stderr, "Unable to open \'%s\' as a PPD file!\n", filename);
    continue;
  }

  printf("FILE: %s\n", filename);
  printf("    language_level = %d\n", ppd->language_level);
  printf("    color_device = %s\n", ppd->color_device ? "TRUE" : "FALSE");
  printf("    variable_sizes = %s\n",
         ppd->variable_sizes ? "TRUE" : "FALSE");
  printf("    landscape = %d\n", ppd->landscape);

  switch (ppd->colorspace)
  {
    case PPD_CS_CMYK :
        puts("    colorspace = PPD_CS_CMYK");
        break;
    case PPD_CS_CMY :
        puts("    colorspace = PPD_CS_CMY");
        break;
    case PPD_CS_GRAY :
        puts("    colorspace = PPD_CS_GRAY");
        break;
```

LISTING 14.4   Continued

```c
    case PPD_CS_RGB :
        puts("    colorspace = PPD_CS_RGB");
        break;
    default :
        puts("    colorspace = <unknown>");
        break;
}

printf("    num_emulations = %d\n", ppd->num_emulations);
for (j = 0; j < ppd->num_emulations; j ++)
  printf("      emulations[%d] = %s\n", j, ppd->emulations[j].name);

printf("    lang_encoding = %s\n", ppd->lang_encoding);
printf("    lang_version = %s\n", ppd->lang_version);
printf("    modelname = %s\n", ppd->modelname);
printf("    ttrasterizer = %s\n",
        ppd->ttrasterizer == NULL ? "None" : ppd->ttrasterizer);
printf("    manufacturer = %s\n", ppd->manufacturer);
printf("    product = %s\n", ppd->product);
printf("    nickname = %s\n", ppd->nickname);
printf("    shortnickname = %s\n", ppd->shortnickname);
printf("    patches = %d bytes\n",
        ppd->patches == NULL ? 0 : strlen(ppd->patches));

printf("    num_groups = %d\n", ppd->num_groups);
for (j = 0, group = ppd->groups; j < ppd->num_groups; j ++, group ++)
{
  printf("      group[%d] = %s\n", j, group->text);

  for (k = 0, option = group->options;
       k < group->num_options;
       k ++, option ++)
  {
    printf("        options[%d] = %s (%s) %s %s %.0f\n", k,
            option->keyword, option->text, uis[option->ui],
            sections[option->section], option->order);

    if (strcmp(option->keyword, "PageSize") == 0 ||
        strcmp(option->keyword, "PageRegion") == 0)
    {
      for (m = option->num_choices, choice = option->choices;
           m > 0;
           m --, choice ++)
```

LISTING 14.4   Continued

```c
      {
        size = ppdPageSize(ppd, choice->choice);

        if (size == NULL)
          printf("                   %s (%s) = ERROR", choice->choice,
                  choice->text);
        else
          printf("                   %s (%s) = %.2fx%.2fin "
                  "(%.1f,%.1f,%.1f,%.1f)", choice->choice,
                  choice->text, size->width / 72.0, size->length / 72.0,
                  size->left / 72.0, size->bottom / 72.0,
                  size->right / 72.0, size->top / 72.0);

        if (strcmp(option->defchoice, choice->choice) == 0)
          puts(" *");
        else
          putchar('\n');
      }
    }
    else
    {
      for (m = option->num_choices, choice = option->choices;
           m > 0;
           m --, choice ++)
      {
        printf("                   %s (%s)", choice->choice, choice->text);

        if (strcmp(option->defchoice, choice->choice) == 0)
          puts(" *");
        else
          putchar('\n');
      }
    }
  }
}

printf("    num_profiles = %d\n", ppd->num_profiles);
for (j = 0; j < ppd->num_profiles; j ++)
  printf("        profiles[%d] = %s/%s %.3f %.3f [ %.3f %.3f %.3f "
         "%.3f %.3f %.3f %.3f %.3f %.3f ]\n",
         j, ppd->profiles[j].resolution, ppd->profiles[j].media_type,
         ppd->profiles[j].gamma, ppd->profiles[j].density,
         ppd->profiles[j].matrix[0][0], ppd->profiles[j].matrix[0][1],
```

LISTING 14.4   Continued

```
                ppd->profiles[j].matrix[0][2], ppd->profiles[j].matrix[1][0],
                ppd->profiles[j].matrix[1][1], ppd->profiles[j].matrix[1][2],
                ppd->profiles[j].matrix[2][0], ppd->profiles[j].matrix[2][1],
                ppd->profiles[j].matrix[2][2]);

    printf("    num_fonts = %d\n", ppd->num_fonts);
    for (j = 0; j < ppd->num_fonts; j ++)
      printf("        fonts[%d] = %s\n", j, ppd->fonts[j]);

    ppdClose(ppd);
  }

  return (0);
}
```

Finding an Option

Call the ppdFindOption()function to find an option in the PPD file:

```
#include <cups/ppd.h>
...
ppd_file_t    *ppd;
ppd_option_t *option;
...
option = ppdFindOption(ppd, "name");
```

The ppd argument is a pointer to the ppd_file_t structure. The name argument is the name of the option. If the option exists, a pointer to the ppd_option_t structure for that option will be returned. Otherwise, a NULL pointer is returned.

Finding a Choice

Call the cupsFindChoice() function to find a particular option choice:

```
ppd_option_t *option;
ppd_choice_t *choice;
...
choice = ppdFindChoice(option, "Custom");
```

The first argument is a pointer to the ppd_option_t structure as returned by ppdFindOption(). The second argument is the name of the choice.

The return value is a pointer to the ppd_choice_t structure for the named choice, or NULL if the choice does not exist.

A similar function is cupsFindMarkedChoice(), which finds the currently marked choice for the option:

```
ppd_file_t   *ppd;
ppd_choice_t *choice;
...
choice = ppdFindMarkedChoice(ppd, "PageSize");
```

Instead of passing the option structure pointer, the first argument is a pointer to the `ppd_file_t` structure. The option name follows.

The return value is a pointer to the `ppd_choice_t` structure for the first choice that is marked, or `NULL` if no choice is marked or the option doesn't exist.

Marking Options

Each option choice has a marked state associated with it. Marked options can be sent to a printer or displayed to the user.

Before marking any user-defined options, call the `ppdMarkDefaults()` function to mark the default options from the PPD file:

```
#include <cups/ppd.h>
...
ppd_file_t *ppd;
...
ppdMarkDefaults(ppd);
```

Then call the `ppdMarkOption()` function to mark individual options:

```
#include <cups/ppd.h>
...
ppd_file_t *ppd;
int        conflicts;
...
conflicts = ppdMarkOption(ppd, "name", "value");
```

The `name` and `value` strings choose a particular option and choice, respectively. The return value is 0 if no conflicts are created by the selection.

CUPS also provides the `cupsMarkOptions()` function for marking all options in a printer option array:

```
#include <cups/cups.h>
...
ppd_file_t    *ppd;
int           num_options;
cups_option_t *options;
int           conflicts;
...
conflicts = cupsMarkOptions(ppd, num_options, options);
```

The cupsMarkOptions() function also handles mapping the IPP options to PPD options. The return value is the number of conflicts present.

Conflicts

PPD files support specification of conflict conditions between different options. Conflicts are stored in ppd_conflict_t structures, which specify the options that conflict with each other.

The ppdMarkOption() and cupsMarkOptions() functions return the number of conflicts with the currently marked options.

You can also call the ppdConflicts() function to get the number of conflicts after you have marked all of the options:

```
#include <cups/cups.h>

...

ppd_file_t *ppd;
int        conflicts;

...

conflicts = ppdConflicts(ppd);
```

The return value is the number of conflicting options, or 0 if no conflicts exist. Due to the symmetrical nature of these conflicts (A conflicts with B, so B conflicts with A), the conflict count will always be an even number.

Page Sizes

PPD files specify all of the available page sizes and the physical margins associated with them. These sizes are stored in ppd_size_t structures and are available in the num_sizes and sizes members of the ppd_file_t structure. You can look up a particular page size with the ppdPageWidth(), ppdPageLength(), and ppdPageSize() functions:

```
#include <cups/ppd.h>

...

ppd_file_t *ppd;
ppd_size_t *size;
float      width;
float      length;

...

size   = ppdPageSize(ppd, "size");
width  = ppdPageWidth(ppd, "size");
length = ppdPageLength(ppd, "size");
```

The size string is the named page size option. The width and length are in points; there are 72 points per inch. The ppd_size_t structure contains the width, length, and margin information. Table 14.4 lists the members of the ppd_size_t structure.

TABLE 14.4   PPD Size Structure Members

Name	Type	Description
marked	int	An indication of whether the page size is selected
name	char[41]	Media size option name
width	float	Width of media in points
length	float	Length of media in points
left	float	Left printable margin in points
bottom	float	Bottom printable margin in points
right	float	Right printable margin in points
top	float	Top printable margin in points

Custom Page Sizes

Besides the standard page sizes listed in a PPD file, some printers support variable or custom page sizes. Unless the variables_sizes member of the ppd_file_t structure is zero, the custom_min, custom_max, and custom_margins members of the ppd_file_t structure define the limits of the variable sizes.

To get the resulting media size, use a page size string of Custom.WIDTHxLENGTH, where WIDTH and LENGTH are integer values in points:

```
Custom.612x792  =  8.5 inches wide, 11 inches long
Custom.1224x792  =  17 inches wide, 11 inches long
```

Temporary Files

Many applications need to create and use temporary files to store intermediate data. Because the availability, usefulness, and security of temporary file functions vary from operating system to operating system, CUPS provides its own temporary file functions for applications to use.

Both of the functions use the TMPDIR environment variable to determine where to place temporary files. If the TMPDIR environment variable is not set, the temporary files will be placed in the /var/tmp directory for normal users and /var/spool/cups/tmp for the root user.

The first function is appropriately called cupsTempFile(). It generates a single temporary filename into a string you pass to it:

```
char filename[1024];
FILE *fp;

...
```

```
if (cupsTempFile(filename, sizeof(filename)) == NULL)
  puts("Unable to create temporary filename!");

fp = fopen(filename, "w");
```

When CUPS generates the temporary file, it creates a placeholder file that only you can access. If `cupsTempFile()` is unable to safely create a temporary file, a `NULL` pointer is returned. Otherwise, a pointer to your filename string is returned.

After getting your temporary filename, you can open it or delete it as you like.

If you will be opening the temporary file right away, the `cupsTempFd()` function is probably a better choice:

```
char filename[1024];
int  fd;
FILE *fp;
...
fd = cupsTempFd(filename, sizeof(filename));
if (fd < 0)
  puts("Unable to create temporary filename!");

fp = fdopen(fd, "w");
```

If the temporary file could be created, `cupsTempFd()` returns a *file descriptor* (a number representing the opened file) for the temporary file opened in read/write mode. Otherwise, it returns −1 to indicate the error.

After you have the file descriptor, use the `fdopen()` function to associate it with a `FILE *` as needed.

Encryption Support

When configured to support encryption, CUPS can provide 128-bit encryption of all requests sent and received from the server. The CUPS API provides two functions for querying and setting the default encryption mode. The `cupsEncryption()` function gets the current encryption setting:

```
http_encryption_t encryption;
...
encryption = cupsEncryption();
```

The encryption value is an enumeration that specifies when encryption will be performed:

`HTTP_ENCRYPT_IF_REQUESTED`: Only encrypt requests if the server wants to

`HTTP_ENCRYPT_NEVER`: Newer encrypt requests

HTTP_ENCRYPT_REQUIRED: Upgrade to encryption before sending a request

HTTP_ENCRYPT_ALWAYS: Use encryption as soon as the server is contacted

The HTTP_ENCRYPT_ALWAYS value is used when encrypting using the SSL protocol, whereas the HTTP_ENCRYPT_REQUIRED and HTTP_ENCRYPT_IF_REQUESTED values use the TLS protocol. The normal setting is HTTP_ENCRYPT_IF_REQUESTED, but it can be overridden by the CUPS_ENCRYPTION environment variable and the Encryption directive in the client.conf or ~/.clientrc files.

The cupsSetEncryption()function sets the default encryption mode. For example, to change the print program earlier in this chapter to always print with encryption, simply add the following line to the top of the main() function:

```
cupsSetEncryption(HTTP_ENCRYPT_REQUIRED);
```

The lp and lpr programs supplied with CUPS use this function to enable encryption when the "-E" option is specified on the command line.

Users, Servers, and Ports

CUPS provides several functions to access and set the current username, server, and port number that are used by the other API functions.

Getting and Setting the Current Username

The current username is normally your login username. The cupsUser() function returns the current username:

```
const char *username;
...
username = cupsUser();
```

As you can see, there isn't much to the interface. You will get the current username, or if the current username is unknown, you'll get the string "unknown".

Use the cupsSetUser() function to change the current username:

```
cupsSetUser("johndoe");
```

Again, there isn't much to the interface, and your only obligation is to provide the username string.

Getting and Setting the Current Server

The current server is normally "localhost", but it can be changed via the CUPS_SERVER environment variable or the client.conf and ~/.clientrc files. The cupsServer() function returns the current server:

```
const char *server;
...
server = cupsServer();
```

The `cupsServer()` function will never return a `NULL` pointer.

Use the `cupsSetServer()` function to change the current server:

```
cupsSetServer("foo.bar.com");
```

The server name string can be a hostname or an IP address.

Getting and Setting the IPP Port

The current IPP port is normally 631, the default port number for the Internet Printing Protocol. This port can be overridden using the `IPP_PORT` environment variable or by adding an "ipp" entry in the `/etc/services` file. The `ippPort()` function returns the current port number:

```
int port;
...
port = ippPort();
```

Use the `ippSetPort()` function to change the default port:

```
ippSetPort(8631);
```

Callback Functions

CUPS supports authentication of any request, including submission of print jobs. The default mechanism for getting the username and password is to use the login user and a password from the console.

To support other types of applications, and in particular graphical user interfaces (GUIs), the CUPS API provides a callback mechanism.

The `cupsSetPasswordCB()` function is used to set a password callback in your program. Only one function can be used at any time. The callback function accepts a single string argument (the password prompt) and must return a pointer to the password string, or `NULL` if the operator cancelled the operation.

When combined with the `cupsSetUser()` function, the password callback can provide the username and password for authentication:

```
#include <cups/cups.h>
...
const char *                        /* O - Password */
```

```
my_password_cb(const char *prompt) /* I - Password prompt */
{
  char  user[65];                  /* Username string */

  /* Show the password prompt. */
  puts(prompt);

  /* Get a username from the user */
  printf("Username: ");
  if (fgets(user, sizeof(user), stdin) == NULL)
    return (NULL);

  /* Strip the newline from the string and set the user */
  user[strlen(user) - 1] = '\0';
  cupsSetUser(user);

  /* Use getpass() to ask for the password... */
  return (getpass("Password: "));
}
...
cupsSetPasswordCB(my_password_cb);
```

Error Handling

If any of the CUPS API printing functions returns an error, the reason for that error can be found by calling cupsLastError() and ippErrorString(). The cupsLastError() function returns the last IPP error code that was encountered. The ippErrorString() converts the error code to a message string suitable for presentation to the user:

```
#include <cups/cups.h>
...
int jobid;
...
if (jobid == 0)
  printf("Unable to print file: %s\n", cupsErrorString(cupsLastError()));
```

Summary

The CUPS API provides many functions for applications to query destinations; send and manage print jobs; discover printer options and capabilities; and control encryption, username, password, server, and port settings.

An application can get a simple list of printers or get a list of real and virtual destinations, along with the options to use for each. Printer options can be managed alone or in conjunction with destinations. Printer, class, instance, option, and choice names are not case sensitive.

Jobs can be cancelled or monitored via the CUPS API. Each job has an associated number that is used to identify the job uniquely on each server. The CUPS API supports listing of all jobs, jobs on a printer, and jobs for the current user.

PPD files describe the printers in CUPS. The CUPS API provides functions for loading, querying, and controlling printers via their PPD files. PPD files contain groups of options with one or more choices associated with them. Options can be constrained against other options to enforce certain policies or limitations in the printer.

Temporary files can be managed using the CUPS API. This is important because the way temporary files are created is different on many systems, and CUPS ensures that the file is created safely with a unique name.

The current encryption mode, user, server, port, and password callback can be controlled using a few simple functions in the CUPS API. The password callback is used to provide support for alternate usernames as well as GUI applications.

In the next chapter you'll get under the hood and learn how to directly interact with the CUPS server using IPP requests.

CHAPTER 15

Sending IPP Requests Using CUPS

This chapter covers the CUPS IPP interface and describes how to manage IPP attributes, send requests, and process responses.

In Chapter 14, "Using CUPS API Functions," you learned how to use the CUPS API to access printers and printer information, manage printer options, and manage print jobs. With all of these functions, you might wonder why you would even need to bother sending your own IPP requests or even reading this chapter.

A simple answer is that you might not need to send IPP requests at all from your applications. After all, the CUPS API *does* provide most of what an application needs to support basic printing.

That said, it is sometimes important to understand *how* these functions are implemented within the IPP layer. Also, if your application does do more than basic printing, such as printer, class, or job administration, then the direct IPP interfaces are the only way to do it.

Finally, many of the interfaces presented here can be used beyond printing. For example, the HTTP functions can be used to implement a simple Web browser that supports both normal (http) and encrypted (https) communications.

The CUPS Low-Level APIs

The CUPS low-level APIs consist of a collection of Hypertext Transfer Protocol (HTTP) and Internet Printing Protocol (IPP) functions and data structures that allow you to manage HTTP and IPP communications.

Each of these interfaces is based on a finite state machine that operates for the duration of the request to and response from the server. Because these interfaces are general-purpose, the server also uses them to manage the connections with the client.

A single HTTP "object" (really a C structure for portability) of type `http_t` is used to manage the HTTP communications while two IPP objects of type `ipp_t` are used to manage the IPP request and response, respectively. Figure 15.1 shows the relationship between the HTTP and IPP interfaces.

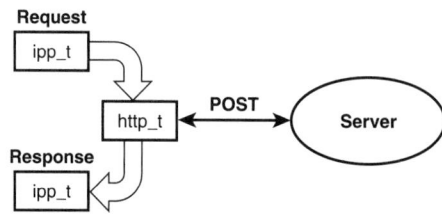

FIGURE 15.1

IPP data flow over HTTP connections.

To send an IPP request to a server, an application first builds the request in the `ipp_t` object. It then opens a connection to the server, which is managed by the `http_t` object. The IPP request is then sent to the server with an HTTP POST operation, with the response returned and stored in the second `ipp_t` object.

HTTP Functions

CUPS provides many functions for managing HTTP connections with a server. Most of these functions deal with the `http_t` structure, which manages an HTTP "object" or connection with a server. A new HTTP object must be created for every server with which you communicate. Table 15.1 lists the HTTP functions.

TABLE 15.1   The CUPS HTTP Functions

Name	Description
httpBlocking()	Sets blocking or non-blocking operation on the connection
httpCheck()	Checks for data coming from the server
httpClearFields()	Clears the HTTP field values
httpClose()	Disconnects from the server and deletes the HTTP object
httpConnect()	Creates an HTTP object and connects to the named server
httpConnectEncrypt()	Creates an HTTP object and connects using the specified encryption method
httpDecode64()	Converts a string from Base64 encoding
httpDelete()	Sends a DELETE request to the server
httpEncode64()	Converts a string to Base64 encoding
httpEncryption()	Sets the encryption mode of the connection
httpError()	Returns a text string for the current error
httpFlush()	Clears any remaining data from the server
httpGet()	Sends a GET request to the server
httpGetDateString()	Returns an HTTP date/time string from a Unix time value
httpGetDateTime()	Returns a Unix time value from an HTTP date/time string
httpGetField()	Gets an HTTP field value
httpGetLength()	Gets the content length from the server response
httpGetSubField()	Gets a sub-field value from a field
httpHead()	Sends a HEAD request to the server
httpInitialize()	Initializes the HTTP module
httpMD5()	Computes the MD5 sum of the username, realm, and password
httpMD5Final()	Computes the final MD5 sum containing the nonce, method, and request URI
httpMD5String()	Converts an MD5 sum to a string value

TABLE 15.1 Continued

Name	Description
httpOptions()	Sends an OPTIONS request to the server
httpPost()	Sends a POST request to the server
httpPut()	Sends a PUT request to the server
httpRead()	Reads data from the server
httpReconnect()	Reconnects to the server
httpSeparate()	Separates a URL into its component parts
httpSetField()	Sets an HTTP field value
httpStatus()	Returns a string for the current status
httpTrace()	Sends a TRACE request to the server
httpUpdate()	Updates the current state of the connection based on data from the server
httpWrite()	Writes data to the server

Creating an HTTP Object

Before you can perform HTTP operations, you must first create an HTTP object. CUPS provides two functions to do this.

The first is httpConnect(), which connects to an HTTP server without encryption and returns a new HTTP object if the connection could be made, or NULL if the server did not respond:

```
http_t *http;
...
http = httpConnect("hostname", port);
```

The hostname argument is the name of the server with which you want to connect; this name can also be the IP address in dotted notation, such as 127.0.0.1. The port argument is the port number to use; for IPP, the port number is usually 631.

The second function is httpConnectEncrypt(), which connects to an HTTP server using the specified level of encryption:

```
http_t *http;
...
http = httpConnectEncrypt("hostname", port, encryption);
```

The encryption parameter is an enumeration that specifies whether to use encryption initially or allow an upgrade at the server's request. Table 15.2 lists the available values.

TABLE 15.2   Encryption Enumeration Values for `httpConnectEncrypt()`

Name	Description
HTTP_ENCRYPT_IF_REQUESTED	Encrypt if the server asks for it.
HTTP_ENCRYPT_NEVER	Never encrypt, even if the server asks for it.
HTTP_ENCRYPT_REQUIRED	Encrypt after the connection is established using the HTTP Upgrade TLS protocols.
HTTP_ENCRYPT_ALWAYS	Encrypt after the connection is established using the SSL protocol.

You can also set the encryption mode after you have created the HTTP object with the `httpEncryption()` function:

```
http_t *http;
...
http = httpConnect("hostname", port);
...
httpEncryption(http, HTTP_ENCRYPT_REQUIRED);
```

NOTE:

If you switch to the HTTP_ENCRYPT_ALWAYS mode, the HTTP object must reconnect to the server and then initiate encryption. For this reason, it is often better to use `httpConnectEncrypt()` to avoid the extra startup time caused by the connect-disconnect–connect-encrypt process.

Destroying a HTTP Object

After you have performed all of the HTTP or IPP requests you need with an HTTP object, you can disconnect from the server and destroy the object using the `httpClose()` function:

```
http_t *http;
...
httpClose(http);
```

Sending an HTTP Request

After you have created your HTTP object, you can send a variety of HTTP requests using the CUPS API functions. CUPS provides seven functions for each of the standard HTTP request methods. Table 15.3 lists the HTTP methods and the corresponding CUPS functions.

TABLE 15.3   CUPS Functions for Each HTTP Method

HTTP Method	CUPS Function
DELETE	httpDelete()
GET	httpGet()
HEAD	httpHead()
OPTIONS	httpOptions()
POST	httpPost()
PUT	httpPut()
TRACE	httpTrace()

All of these functions take an HTTP object pointer and the resource name for the request line. For example, to GET the home page on the server, you would use:

```
http_t *http;
...
httpGet(http, "/");
```

The HTTP request sent to the server would look like this:

```
GET / HTTP/1.1 CR LF
Host: hostname CR LF
CR LF
```

Obtaining the Server Response

After you have sent the request, use the httpUpdate() function to update the current state until you get something other than an HTTP_CONTINUE status:

```
http_t      *http;
http_state_t status;
...
httpGet(http, "/");
while ((status = httpUpdate(http)) != HTTP_CONTINUE);
```

The status variable is an enumeration of all the standard HTTP status codes. Code 100 (HTTP_CONTINUE) is returned until a final request status is received from the server.

Reading Data from the Server

After you have received the status code from the server, you can read the response data using the httpRead() function:

```
http_t *http;
int    bytes;
char   buffer[1024];
```

```
...
while ((bytes = httpRead(http, buffer, sizeof(buffer) - 1) > 0)
{
  buffer[bytes] = '\0';
  fputs(buffer, stdout);
}
```

The first argument is the HTTP object pointer. This is followed by the pointer to the buffer for the data and the size of the buffer, respectively.

The HTTP object keeps track of the content length or chunking of the response and will return 0 when you have read all of the data.

Setting HTTP Request Fields

Some requests require additional information to be properly handled. For example, a POST operation requires Content-Type and Content-Length or Transfer-Encoding parameters to tell the server the format and length of the request data.

The httpSetField() function sets a field value that will be sent to the server. Typically, you will also call the httpClearFields() function first to initialize all fields to the empty string:

```
http_t *http;
...
httpClearFields(http);
httpSetField(http, field, "value");
httpPost(http, "resource");
```

The field argument is an enumeration representing the field name. Table 15.4 lists the supported fields and the enumeration name. The value argument is the string value for the field.

TABLE 15.4   HTTP Field Value Names

CUPS Name	HTTP Name
HTTP_FIELD_ACCEPT_LANGUAGE	Accept-Language
HTTP_FIELD_ACCEPT_RANGES	Accept-Ranges
HTTP_FIELD_AUTHORIZATION	Authorization
HTTP_FIELD_CONNECTION	Connection
HTTP_FIELD_CONTENT_ENCODING	Content-Encoding
HTTP_FIELD_CONTENT_LANGUAGE	Content-Language
HTTP_FIELD_CONTENT_LENGTH	Content-Length
HTTP_FIELD_CONTENT_LOCATION	Content-Location

TABLE 15.4 Continued

CUPS Name	HTTP Name
HTTP_FIELD_CONTENT_MD5	Content-MD5
HTTP_FIELD_CONTENT_RANGE	Content-Range
HTTP_FIELD_CONTENT_TYPE	Content-Type
HTTP_FIELD_CONTENT_VERSION	Content-Version
HTTP_FIELD_DATE	Date
HTTP_FIELD_HOST	Host
HTTP_FIELD_IF_MODIFIED_SINCE	If-Modified-Since
HTTP_FIELD_IF_UNMODIFIED_SINCE	If-Unmodified-Since
HTTP_FIELD_KEEP_ALIVE	Keep-Alive
HTTP_FIELD_LAST_MODIFIED	Last-Modified
HTTP_FIELD_LINK	Link
HTTP_FIELD_LOCATION	Location
HTTP_FIELD_RANGE	Range
HTTP_FIELD_REFERER	Referer
HTTP_FIELD_RETRY_AFTER	Retry-After
HTTP_FIELD_TRANSFER_ENCODING	Transfer-Encoding
HTTP_FIELD_UPGRADE	Upgrade
HTTP_FIELD_USER_AGENT	User-Agent
HTTP_FIELD_WWW_AUTHENTICATE	WWW-Authenticate

Obtaining HTTP Request Fields

After you have submitted an HTTP request and received a response from the server, the HTTP object will contain the request fields from the response. You can access these fields using the httpGetField() function:

```
http_t        *http;
http_status_t status;
...
httpGet(http, "resource");
while ((status = httpUpdate(http)) == HTTP_CONTINUE);
printf("Content-Type is %s\n",
      httpGetField(http, HTTP_FIELD_CONTENT_TYPE));
printf("Content-Length is %s\n",
      httpGetField(http, HTTP_FIELD_CONTENT_LENGTH));
```

The return value is always a non–NULL string; the string will be empty for fields that are not specified by the server.

Some fields, such as the WWW-Authenticate field, can contain sub-values. For example, a server might return the following:

```
WWW-Authenticate: Basic realm="Foobar"
```

To access the "realm" sub-field, call httpGetSubField() with the HTTP_FIELD_WWW_AUTHENTICATE field enumeration and the "realm" sub-field name:

```
realm = httpGetSubField(http, HTTP_WWW_AUTHENTICATE, "realm");
```

Writing Data to the Server

After sending a POST or PUT request, you'll need to write data to the server using the httpWrite() function:

```
http_t *http;
...
httpPost(http, "resource");
httpWrite(http, buffer, length);
```

The first argument is a pointer to the HTTP object. After the HTTP object are the pointer to the data buffer and the length of the data in bytes.

Unlike the write() or send() functions, httpWrite() sends fragments as necessary until the entire buffer is written to the server. httpWrite() also handles chunking of data if you set the Transfer-Encoding field to "chunked" before sending your request:

```
http_t *http;
...
httpSetField(http, HTTP_FIELD_TRANSFER_ENCODING, "chunked");
httpPost(http, "resource");
httpWrite(http, buffer, 123);
httpWrite(http, buffer, 456);
httpWrite(http, buffer, 0);
```

This example sends two chunks of data, 123 and 456 bytes each, followed by a 0-length chunk. The 0-length chunk instructs the server that the client has sent all data.

NOTE:

You must set the Content-Length (HTTP_FIELD_CONTENT_LENGTH) or Transfer-Encoding (HTTP_FIELD_TRANSFER_ENCODING) fields to indicate the amount of data to be sent to the server.

The Content-Length field contains the total number of bytes that will be sent. Use this field when you know the total size of the data before sending the request.

The Transfer-Encoding field can be set to "chunked" to tell the server that you will be sending chunks of data. Use this field when you don't know the total size of the data before sending the request.

When sending chunked data, a zero-length httpWrite() is mandatory. When sending data with a Content-Length, a zero-length httpWrite() is optional.

Handling Errors

When errors occur, your program will get either an HTTP_ERROR status from httpUpdate() or an error code from the server.

Use the httpError() function to check the error condition that the HTTP_ERROR status reports. The error number is a system error code, so you can use the strerror() function to retrieve a text message for the error:

```
http_t          *http;
http_status_t status;
...
while ((status = httpUpdate(http)) == HTTP_CONTINUE);
...
if (status == HTTP_ERROR)
{
  printf("The following system error occurred:\n\t%s\n",
        strerror(httpError(http)));
}
```

For HTTP status codes, use the httpStatus() function to retrieve the standard message for that status:

```
http_t          *http;
http_status_t status;
...
while ((status = httpUpdate(http)) == HTTP_CONTINUE);
...
if (status != HTTP_OK && status != HTTP_ERROR)
{
  printf("The following HTTP error occurred:\n\t%s\n",
        httpStatus(status));
}
```

Handling Authentication

When the server returns a 401-status code (HTTP_UNAUTHORIZED), your program should ask the user for a username and password and then resubmit your request with the authentication information.

For Basic authentication, the username and password are formatted as "username:password" and then base-64 encoded. You can use the `httpEncode64()` function to generate the necessary authentication information for the server:

```
http_t         *http;
http_status_t  status;
char           username[33];
char           *password;
char           userpass[66];
char           encoded[255];
...
httpGet(http, "/");
while ((status = httpUpdate(http)) == HTTP_CONTINUE);
if (status == HTTP_UNAUTHORIZED)
{
  printf("Username: ");
  gets(username);
  password = getpass("Password: ");
  sprintf(userpass, "%s:%s", username, password);
  strcpy(encoded, "Basic ");
  httpEncode64(encoded + 6, userpass);

  httpFlush(http);
  httpClearFields(http);
  httpSetField(http, HTTP_FIELD_AUTHORIZATION, encoded);
  httpGet(http, "/");
  while ((status = httpUpdate(http)) == HTTP_CONTINUE);
}
```

You ask for a username and password when you get an HTTP_UNAUTHORIZED status from `httpUpdate()`. After you have the username and password, use `sprintf()` to combine the two strings and `httpEncode64()` to convert the combined string into a base-64 encoded string for authentication. The output string is the first argument followed by the input string, just like `strcpy()`.

For Digest authentication, the password is not passed "in the clear." Instead, the username, password, realm, and other information are combined and an MD5 sum of the string is computed. The MD5 sum is then sent to the server along with other supporting fields.

The `httpMD5()` and `httpMD5Final()` functions are used to do most types of Digest authentication. To compute the MD5 sum, you first retrieve the "realm" and "nonce" sub-fields from the WWW-Authenticate field:

```
http_t *http;
char    nonce[256];
char    realm[256];
```

```
...
httpGetSubField(http, HTTP_FIELD_WWW_AUTHENTICATE, "realm", realm);
httpGetSubField(http, HTTP_FIELD_WWW_AUTHENTICATE, "nonce", nonce);
```

Next, we call the httpMD5() function to compute the initial password sum:

```
char username[33];
char *password;
char encoded[33];
...
httpMD5(cupsUser(), realm, password, encoded);
```

Then we combine the password sum with the "nonce" value, request method, and resource path using the httpMD5Final() function:

```
char resource[HTTP_MAX_URI];
...
httpMD5Final(nonce, "POST", resource, encoded);
```

The resulting string in the encoded variable is the MD5 response string that will be passed to the server. This authentication string also needs the username, "realm", and "nonce" values to validate the authentication:

```
char authstring[256];
...
snprintf(authstring, sizeof(authstring),
        "Digest username=\"%s\", realm=\"%s\", nonce=\"%s\", "
        "response=\"%s\"", username, realm, nonce, encoded);
```

To handle both Basic and Digest authentication, just check the first word of the WWW-Authenticate field using strncmp():

```
if (strncmp(httpGetField(http, HTTP_FIELD_WWW_AUTHENTICATE),
            "Basic", 5) == 0)
{
  /* Do Basic authentication */
  ...
}
else
{
  /* Do Digest authentication */
  ...
}
```

Upgrading to Encryption

When the server returns a 426–status code (HTTP_UPGRADE_REQUIRED), your program should switch to encrypted communications. The easiest way to do this is to use the httpEncryption() function described earlier:

```
http_t *http;
http_status_t status;
...
httpGet(http, "/");
while ((status = httpUpdate(http)) == HTTP_CONTINUE);
if (status == HTTP_UPGRADE_REQUIRED)
{
  httpFlush(http);
  httpEncryption(http, HTTP_ENCRYPT_REQUIRED);
  httpClearFields(http);
  httpSetField(http, HTTP_FIELD_AUTHORIZATION, encoded);
  httpGet(http, "/");
  while ((status = httpUpdate(http)) == HTTP_CONTINUE);
}
```

The httpFlush() function is described in a later section.

Handling Proxy Servers

Normally, CUPS sets the Host field to the name of the server associated with the HTTP object. This is fine if you are communicating directly with the server, but if you are using a proxy server, you'll need to set the Host field to the name of the destination server. An HTTP GET request for http://www.foo.com/ that uses a proxy server bar.com would look something like this:

```
GET http://www.foo.com/ HTTP/1.1 CR LF
Host: www.foo.com CR LF
CR LF
```

To do this with the CUPS HTTP functions, use the following:

```
http_t        *http;
http_status_t status;
...
http = httpConnect("bar.com", 80);
...
httpClearFields(http);
httpSetField(http, HTTP_FIELD_HOST, "www.foo.com");
httpGet(http, "http://www.foo.com/");
while ((status = httpUpdate(http)) == HTTP_CONTINUE);
```

The `httpUpdate()` function handles any messages from intermediate proxy servers for you automatically.

Other Useful Functions

Aside from handling the low-level protocol issues, CUPS provides some HTTP convenience functions as well. The first is `httpSeparate()`, which separates a URL into its components:

```
char  url[HTTP_MAX_URI];
char  scheme[HTTP_MAX_URI];
char  userpass[HTTP_MAX_URI];
char  server[HTTP_MAX_URI];
int   port;
char  resource[HTTP_MAX_URI];
...
httpSeparate(url, scheme, userpass, server, &port, resource);
```

The first argument is the URL string to separate. This is followed by the `scheme` (http), `userpass` (username:password), and `server` (hostname) string buffers, a pointer to a `port` number integer (80), and finally, the `resource` string (/).

The input URL is unchanged by `httpSeparate()`. Each of the other string buffers must be at least `HTTP_MAX_URI` characters in length to avoid potential buffer overflows.

Newer versions of CUPS add an `httpSeparateLen()` function, which enables you to specify the sizes of the string buffers. Each output string is followed by the size of the buffer; one `nul` character is reserved from this buffer to ensure that the strings are `nul`-terminated:

```
httpSeparateLen(url, scheme, sizeof(scheme), userpass, sizeof(userpass),
                server, sizeof(server), &port, resource, sizeof(resource));
```

NOTE:

The `httpSeparate()` function is obsolete in CUPS 1.2 and will be removed in a future release of CUPS.

Another useful function is `httpFlush()`. It reads all pending data from a server and is especially useful for flushing the text of error messages from the server:

```
http_t *http;
...
httpFlush(http);
```

Implementing a Simple Web Browser

Now that you have explored the HTTP functions, you have enough information to implement a simple text-based Web browser using them. You will start by using `httpSeparate()` to get the hostname, port, and resource name for the page:

```
char  scheme[HTTP_MAX_URI];
char  userpass[HTTP_MAX_URI];
char  server[HTTP_MAX_URI];
int   port;
char  resource[HTTP_MAX_URI];
...
httpSeparate(argv[1], scheme, userpass, server, &port, resource);
```

Next, connect to the server using `httpConnectEncrypt()`:

```
http_t *http;
...
if ((http = httpConnectEncrypt(server, port, encryption)) == NULL)
...
```

Then send a GET request to the server using `httpGet()`:

```
http_status_t status;
...
httpGet(http, resource);
while ((status = httpUpdate(http)) == HTTP_CONTINUE);
```

If the status is HTTP_UNAUTHORIZED, ask for a username and password. If it is HTTP_UPGRADE_REQUIRED, upgrade to TLS encryption.

Finally, read the response from the server and send it to the standard output:

```
char  buffer[1024];
int   bytes;
...
while ((bytes = httpRead(http, buffer, sizeof(buffer) - 1)) > 0)
{
  buffer[bytes] = '\0';
  fputs(buffer, stdout);
}
```

This is perhaps not the best way of viewing a Web page, but it demonstrates the process. Listing 15.1 shows the source for the browse program. After compiling the program, run it with a URL on the command line:

```
./browse http://localhost:631 ENTER
<HTML>
...
</HTML>
```

LISTING 15.1   The browse.c Source File

```c
/* Include CUPS header files */
#include <cups/cups.h>


/*
 * 'main()' - Get and display a Web page.
 */

int                     /* O - Exit status */
main(int  argc,         /* I - Number of command-line arguments */
     char *argv[]) /* I - Command-line arguments */
{
  http_t            *http;
  http_status_t     status;
  char              scheme[HTTP_MAX_URI];
  char              userpass[HTTP_MAX_URI];
  char              server[HTTP_MAX_URI];
  int               port;
  char              resource[HTTP_MAX_URI];
  http_encryption_t encryption;
  char              username[33];
  char              *password;
  char              encoded[255];
  int               bytes;
  char              buffer[1024];


  /* Check the command line. */
  if (argc != 2)
  {
    puts("Usage: browse <URL>");
    return (1);
  }

  /* Separate the URL into its components. */
  httpSeparate(argv[1], scheme, userpass, server, &port, resource);
```

LISTING 15.1   Continued

```c
/* Determine if we need to use SSL. */
if (strcmp(scheme, "https") == 0)
  encryption = HTTP_ENCRYPT_ALWAYS;
else
  encryption = HTTP_ENCRYPT_IF_REQUESTED;

/* Connect to the server. */
if ((http = httpConnectEncrypt(server, port, encryption)) == NULL)
{
  perror(server);
  return (1);
}

/* Encode the userpass string. */
if (userpass[0])
{
  strcpy(encoded, "Basic ");
  httpEncode64(encoded + 6, userpass);
}
else
  encoded[0] = '\0';

/* Send a GET request, retrying as necessary... */
do
{
  /* Set HTTP fields and send the request. */
  httpClearFields(http);
  httpSetField(http, HTTP_FIELD_AUTHORIZATION, encoded);
  httpGet(http, resource);

  /* Wait for a response from the server. */
  while ((status = httpUpdate(http)) == HTTP_CONTINUE);

  /* Do authentication or encryption as needed. */
  if (status == HTTP_UNAUTHORIZED)
  {
    /* Get the username and password. */
    printf("Username: ");
    if (gets(username) == NULL)
      break;

    if ((password = getpass("Password: ")) == NULL)
```

LISTING 15.1   Continued

```c
      break;

    /* Encode the username and password */
    sprintf(userpass, "%s:%s", username, password);
    strcpy(encoded, "Basic ");
    httpEncode64(encoded + 6, userpass);

    /* Flush the error message. */
    httpFlush(http);
  }
  else if (status == HTTP_UPGRADE_REQUIRED)
  {
    /* Flush the error message. */
    httpFlush(http);

    /* Upgrade to encryption */
    httpEncryption(http, HTTP_ENCRYPT_REQUIRED);
  }
}
while (status == HTTP_UPGRADE_REQUIRED ||
       status == HTTP_UNAUTHORIZED);

/* Now display the system error or data from the server. */
if (status == HTTP_ERROR)
{
  printf("A system error occurred:\n\t%s\n",
         strerror(httpError(http)));
}
else
{
  while ((bytes = httpRead(http, buffer, sizeof(buffer) - 1)) > 0)
  {
    buffer[bytes] = '\0';
    fputs(buffer, stdout);
  }
}

/* Close the server connection and delete the HTTP object. */
httpClose(http);

/* Return with no error */
return (0);
}
```

IPP Functions

The CUPS IPP interface is simpler than the HTTP interface. The CUPS IPP interface doesn't have to deal with as many states or special protocol issues, such as authentication.

The IPP Object Structure

Each IPP request or response is represented by the `ipp_t` "object" structure, which contains the IPP header and a linked list of attributes. Table 15.5 shows the members of the `ipp_t` structure.

TABLE 15.5   The `ipp_t` Structure

Name	Type	Description
state	ipp_state_t	The current state of the IPP object
request	ipp_request_t	The IPP request or response header
attrs	ipp_attribute_t *	The first attribute in the object
last	ipp_attribute_t *	The last attribute in the object
current	ipp_attribute_t *	The current attribute in the object
curtag	ipp_tag_t	The current group tag

The IPP Object State

The `state` member provides the current state of the object and is used when reading and writing the object. Table 15.6 lists the states.

TABLE 15.6   IPP Object States

Name	Description
IPP_ERROR	An error occurred.
IPP_IDLE	Nothing is happening or request completed.
IPP_HEADER	The request header needs to be sent or received.
IPP_ATTRIBUTE	One or more attributes need to be sent or received.
IPP_DATA	All attributes have been sent or received. IPP request data follows.

Normally, an application will look for the `IPP_ERROR` or `IPP_DATA` states, which indicate that all IPP data has been sent or received. The application then sends or receives any remaining data, such as a file for printing.

The Request and Response Header

Each IPP request or response starts with a 10-byte header containing the protocol version, operation or status, and request ID. This information is stored in a union of type ipp_request_t. Table 15.7 shows the request and response members of this union.

TABLE 15.7   The IPP Request Header Members

Name	Type	Description
any.version	ipp_uchar_t [2]	The protocol version number
any.request_id	int	The request ID number
op.operation_id	ipp_op_t	The operation code for the request
status.status_code	ipp_status_t	The status code for the response

The any.version member contains the IPP protocol version number. The first element of the array will always be 1. The second can be 0 or 1 depending on whether the request or response is IPP/1.0 or IPP/1.1.

The op.operation_id contains an enumeration value for the operation in a request. Table 15.8 lists the defined operation names.

TABLE 15.8   CUPS Operation Names Mapped to IPP Operations

CUPS Name	IPP Name
IPP_PRINT_JOB	Print-Job
IPP_PRINT_URI	Print-URI
IPP_VALIDATE_JOB	Validate-Job
IPP_CREATE_JOB	Create-Job
IPP_SEND_DOCUMENT	Send-Document
IPP_SEND_URI	Send-URI
IPP_CANCEL_JOB	Cancel-Job
IPP_GET_JOB_ATTRIBUTES	Get-Job-Attributes
IPP_GET_JOBS	Get-Jobs
IPP_GET_PRINTER_ATTRIBUTES	Get-Printer-Attributes
IPP_HOLD_JOB	Hold-Job
IPP_RELEASE_JOB	Release-Job
IPP_RESTART_JOB	Restart-Job
IPP_PAUSE_PRINTER	Pause-Printer
IPP_RESUME_PRINTER	Resume-Printer
IPP_PURGE_JOBS	Purge-Jobs
IPP_SET_PRINTER_ATTRIBUTES	Set-Printer-Attributes
IPP_SET_JOB_ATTRIBUTES	Set-Job-Attributes

TABLE 15.8 Continued

CUPS Name	IPP Name
IPP_GET_PRINTER_SUPPORTED_VALUES	Get-Printer-Supported-Values
IPP_CREATE_PRINTER_SUBSCRIPTION	Create-Printer-Subscription
IPP_CREATE_JOB_SUBSCRIPTION	Create-Job-Subscription
IPP_GET_SUBSCRIPTION_ATTRIBUTES	Get-Subscription-Attributes
IPP_GET_SUBSCRIPTIONS	Get-Subscriptions
IPP_RENEW_SUBSCRIPTION	Renew-Subscription
IPP_CANCEL_SUBSCRIPTION	Cancel-Subscription
IPP_GET_NOTIFICATIONS	Get-Notifications
IPP_SEND_NOTIFICATIONS	Send-Notifications
IPP_GET_PRINT_SUPPORT_FILES	Get-Printer-Support-Files
IPP_ENABLE_PRINTER	Enable-Printer
IPP_DISABLE_PRINTER	Disable-Printer
IPP_PAUSE_PRINTER_AFTER_CURRENT_JOB	Pause-Printer-After-Current-Job
IPP_HOLD_NEW_JOBS	Hold-New-Jobs
IPP_RELEASE_HELD_NEW_JOBS	Release-Held-New-Jobs
IPP_DEACTIVATE_PRINTER	Deactivate-Printer
IPP_ACTIVATE_PRINTER	Activate-Printer
IPP_RESTART_PRINTER	Restart-Printer
IPP_SHUTDOWN_PRINTER	Shutdown-Printer
IPP_STARTUP_PRINTER	Startup-Printer
IPP_REPROCESS_JOB	Reprocess-Job
IPP_CANCEL_CURRENT_JOB	Cancel-Current-Job
IPP_SUSPEND_CURRENT_JOB	Suspend-Current-Job
IPP_RESUME_JOB	Resume-Job
IPP_PROMOTE_JOB	Promote-Job
IPP_SCHEDULE_JOB_AFTER	Schedule-Job-After
CUPS_GET_DEFAULT	CUPS-Get-Default
CUPS_GET_PRINTERS	CUPS-Get-Printers
CUPS_ADD_PRINTER	CUPS-Add-Printer
CUPS_DELETE_PRINTER	CUPS-Delete-Printer
CUPS_GET_CLASSES	CUPS-Get-Classes
CUPS_ADD_CLASS	CUPS-Add-Class
CUPS_DELETE_CLASS	CUPS-Delete-Class
CUPS_ACCEPT_JOBS	CUPS-Accept-Jobs
CUPS_REJECT_JOBS	CUPS-Reject-Jobs
CUPS_SET_DEFAULT	CUPS-Set-Default
CUPS_GET_DEVICES	CUPS-Get-Devices

TABLE 15.8   Continued

CUPS Name	IPP Name
CUPS_GET_PPDS	CUPS-Get-PPDs
CUPS_MOVE_JOB	CUPS-Move-Job
CUPS_ADD_DEVICE	CUPS-Add-Device
CUPS_DELETE_DEVICE	CUPS-Delete-Device

The `status.status_code` member contains an enumeration value for the status in a response. Table 15.9 lists the defined status code names.

TABLE 15.9   CUPS Status Codes to IPP Status Code Names

CUPS Name	IPP Name
IPP_OK	successful-ok
IPP_OK_SUBST	successful-ok-ignored-or-substituted-attributes
IPP_OK_CONFLICT	successful-ok-conflicting-attributes
IPP_OK_IGNORED_SUBSCRIPTIONS	successful-ok-ignored-subscriptions
IPP_OK_IGNORED_NOTIFICATIONS	successful-ok-ignored-notifications
IPP_OK_TOO_MANY_EVENTS	successful-ok-too-many-events
IPP_OK_BUT_CANCEL_SUBSCRIPTION	successful-ok-but-cancel-subscription
IPP_REDIRECTION_OTHER_SITE	redirection-other-site
IPP_BAD_REQUEST	client-error-bad-request
IPP_FORBIDDEN	client-error-forbidden
IPP_NOT_AUTHENTICATED	client-error-not-authenticated
IPP_NOT_AUTHORIZED	client-error-not-authorized
IPP_NOT_POSSIBLE	client-error-not-possible
IPP_TIMEOUT	client-error-timeout
IPP_NOT_FOUND	client-error-not-found
IPP_GONE	client-error-gone
IPP_REQUEST_ENTITY	client-error-request-entity-too-large
IPP_REQUEST_VALUE	client-error-request-value-too-long
IPP_DOCUMENT_FORMAT	client-error-document-format-not-supported
IPP_ATTRIBUTES	client-error-attributes-or-values-not-supported
IPP_URI_SCHEME	client-error-uri-scheme-not-supported
IPP_CHARSET	client-error-charset-not-supported
IPP_CONFLICT	client-error-conflicting-attributes
IPP_COMPRESSION_NOT_SUPPORTED	client-error-compression-not-usupported
IPP_COMPRESSION_ERROR	client-error-compression-error
IPP_DOCUMENT_FORMAT_ERROR	client-error-document-format-error

TABLE 15.9   Continued

CUPS Name	IPP Name
IPP_DOCUMENT_ACCESS_ERROR	client-error-document-access-uerror
IPP_ATTRIBUTES_NOT_SETTABLE	client-error-attributes-not-settable
IPP_IGNORED_ALL_SUBSCRIPTIONS	client-error-ignored-all-subscriptions
IPP_TOO_MANY_SUBSCRIPTIONS	client-error-too-many-subscriptions
IPP_IGNORED_ALL_NOTIFICATIONS	client-error-ignored-all-notifications
IPP_PRINT_SUPPORT_FILE_NOT_FOUND	client-error-print-support-file-not-found
IPP_INTERNAL_ERROR	server-error-internal-error
IPP_OPERATION_NOT_SUPPORTED	server-error-operation-not-supported
IPP_SERVICE_UNAVAILABLE	server-error-service-unavailable
IPP_VERSION_NOT_SUPPORTED	server-error-version-not-supported
IPP_DEVICE_ERROR	server-error-device-error
IPP_TEMPORARY_ERROR	server-error-temporary-error
IPP_NOT_ACCEPTING	server-error-not-accepting-jobs
IPP_PRINTER_BUSY	server-error-busy
IPP_ERROR_JOB_CANCELLED	server-error-job-canceled
IPP_MULTIPLE_JOBS_NOT_SUPPORTED	server-error-multiple-document-jobs-not-supported
IPP_PRINTER_IS_DEACTIVATED	server-error-printer-is-deactivated

The `any.request_id` field is the client-supplied request ID number that is returned with the response from the server.

Attribute Data

The `attrs`, `last`, and `current` members point to attributes in the IPP object. The `attrs` member points to the first element in the list of attributes and can be used as a starting point for searches. It is often used to collect groups of attributes, such as when showing a list of print jobs.

The `last` member points to the last element in the list of attributes and is used by the "add" functions when adding an attribute to the IPP object. Most programs shouldn't touch this member.

The `current` member specifies the current attribute in the object. It is used when writing attributes with `ippWrite()` or finding attributes using `ippFindAttribute()` and `ippFindNextAttribute()`.

Each attribute is stored in an `ipp_attribute_t` structure and consists of the value and group tags for the attribute, the name of the attribute, the number of values, and an array of values. Table 15.10 shows the members of the `ipp_attribute_t` structure.

TABLE 15.10   The IPP Attribute Structure

Name	Type	Description
group_tag	ipp_tag_t	The group tag for the attribute
value_tag	ipp_tag_t	The value tag for the attribute
name	char *	The name of the attribute
num_values	int	The number of values in the attribute
values	ipp_value_t []	The values in the attribute

The group_tag member is an enumeration representing the IPP group tag. Table 15.11 lists the valid values.

TABLE 15.11   IPP Group Tags and Their CUPS Enumeration Names

CUPS Name	IPP Name
IPP_TAG_OPERATION	operation-attributes-tag
IPP_TAG_JOB	job-attributes-tag
IPP_TAG_END	end-of-attributes-tag
IPP_TAG_PRINTER	printer-attributes-tag
IPP_TAG_UNSUPPORTED_GROUP	unsupported-attributes-tag
IPP_TAG_SUBSCRIPTION	subscription-attributes-tag
IPP_TAG_EVENT_NOTIFICATION	event-notification-attributes-tag

The value_tag member is an enumeration representing the IPP value tag. Table 15.12 lists the valid values.

TABLE 15.12   IPP Value Tags and Their CUPS Enumeration Names

CUPS Name	IPP Name
IPP_TAG_UNSUPPORTED_VALUE	unsupported
IPP_TAG_DEFAULT	default
IPP_TAG_UNKNOWN	unknown
IPP_TAG_NOVALUE	no-value
IPP_TAG_NOTSETTABLE	not-settable
IPP_TAG_DELETEATTR	delete-attribute
IPP_TAG_ADMINDEFINE	admin-define
IPP_TAG_INTEGER	integer
IPP_TAG_BOOLEAN	boolean
IPP_TAG_ENUM	enum
IPP_TAG_STRING	octetString

TABLE 15.12   Continued

CUPS Name	IPP Name
IPP_TAG_DATE	dateTime
IPP_TAG_RESOLUTION	resolution
IPP_TAG_RANGE	rangeOfInteger
IPP_TAG_BEGIN_COLLECTION	begCollection
IPP_TAG_TEXTLANG	textWithLanguage
IPP_TAG_NAMELANG	nameWithLanguage
IPP_TAG_END_COLLECTION	endCollection
IPP_TAG_TEXT	textWithoutLanguage
IPP_TAG_NAME	nameWithoutLanguage
IPP_TAG_KEYWORD	keyword
IPP_TAG_URI	uri
IPP_TAG_URISCHEME	uriScheme
IPP_TAG_CHARSET	charset
IPP_TAG_LANGUAGE	naturalLanguage
IPP_TAG_MIMETYPE	mimeMediaType
IPP_TAG_MEMBERNAME	memberAttrName

Each value is stored in a union type called `ipp_value_t`. Table 15.13 shows the members of the `ipp_value_t` union.

TABLE 15.13   IPP Value Members

Name	Type	Description
integer	int	The integer or enum value
boolean	char	The boolean value
date	ipp_uchar_t [11]	The dateTime value
resolution.xres	int	The horizontal resolution value
resolution.yres	int	The vertical resolution value
resolution.units	ipp_res_t	The resolution units
range.lower	int	The lower value for a rangeOfInteger attribute
range.upper	int	The upper value for a rangeOfInteger attribute
string.charset	char *	The charset value for a textWithLanguage or nameWithLanguage attribute
string.text	char *	The string value for any string attribute
collection.attrs	ipp_t *	The IPP object for a collection attribute

The `resolution.units` member is an enumeration specifying the resolution in dots per inch (`IPP_RES_PER_INCH`) or centimeters (`IPP_RES_PER_CM`).

Creating an IPP Object

IPP objects are used to send requests and receive responses. Use the `ippNew()` function to create an IPP object:

```
ipp_t *ipp;
...
ipp = ippNew();
```

The return value is a new pointer to an `ipp_t` structure or `NULL` if the memory for creating the object was low.

Deleting an IPP Object

After you are finished with an IPP object, use the `ippDelete()` function to destroy it:

```
ipp_t *ipp;
...
ippDelete(ipp);
```

The `ippDelete()` function does not return a value.

Adding a Value to an IPP Object

CUPS provides several functions to add values to an IPP object. Table 15.14 lists these functions.

TABLE 15.14   CUPS Functions for Adding IPP Attributes

Name	Description
ippAddBoolean()	Adds a single boolean value
ippAddBooleans()	Adds one or more boolean values
ippAddCollection()	Adds a single collection value
ippAddCollections()	Adds one or more collection values
ippAddDate()	Adds a single dateTime value
ippAddInteger()	Adds a single integer or enum value
ippAddIntegers()	Adds one or more integer or enum values
ippAddRange()	Adds a single rangeOfInteger value
ippAddRanges()	Adds one or more rangeOfInteger values
ippAddResolution()	Adds a single resolution value
ippAddResolutions()	Adds one or more resolution values
ippAddString()	Adds a single string value
ippAddStrings()	Adds one or more string values

The `ippAddBoolean()` function adds a single boolean value to the IPP object:

```
ipp_t *ipp;
...
ippAddBoolean(ipp, group, "name", value);
```

The `ipp` argument is the IPP object pointer. The `group` argument is the group tag enumeration. The `name` string is the attribute name. The `value` argument is the boolean value, which is 0 for `false` and 1 for `true`.

The `ippAddBooleans()` function adds one or more boolean values to the IPP object:

```
ipp_t *ipp;
char   values[10];
...
ippAddBooleans(ipp, group, "name", num_values, values);
```

The `num_values` argument specifies the number of values in the set, whereas the `values` argument is a pointer to the values.

Integer and enum values are added using the `ippAddInteger()` and `ippAddIntegers()` functions. Unlike the boolean value functions, you must also specify the value tag enumeration:

```
ipp_t *ipp;
int    values[10];
...
ippAddInteger(ipp, group, value_tag, "name", value);
ippAddBooleans(ipp, group, value_tag, "name", num_values, values);
```

The `value_tag` argument can be `IPP_TAG_INTEGER` or `IPP_TAG_ENUM`.

String values can have an associated character set; therefore, the `ippAddString()` and `ippAddStrings()` functions also include a character set parameter:

```
ipp_t *ipp;
char   *values[10];
...
ippAddString(ipp, group, value_tag, "name", charset, value);
ippAddStrings(ipp, group, value_tag, "name", num_values, charset, values);
```

The `value_tag` argument can be any string enumeration value. The `charset` argument is the character set to use for the value(s). For the `IPP_TAG_TEXTLANG` and `IPP_TAG_NAMELANG` value tags, the charset will be a string, such as "utf-8". For all other value tags, the `charset` must be a `NULL` pointer. When more than one string is added, all strings share the same charset value.

NOTE:

CUPS currently requires that all `textWithLanguage` and `nameWithLanguage` values use the same character set. This prevents `1setOf` arrays of these values with different encodings; in practice, this is not an issue.

Resolution values are added using the `ippAddResolution()` and `ippAddResolutions()` functions:

```
ipp_t *ipp;
int    xreses[10];
int    yreses[10];
...
ippAddResolution(ipp, group, "name", units, xres, yres);
ippAddResolutions(ipp, group, "name", num_values, units, xreses, yreses);
```

The `units` argument specifies the unit of measurement for all resolutions and can be the `IPP_RES_PER_INCH` or `IPP_RES_PER_CM` enumerations. The `xres` and `yres` arguments specify the horizontal and vertical resolution. The `xreses` and `yreses` arguments specify the arrays for multiple resolutions.

NOTE:

CUPS currently requires that all resolution values use the same units. This prevents `1setOf` arrays of these values with different units; in practice, this is not an issue.

Range values are added using the `ippAddRange()` and `ippAddRanges()` functions:

```
ipp_t *ipp;
int    lowers[10];
int    uppers[10];
...
ippAddRange(ipp, group, "name", lower, upper);
ippAddResolutions(ipp, group, "name", num_values, lowers, uppers);
```

The `lower` and `upper` arguments specify the lower and upper bounds of the range. Similarly, the `lowers` and `uppers` arguments specify the arrays for multiple ranges.

Collection values are stored in IPP sub-objects and are added using the `ippAddCollection()` and `ippAddCollections()` functions:

```
ipp_t *ipp;
ipp_t *value;
ipp_t *values[10];
...
ippAddCollection(ipp, group, "name", value);
ippAddCollections(ipp, group, "name", num_values, values);
```

The `value` and `values` arguments are pointers to an IPP object or IPP object array that contains the attributes in each collection. Unlike normal IPP objects, collection objects do not use the `group_tag` field; the `group` you specify when adding attributes to the collection's IPP object is ignored. Collections can also contain sub-collections.

NOTE:

IPP collections can be a maximum of 32767 bytes in length. If you try to add a collection with an IPP object longer than 32767 bytes, the collection will not be added.

You can determine the size of the IPP object by calling the `ippCollectionLength()` function.

Determining the Size of an IPP Object

The transmission size of an IPP object can be computed using the `ippLength()` function:

```
ipp_t *ipp;
int    length;
...
length = ippLength(ipp);
```

The return value is the length in bytes. It includes the IPP header and any group tags to be included in the output stream.

Collection values are composed of IPP objects. Unlike normal IPP objects, sub–objects lack the IPP header and group tags; therefore, the collection IPP objects will always be smaller than a regular IPP object. Because the size difference is not constant, the `ippCollectionLength()` function is provided to compute the length of an IPP object in a collection:

```
ipp_t *ipp;
int    length;
...
length = ippCollectionLength(ipp);

if (length > 32767)
  puts("Collection value too large!");
```

The return value is the length in bytes. As noted previously, collection values cannot exceed 32767 bytes.

Finding an Attribute in an IPP Object

After you have added attributes to an IPP object, you can look them up using the `ippFindAttribute()` function:

```
ipp_t           *ipp;
ipp_attribute_t *attr;
...
attr = ippFindAttribute(ipp, "name", value_tag);
```

The `name` argument is the name of the attribute. The `value_tag` argument specifies the required type of the attribute. The special value `IPP_TAG_ZERO` can be used to find an attribute of any type that has the specified name.

If the attribute cannot be found, a `NULL` pointer is returned.

NOTE:

The IPP specification requires that clients and servers support `textWithLanguage` or `nameWithLanguage` values interchangeably with `textWithoutLanguage` and `nameWithoutLanguage` values. To make this possible with CUPS, the `IPP_TAG_TEXT` and `IPP_TAG_NAME` enumerations will match against the corresponding "WithLanguage" values `IPP_TAG_TEXTLANG` and `IPP_TAG_NAMELANG`.

A client (application) need only look at the `string.charset` member of the value to see whether the attribute is a "WithLanguage" or "WithoutLanguage" value.

The `ippFindAttribute()` function finds the first occurrence of the attribute in the IPP object. However, many IPP requests return multiple groups of attributes, each with its own copies of a named attribute. The `ippFindNextAttribute()` function is provided to more easily handle this situation:

```
ipp_t           *ipp;
ipp_attribute_t *attr;
...
for (attr = ippFindAttribute(ipp, "printer-name", IPP_TAG_NAME);
     attr != NULL;
     attr = ippFindNextAttribute(ipp, "printer-name", IPP_TAG_NAME))
  puts(attr->values[0].string.text);
```

The `ippFindNextAttribute()` function takes all of the same arguments as `ippFindAttribute()`, but instead of starting at the beginning of the attribute list, it starts where the last search left off.

Sending an IPP Request

After you have built an IPP object for a request, you write the request data to the server using the `ippWrite()` function:

```
ipp_t           *request;
ipp_state_t     state;
http_t          *http;
http_status_t   status;
```

```
...
httpSetField(http, HTTP_FIELD_TRANSFER_ENCODING, "chunked");
httpPost(http, "resource");

while ((state = ippWrite(http, request)) != IPP_ERROR)
  if (state == IPP_DATA)
  {
    httpWrite(http, "", 0);
    break;

while ((status = httpUpdate(http)) == HTTP_CONTINUE);
```

The `ippWrite()` function accepts a pointer to the HTTP object and a pointer to the IPP object that is sent to the server. The return value is the IPP object state. Normally, this state will be either `IPP_DATA` or `IPP_ERROR`. If `IPP_ERROR` is returned, a write error occurred; the error code can be found using the `httpError()` function:

```
int error = httpError(http);
```

The `IPP_DATA` state indicates that all IPP attributes have been sent and you can send any additional data, such as a print file, to the server immediately. For the preceding example, the `ippWrite()` would be followed by a series of calls to `httpWrite()` to send the print file:

```
FILE *fp;
char buffer[1024];
int  bytes;
...
while ((state = ippWrite(http, request)) != IPP_ERROR)
  if (state == IPP_DATA)
  {
    while ((bytes = fread(buffer, 1, sizeof(buffer), fp)) > 0)
      httpWrite(http, buffer, bytes);

    httpWrite(http, buffer, 0);
    break;
  }

while ((status = httpUpdate(http)) == HTTP_CONTINUE);
```

CAUTION:

If you are sending chunked output, make sure to send the final 0-length block with `httpWrite()`, as shown in the example code.

If you do not send a 0-length block or use the `Content-Length` field, the server will not know that you have finished sending data to it, and the request will not succeed.

Reading the IPP Response

After you have POSTed the IPP request to the server, you can read the response using the ippRead() function:

```
ipp_t          *response;
http_t         *http;
http_status_t status;
...
while ((status = httpUpdate(http)) == HTTP_CONTINUE);

if (status == HTTP_OK)
{
  response = ippNew();
  while ((state = ippRead(http, response)) != IPP_ERROR)
    if (state == IPP_DATA)
    {
      httpFlush(http);
      break;
    }
}
```

Like the ippWrite() function, ippRead() accepts a pointer to the HTTP object and a pointer to the IPP object that will receive the response data from the server. The return value is the IPP object state, normally IPP_ERROR or IPP_DATA.

After you are in the IPP_DATA state, flush or read any remaining data. This will ensure that all data has been read from the server, including the final 0-length chunk. In the example code, you use the httpFlush() function to accomplish this.

Automating IPP Requests

The CUPS API provides two functions called cupsDoRequest() and cupsDoFileRequest() that automate the IPP request sending- and response-gathering process:

```
ipp_t  *request;
ipp_t  *response;
http_t *http;
...
response = cupsDoRequest(http, request, "resource");
...
response = cupsDoFileRequest(http, request, "resource", "filename");
```

Both functions accept a pointer to an HTTP object, a pointer to an IPP request object, and the resource string that is used in the POST request. The IPP request object is destroyed by both functions after the request is successfully sent.

The `cupsDoFileRequest()` also accepts a `filename` string to specify a file to send to the server after the IPP data.

Both functions return a pointer to the IPP object holding the response from the server. If an error occurs, `NULL` is returned and the IPP error code can be found by calling the `cupsLastError()` function.

One advantage of using these functions over your own code is that common errors, such as missing the 0-length block handling code, are avoided. These functions also support authentication using the password callback mechanism described in Chapter 14. This allows your application to fully utilize all authentication, encryption, and error-checking mechanisms without duplicating code.

Building a Real IPP Request

Now that you know the basics, you will write a new program that sends a `CUPS-Get-Printers` request to list all of the available printers on the server. To begin, create the IPP request object:

```
ipp_t *request;
...
request = ippNew();
```

Next, add the required attributes for the request; for `CUPS-Get-Printers`, you must send `attributes-charset` and `attributes-natural-language` attributes:

```
ippAddString(request, IPP_TAG_OPERATION, IPP_TAG_CHARSET,
             "attributes-charset", NULL, "utf-8");
ippAddString(request, IPP_TAG_OPERATION, IPP_TAG_LANGUAGE,
             "attributes-natural-language", NULL, "en");
```

Then initialize the IPP request header by setting the `request.op.operation_id` and `request.any.request_id` fields to `CUPS_GET_PRINTERS` and 1, respectively:

```
request->request.op.operation_id = CUPS_GET_PRINTERS;
request->request.any.request_id  = 1;
```

Finally, send the request using `cupsDoRequest()`:

```
ipp_t   *response;
http_t *http;
...
response = cupsDoRequest(http, request, "/");
```

After you have the response, you can use `ippFindAttribute()` and `ippFindNextAttribute()` to show the names of the printers:

```
ipp_attribute_t *attr;
...
```

```
for (attr = ippFindAttribute(ipp, "printer-name", IPP_TAG_NAME);
     attr != NULL;
     attr = ippFindNextAttribute(ipp, "printer-name", IPP_TAG_NAME))
  puts(attr->values[0].string.text);
```

The completed program is shown in Listing 15.2. After building the program you can run it to see something like the following:

```
./showprinters ENTER
DeskJet
LaserJet
StylusColor
StylusPhoto
```

LISTING 15.2   The showprinters.c Source File

```
/* Include the CUPS header files. */
#include <cups/cups.h>


int             /* O - Exit status */
main(void)
{
  http_t          *http;     /* HTTP object */
  ipp_t           *request;  /* IPP request object */
  ipp_t           *response; /* IPP response object */
  ipp_attribute_t *attr;     /* Current IPP attribute */


  /* Connect to the HTTP server */
  http = httpConnectEncrypt(cupsServer(), ippPort(), cupsEncryption());

  if (http == NULL)
  {
    perror("Unable to connect to server");
    return (1);
  }

  /* Assemble the IPP request */
  request = ippNew();

  ippAddString(request, IPP_TAG_OPERATION, IPP_TAG_CHARSET,
               "attributes-charset", NULL, "utf-8");
```

LISTING 15.2   Continued

```
ippAddString(request, IPP_TAG_OPERATION, IPP_TAG_LANGUAGE,
            "attributes-natural-language", NULL, "en");

request->request.op.operation_id = CUPS_GET_PRINTERS;
request->request.any.request_id  = 1;

/* Send the request and get a response. */
response = cupsDoRequest(http, request, "/");

if (response != NULL)
{
  for (attr = ippFindAttribute(response, "printer-name", IPP_TAG_NAME);
       attr != NULL;
       attr = ippFindNextAttribute(response, "printer-name", IPP_TAG_NAME))
    puts(attr->values[0].string.text);

  ippDelete(response);
}
else
  printf("Unable to get printer list: %s\n",
         ippErrorString(cupsLastError()));

/* Close the connection to the server. */
httpClose(http);
return (0);
}
```

Optimizing Your Requests

Many IPP operations support the requested-attributes attribute, which lists the attributes in which the client is interested. The IPP server can then eliminate those attributes from the response. This elimination often results in faster, more timely responses and reduces the load on the server, client, and network.

For example, the showprinters example can be made much more efficient with the addition of the requested-attributes attribute:

```
ippAddString(request, IPP_TAG_OPERATION, IPP_TAG_KEYWORD,
            "requested-attributes", NULL, "printer-name");
```

The IPP server will then try to limit the response to include only attributes named "printer-name".

NOTE:

The IPP specification does not require that servers honor the `requested-attributes` attribute. The only indication you will see that the attribute has not been honored will be in the `request.status.status_code` field. A value of `IPP_OK_SUBST` (`successful-ok-substituted-attributes`) will be returned.

Use the `requested-attributes` attribute whenever possible, but don't depend on the response containing only the attributes you requested. This will provide the best performance and will make your programs more flexible with different IPP servers.

Summary

CUPS provides a rich set of functions for managing HTTP and IPP objects. Both objects are based on a finite state machine model and maintain an internal state for all modes of operation.

HTTP objects provide an interface to Hypertext Transfer Protocol servers and can be used to manage HTTP or IPP requests. Functions are provided to easily support encryption and authentication.

IPP objects provide an interface for sending and receiving Internet Printing Protocol data via HTTP objects. Each IPP object consists of a 10-byte header followed by a linked list of attribute values.

IPP requests and responses can be easily managed using the `cupsDoRequest()` and `cupsDoFileRequest()` functions. These functions handle the HTTP POST request, any authentication or encryption that needs to be done, the sending of the IPP request and a file to the server (optional), and the receiving of the IPP response.

## CHAPTER 16

Writing File Filters
for CUPS

This chapter describes how to write a file filter for CUPS, which forms the backbone of the CUPS printing process. An example TeX DVI filter is provided, and the HP-GL/2 filter is explained.

What Are File Filters?

File filters are programs that convert files from one or more MIME types to other types. Filters use a common command-line and environment interface that enables them to be joined as needed to print files of any type and to any printer. Printer drivers, which are covered in the next chapter, are special types of filters. Figure 16.1 shows the relationship between print files, filters, printer drivers, and backends.

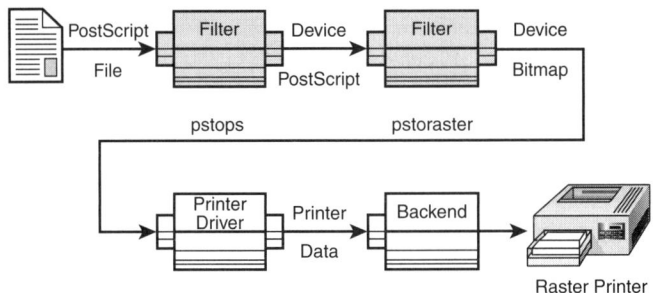

FIGURE 16.1

File filters in a print job.

CUPS provides many filters for converting common file formats into something a printer can use. Table 16.1 lists the standard filters in CUPS.

TABLE 16.1   File filters provided with CUPS

Name	Description
hpgltops	Converts HP-GL and HP-GL/2 files into PostScript
imagetops	Converts image files into PostScript
imagetoraster	Converts image files into raster images for a printer driver
pdftops	Converts PDF files into PostScript
pstops	Filters PostScript files and adds printer commands and options
pstoraster	Converts PostScript files into raster images for a printer driver
texttops	Converts text files into PostScript

The hpgltops Filter

The hpgltops filter converts HP-GL and HP-GL/2 plot files into PostScript. When the plot file contains the PS (plot size) command, the filter can either change the printed page size to match or the fitplot option can be used to scale the plot to the requested page size. If the blackplot option is used, the filter will output only black and white PostScript (no color or grayscale).

The filter uses the printer's PPD file to determine the available page sizes, the printable area and margins, and whether the printer supports color.

The output from the hpgltops filter is normally piped into the pstops filter.

NOTE:

HP-GL and HP-GL/2 are so-called *vector* file formats. Each file consists of a series of initialization commands followed by drawing commands. The drawing commands include PU (pen up), PD (pen down), SP (set pen), PA (plot absolute), and PR (plot relative). A complete reference manual for HP-GL/2 can be found on the Hewlett-Packard developers' Web site at

    http://www.hp-developer-solutions.com/

Most CAD applications produce HP-GL/2 files for printing line drawings and PostScript files for shaded images.

The imagetops Filter

The imagetops filter converts image files to PostScript. It can scale the image to its natural size (the default), or scale it to a percentage of the page size if the scaling option is used, or scale it based on a resolution you specify if the ppi option is used. Labels can be added using the page-label option or via the Classification directive in the cupsd.conf file.

The filter uses the printer's PPD file to determine the available page sizes and printable area, the language level to use, and whether to produce RGB or grayscale image data for the printer. Image data is sent as hexadecimal strings for Level 1 PostScript printers and base-85 encoded strings for Level 2 and 3 PostScript printers.

The output from the imagetops filter is normally sent directly to the backend, so all printer commands and options are included in the PostScript it produces. When a raster printer with page label or classification markings turned on is being used, the output of imagetops is piped into pstoraster for conversion to a series of raster images for the printer driver.

The imagetops filter produces page accounting data ("PAGE:" messages) when printing to a PostScript printer. If the output is going to a non-PostScript printer, then the printer driver is responsible for producing the page comments.

NOTE:

PostScript printers support one of three language levels. Level 1 printers represent the original PostScript printers such as the Apple LaserWriter. Level 2 printers are by far the most prevalent PostScript printers in use today. Level 3 printers appeared on the market late in 2000 and will likely dominate the PostScript printer market in a few years.

Each language level supports a number of different features as well as a common core language. The Adobe PostScript Language Reference Manual is required reading for anyone who wants to write a filter that produces PostScript, as is the Adobe Document Structuring Conventions specification. You can find these on-line at

```
http://partners.adobe.com/asn/developer/technotes/main.html
```

The `imagetoraster` Filter

The `imagetoraster` filter converts image files to a series of raster images. It can scale the image to its natural size (the default), or scale it to a percentage of the page size if you use the `scaling` option, or scale it based on a resolution you specify with the `ppi` option. Labels can be added using the `page-label` option or via the `Classification` directive in the `cupsd.conf` file.

The filter uses the printer's PPD file to determine the available page sizes, printable area, and the type of raster data to send to the printer driver. Color profile information in the PPD file is also used; for CUPS 1.1, the filter supports a CMY transform matrix with a lookup table to control the overall gamma and density correction of the raster data. In CUPS 1.2, the PPD file can specify ICC profiles for each resolution, color model, and media type; these profiles determine the colorspace for the raster data that is sent to the printer driver.

The output from the `imagetoraster` filter is piped into the printer driver, which converts the raster images into printed pages.

NOTE:

The `imagetops` and `imagetoraster` filters use the `cupsimage` library to read and convert image files. This library supports reading of BMP, GIF, JPEG, PhotoCD, portable anymap (PBM, PGM, PNM, PPM), PNG, SGI RGB, Sun Raster, and TIFF image files.

The `pdftops` Filter

The `pdftops` filter is based on the Xpdf software from Derek B. Noonburg and converts Adobe Portable Document Format (PDF) files into PostScript. It scales pages in the PDF document to the requested page size.

The filter uses the printer's PPD file to determine the available page sizes, printable area, and language level of the printer.

The output from the `pdftops` filter is piped into the `pstops` filter.

NOTE:

The PDF format is probably the most popular format for sharing complex documents electronically, and is quickly becoming the standard for pre-press and other printing applications. The primary reason for its popularity is its portability and open format—PDF can be used anywhere for anything.

Apple's MacOS X uses PDF as the basis of its printing architecture, and the GNOME project may use it in a future incarnation of that desktop environment. Even the final proofing for this book was done with PDF files!

Adobe maintains a public specification for the PDF format online at:

        http://partners.adobe.com/asn/developer/technotes/main.html

The PDFzone Web site is a great place to find PDF software and information as well:

        http://PDFzone.com

The `pstops` Filter

Most print files go through the `pstops` filter. This filter takes a PostScript print file, separates it into pages, and then reassembles the pages with the necessary printer commands, options, and glue to produce the desired print job.

With the `pstops` filter, you can use the `page-ranges` option to print ranges of pages, the `page-set` option to print the even or odd pages, the `page-label` option and `Classification` directive to produce page labels and classification markings, and the `number-up` option to place multiple pages on a single output page.

The filter uses the printer's PPD file to determine the available page sizes and the printable area and margins. The PPD file also provides the commands and other data that the printer needs before the job and each page.

The `pstops` filter generates accounting information ("`PAGE:`" messages) when it is outputting to a PostScript printer.

The output of the `pstops` filter is piped to the printer's backend for PostScript printers or to the `pstoraster` filter for non-PostScript printers.

NOTE:

The pstops filter depends on comments in the PostScript file to determine where each page begins and ends in the document. These comments follow a format described in the Adobe Document Structuring Conventions (DSC) specification, available online at

http://partners.adobe.com/asn/developer/technotes/main.html

If you try to print a PostScript file that does not have these comments, the pstops filter treats the file as if it has a single page. It does not support the page filtering options or page accounting.

The pstoraster Filter

The pstoraster filter converts PostScript files to raster images for printer drivers. Based on the PostScript and comments embedded in it, the filter can produce raster data for small letter-size inkjet printers and large 50" wide plotters alike. The current filter supports PostScript language levels 1 through 3.

The filter uses the printer's PPD file to determine the available page sizes, printable area, and the type of raster data to send to the printer driver. Color profile information in the PPD file is also used; for CUPS 1.1, the filter supports a CMY transform matrix with a lookup table to control the overall gamma and density correction of the raster data. In CUPS 1.2, the PPD file can specify ICC profiles for each resolution, color model, and media type; these profiles determine the colorspace for the raster data that is sent to the printer driver.

The output from the pstoraster filter is piped into the printer driver, which converts the raster images into printed pages.

NOTE:

The pstoraster filter is based on the GNU Ghostscript PostScript interpreter and graphics library. On the frontend, the pstoraster filter supports the CUPS filter interface rather than the standard Ghostscript command-line options so that Ghostscript can be used without a shell script wrapper or helper application.

On the backend the clunky printer drivers included with Ghostscript have been replaced by a single CUPS raster driver called cups. This raster driver generates raster data suitable for use with CUPS printer drivers, and enables multiple raster filters to share the same printer driver.

The pstoraster filter also includes many bug fixes to the standard GNU Ghostscript distribution. An ESP Ghostscript project was therefore started on SourceForge to maintain a single GPL'd version of Ghostscript that contains all the latest drivers, fixes, and enhancements. The project is available online at

http://espgs.sourceforge.net

This Ghostscript distribution is used by several Linux distributors and includes the patches, fixes, and drivers from them all. The distribution also includes a version of `pstoraster` that can be used with CUPS but still shares all the same library, executable, and data files from the standard Ghostscript. Using this version helps to minimize disk space requirements.

The `texttops` Filter

The `texttops` filter converts text files to PostScript. With it, you can use the `columns` option to print multiple columns of text, the `prettyprint` option to highlight keywords and print a fancy header, and the `wrap` option to wrap text. The `cpi` and `lpi` options determine the size of the text.

The filter uses the printer's PPD file to determine the available page sizes and the printable area and margins. The PPD file also provides a list of the available fonts. If the text file requires a font that is not available on the printer, the font is embedded in the document.

The `texttops` filter handles the usual overstrike methods of underlining and boldfacing with either the carriage return or backspace characters. Form feed characters eject the current page.

When you use the `prettyprint` option with text files, the filter uses the CONTENT_TYPE environment variable to determine how to highlight the syntax in the file. These rules are currently hardcoded into the filter.

The output of the `texttops` filter is piped into the `pstops` filter for further processing before it goes to the printer.

NOTE:

The `texttops` filter is designed to support a generic text engine that constructs a page of text and a language module that produces the output.

The `texttops` filter provides the PostScript language module. Later in chapter 17 you will see the text engine used to build a PCL language module for Hewlett-Packard laser printers.

The CUPS Filter Architecture

CUPS filters form the backbone of the printing system's capability to support any type of printer. The scheduler chooses filters that convert the print file into something that can be printed. Filters can be any program or script the system can execute.

Aside from the filter programs themselves, the scheduler reads MIME type and conversion files that describe the supported file types and filters on the system. The standard filters described in the preceding section are listed in the `mime.types` and `mime.convs` files. These files equip the scheduler to determine the least-cost filtering solution for the print file.

Each filter program is piped into the next, and status and other messages are written to the standard error file. The first filter in the chain reads the file specified on the command line. The filters that follow must read from the standard input file.

Command-Line Arguments

Each filter program uses a command-line interface that was inherited from the System V printing system. Every filter is provided with exactly six or seven command-line arguments:

```
printer job user title copies options filename
printer job user title copies options
```

The first filter is run with seven arguments, while each filter after the first in the chain only gets six arguments. This enables the first filter to read the print file directly, while each additional filter reads the results from the previous filter on the standard input.

- The `printer` argument (`argv[0]`) is the name of the printer queue, which is the value of the `printer-name` attribute.

NOTE:

Shell interpreters replace the `printer` argument (`$0`) with the name of the shell script. If you need the printer name in your shell script, use the corresponding environment variable listed in the next section.

- The `job` argument (`argv[1]`) provides the numeric job ID for the job being printed. It is the value of the job's `job-id` attribute.
- The `user` argument (`argv[2]`) provides the username associated with the job. It is the value of the job's `job-originating-user-name` attribute.
- The `title` argument (`argv[3]`) provides the name or title associated with the job. It is the value of the job's `job-name` attribute.
- The `copies` argument (`argv[4]`) provides the number of copies to be printed. It is the value of the job's `number-copies` attribute.
- The `options` argument (`argv[5]`) is a string representation of the job template attributes separated by spaces. Boolean attributes are provided as "name" for true values and "noname" for false values. All other attributes are provided as "name=value" for single-valued attributes and "name=value1,value2,...,valueN" for `1setOf` attributes. The `cupsParseOptions()` function can be used to convert this string to an array of CUPS options, as follows:

```
int          num_options;
cups_option_t *options;
```

```
...
num_options = 0;
options     = NULL;
num_options = cupsParseOptions(argv[5], num_options, &options);
```

- The `filename` argument (`argv[6]`) is provided to the first filter only. It specifies the print file that is to be converted.

NOTE:

All filters must be prepared to read the print file from the standard input. If the filter requires random access to the file data, it must copy the print file on the standard input to a temporary file.

Environment Variables

Every filter receives a fixed set of environment variables that the filter can use. Table 16.2 lists the environment variables.

TABLE 16.2   Environment variables passed to CUPS filters

Name	Description
CHARSET	The character set used by the client for this print file.
CLASSIFICATION	The current system-high classification level, such as "unclassified." Provided only when used.
CONTENT_TYPE	The original document format, such as "application/postscript."
CUPS_DATADIR	The location of CUPS data files.
CUPS_FONTPATH	The locations of CUPS font files.
CUPS_SERVERROOT	The location of CUPS configuration files.
DEVICE_URI	The output device URI.
LANG	The language used by the client for this print file.
LD_LIBRARY_PATH	The dynamic load path. Provided only when used.
PATH	The execution path exported to the filter.
PPD	The full filename of the printer's PPD file.
PRINTER	The name of the printer queue.
RIP_CACHE	The maximum amount of memory each filter should use.
SOFTWARE	The name of the CUPS software, typically "CUPS/1.1."
TMPDIR	The directory for temporary files.
TZ	The local time zone.
USER	The name of the filter user.

The CLASSIFICATION and LD_LIBRARY_PATH environment variables are set only if they are defined in the scheduler. The CLASSIFICATION environment variable corresponds to the Classification directive, as follows:

Classification secret

The LD_LIBRARY_PATH environment variable is inherited from the environment of the scheduler, as follows:

LD_LIBRARY_PATH=/foo/bar; export LD_LIBRARY_PATH *ENTER*
cupsd *ENTER*

All other environment variables are guaranteed to be present and use default values when they are not otherwise configured in the cupsd.conf file.

Security Considerations

Filters are normally run as non-privileged users, so the major security consideration is resource utilization: filters should not depend on unlimited amounts of memory and disk space.

You should also be careful when creating or modifying files from your filter. If you need to create a temporary file, use the TMPDIR environment variable to determine where to locate the file.

Finally, design your filters to handle buffer overflow conditions. In particular, be very conservative about using the gets(), sprintf(), strcat(), and strcpy() functions, which often are the source of buffer overflow risks. If you handle potential buffer overflow situations (even if you believe they will never happen), you will make your filter more reliable.

NOTE:

Do not create setuid or setgid filter programs. Most filters are accessible to any user, so these programs might be used to bypass system security and access (or change) files and programs on the system.

Users and Groups

The default CUPS configuration runs filters as user "lp" and group "other." You can use the User and Group directives in the cupsd.conf file to change this, as follows:

User foo
Group bar

These accounts and groups should be unprivileged to prevent unwanted security risks.

Temporary Files

Temporary files should be created in the directory specified by the TMPDIR environment variable. The cupsTempFile() and cupsTempFd() functions can be used to safely create temporary files in this directory.

Temporary files should be removed when your filter program is finished so that disk space is not wasted.

Sending Messages to the User

The CUPS scheduler collects messages the filter sends to the standard error file. These messages are relayed to the user based upon the scheduler LogLevel directive.

An initial prefix string sent on each line determines the type of message. Table 16.3 lists the available prefixes.

TABLE 16.3   Message string prefixes for CUPS filters

Prefix	Description
DEBUG:	A debugging message
DEBUG2:	A detailed debugging message
ERROR:	An error message
INFO:	An informational message
PAGE:	A page accounting message
WARNING:	A warning message

If the line of text does not begin with any of the above prefixes, it is treated as a DEBUG: message. DEBUG:, DEBUG2:, ERROR:, INFO:, and WARNING: messages are copied to the printer-state-message attribute for the printer.

The DEBUG:, DEBUG2:, ERROR:, and WARNING: messages can also be logged to the error_log file. The LogLevel directive determines which messages get logged, as follows:

LogLevel debug

PAGE: messages contain page accounting information. Each PAGE: message is logged to the page_log file and used to update the job's job-impressions-completed attribute.

NOTE:

Filters, printer drivers, and backends share a single status pipe on the standard error file with the server. To avoid problems with message corruption, always disable buffering of the standard error file or flush the file after writing a message line. Also, the server accepts messages of up to only 1k in length. The server breaks up and may misinterpret longer lines.

Page Accounting

Page accounting messages (PAGE:) are used to inform the server when one or more pages are printed. Each line has the following form:

```
PAGE: page-number copy-count
```

The page-number field is the current page number, starting at 1. The copy-count field specifies the number of copies of the page that were produced.

Only the last filter to do page-based processing should generate page accounting messages. For example, the pstops filter generates PAGE: messages when it prints to a PostScript printer, but does not generate these messages when it prints to a non-PostScript printer, because the printer driver generates them instead.

NOTE:

The page accounting that CUPS currently provides depends on the accurate generation of PAGE: comments from filters. This is widely considered to be a limitation of the accounting system in CUPS.

CUPS 1.2 adds a new interface that enables intelligent backends to collect page accounting information from the printer itself. When a backend provides page accounting information, the PAGE: comments from the filters are ignored.

Copy Generation

The copies (argv[4]) argument specifies the number of copies of the input file that should be produced. The multiple-document-handling option specifies whether the copies should be collated (separate-documents-collated-copies) or uncollated (separate-documents-uncollated-copies).

In general, you should generate copies only if the filename (argv[6]) argument is supplied. The only exception to this rule is when you use filters that produce PostScript output that the pstops filter then filters. This includes the hpgltops and texttops filters included with CUPS.

When collated copies are being generated, the presence of the Collate option in the PPD file indicates that the printer is capable of producing collated copies on its own:

```
ppd_file_t *ppd;
ppd_option_t *option;
...
option = ppdFindOption(ppd, "Collate");
```

If you are generating uncollated copies for non–PostScript printers, the `manual_copies` member of the `ppd_file_t` structure indicates whether the printer can generate copies on its own:

```
ppd_file_t *ppd;
...
if (ppd->manual_copies)
  puts("The printer can't generate copies on its own.");
```

Configuration and Data Files

Configuration files are usually stored in the `/etc/cups` directory. Filters that provide their own configuration files should use the `CUPS_SERVERROOT` environment variable to locate the configuration files rather than hardcode a particular directory.

The normal convention for filter configuration files is to use the name of the filter with an extension of `.conf`. For example, the `pdftops` filter looks for a file named `pdftops.conf`.

Similarly, data files are usually stored under `/usr/share/cups`. The `CUPS_DATADIR` environment variable contains the actual directory in use.

MIME Types and Filters

After you have written a filter, you must register it and the file format(s) it supports with the scheduler. The standard file types and filters are defined in the `mime.types` and `mime.convs` files, which are usually located in the `/etc/cups` directory.

The scheduler reads all files with the `.types` and `.convs` extensions in the `/etc/cups` directory on startup.

NOTE:

The Multimedia Internet Mail Exchange (MIME) specifications define how to identify and transmit different types of data. The *MIME media type* is a string that identifies the format of a file and may include optional information such as the file's character set or encoding.

MIME types consist of a content type (text, application, image, and so forth) and sub-type (html, postscript, gif, and so forth), separated by a slash (/):

```
text/html
application/postscript
image/gif
```

Any optional information follows the sub-type. The semi-colon (;) and comma (,) are used as separators:

```
text/plain; charset=utf-8, language=en
```

MIME types are registered with the Internet Assigned Numbers Authority (IANA) and are listed online at the following links:

```
http://www.iana.org/
http://www.isi.edu/in-notes/iana/assignments/media-types/media-types
```

The MIME Type File Format

Each `.types` file defines file types for the scheduler; the `mime.types` file defines the standard file types.

Each line of a `.types` file starts with the MIME type and may be followed by one or more file type recognition rules. For example, the `text/html` file type is defined as

```
text/html        html htm \
                 printable(0,1024) + \
                 (string(0,"<HTML>") string(0,"<!DOCTYPE"))
```

The first two rules say that any file with an extension of `.html` or `.htm` is an HTML file. The third rule says that any file whose first 1024 characters are printable text and starts with the strings `<HTML>` or `<!DOCTYPE` is an HTML file as well.

The first two rules deal solely with the name of the file being typed. This is useful when the original filename is known, such as when you view a file in your Web browser.

For print files, however, the server doesn't have a filename to work with. The third rule takes care of this possibility and automatically figures out the file type based upon the contents of the file, instead.

As shown in the text/html example, rules can span multiple lines if you use the backslash (\) character. A more complex example is the image/jpeg rules:

```
image/jpeg       jpeg jpg jpe string(0,<FFD8FF>) &&\
                 (char(3,0xe0) char(3,0xe1) char(3,0xe2) char(3,0xe3)\
                  char(3,0xe4) char(3,0xe5) char(3,0xe6) char(3,0xe7)\
                  char(3,0xe8) char(3,0xe9) char(3,0xea) char(3,0xeb)\
                  char(3,0xec) char(3,0xed) char(3,0xee) char(3,0xef))
```

This rule states that any file with an extension of `.jpeg`, `.jpg`, or `.jpe` is a JPEG file. In addition, any file starting with the hexadecimal string `<FFD8FF>` (JPEG Start-Of-Image), followed by a character between and including `0xe0` and `0xef` (JPEG APPn markers), is also a JPEG file.

Table 16.4 lists the available tests that can be used for a file type.

TABLE 16.4   MIME type recognition rules for CUPS

Rule	Description
(expr)	Parenthesis for expression grouping
"+"	Logical AND
"," or whitespace	Logical OR
"!"	Logical NOT
ascii(offset,length)	True if bytes are valid printable ASCII (CR, NL, TAB, BS, 32–126)
char(offset,value)	True if byte is identical
contains(offset,range,"string")	True if the range of bytes contains the string
extension	Pattern match on "extension"
int(offset,value)	True if 32-bit integer is identical (network or "big-endian" byte order)
locale("string")	True if current locale matches string
match("pattern")	Pattern match on filename
printable(offset,length)	True if bytes are printable 8-bit chars (CR, NL, TAB, BS, 32–126, 128–254)
short(offset,value)	True if 16-bit integer is identical (network or "big-endian" byte order)
string(offset,"string")	True if bytes are identical to string

All numeric values can be in decimal (123), octal (0123), or hexadecimal (0x123) format as desired. Strings can be in quotes, all by themselves, as a string of hexadecimal values, or some combination:

```
"string"
'string'
string
<737472696e67>
<7374>ring
```

NOTE:

MIME types should be added to a new .types file. *Never* add types to the mime.types file, because that file is overwritten when CUPS is installed or upgraded.

MIME type files should use the product, format, or filter name, for example:

```
acme-word.types
msword.types
mswordtops.types
```

The MIME Filter File Format

Each .convs file defines filters for the scheduler; the mime.convs file defines the standard file filters.

Each line of a .convs file consists of

```
source destination cost program
```

The source field is the input MIME type. It optionally can use wildcards for the type or sub-type, for example:

```
text/plain
image/*
*/postscript
```

The destination field is the output MIME type. It cannot use wildcards.

The cost field defines a relative cost, from 1 to 100, for the filtering operation. The cost is used to choose between two different sets of filters when converting a file. For example, to convert from image/jpeg to application/vnd.cups-raster, the scheduler could use the imagetops and pstoraster filters for a total cost of 166, or the imagetoraster filter for a total cost of 100 (see Figure 16.2).

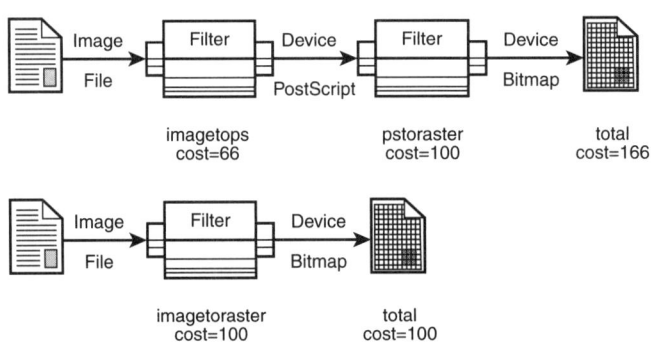

FIGURE 16.2

Finding the best filters to run for a file.

The program field defines which filter program should be run; the special program "-" can be used to make two file types equivalent.

The following lines are from the mime.convs file that comes with CUPS:

```
text/plain                     application/postscript       33  texttops
application/vnd.cups-postscript application/vnd.cups-raster  100 pstoraster
```

```
image/*                        application/vnd.cups-postscript 66  imagetops
image/*                        application/vnd.cups-raster        100 imagetoraster
application/octet-stream       application/vnd.cups-raw          0  -
```

As you can see, the filters that produce CUPS raster data (`application/vnd.cups-raster`) have the highest cost. The last line is the raw filter, which has a cost of 0 because no processing needs to be done.

Writing a Script-Based TeX DVI Filter

This first filter converts TeX DVI files to PostScript for printing. There is already an excellent program for doing this called `dvips`, but it doesn't support CUPS directly.

To use it you need to write a "wrapper" script called `dvitops` that converts the CUPS arguments and interface for `dvips`. Because `dvips` requires random access to the DVI file, the first task is to copy the standard input to a temporary file if no filename is provided to the script:

```
# Copy stdin to a temp file as necessary...
if test $# -lt 6; then
    filename=$TMPDIR/$$.dvi
    cat >$filename
else
    filename=$6
fi
```

Then run the `dvips` program to convert the file to PostScript:

```
dvips -R -q -o - $filename
```

Finally, remove the temporary file if you created one. The complete filter is shown in Listing 16.1.

LISTING 16.1   The CUPS *dvitops* filter script

```
#!/bin/sh
#
# CUPS wrapper script for dvips
#

# Copy stdin to a temp file as necessary...
if test $# -lt 6; then
    filename=$TMPDIR/$$.dvi
    cat >$filename
```

LISTING 16.1   Continued

```
    else
        filename=$6
    fi

    # Run dvips to convert to PostScript, sending the output to
    # stdout...
    dvips -R -q -o - $filename

    # Remove temp file as necessary...
    if test $# -lt 6; then
        rm -f $filename
    fi
```

To use the dvitops filter, you need to create .types and .convs files for the filter. Because you have only one filter and file type, you should use the filter name as the prefix for these files, or dvitops.types and dvitops.convs.

The dvitops.types file should contain an entry for the DVI file type; because this file type has not been registered with IANA, the sub-type name has an "x-" prefix:

```
application/x-dvi dvi string(0,<F702>)
```

The recognition rules state that any file with a .dvi extension or starting with the string <F702> is a DVI file.

The dvitops.convs file should contain a line for the dvitops filter:

```
application/x-dvi application/postscript 50 dvitops
```

Use a cost of 50 for the filter, which is a good starting value if you do not know the actual cost of a particular filter.

To install the filter, start by copying the files you have created from the current directory to the /etc/cups and /usr/lib/cups/filter directories:

cp dvitops.types /etc/cups *ENTER*
cp dvitops.convs /etc/cups *ENTER*
cp dvitops /usr/lib/cups/filter *ENTER*

Then restart the cupsd process using the provided init script or by sending it a HUP signal:

/etc/init.d/cups restart *ENTER*
kill -HUP pid *ENTER*

Congratulations—you can now print DVI files!

PostScript Output

Filters that produce PostScript output must generate output conforming to the Adobe Document Structuring Conventions (DSC), version 3.0. PostScript files that conform to the DSC include comments that enable the PostScript filter to correctly perform page accounting, copy generation, N-up printing, and so forth. Some printers also require them to print the file.

To generate conforming files, start each file with the following header:

```
%!PS-Adobe-3.0
%%BoundingBox: left bottom right top
%%Pages: (atend)
%%EndComments
```

The left, bottom, right, and top values define the bounding box for the entire document. The bounding box defines the area that contains print data. The values are integers in points from the lower left corner of the page (see Figure 16.3).

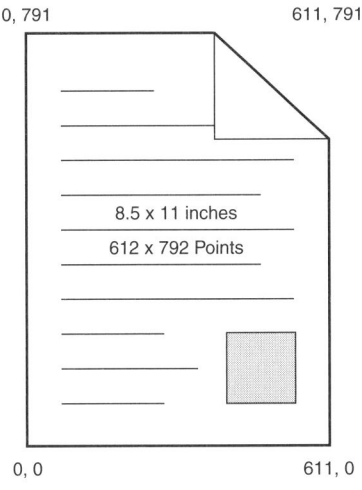

0, 791   611, 791

8.5 x 11 inches

612 x 792 Points

0, 0   611, 0

FIGURE 16.3

The PostScript page coordinate system.

Filters are free to define the bounding box as the entire area of the selected page size. For example, a filter could generate the right and top values using the ppdPageWidth() and ppdPageLength() functions:

```
ppd_file_t *ppd;
int        width;
int        length;
```

```
...
width = ppdPageWidth(ppd, NULL);
length = ppdPageLength(ppd, NULL);

printf("%%%%BoundingBox: 0 0 %d %d\n", width, length);
```

Document setup commands follow the header, and pages follow the document setup commands. The following lines must surround each page in the PostScript output:

```
%%Page: label number
gsave
... your output goes here ...
grestore
showpage
```

The `number` field specifies the page number. The page number starts at 1 and must increase throughout the file. The `label` field specifies a human-readable page number but is usually the same as the `number` field.

The end of the PostScript output must contain the following lines:

```
%%Trailer
%%Pages: number-pages
%%EOF
```

The `number-pages` field specifies the total number of pages in the document.

NOTE:

Never set the copy count or use the `copypage` operator in your PostScript output. These prevent page accounting from working, and you may not get the results you expect.

Also, each PostScript language level supports a number of different features as well as a common core language. The Adobe PostScript Language Reference Manual is required reading for anyone who wants to write a filter that produces PostScript, as is the Adobe Document Structuring Conventions specification. You can find these online at:

> http://partners.adobe.com/asn/developer/technotes/main.html

Use the `language_level` member of the `ppd_file_t` structure to determine what level of PostScript the printer supports. If you use a newer language feature than the printer supports, you probably won't get any output—not even an error page.

Raster Output

Some filters use the `cupsimage` library to produce raster output for printer drivers. The `imagetoraster` and `pstoraster` filters both use this library to produce raster output.

CUPS raster data consists of a file header followed by one or more pages of raster data. Each page contains a page header followed by pixel data. Figure 16.4 shows the general organization of the raster stream.

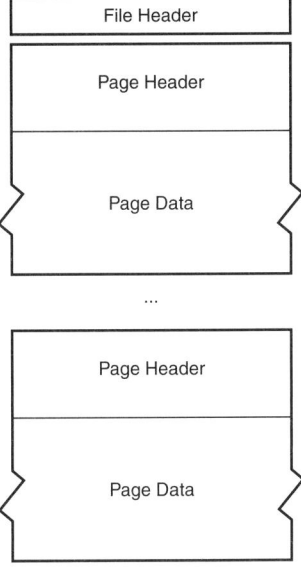

FIGURE 16.4

The CUPS raster stream.

CUPS provides several functions for writing raster streams. These functions, along with the data structures and constants used in raster files, are defined in the `<cups/raster.h>` header file. Table 16.5 lists the functions that are provided in CUPS for writing raster output.

TABLE 16.5   CUPS functions for writing raster data to printer drivers

Name	Description
`cupsRasterClose()`	Closes a raster stream
`cupsRasterOpen()`	Opens a raster stream for writing
`cupsRasterWriteHeader()`	Writes a raster header to a stream
`cupsRasterWritePixels()`	Writes pixel data to a stream

Opening and Closing Raster Streams

The `cupsRasterOpen()` function opens a raster stream for writing:

```
cups_raster_t *ras;
...
ras = cupsRasterOpen(1, CUPS_RASTER_WRITE);
```

The first argument is the file descriptor for the raster stream; this is normally 1 for the standard output file. The second argument specifies the open mode—the `CUPS_RASTER_WRITE` constant specifies that you will be writing raster data.

The return value is a pointer to a `cups_raster_t` structure, which is used to keep the state of the raster stream. If the stream cannot be opened, a `NULL` pointer is returned.

When you have finished writing raster data, call the `cupsRasterClose()` function to close the stream:

```
cupsRasterClose(ras);
```

Writing the Page Header

Before you write the raster data for a page, you must write a page header. The `cupsRasterWriteHeader()` function writes a single page header to the raster stream:

```
cups_raster_t *ras;
cups_page_header_t header;
...
cupsRasterWriteHeader(ras, &header);
```

The `ras` argument is the raster stream. The `header` argument specifies a pointer to the page header structure. The return value is 0 on success and –1 on error.

The page header is encapsulated in the `cups_page_header_t` structure as shown in Table 16.6.

TABLE 16.6   The CUPS raster page header structure

Name	Type	Description
AdvanceDistance	unsigned	The amount to advance the media in points
AdvanceMedia	cups_adv_t	How to advance the media
Collate	cups_bool_t	Whether to collate the output
CutMedia	cups_cut_t	How to cut the media
Duplex	cups_bool_t	Whether to duplex the output
HWResolution	unsigned [2]	The horizontal and vertical resolution in pixels per inch
ImagingBoundingBox	unsigned [4]	The bounding box for the imaged area in points
InsertSheet	cups_bool_t	Whether to insert a sheet before each copy

TABLE 16.6   Continued

Name	Type	Description
Jog	cups_jog_t	How to jog the output
LeadingEdge	cups_edge_t	The leading edge of the media
Margins	unsigned [2]	The lower left margins of the media
ManualFeed	cups_bool_t	Whether to use the manual feed slot
MediaClass	char [64]	The MediaClass string
MediaColor	char [64]	The MediaColor string
MediaPosition	unsigned	The media source
MediaType	char [64]	The MediaType string
MediaWeight	unsigned	The media weight in grams/m²
MirrorPrint	cups_bool_t	Whether to mirror the print
NegativePrint	cups_bool_t	Whether to invert the print
NumCopies	unsigned	The number of copies to print
Orientation	cups_orient_t	The orientation of the job
OutputFaceUp	cups_bool_t	Whether to print the job face-up
OutputType	char [64]	The OutputType string
PageSize	unsigned [2]	The width and length of the page in points
Separations	cups_bool_t	Whether to produce separations (one page per color plane)
TraySwitch	cups_bool_t	Whether to automatically switch trays based on the PageSize, MediaType, and MediaWeight options
Tumble	cups_bool_t	Whether to rotate the back side of duplexed pages
cupsBitsPerColor	unsigned	The number of bits per color
cupsBitsPerPixel	unsigned	The number of bits per pixel
cupsBytesPerLine	unsigned	The number of bytes per line of pixels
cupsColorOrder	cups_order_t	The ordering of color values
cupsColorSpace	cups_cspace_t	The colorspace for the color values
cupsCompression	unsigned	A driver-specific compression mode code
cupsHeight	unsigned	The height of the page in pixels
cupsMediaType	unsigned	The media type expressed as an integer
cupsRowCount	unsigned	The number of rows to write in one pass
cupsRowFeed	unsigned	The number of rows to feed between passes
cupsRowStep	unsigned	The number of rows between jets on the print head
cupsWidth	unsigned	The width of the page in pixels

Most of the members of the page header structure correspond directly with a PostScript page device dictionary attribute. The cups members define information specifically for the raster data.

The cupsColorSpace field specifies the output colorspace. Table 16.7 lists the supported colorspaces.

TABLE 16.7   Colorspaces supported by CUPS

Name	Description
CUPS_CSPACE_CMY	Cyan, magenta, yellow
CUPS_CSPACE_CMYK	Cyan, magenta, yellow, black
CUPS_CSPACE_GMCK	Gold, magenta, yellow, black
CUPS_CSPACE_GMCS	Gold, magenta, yellow, silver
CUPS_CSPACE_GOLD	Gold foil
CUPS_CSPACE_ICC1	1 channel of ICC color data (CUPS 1.2 only)
CUPS_CSPACE_ICC2	2 channels of ICC color data (CUPS 1.2 only)
CUPS_CSPACE_ICC3	3 channels of ICC color data (CUPS 1.2 only)
CUPS_CSPACE_ICC4	4 channels of ICC color data (CUPS 1.2 only)
CUPS_CSPACE_ICC5	5 channels of ICC color data (CUPS 1.2 only)
CUPS_CSPACE_ICC6	6 channels of ICC color data (CUPS 1.2 only)
CUPS_CSPACE_ICC7	7 channels of ICC color data (CUPS 1.2 only)
CUPS_CSPACE_ICC8	8 channels of ICC color data (CUPS 1.2 only)
CUPS_CSPACE_K	Black/grayscale
CUPS_CSPACE_KCMY	Black, cyan, magenta, yellow
CUPS_CSPACE_KCMYcm	Black, cyan, magenta, yellow, light-cyan, light magenta
CUPS_CSPACE_RGB	Red, green, blue
CUPS_CSPACE_RGBA	Red, green, blue, alpha
CUPS_CSPACE_SILVER	Silver foil
CUPS_CSPACE_W	White/luminance
CUPS_CSPACE_WHITE	White ink (as black)
CUPS_CSPACE_YMC	Yellow, magenta, cyan
CUPS_CSPACE_YMCK	Yellow, magenta, cyan, black

The cupsColorOrder field specifies the organization of the color values. Figure 16.5 shows the different color orders.

The cupsBitsPerColor field specifies the number of bits per color that are provided. CUPS 1.1 and earlier support values of 1, 2, 4, and 8 bits per color. CUPS 1.2 supports 16 bits per color when using ICC color profiles and colorspaces.

CUPS_ORDER_CHUNKED

CMYK CMYK CMYK CMYK CMYK CMYK CMYK CMYK CMYK CMYK
CMYK CMYK CMYK CMYK CMYK CMYK CMYK CMYK CMYK CMYK
CMYK CMYK CMYK CMYK CMYK CMYK CMYK CMYK CMYK CMYK
CMYK CMYK CMYK CMYK CMYK CMYK CMYK CMYK CMYK CMYK
CMYK CMYK CMYK CMYK CMYK CMYK CMYK CMYK CMYK CMYK
CMYK CMYK CMYK CMYK CMYK CMYK CMYK CMYK CMYK CMYK

CUPS_ORDER_BANDED

CCCCCCCCCC	MMMMMMMM	YYYYYYYYYY	KKKKKKKKKK
CCCCCCCCCC	MMMMMMMM	YYYYYYYYYY	KKKKKKKKKK
CCCCCCCCCC	MMMMMMMM	YYYYYYYYYY	KKKKKKKKKK
CCCCCCCCCC	MMMMMMMM	YYYYYYYYYY	KKKKKKKKKK
CCCCCCCCCC	MMMMMMMM	YYYYYYYYYY	KKKKKKKKKK
CCCCCCCCCC	MMMMMMMM	YYYYYYYYYY	KKKKKKKKKK

CUPS_ORDER_PLANAR

CCCCCCCCCCCCCCCCCCCCCCCCCCCCCCCCCCCCCCCCCC
CCCCCCCCCCCCCCCCCCCCCCCCCCCCCCCCCCCCCCCCCC
CCCCCCCCCCCCCCCCCCCCCCCCCCCCCCCCCCCCCCCCCC
CCCCCCCCCCCCCCCCCCCCCCCCCCCCCCCCCCCCCCCCCC

MMMMMMMMMMMMMMMMMMMMMMMMMMMMMMMMMMMMMMMMMM
MMMMMMMMMMMMMMMMMMMMMMMMMMMMMMMMMMMMMMMMMM
MMMMMMMMMMMMMMMMMMMMMMMMMMMMMMMMMMMMMMMMMM
MMMMMMMMMMMMMMMMMMMMMMMMMMMMMMMMMMMMMMMMMM

YYYYYYYYYYYYYYYYYYYYYYYYYYYYYYYYYYYYYYYYYY
YYYYYYYYYYYYYYYYYYYYYYYYYYYYYYYYYYYYYYYYYY
YYYYYYYYYYYYYYYYYYYYYYYYYYYYYYYYYYYYYYYYYY
YYYYYYYYYYYYYYYYYYYYYYYYYYYYYYYYYYYYYYYYYY

KKKKKKKKKKKKKKKKKKKKKKKKKKKKKKKKKKKKKKKKKK
KKKKKKKKKKKKKKKKKKKKKKKKKKKKKKKKKKKKKKKKKK
KKKKKKKKKKKKKKKKKKKKKKKKKKKKKKKKKKKKKKKKKK
KKKKKKKKKKKKKKKKKKKKKKKKKKKKKKKKKKKKKKKKKK

FIGURE 16.5

CUPS raster color orders.

NOTE:

Writing raster data can be tricky. A properly written filter can scan the commands in a PPD file to determine the correct values for the various fields in the page header.

Consult the main source file for the `imagetoraster` filter for a sample implementation that scans the PPD file for the page header values; it can be found in the file `filter/imagetoraster.c`.

Writing the Page Data

The cupsRasterWritePixels() function is used to write the raster data for the page:

```
cups_raster_t *ras;
unsigned char buffer[1024];
...
cupsRasterWritePixels(ras, buffer, length);
```

The ras argument points to the raster stream. The buffer argument points to the pixel data. The length argument specifies the number of bytes to write.

The return value is the number of bytes written or –1 for an error.

NOTE:

The cupsRasterWritePixels() function does not do any checking to make sure that you have written the correct amount of raster data. It is very easy to write too much or too little data, so be careful to write exactly the right number of bytes.

The total number of bytes of raster data should normally equal the product of the cupsBytesPerLine and cupsHeight members of the page header. The only exception is when the color order is CUPS_ORDER_PLANAR, in which case the count must also be multiplied by the number of color planes.

Dissecting the HP-GL/2 Filter

The HP-GL/2 filter (hpgltops) provided with CUPS is a complex program that converts HP-GL/2 files into PostScript output. Because it produces PostScript output that is passed to the pstops filter, it does not need to handle copy generation or writing printer options from the printer's PPD file.

Initializing the Filter

The first task of any filter is to ensure that the correct number of command-line arguments is present:

```
if (argc < 6 || argc > 7)
{
  fputs("ERROR: hpgltops job-id user title copies options [file]\n", stderr);
  return (1);
}
```

After this you open the print file or read from the standard input as needed:

```
FILE *fp;
/*
 * If we have 7 arguments, print the file named on the command-line.
 * Otherwise, send stdin instead...
 */

if (argc == 6)
  fp = stdin;
else
{
 /*
  * Try to open the print file...
  */

  if ((fp = fopen(argv[6], "rb")) == NULL)
  {
    perror("ERROR: unable to open print file - ");
    return (1);
  }
}
```

After the print file has been opened, options can be processed using the `cupsParseOptions()` and `cupsGetOption()` functions:

```
int            num_options;
cups_option_t *options;
const char    *val;

/*
 * Process command-line options and write the prolog...
 */

options     = NULL;
num_options = cupsParseOptions(argv[5], 0,

if ((val = cupsGetOption("blackplot", num_options, options)) != NULL)
  shading = 0;

if ((val = cupsGetOption("fitplot", num_options, options)) != NULL)
  FitPlot = 1;

if ((val = cupsGetOption("penwidth", num_options, options)) != NULL)
  PenWidth = (float)atoi(val) * 0.001f;
```

After the options have been processed, the filter writes the standard PostScript header to the standard output file:

```c
void
OutputProlog(char  *title,      /* I - Job title */
             char  *user,       /* I - Username */
             int   shading)     /* I - Type of shading */
{
  FILE          *prolog;        /* Prolog file */
  char          line[255];      /* Line from prolog file */
  const char    *datadir;       /* CUPS_DATADIR environment variable */
  char          filename[1024]; /* Name of prolog file */
  time_t        curtime;        /* Current time */
  struct tm     *curtm;         /* Current date */


  curtime = time(NULL);
  curtm   = localtime(&curtime);

  puts("%!PS-Adobe-3.0");
  printf("%%%%BoundingBox: %.0f %.0f %.0f %.0f\n",
         PageLeft, PageBottom, PageRight, PageTop);
  puts("%%Pages: (atend)");
  printf("%%%%LanguageLevel: %d\n", LanguageLevel);
  puts("%%DocumentData: Clean7Bit");
  puts("%%DocumentSuppliedResources: procset hpgltops 1.1 0");
  puts("%%DocumentNeededResources: font Courier Helvetica");
  puts("%%Creator: hpgltops/" CUPS_SVERSION);
  strftime(line, sizeof(line), CUPS_STRFTIME_FORMAT, curtm);
  printf("%%%%CreationDate: %s\n", line);
  printf("%%%%Title: %s\n", title);
  printf("%%%%For: %s\n", user);
  if (Orientation & 1)
    puts("%%Orientation: Landscape");
  puts("%%EndComments");
  puts("%%BeginProlog");
  printf("/DefaultPenWidth %.2f def\n", PenWidth * 72.0 / 25.4);
  puts("3.0 setmiterlimit");
  if (!shading) /* Black only */
    puts("/setrgbcolor { pop pop pop } bind def");
  else if (!ColorDevice) /* Greyscale */
    puts("/setrgbcolor { 0.08 mul exch 0.61 mul add exch 0.31 mul add setgray }
bind def\n");
```

```
  if ((datadir = getenv("CUPS_DATADIR")) == NULL)
    datadir = CUPS_DATADIR;

  snprintf(filename, sizeof(filename), "%s/data/HPGLprolog", datadir);

  if ((prolog = fopen(filename, "r")) == NULL)
  {
    fprintf(stderr, "ERROR: Unable to open HPGL prolog \"%s\" for reading - %s\n",
            filename, strerror(errno));
    exit(1);
  }

  while (fgets(line, sizeof(line), prolog) != NULL)
    fputs(line, stdout);

  fclose(prolog);

  puts("%%EndProlog");

  IN_initialize(0, NULL);
}
```

Next, the filter reads the plot file, sending PostScript drawing commands as needed. When it sees the PG (page eject) command, it sends a showpage command. Each page is wrapped in the standard DSC comments described earlier.

When all plot data has been read, the standard PostScript trailer is written:

```
void
OutputTrailer(void)
{
  if (PageDirty)
    PG_advance_page(0, NULL);

  puts("%%Trailer");
  printf("%%%%Pages: %d\n", PageCount);
  puts("%%EOF");
}
```

Finally, the filter closes the print file (as needed) and returns 0 to the scheduler:

```
if (fp != stdin)
  fclose(fp);

return (0);
```

Summary

File filters form the backbone of the CUPS printing process. They convert print files into something a printer can understand. Rather than one monolithic program that handles every format, smaller single-purpose filters are provided. These filters are piped together so that you can obtain the necessary output formats.

Filters use a common interface to handle printing and provide status information to the user and scheduler. The cups library provides the essential functions you need to develop CUPS filters. Filters can also be written using shell scripts wrapped around existing programs, usually with little or no difference in performance or capabilities.

Filters that write PostScript must follow the Adobe Document Structuring Conventions to ensure that the PostScript output works with all other filters and printers.

Filters that write raster data use the cupsimage library to write the raster stream to the printer driver. Raster filters are probably the most complex to write, but the source code for the CUPS imagetoraster filter can serve as a sample implementation for other filters, reducing development time.

CHAPTER 17

Writing Printer Drivers for CUPS

This chapter describes how to write printer drivers for CUPS, including an advanced version of the HP PCL driver included with CUPS.

Overview

Printer drivers in CUPS are filter programs that are associated with a particular printer. Each printer driver consists of a PostScript printer description (PPD) file and one or more filter programs that convert intermediate files into printable data. Figure 17.1 shows the organization of typical printer drivers.

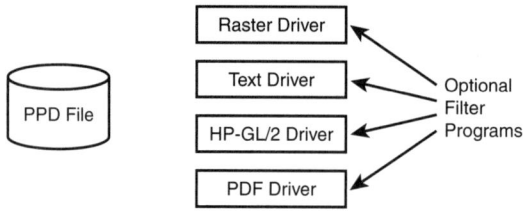

FIGURE 17.1

CUPS printer driver architecture.

PostScript printers generally need no additional filters because the built-in PostScript filters can usually handle everything that is needed. However, some PostScript printers can print other types of files directly, such as PDF files to a Level 3 PostScript printer. Filters can therefore be used to provide enhanced printing support, even for PostScript printers.

Non-PostScript printers generally provide a raster driver filter to convert the CUPS raster data into a format that the printer can understand. As you'll see later in this chapter, you can also add other driver filters to provide enhanced printing support.

Understanding PostScript Printer Description (PPD) Files

PPD files provide the basis for all printer drivers in CUPS. A PPD file is composed of plain text and includes four basic sections:

- Printer identification
- Constraints
- Options
- Fonts

Each line in the file may be terminated by a linefeed (LF) for Unix, a carriage return (CR) for MacOS, or a CR and LF for Windows. Comment lines begin with the string "*%" and continue to the end of the line.

The Printer Identification Section

The printer identification section begins with the standard PPD header:

```
*PPD-Adobe: "4.3"
```

The *PPD-Adobe: attribute identifies the file as a PPD file, and the "4.3" value identifies the version of the PPD specification to which the PPD file conforms.

NOTE:

Adobe maintains the PostScript printer description file specification online at

```
http://partners.adobe.com/asn/developer/technotes/main.html
```

The printer identification attributes follow the header:

```
*FormatVersion: "4.3"
*FileVersion:   "1.1"
*LanguageVersion: English
*LanguageEncoding: ISOLatin1
*PCFileName:    "LASERJET.PPD"
*Manufacturer:  "ESP"
*Product:       "(CUPS v1.1)"
*ModelName:     "HP LaserJet Series"
*ShortNickName: "HP LaserJet Series"
*NickName:      "HP LaserJet Series CUPS v1.1"
*PSVersion:     "(3010.000) 550"
*LanguageLevel: "3"
*ColorDevice:   False
*DefaultColorSpace: Gray
*FileSystem:    False
*Throughput:    "8"
*LandscapeOrientation: Plus90
*VariablePaperSize: False
*TTRasterizer:  Type42
```

As you can see, all attributes in a PPD file start with the "*" character. The FormatVersion attribute specifies the specification version for the file and must match the version number on the first line.

The LanguageLevel attribute specifies the PostScript level that is supported. For raster drivers this should always be 3.

The NickName attribute specifies the common name for the printer. This is the name that is presented to the user in the Web interface, and also when you run the lpinfo command.

The ColorDevice attribute specifies whether the printer supports color. Use a value of True for color printers and False for grayscale printers.

Aside from the required attributes, CUPS printer drivers also provide additional attributes that identify the filters and other information unique to that printer:

```
*cupsVersion:    1.1
*cupsManualCopies: True
*cupsFilter:     "application/vnd.cups-raster 0 rastertohp"
*cupsModelNumber: 2
*cupsFlipDuplex: True
*cupsColorProfile -/-:   "1.0 1.5 1.0 -0.25 -0.2 -0.25 1.0 -0.2 -0.25 -0.25 0.9"
```

The cupsVersion attribute specifies the version of CUPS for which the driver was developed. Use only the major and minor version numbers (1.0, 1.1, 1.2, and so forth).

The cupsManualCopies attribute specifies whether the printer or driver can produce copies on its own. The imagetoraster and pstoraster filters use this attribute to determine if copies must be generated for the driver.

The cupsFilter attribute specifies a filter that is to be used for printing. The format is

```
source cost filter
```

where source is the MIME type of the source file, cost is the relative cost of using the filter, and filter is the name of the filter program. The destination type is assumed to be the printer's native format.

The cupsModelNumber attribute provides a number to the printer driver to differentiate the printer from other printers that use the same driver filters. This attribute is often used to determine which version of a command set is used with a printer.

The cupsFlipDuplex attribute specifies that duplexed page images must be rotated 180 degrees. This is used for double-sided printing support for some inkjet printers.

The cupsColorProfile attribute specifies a color profile for the printer. The attribute lists a resolution and media type as well as the profile:

```
*cupsColorProfile resolution/mediatype: "profile"
```

The resolution field specifies the Resolution option name for this profile, whereas the mediatype field specifies the MediaType option name. The profile string can be a list of gamma, density, and CMY transform matrix values, or the name of an ICC profile file. (ICC profile files are supported only in CUPS 1.2.)

Constraints

PPD files can also contain constraint attributes. Constraints basically tell the driver or user interface that two options are incompatible. Each constraint is described by a `UIConstraint` attribute:

```
*UIConstraints: *PageSize Executive *InputSlot Envelope
*UIConstraints: *PageSize Letter *InputSlot Envelope
*UIConstraints: *PageSize Legal *InputSlot Envelope
*UIConstraints: *PageSize Tabloid *InputSlot Envelope
*UIConstraints: *PageSize A3 *InputSlot Envelope
*UIConstraints: *PageSize A4 *InputSlot Envelope
*UIConstraints: *PageSize A5 *InputSlot Envelope
*UIConstraints: *PageSize B5 *InputSlot Envelope
*UIConstraints: *Duplex *Option1 False
```

The value of the constraint can be two options and choices, where the option names start with an asterisk (*) and the option choices do not:

```
*UIConstraints: *PageSize Executive *InputSlot Envelope
```

This constraint says that you can't choose `Executive` page sizes when printing from the `Envelope` feeder.

Constraints can also apply to any choice of a particular option. For example, the `Duplex` option may depend on the presence of a duplex attachment in the printer. The following rule specifies that if the duplexer is not installed (`Option1` = `False`) then no duplex option can be chosen:

```
*UIConstraints: *Duplex *Option1 False
```

NOTE:

CUPS does not enforce constraints when printing. Constraints must be managed and resolved by the user interface, because there is usually no way to specify preferences or intentions for automatic resolution of constraints by the driver or other filters. Be prepared to handle unsupported option combinations in your driver gracefully.

Options

PPD files can contain any number of options and option groups. Each option can be a Boolean value (`Boolean`), allow a choice from a list (`PickOne`), or allow multiple choices (`PickMany`). The `*OpenUI` keyword starts a new option:

```
*OpenUI *option/text: type
```

The `option` field specifies the name of the option and can consist of up to 40 letters and numbers. Option names are case sensitive, although CUPS supports a non-case-sensitive option selection for convenience.

The `text` field specifies the human-readable name for the option. It can contain any text including spaces. The colon (:) and all 8-bit text characters must be represented as hexadecimal values:

```
*OpenUI Foo/Foo<2E>: type
```

The `type` field specifies the option type: `Boolean`, `PickOne`, or `PickMany`.

Next comes the `*OrderDependency` keyword, which indicates the relative order of the commands for the option:

```
*OrderDependency: order section *option
```

Again, `option` is the name of the option. The `order` field specifies the relative order of the commands for the option. For example, if `Option1` has an order value of 10 and `Option2` has an order value of 5, the commands for `Option2` are sent before the commands for `Option1`.

The `section` field specifies when to send the commands and can be one of the values listed in Table 17.1.

TABLE 17.1   PPD section names for options

Name	Description
AnySetup	The options must be included in the `DocumentSetup` or `PageSetup` sections.
DocumentSetup	The options must be included in the `DocumentSetup` section.
ExitServer	The options must be sent as a separate job before the rest of the print file.
JCLSetup	The options must be sent with the JCL commands.
PageSetup	The options must be included in the `PageSetup` section.
Prolog	The options must be included in the `Prolog` section.

The section names correspond to the Adobe document structuring conventions specification.

NOTE:

Adobe maintains the document structuring conventions specification online at

http://partners.adobe.com/asn/developer/technotes/main.html

After the `*OrderDependency` keyword comes the default value for the option:

`*Defaultoption: choice`

where `option` is the option name and `choice` is the name of the default choice.

Following the default value are the actual choices for the option:

`*option choice/text: "command"`

The `choice` field is a string of up to 40 letters and numbers and is case sensitive. The `text` field is the human-readable string for the choice. The `command` string is the command that is to be sent to the printer or driver when this choice is selected.

Finally, the `*CloseUI` keyword finishes the option definition:

`*CloseUI: *option`

Page Sizes

Page sizes are described by four sets of options. The first two are the `PageSize` and `PageRegion` options:

```
*OpenUI *PageSize/Media Size: PickOne
*OrderDependency: 10 AnySetup *PageSize
*DefaultPageSize: Letter
*PageSize Letter/US Letter: "<</PageSize[612 792]/ImagingBBox null>>setpagedevice"
*PageSize A4/A4: "<</PageSize[595 842]/ImagingBBox null>>setpagedevice"
*CloseUI: *PageSize

*OpenUI *PageRegion: PickOne
*OrderDependency: 10 AnySetup *PageRegion
*DefaultPageRegion: Letter
*PageRegion Letter/US Letter: "<</PageSize[612 792]/ImagingBBox
null>>setpagedevice"
*PageRegion A4/A4: "<</PageSize[595 842]/ImagingBBox null>>setpagedevice"
*CloseUI: *PageRegion
```

Traditionally the `PageRegion` option is used for manual feed prints whereas the `PageSize` option is used for normal prints; that use, however, is obsolete. Modern printers and drivers provide identical `PageSize` and `PageRegion` options.

The third option is `ImageableArea`. It defines the bounding box for the printable area of each page size:

```
*DefaultImageableArea: Letter
*ImageableArea Letter/US Letter: "18 36 594 786"
*ImageableArea A4/A4: "18 36 577 836"
```

The values for these options provide the left, bottom, right, and top coordinates in points.

Finally, the `PaperDimension` option lists the physical dimensions of each page size:

```
*DefaultPaperDimension: Letter
*PaperDimension Letter/US Letter: "612 792"
*PaperDimension A4/A4:   "595 842"
```

The values are the width and length of the page in points.

Fonts

The final section of the PPD file contains a list of fonts that the printer supports. Each line specifies a font name, encoding, version, charset, and status:

```
*Font fontname: encoding "(version)" charset status
```

The `fontname` field is the name of the PostScript font.

The `encoding` field is usually either `Standard` for normal fonts or `Special` for fonts such as `Symbol` and `Zapf-Dingbats`. You can find the complete list of possible encodings in the PPD specification.

The `version` string provides a version number for the font.

The `charset` string specifies what characters are in the font. The `Standard` charset specifies that the font is capable of representing most Latin characters. The `Extended` character set adds characters for Cyrillic and other eastern European languages. The `Special` character set is used for fonts such as `Symbol` and `Zapf-Dingbats`.

The status field specifies whether the font is resident on the printer (`ROM`) or needs to be downloaded to the printer (`Disk`).

NOTE:

CUPS currently tracks only the presence of fonts on the printer and not the specific encoding, version, charset, or status of the fonts. This may change in future versions of CUPS.

Writing a Text Driver for HP Printers

Chapter 16 explained that the `texttops` filter was designed to support other output languages in addition to PostScript. Because HP PCL printers support both portrait and landscape text, you can add a language module for PCL printers fairly easily and speed up text printing in the process!

First, create a new filter module called `texttohp.c`. This filter will link against the `textcommon.c` and `common.c` modules used by the CUPS filters.

The `main()` function for the `texttohp.c` module needs to call the `TextMain()` function to do the printing:

```
int                    /* O - Exit status */
main(int  argc,     /* I - Number of command-line arguments */
     char *argv?) /* I - Command-line arguments */
{
  /* Print stuff. */
  return (TextMain("texttohp", argc, argv));
}
```

After calling `TextMain()`, you need to define three functions—`WriteEpilogue()`, `WriteProlog()`, and `WritePage()`—that will handle printing and setup of the PCL text data.

The `WriteEpilogue()` Function

The `WriteEpilogue()` function is responsible for sending any post-job commands to the printer and for freeing the page buffer. For this PCL filter you will send the PCL reset sequence `ESC E`, free the page buffer, and return:

```
void
WriteEpilogue(void)
{
  printf("\033E");

  free(Page[0]);
  free(Page);
}
```

The `WriteProlog()` Function

The `WriteProlog()` function sends any initialization commands that the printer needs, computes the number of columns and rows for the page buffer, and allocates the page buffer.

First, adjust the margins if you intend to display a page label or classification:

```
/* Adjust margins as necessary for page labels. */
if (classification || label)
{
  /* Leave room for labels. */
  PageBottom += 144.0 / LinesPerInch;
  PageTop    -= 144.0 / LinesPerInch;
}
```

Next, initialize the strings that are to be used in the header and footer of each page:

```
/* Set the printing time. */
curtime = time(NULL);
curtm   = localtime(&curtime);
strftime(file_date, sizeof(file_date), "%c", curtm);

/* Set the title... */
strncpy(file_title, title, sizeof(file_title) - 1);
file_title[sizeof(file_title) - 1] = '\0';
```

Then compute the size of the page in rows and columns:

```
/* Figure out the page size. */
SizeColumns = (PageRight - PageLeft) / 72.0 * CharsPerInch;
SizeLines   = (PageTop - PageBottom) / 72.0 * LinesPerInch;
```

and allocate the memory needed by the page:

```
/* Allocate memory for the page buffer */
Page    = calloc(sizeof(lchar_t *), SizeLines);
Page[0] = calloc(sizeof(lchar_t), SizeColumns * SizeLines);
for (line = 1; line < SizeLines; line ++)
  Page[line] = Page[0] + line * SizeColumns;
```

Multi-column text uses some additional parameters that define the column and gutter (the space between the columns) widths:

```
if (PageColumns > 1)
{
  ColumnGutter = CharsPerInch / 2;
  ColumnWidth  = (SizeColumns - ColumnGutter * (PageColumns - 1)) /
                  PageColumns;
}
else
  ColumnWidth = SizeColumns;
```

The classification labels use a pretty straightforward mapping from the classification name the scheduler provides to English words:

```
/* Set any classification/label strings... */
memset(file_notice, 0, sizeof(file_notice));

if (classification || label)
{
  if (classification)
  {
    if (strcmp(classification, "confidential") == 0)
      classification = "CONFIDENTIAL";
    else if (strcmp(classification, "classified") == 0)
      classification = "CLASSIFIED";
    else if (strcmp(classification, "secret") == 0)
      classification = "SECRET";
    else if (strcmp(classification, "topsecret") == 0)
      classification = "TOP SECRET";
    else if (strcmp(classification, "unclassified") == 0)
      classification = "UNCLASSIFIED";
  }

  if (classification && label)
    snprintf(s, sizeof(s), "%s - %s", classification, label);
  else if (classification)
  {
    strncpy(s, classification, sizeof(s) - 1);
    s[sizeof(s) - 1] = '\0';
  }
  else
  {
    strncpy(s, label, sizeof(s) - 1);
    s[sizeof(s) - 1] = '\0';
  }
```

After you have the words, convert the characters to the text filter's lchar_t structures so they can be printed in boldface text:

```
  for (ptr = s, lptr = file_notice + (SizeColumns - strlen(s)) / 2;
       *ptr;
       ptr ++, lptr ++)
  {
    lptr->ch   = *ptr;
    lptr->attr = ATTR_BOLD;
  }
}
```

Finally, initialize the printer using a series of PCL commands.

The `WritePage()` Function

The `WritePage()` function provides the "guts" for the filter. It handles actually writing each page to the printer. The first thing is to send a PAGE: message to the scheduler for the page you are about to send to the printer:

```
NumPages ++;

fprintf(stderr, "PAGE: %d %d\n", NumPages, Copies);
```

After you prep the printer for the page, call a local function called `write_line()` to actually write each line to the printer. Each character in a line on the page is stored in an `lchar_t` structure, which contains the character and attributes for the character. The `write_line()` function scans a line for characters that use the same attributes and writes each fragment using the local function `write_string()`.

After all the lines have been written, eject the page, clear the page buffer, and return:

```
/* Eject the page. */
putchar(0x0c);

/* Clear the page. */
memset(Page[0], 0, sizeof(lchar_t) * SizeColumns * SizeLines);
```

Using the `texttohp` Filter

Listing 17.1 shows the completed `texttohp.c` module. Because it is based on the CUPS `texttops` filter, you need to copy the `common.h`, `common.c`, `textcommon.h`, and `textcommon.c` source files and build `texttohp` using these files as well:

cc -o texttohp texttohp.c testcommon.c common.c -lcups *ENTER*

The Chapter 17 example directory also includes a `Makefile` and copies of these files to make building the filter easier:

make texttohp *ENTER*

After you have built the `texttohp` filter, copy it to the CUPS filter directory:

cp texttohp /usr/lib/cups/filter *ENTER*

Then add the following line to the `laserjet.ppd` and `deskjet.ppd` files in the `/usr/share/cups/model` directory:

```
cupsFilter: "text/* 0 texttohp"
```

This tells the scheduler that it can use the text filter to print text files faster.

Finally, re-add the printers that use the `laserjet.ppd` or `deskjet.ppd` drivers to register the new filters.

LISTING 17.1   The "texttohp.c" text driver module

```c
/* Include necessary headers... */
#include "textcommon.h"


/* Local functions... */

static void write_line(int row, lchar_t *line);
static void write_string(int col, int row, int len, lchar_t *s);

/* Local globals... */

static char    file_date[255],
               file_title[255];
static lchar_t file_notice[255]; /* Class + caveat */


/*
 * 'main()' - Main entry for text to HP-PCL filter.
 */

int                    /* O - Exit status */
main(int  argc,        /* I - Number of command-line arguments */
     char *argv?) /* I - Command-line arguments */
{
  /* Print stuff. */
  return (TextMain("texttohp", argc, argv));
}


/*
 * 'WriteEpilogue()' - Write the HP-PCL file epilogue.
 */

void
WriteEpilogue(void)
{
  printf("\033E");
```

LISTING 17.1   Continued

```c
    free(Page[0]);
    free(Page);
}


/*
 * 'WritePage()' - Write a page of text.
 */

void
WritePage(void)
{
  float left,       /* Left margin */
        width;      /* Width of page */
  int   line;       /* Current line */
  char  page[255];  /* Page number */


  NumPages ++;

  fprintf(stderr, "PAGE: %d %d\n", NumPages, Copies);

  /* Print the shaded header as needed. */
  if (PrettyPrint)
  {
    sprintf(page, "%d", NumPages);

    if (!Duplex || (NumPages & 1))
      left = PageLeft * 10.0f;
    else
      left = (PageWidth - PageRight) * 10.0f;

    width = (PageRight - PageLeft) * 10.0f;

    printf("\033(s3B");
    printf("\033&a%.0fH\033&a360V", left);

    printf("\033*c%.0fH\033*c%.0fV", width, 720.0f * 2.0f / LinesPerInch);
    printf("\033*c10G\033*c2P");

    printf("\033&a%.0fV", 360.0f + 1.343f * 720.0f / LinesPerInch);
```

LISTING 17.1   Continued

```
  if (!Duplex || (NumPages & 1))
  {
    printf("\033&a%.0fH%s", left + 720.0f / CharsPerInch, file_title);
    printf("\033&a%.0fH%s",
           left + 0.5 * (width - 720.0f / CharsPerInch * strlen(file_date)),
           file_date);
    printf("\033&a%.0fH%s",
           left + width - 720.0f / CharsPerInch * (strlen(page) + 1), page);
  }
  else
  {
    printf("\033&a%.0fH%s", left + 720.0f / CharsPerInch, page);
    printf("\033&a%.0fH%s",
           left + 0.5 * (width - 720.0f / CharsPerInch * strlen(file_date)),
           file_date);
    printf("\033&a%.0fH%s",
           left + width - 720.0f / CharsPerInch * (strlen(file_title) + 1),
           file_title);
  }
}


/* Classification/label stuff... */
write_line(-2, file_notice);

/* Then all the lines. */
for (line = 0; line < SizeLines; line ++)
  write_line(line, Page[line]);

/* Classification/label stuff. */
write_line(SizeLines + 1, file_notice);

/* Eject the page. */
putchar(0x0c);

/* Clear the page. */
memset(Page[0], 0, sizeof(lchar_t) * SizeColumns * SizeLines);
}


/*
 * 'WriteProlog()' - Write the HP-PCL file prolog with options.
 */
```

LISTING 17.1   Continued

```
void
WriteProlog(const char *title,           /* I - Title of job */
            const char *user,            /* I - Username */
            const char *classification,  /* I - Classification */
            const char *label,           /* I - Page label */
            ppd_file_t *ppd)             /* I - PPD file info */
{
  int           line;               /* Current output line */
  char          *charset;           /* Character set string */
  time_t        curtime;            /* Current time */
  struct tm     *curtm;             /* Current date */
  ppd_choice_t  *input_slot;        /* InputSlot option (if any) */
  char          *temp;              /* MediaPosition string (if any) */
  int           pos;                /* MediaPosition value (if any) */
  char          s[255],             /* Classification/label string */
                *ptr;               /* Pointer into string */
  lchar_t       *lptr;              /* Pointer into line */


  /* Don't use the user argument. */
  (void)user;

  /* Adjust margins as necessary for page labels. */
  if (classification || label)
  {
    /* Leave room for labels. */
    PageBottom += 144.0 / LinesPerInch;
    PageTop    -= 144.0 / LinesPerInch;
  }

  /* Set the printing time. */
  curtime = time(NULL);
  curtm   = localtime(&curtime);
  strftime(file_date, sizeof(file_date), "%c", curtm);

  /* Set the title... */
  strncpy(file_title, title, sizeof(file_title) - 1);
  file_title[sizeof(file_title) - 1] = '\0';

  /* Figure out the page size. */
  SizeColumns = (PageRight - PageLeft) / 72.0 * CharsPerInch;
  SizeLines   = (PageTop - PageBottom) / 72.0 * LinesPerInch;
```

LISTING 17.1   Continued

```c
/* Allocate memory for the page buffer */
Page     = calloc(sizeof(lchar_t *), SizeLines);
Page[0] = calloc(sizeof(lchar_t), SizeColumns * SizeLines);
for (line = 1; line < SizeLines; line ++)
  Page[line] = Page[0] + line * SizeColumns;

if (PageColumns > 1)
{
  ColumnGutter = CharsPerInch / 2;
  ColumnWidth  = (SizeColumns - ColumnGutter * (PageColumns - 1)) /
                 PageColumns;
}
else
  ColumnWidth = SizeColumns;

/* Set any classification/label strings... */
memset(file_notice, 0, sizeof(file_notice));

if (classification || label)
{
  if (classification)
  {
    if (strcmp(classification, "confidential") == 0)
      classification = "CONFIDENTIAL";
    else if (strcmp(classification, "classified") == 0)
      classification = "CLASSIFIED";
    else if (strcmp(classification, "secret") == 0)
      classification = "SECRET";
    else if (strcmp(classification, "topsecret") == 0)
      classification = "TOP SECRET";
    else if (strcmp(classification, "unclassified") == 0)
      classification = "UNCLASSIFIED";
  }

  if (classification && label)
    snprintf(s, sizeof(s), "%s - %s", classification, label);
  else if (classification)
  {
    strncpy(s, classification, sizeof(s) - 1);
    s[sizeof(s) - 1] = '\0';
  }
```

LISTING 17.1   Continued

```c
    else
    {
      strncpy(s, label, sizeof(s) - 1);
      s[sizeof(s) - 1] = '\0';
    }

    for (ptr = s, lptr = file_notice + (SizeColumns - strlen(s)) / 2;
         *ptr;
         ptr ++, lptr ++)
    {
      lptr->ch   = *ptr;
      lptr->attr = ATTR_BOLD;
    }
  }

  /* Set the actual media size and character sizes... */
  printf("\033E");
  printf("\033&l%dX", Copies);
  printf("\033&l%dO", Orientation);

  switch ((int)(PageLength + 0.5f))
  {
    case 540 : /* Monarch Envelope */
        printf("\033&l80A");
        break;

    case 624 : /* DL Envelope */
        printf("\033&l90A");
        break;

    case 649 : /* C5 Envelope */
        printf("\033&l91A");
        break;

    case 684 : /* COM-10 Envelope */
        printf("\033&l81A");
        break;

    case 709 : /* B5 Envelope */
        printf("\033&l100A");
        break;
```

LISTING 17.1   Continued

```
case 756 : /* Executive */
    printf("\033&l1A");
    break;

case 792 : /* Letter */
    printf("\033&l2A");
    break;

case 842 : /* A4 */
    printf("\033&l26A");
    break;

case 1008 : /* Legal */
    printf("\033&l3A");
    break;

case 1191 : /* A3 */
    printf("\033&l27A");
    break;

case 1224 : /* Tabloid */
    printf("\033&l6A");
    break;

default :
    /* Set page length */
    printf("\033&l%.2fP", PageLength / 12.0);
    break;
}

printf("\033&l0L"); /* Turn off perforation skip */
printf("\033&l0E"); /* Reset top margin to 0 */

if ((input_slot = ppdFindMarkedChoice(ppd, "InputSlot")) != NULL)
{
  if ((temp = strstr(input_slot->code, "/cupsMediaPosition")) != NULL)
    if ((pos = atoi(temp + 19)) != 0)
      printf("\033&l%dH", pos);
}

printf("\033&l%dS", Duplex + (Orientation & 1));
printf("\033(s%dH", CharsPerInch);
printf("\033(s%.2fV", 72.0f / (float)LinesPerInch);
```

LISTING 17.1   Continued

```
  if (ColorDevice)
    printf("\033*r3U");

 /*
  * Get the output character set; if it is undefined or "us-ascii", do
  * nothing because we can use the default encoding...
  */

  charset = getenv("CHARSET");
  if (charset != NULL && strcmp(charset, "us-ascii") != 0)
  {
    /* Set the HP-PCL character set to ISO-8859-1. */
    printf("\033(0N");
  }
}


/*
 * 'write_line()' - Write a row of text.
 */

static void
write_line(int      row,   /* I - Row number (0 to N) */
           lchar_t *line) /* I - Line to print */
{
  int      col;             /* Current column */
  int      attr;            /* Current attribute */
  lchar_t *start;           /* First character in sequence */


  for (col = 0, start = line; col < SizeColumns;)
  {
    while (col < SizeColumns && (line->ch == ' ' || line->ch == 0))
    {
      col ++;
      line ++;
    }

    if (col >= SizeColumns)
      break;

    attr  = line->attr;
    start = line;
```

LISTING 17.1   Continued

```
    while (col < SizeColumns && line->ch != 0 && attr == line->attr)
    {
      col ++;
      line ++;
    }

    write_string(col - (line - start), row, line - start, start);
  }
}


/*
 * 'write_string()' - Write a string of text.
 */

static void
write_string(int     col, /* I - Start column */
             int     row, /* I - Row */
             int     len, /* I - Number of characters */
             lchar_t *s)  /* I - String to print */
{
  float    x, y;          /* Position of text */
  unsigned attr;          /* Character attributes */


  /* Position the text and set the font. */
  if (Duplex && (NumPages & 1) == 0)
  {
    x = (PageWidth - PageRight) * 10.0;
    y = (PageLength - PageTop) * 10.0;
  }
  else
  {
    x = PageLeft * 10.0;
    y = (PageLength - PageTop) * 10.0;
  }

  if (PrettyPrint)
    y += 3.0f * 720.0f / (float)LinesPerInch;

  x += (float)col * 720.0f / (float)CharsPerInch;
  y += (float)(row + 0.843f) * 720.0f / (float)LinesPerInch;
```

LISTING 17.1   Continued

```
attr = s->attr;

if (attr & ATTR_RAISED)
  y -= 360.0 / (float)LinesPerInch;
else if (attr & ATTR_LOWERED)
  y += 360.0 / (float)LinesPerInch;

printf("\033&a%.0fH", x);
printf("\033&a%.0fV", y);

if (attr & ATTR_BOLD)
  printf("\033(s3B\033(s0S");
else if (attr & ATTR_ITALIC)
  printf("\033(s0B\033(s1S");
else
  printf("\033(s0B\033(s0S");

if (attr & ATTR_UNDERLINE)
  printf("\033&d0D");
else
  printf("\033&d@");

if (ColorDevice && PrettyPrint)
{
  if (attr & ATTR_BOLD)
    printf("\033*v4S");
  else if (attr & ATTR_ITALIC)
    printf("\033*v2S");
  else
    printf("\033*v0S");
}

/* Write the string. */
while (len > 0)
{
  putchar(s->ch);

  len --;
  s ++;
}
}
```

Reading Raster Data

All raster printer drivers need to read raster images for each page in the job. The cupsimage library provides several functions for reading streams of raster data. Table 17.2 lists the raster functions.

TABLE 17.2   CUPS raster reading functions

Name	Description
cupsRasterClose()	Closes a raster stream.
cupsRasterOpen()	Opens a raster stream.
cupsRasterReadHeader()	Reads a page header from the stream.
cupsRasterReadPixels()	Reads pixel data from the stream.

Opening a Raster Stream

The cupsRasterOpen() function initializes a cups_raster_t structure for reading raster data from a filter:

```
cups_raster_t *ras;
...
ras = cupsRasterOpen(0, CUPS_RASTER_READ);
```

The first argument specifies the file descriptor from which to read; the 0 value means to read from the standard input file.

The second argument specifies the open mode. Use CUPS_RASTER_READ to read from a raster stream.

The return value is a pointer to a cups_raster_t structure.

Closing a Raster Stream

After you finish reading from the raster stream, call cupsRasterClose() to free the memory used for the stream:

```
cups_raster_t *ras;
...
cupsRasterClose(ras);
```

Reading the Page Header

The cupsRasterReadHeader() function reads a page header from the raster stream:

```
cups_raster_t      *ras;
cups_page_header_t header;
...
while (cupsRasterReadHeader(ras, &header) >= 0)
{
  /* Process page data */
}
```

The ras argument is the raster stream pointer. The header argument is a pointer to a cups_page_header_t structure that contains information about the page being printed.

The return value is 1 if the read was successful or 0 on end-of-file or any other error.

Reading Pixel Data

After you have read the page header you can read the page data using the cupsRasterReadPixels() function:

```
cups_raster_t *ras;
unsigned char buffer[1024];
...
cupsRasterReadPixels(ras, buffer, length);
```

The ras argument points to the raster stream. The buffer argument points to the buffer that will hold the raster data. The length argument specifies the number of bytes to read.

The return value is the number of bytes read or 0 on end-of-file or an error.

NOTE:

The cupsRasterReadPixels() function does not do any checking to make sure that you do not read past the end of a page of data. It is up to you to make sure that your filter reads only as much data as there is in the page.

The cupsBytesPerLine and cupsHeight members of the cups_page_header_t structure define the normal size of the page in bytes. The only exception is for pages whose cupsColorOrder member is set to CUPS_ORDER_PLANAR, in which case you also need to handle multiple planes of data, one for each color.

Adding Dithering to the HP-PCL Driver

One problem with the sample drivers included with CUPS is that they do not provide their own dithering algorithms. This results in poor quality if you use these drivers to print images.

Your second addition to the Hewlett-Packard drivers will be a Floyd-Steinberg dithering algorithm. This type of algorithm is also called a "blue-noise" or "error-diffusion" dithering algorithm.

NOTE:

Dithering (or halftoning) is a complex subject, and whole books have been written on it. Dithering produces a pattern of dots that approximate the color or shade of gray that you want to produce.

The algorithm presented here is suitable for most types of printers, but does suffer from "waterfall" effects common with error-diffusion dithers. One of the best books that describes this problem is Robert Ulichney's *Digital Halftoning* (ISBN 0-262-21009-6.)

Basics of Error-Diffusion Dithering Algorithms

Error-diffusion dithering algorithms work by spreading an error value between adjacent pixels. The error value is the difference between the printed pixel and the original pixel.

A typical implementation maintains an error buffer of the required size and scans from left to right and then right to left on alternate lines. A random value is often added or multiplied with the error value to improve the quality of the error-diffusion dither.

The first thing you need for any error-diffusion dither is an error buffer. For the HP-PCL driver you need two lines of four buffers, one each for the cyan, magenta, yellow, and black colors that can be used:

```
int *ErrorBuffers[2][4];
...
SetupPage(...)
{
  int plane;
...
  ErrorBuffers[0][0] = calloc(sizeof(int), header->cupsWidth + 2);
  for (plane = 1; plane < NumPlanes; plane ++)
    ErrorBuffers[0][plane] = ErrorBuffers[0][0] +
                             plane * (header->cupsWidth + 2);

  ErrorBuffers[1][0] = calloc(sizeof(int), header->cupsWidth + 2);
  for (plane = 1; plane < NumPlanes; plane ++)
    ErrorBuffers[1][plane] = ErrorBuffers[1][0] +
                             plane * (header->cupsWidth + 2);
}
```

Because the printer accepts one bit per pixel rather than eight, you also need an input buffer for the 8-bit data:

```
unsigned char *Pixels[4];
...
```

```
SetupPage(...)
{
  int plane;
...
  Pixels[0] = malloc(header->cupsBytesPerLine);
  for (plane = 1; plane < NumPlanes; plane ++)
    Pixels[plane] = Pixels[0] + plane * header->cupsBytesPerLine / NumPlanes;
}
```

Implementing the Floyd-Steinberg Algorithm

The Floyd-Steinberg dithering algorithm spreads the error over four adjacent pixels. Figure 17.2 shows the layout and weight of each pixel.

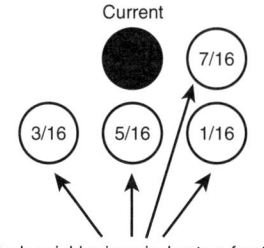

Current

7/16

3/16   5/16   1/16

Each neighboring pixel gets a fraction
of the error value. All error values
add up to 1:

7/16 + 5/16 + 3/16 + 1/16 = 16/16 = 1

FIGURE 17.2

The Floyd-Steinberg error-diffusion dither.

The new function that implements this algorithm is called `DitherLine()`. It is called once for each color plane in the line. The dithering code itself starts with the computation of the current error value:

```
/* Compute the error for this pixel. */
error = *pixels + *error0 / 128;
```

The error value is a number greater than 127 if the pixel should be set and a number less than 128 if the pixel should not be set:

```
/* Set the dithered pixel value (0 or 1). */
if (error < 128)
  *pixels = 0;
else
{
  error   = 255 - error;
  *pixels = 1;
}
```

The remaining error value is then scaled by a random amount:

```
/* Randomize the error value. */
error *= (rand() % 5) + 6;
```

The random multiplier is centered around 8. When combined with the Floyd–Steinberg divisor of 16 the result is a scaling of 128. This is the same value you used for the divisor of the error value in the first step.

Now that you have the scaled error value, add portions of it to the neighboring pixels, spreading a total of 16 portions to 4 pixels:

```
/* Spread the error around. */
error0[0]  = 0;
error0[1]  += 7 * error;
error1[-1] += 3 * error;
error1[0]  += 5 * error;
error1[1]  += error;
```

Repeat this process for every pixel on the line. The completed DitherLine() function is shown in Listing 17.2.

LISTING 17.2   The new DitherLine() function

```
void
DitherLine(unsigned char *pixels, /* IO - Pixels on the line */
           int            width,   /* I  - Width of the line */
           int            plane,   /* I  - Color plane */
           int            y)       /* I  - Current row on the line */
{
  int  error,                      /* Current error value */
       *error0,                    /* Pointer to current error line */
       *error1;                    /* Pointer to next error line */
```

LISTING 17.2   Continued

```c
if (y & 1)
{
  /* Dither right to left. */
  error0 = ErrorBuffers[1][plane] + width;
  error1 = ErrorBuffers[0][plane] + width;

  pixels += width - 1;

  while (width > 0)
  {
    /* Compute the error for this pixel. */
    error = *pixels + *error0 / 128;

    /* Set the dithered pixel value (0 or 1). */
    if (error < 128)
      *pixels = 0;
    else
    {
      error   = 255 - error;
      *pixels = 1;
    }

    /* Randomize the error value. */
    error *= (rand() % 5) + 6;

    /* Spread the error around. */
    error0[0]  = 0;
    error0[-1] += 7 * error;
    error1[1]  += 3 * error;
    error1[0]  += 5 * error;
    error1[-1] += error;

    /* Move to the next pixel */
    pixels --;
    error0 --;
    error1 --;
    width --;
  }
}
else
{
  /* Dither left to right. */
  error0 = ErrorBuffers[0][plane] + 1;
```

LISTING 17.2   Continued

```
  error1 = ErrorBuffers[1][plane] + 1;

  while (width > 0)
  {
    /* Compute the error for this pixel. */
    error = *pixels + *error0 / 128;

    /* Set the dithered pixel value (0 or 1). */
    if (error < 0)
      *pixels = 0;
    else
    {
      error   = 255 - error;
      *pixels = 1;
    }

    /* Randomize the error value. */
    error *= (rand() % 5) + 6;

    /* Spread the error around. */
    error0[0]  = 0;
    error0[1]  += 7 * error;
    error1[-1] += 3 * error;
    error1[0]  += 5 * error;
    error1[1]  += error;

    /* Move to the next pixel */
    pixels ++;
    error0 ++;
    error1 ++;
    width --;
  }
 }
}
```

Updating the PPD Files

Now that you have added the dithering code to the rastertohp driver, you need to add
some commands to the existing PPD files to use the new dithering algorithm.

The cupsBitsPerColor attribute specifies how many bits are passed to the driver for each color. Use a PostScript setpagedevice command to set this attribute for the options:

```
<</cupsBitsPerColor bits>>setpagedevice
```

where bits is the number of bits you want: 1 or 8.

You could add this command to an existing option; however the PPD specification includes a BitsPerPixel option that is specifically suited to the task. The option looks like the following in each PPD file:

```
*OpenUI *BitsPerPixel/Output Quality: PickOne
*OrderDependency: 10 AnySetup *BitsPerPixel
*DefaultBitsPerPixel: 8
*BitsPerPixel 1/Draft: "<</cupsBitsPerColor 1>>setpagedevice"
*BitsPerPixel 8/High: "<</cupsBitsPerColor 8>>setpagedevice"
*CloseUI: *BitsPerPixel
```

Add this option to both the laserjet.ppd and deskjet.ppd files to enable the dithering code.

Installing the New HP-PCL Raster Driver

To install the new driver, start by copying the rastertohp filter to the CUPS filter directory:

cp rastertohp /usr/lib/cups/filter *ENTER*

Then copy the PPD files to the model directory:

cp *.ppd /usr/share/cups/model *ENTER*

Finally, re-add any HP printers to use these new PPD files with the following command:

lpadmin -p name -m filename.ppd *ENTER*

Summary

CUPS printer drivers are composed of a PPD file and one or more filter programs specifically for the printer. PostScript printers can use the standard CUPS filters and do not need additional filter programs to drive them.

Non-PostScript printers generally have a raster filter and may also provide text, HP-GL/2, PDF, and other types of filters for various file formats. The text filter presented in this chapter shows how a printer driver can provide accelerated printing for specific types of files.

Dithering algorithms enable a printer driver to provide higher quality output than the basic raster filters support. The dithering algorithm presented in this chapter shows how to add dithering to printer drivers without a lot of work.

## CHAPTER 18

Writing Backends
for CUPS

Backends do the actual communication with printers, detecting and sending print jobs on demand. This chapter describes how to write a backend for CUPS, including a shell script-based backend for Ethertalk printers.

Overview

Backends are special filters that communicate with printers directly. Backends are the final arbiters of print data, doing whatever is necessary to get the print data to the printer. Figure 18.1 shows the role every backend plays.

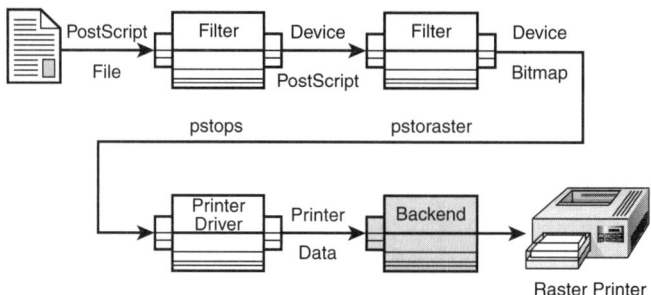

FIGURE 18.1

The role of backends in a print job.

All requirements and advice for filters apply to backends. However, because backends communicate directly with printers, they have some unique requirements.

Security Considerations

Each backend is normally run as the root user, so special care must be taken to avoid potential security violations. In particular, remember that a backend can manipulate disk files, devices, and other resources that have the potential to damage a system or printer.

With backends that run external programs, and script-based backends in particular, you should be especially careful about buffer overflows and other backdoors into the system. Remember, the backend is being run in response to an unprivileged user sending a print job—this can be from a local user or remote system, so any security exploit can be dangerous!

Command-Line Arguments

In addition to the standard filter arguments, backends that are run with no arguments are also used to get a list of available devices. This discovery process is described later in this chapter.

Page Accounting

Backend filters generally do not do page accounting; at a minimum, however, they should produce a single page message for each copy that is produced when a filename is present on the command line. When a filename is present on the command-line, it indicates the user selected "raw" printing and no other accounting information is possible.

If a backend can retrieve page accounting information from the printer, it must send one or more PAGE: messages to the scheduler with the word "total" rather than the copy count:

```
PAGE: 15 total
```

These PAGE: messages set the job-impressions-completed value directly, so each PAGE: message must contain the total number of pages, not just the current page and copies.

Exclusive Access

Backends that talk to local character or block devices should open the device file in exclusive mode (O_EXCL) to cooperate with other printers defined for the same device. If the file cannot be opened and the error number is EAGAIN or EBUSY, the backend should sleep for a certain amount of time, and then retry the open() call indefinitely:

```
int fd;
...
do
{
  if ((fd = open("/dev/filename", O_RDWR | O_EXCL)) < 0)
  {
    if (errno != EAGAIN && errno != EBUSY)
      break;

    sleep(10);
  }
}
while (fd < 0);
```

Retries

All backends must retry connections to the device. This includes backends that talk to local character or block devices, because the user may define more than one printer queue pointing to the same physical device.

NOTE:

Retries are necessary for character and block devices just as much as for network devices. Some local devices may not be ready immediately, or may not respond until the printer is put on-line.

Also, when a properly written backend opens the local device with the O_EXCL option, it will only be successful if no other backend is currently using the device. For example, this allows for two or more print queues to point to the same parallel port. Without the O_EXCL option and retries, the output from both queues could go to the printer simultaneously, resulting in garbled prints.

To prevent excess CPU utilization, the backend should go to sleep for an amount of time between retries; the CUPS-supplied backends retry once every 10 to 30 seconds.

Dissecting the Serial Port Backend

The serial port backend provides support for serial printers. Because it does everything a good backend needs to do, it provides an excellent example of how to write a backend.

Supporting Device Discovery

As previously noted, backends are special filter programs that talk to printer devices. Another task a backend must perform is listing the available devices it supports. The backend lists the available devices when no additional arguments are supplied on the command line; for example:

```
/usr/lib/cups/backend/serial ENTER
serial serial:/dev/ttyS0?baud=115200 "Unknown" "Serial Port #1"
serial serial:/dev/ttyS1?baud=115200 "Unknown" "Serial Port #2"
serial serial:/dev/ttyS2?baud=115200 "Unknown" "Serial Port #3"
serial serial:/dev/ttyS3?baud=115200 "Unknown" "Serial Port #4"
```

The serial backend lists devices by looking at serial port files in the /dev directory, by consulting a hardware inventory (IRIX and Linux), and in some cases by trying to open the ports to see whether they actually exist.

After it finds a serial port it writes a single line for each port to the standard error file. Each line looks something like this:

```
class device-uri "model" "description"
```

The class field identifies the class of device that can be used to categorize it in user interfaces. CUPS currently recognizes the following classes:

- file. A disk file.
- direct. A parallel or fixed-rate serial data port, currently used for Centronics, IEEE-1284, and USB printer ports.

- `serial`. A variable-rate serial port.
- `network`. A network connection, typically via AppSocket, HTTP, IPP, LPD, or SMB/CIFS protocols.

The `device-uri` field appears after the class. This field is the URI that the user should use to select the port or device. For serial ports, the "baud=115200" on the end of the device URI specifies the maximum baud rate supported by the port. The actual value varies based on the speed the user selects for the printer.

The last two fields are the `model` and `description` strings for the device. A model name of "Unknown" means that the printer model is unknown; otherwise, the device should provide the make and model for the printer, such as "HP DeskJet." This enables users and software to choose an appropriate printer driver more easily.

The `description` field provides a human-readable description for the device, such as "Serial Port #1."

Opening the Serial Port

As noted previously, all backends should open device files in exclusive mode, and retry as needed until the port is available. The serial backend does this with a do-while loop, as follows:

```
int  fd;
char resource[HTTP_MAX_URI];
...
do
{
  if ((fd = open(resource, O_WRONLY | O_NOCTTY | O_EXCL)) == -1)
  {
    if (errno == EBUSY)
    {
      fputs("INFO: Serial port busy; will retry in 30 seconds...\n", stderr);
      sleep(30);
    }
    else
    {
      perror("ERROR: Unable to open serial port device file");
      return (1);
    }
  }
}
while (fd < 0);
```

If the port is busy or in use by another process, the backend goes to sleep for 30 seconds and then tries again. If another error is detected, a message is sent to the user and the backend aborts the print job until the problem can be corrected.

Writing Data to the Port

Network and character devices pose an interesting problem when a backend writes data to the port: they may not be able to write all the bytes in your buffer before returning. To work around this problem your backend must loop until all bytes have been written to the device:

```
while (nbytes > 0)
{
  if ((wbytes = write(fd, bufptr, nbytes)) < 0)
    if (errno == ENOTTY)
      wbytes = write(fd, bufptr, nbytes);

  if (wbytes < 0)
  {
    perror("ERROR: Unable to send print file to printer");
    break;
  }

  nbytes -= wbytes;
  bufptr += wbytes;
}
```

The check for the ENOTTY error is needed on some platforms to clear an error from a previous ioctl() call.

Finishing Up

After the backend has sent the print file, return 0 if the file printed successfully or 1 if it did not. This enables the scheduler to stop the print job if there is a device error, preserving the print job for later printing after the problem has been corrected.

Writing a Script-Based Backend

As long as you pay attention to security, using scripts can be a great way to write backends that use existing programs. Backends for e-mailing print files and generating PDF files on the fly are available on the CUPS Web site. All these backends were built using scripts and other programs.

If you have any Ethertalk printers, you probably know what a hassle it is to print to them from a UNIX machine. Among the free Ethertalk solutions are the Columbia Appletalk Package (CAP) and the Netatalk software.

Both software packages support printing to Ethertalk printers using a command-line program. To support these printers from CUPS, all you need to do is write a script to collect the print file and then send the print job.

The beginning of the backend script checks the command line for arguments; if none are supplied then it outputs a device discovery line:

```
# No arguments means show available devices...
if test ${#argv} = 0; then
    echo "network cap \"Unknown\" \"Mac OS Printer via CAP\""
    exit 0
fi
```

Next, the script should collect any arguments it needs and copy the print file to a temporary file as necessary to accommodate retries and copy generation:

```
# Collect arguments...
user=$2
copies=$4

if test ${#argv} = 5; then
    # Get print file from stdin; copies have already been handled...
    file=/var/tmp/$$.prn
    copies=1
    cat > $file
else
    # Print file is on command line...
    file=$6
fi
```

For the CAP software, you need to create a cap.printers file that contains the following entry:

```
name=resource:LaserWriter@server
```

To extract this information from the PRINTER and DEVICE_URI environment variables, use the awk command to split the fields and build the line you need:

```
# Create a dummy cap.printers file for this printer based
# upon a device URI of "cap://server/printer"...
echo $PRINTER/$DEVICE_URI | \
    awk -F/ '{print $1 "=" $5 ":LaserWriter@" $4}' > /var/tmp/$$.cap

CAPPRINTERS=/var/tmp/$$.cap; export CAPPRINTERS
```

Finally, use the `papif` command to send the file. When printing a file that was named on the command line, loop until you have printed all copies:

```
# Send the file to the printer, once for each copy. This assumes that you
# have properly initialized the cap.printers file...
while [ $copies -gt 0 ]; do
    papif -n $user < $file

    copies=`expr $copies - 1`
done
```

The complete script is shown in Listing 18.1. To install the script, copy it to the CUPS backend directory:

cp cap /usr/lib/cups/backend *ENTER*

LISTING 18.1   The CAP backend script

```
#!/bin/sh
#
# Usage: cap job user title copies options [filename]
#

# No arguments means show available devices...
if test ${#argv} = 0; then
    echo "network cap \"Unknown\" \"Mac OS Printer via CAP\""
    exit 0
fi

# Collect arguments...
user=$2
copies=$4

if test ${#argv} = 5; then
    # Get print file from stdin; copies have already been handled...
    file=/var/tmp/$$.prn
    copies=1
    cat > $file
else
    # Print file is on the command line...
    file=$6
fi

# Create a dummy cap.printers file for this printer based
```

LISTING 18.1   Continued

```
# upon a device URI of "cap://server/printer"...
echo $PRINTER/$DEVICE_URI | \
    awk -F/ '{print $1 "=" $5 ":LaserWriter@" $4}' > /var/tmp/$$.cap

CAPPRINTERS=/var/tmp/$$.cap; export CAPPRINTERS

# Send the file to the printer, once for each copy. This assumes that you
# have properly initialized the cap.printers file...
while [ $copies -gt 0 ]; do
    papif -n $user < $file

    copies=`expr $copies - 1`
done

# Remove any temporary files...
if test ${#argv} = 5; then
    /bin/rm -f $file
fi

/bin/rm -f /var/tmp/$$.cap

exit 0
```

Summary

Backends are special filters that communicate directly with printers. Backends have special security and page accounting requirements that should be closely scrutinized to avoid problems.

Backends can be programs or scripts. Programs provide the most control over devices, whereas scripts offer easier integration with existing software.

CHAPTER **19**

Writing Notifiers for CUPS

This chapter describes how to write a notifier for CUPS and how the `mailto` notifier works.

What Are Notifiers?

Notifiers are programs that send IPP notifications via various protocols. CUPS provides notifier programs for the `indp` and `mailto` protocols. The `ippget` protocol is implemented as an internal method because it uses an HTTP connection from the recipient.

Notifiers are fairly simple programs and merely need to read IPP event messages and send them to the recipient. The CUPS API includes functions for reading and decoding these messages.

Notification and notifier support is available starting with CUPS 1.2.

The CUPS Notifier Architecture

Each notifier program uses a common interface. Notifiers are located in the `/usr/lib/cups/notifier` directory and are executed as needed to send notifications to the notification recipient. There is generally one notifier process per subscription. Figure 19.1 shows the CUPS notification architecture.

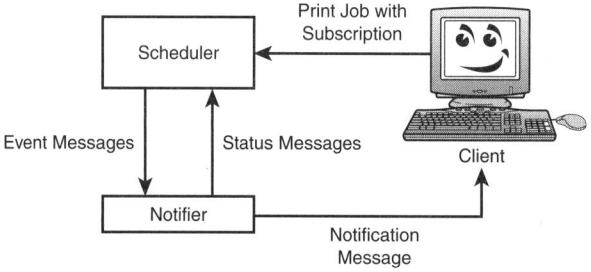

FIGURE 19.1

Sending notification events via CUPS notifiers.

Event messages are piped from the scheduler to each notifier via the standard input file. Status and error messages are piped from the notifier's standard output and standard error files to the scheduler.

The scheduler scans the `/usr/lib/cups/notifier` directory to determine the list of available notification schemes. The `ippget` scheme is always available because it is an internal method in the server.

Command-Line Arguments

Each notifier program is provided with exactly three command-line arguments:

```
notifier recipient-uri notify-user-data
```

The recipient-uri argument (argv[1]) is the recipient for the notification; for example, mailto:joe@foo.bar.com.

The notify-user-data argument (argv[2]) provides an opaque string of data that the client wants in the notification. To ensure that this data is not altered, the string is base-64 encoded and can be decoded using the httpDecode() function.

Environment Variables

Every notifier receives a fixed set of environment variables that the notifier can use. Table 19.1 lists the environment variables.

TABLE 19.1   Environment variables passed to CUPS notifiers

Name	Description
CHARSET	The character set used by the client for this print file.
CLASSIFICATION	The current system-high classification level, such as "unclassified." Provided only when used.
CUPS_DATADIR	The location of CUPS data files.
CUPS_SERVERROOT	The location of CUPS configuration files.
LANG	The language used by the client for this print file.
LD_LIBRARY_PATH	The dynamic load path. Provided only when used.
PATH	The execution path exported to the notifier.
SOFTWARE	The name of the CUPS software, typically "CUPS/1.2."
TMPDIR	The directory for temporary files.
TZ	The local time zone.
USER	The name of the notifier user.

The CLASSIFICATION and LD_LIBRARY_PATH environment variables are set only if they are defined in the scheduler. The CLASSIFICATION environment variable corresponds to the Classification directive:

```
Classification secret
```

The LD_LIBRARY_PATH environment variable is inherited from the environment of the scheduler:

```
LD_LIBRARY_PATH=/foo/bar; export LD_LIBRARY_PATH ENTER
cupsd ENTER
```

All other environment variables are guaranteed to be present and use default values when they are not otherwise configured in the `cupsd.conf` file.

Reading Event Data

Event data is provided via a pipe to the standard input file. Notifiers use the `ippReadFile()` function and must then read zero or more notification messages. When an end-of-file or broken pipe error is seen, the notifier should exit immediately. Otherwise, it should continue reading new messages and sending notifications indefinitely.

Sending Messages to the Scheduler

The CUPS scheduler collects messages that the notifier sends to the standard output and standard error files. These messages are stored in the `error_log` file based upon the scheduler `LogLevel` directive.

An initial prefix string sent with each message line determines the type of message. Table 19.2 lists the available prefixes.

TABLE 19.2   Message string prefixes for CUPS notifiers

Prefix	Description
DEBUG:	A debugging message
DEBUG2:	A detailed debugging message
ERROR:	An error message
INFO:	An informational message
WARNING:	A warning message

If the line of text does not begin with any of the above prefixes, it is treated as a `DEBUG:` message.

Return Values

The notifier should return a status of 0 when there are no new messages to receive or non-zero if a fatal error has occurred.

NOTE:

If the notifier detects a temporary error in making a notification to the recipient, *it must not exit*. Only fatal errors should trigger an exit with a non-zero status code.

Security Considerations

Notifiers are normally run as non-privileged users, so the major security consideration is resource utilization—notifiers should not depend on unlimited amounts of processor, memory, and disk space.

You should also be careful when creating or modifying files from your notifier. If you need to create a temporary file, use the TMPDIR environment variable to determine where to locate the file.

Finally, design your notifers to handle buffer overflow conditions. In particular, be very conservative about using the gets(), sprintf(), strcat(), and strcpy() functions, which often are the source of buffer overflow risks. Always code around potential buffer overflow situations, even if you believe they will never happen. Your notifier will be more reliable.

NOTE:

Do not create setuid or setgid notifier programs. Most notifiers are accessible to any user, so these programs might be used to bypass system security and access (or change) files and programs on the system.

Users and Groups

The default CUPS configuration runs notifiers as user "lp" and group "other." You can use the User and Group directives in the cupsd.conf file to change this, as follows:

```
User foo
Group bar
```

These accounts and groups should be unprivileged to prevent unwanted security risks.

Temporary Files

You should create temporary files in the directory specified by the TMPDIR environment variable. You can use the cupsTempFile() and cupsTempFd() functions to safely create temporary files in this directory.

Temporary files should be removed when your notifier program is finished, so that disk space is not wasted.

Configuration and Data Files

Configuration files are usually stored in the /etc/cups directory. Notifiers that provide their own configuration files should use the CUPS_SERVERROOT environment variable to locate the configuration files rather than hardcode a particular directory.

The normal convention for notifier configuration files is to use the name of the notifier with an extension of .conf. For example, the `mailto` notifier looks for a file named `mailto.conf`.

Similarly, data files are usually stored under /usr/share/cups. The `CUPS_DATADIR` environment variable contains the actual directory in use.

Retries

In general, notifiers should be written to retry event notifications that involve a state change, but not retry "progress" messages, which have a particularly short life. Retries must not interfere with reading new event messages, because one or more messages could be lost.

Dissecting the `mailto` Notifier

The `mailto` notifier is probably the most popular and most used. Typically, the `-m` option for the `lp` or `lpr` commands is used to schedule a `mailto` notification, as follows:

```
lp -m filename ENTER
lpr -m filename ENTER
```

Each notification is e-mailed to the recipient via the Simple Mail Transport Protocol (SMTP). To prevent mail abuse, only state change events are sent to the recipient—otherwise, you could get an e-mail for every progress update for a job—1%, 2%, and so forth.

The notifier starts by reading the `mailto.conf` configuration file. Table 19.3 lists the configuration directives used in that file.

TABLE 19.3 Configuration directives for the `mailto` notifier

Name	Description
Cc	A carbon-copy address for the message; useful for logging all e-mail notifications.
From	The `From:` address in outgoing e-mails; default is "lp@servername."
SMTPServer	The hostname of the mail server; default is "localhost."
Subject	The prefix for the `Subject:` line in the message.

Next it uses the `ippReadFile()` function to read a notification message from the standard input file, as follows:

```
ipp_t       *msg;
ipp_state_t state;
...
do
```

```
{
  msg = ippNew();
  while ((state = ippReadFile(msg, 0)) != IPP_ERROR)
    if (state == IPP_DATA)
      break;
```

If the read was successful, the notifier uses the `cupsNotifySummary()` and `cupsNotifyText()` functions to create subject and message strings for the recipient:

```
char            *subject;
char            *text;
cups_language_t *lang;
...
lang = cupsLangDefault();
...
if (state == IPP_DATA)
{
  subject = cupsNotifySubject(lang, msg);
  text    = cupsNotifyText(lang, msg);
  email_message(argv[1] + 7, subject, text);
  free(subject);
  free(text);
}
```

Both functions take a `cups_language_t` pointer to localize the strings and an `ipp_t` pointer for the event message itself.

The return value is a pointer to a string that must be freed after its use with the `free()` function.

Finally, the notifier loops back to read another message. When an end-of-file (0) or broken pipe (`EPIPE`) error is seen, the notifier shuts down, returning 0.

Summary

Notifiers provide a way for CUPS to notify users or programs about state changes in the server, a printer, or a job. The `ippget` notification scheme is implemented internally in the CUPS server, whereas all other CUPS notifiers are external programs that receive events on their standard input files.

Notifiers receive messages from the scheduler and send notifications. Each notifier receives three arguments, including the recipient URI and user data for the subscription.

CUPS provides several functions to convert notification messages into human-readable text. These functions are used by the `mailto` notifier and can be used by other text-based notification schemes not provided in the CUPS distribution.

PART IV

Appendices

APPENDIX A

Configuration File Directives

This appendix summarizes the configuration directives used for all the CUPS configuration files.

classes.conf

The CUPS scheduler (cupsd) uses the classes.conf file to store the list of available printer classes. This file contains only locally defined classes and not remote or implicit classes that are created automatically.

Accepting

Examples

```
<Class foo>
...
Accepting yes
</Class>

<Class bar>
...
Accepting no
</Class>
```

Description

The Accepting directive defines the initial Boolean value for the printer-is-accepting-jobs attribute. This directive must appear inside a Class or DefaultClass definition.

AllowUser

Examples

```
<Class name>
...
AllowUser foo
AllowUser bar
</Class>
```

Description

The AllowUser directive adds a username to the requesting-user-name-allowed attribute. This directive must appear inside a Class or DefaultClass definition.

Class

Examples

```
<Class name>
...
</Class>
```

Description

The Class directive begins a printer class definition.

DefaultClass

Examples

```
<DefaultClass name>
...
</Class>
```

Description

The DefaultClass directive begins a printer class definition for the default server destination.

DenyUser

Examples

```
<Class name>
...
DenyUser foo
DenyUser bar
</Class>
```

Description

The DenyUser directive adds a username to the requesting-user-name-denied attribute. This directive must appear inside a Class or DefaultClass definition.

Info

Examples

```
<Class name>
...
Info My Class
</Class>
```

Description

The Info directive defines the string for the printer-info attribute. This directive must appear inside a Class or DefaultClass definition.

JobSheets

Examples

```
<Class name>
...
JobSheets none,standard
</Class>
```

Description

The JobSheets directive specifies the default banner pages to print before and after a print job. This directive must appear inside a Class or DefaultClass definition.

KLimit

Examples

```
<Class name>
...
KLimit 1234
</Class>
```

Description

The KLimit directive defines the value of the job-k-limit attribute. This directive must appear inside a Class or DefaultClass definition.

Location

Examples

```
<Class name>
...
Location Building 1234
</Class>
```

Description

The Location directive defines the string for the printer-location attribute. This directive must appear inside a Class or DefaultClass definition.

PageLimit

Examples

```
<Class name>
...
PageLimit 1234
</Class>
```

Description

The PageLimit directive defines the value of the job-page-limit attribute. This directive must appear inside a Class or DefaultClass definition.

Printer

Examples

```
<Class name>
...
Printer foo
Printer bar
Printer foo@bar
</Class>
```

Description

The Printer directive adds a printer to the class. This directive must appear inside a Class or DefaultClass definition.

QuotaPeriod

Examples

```
<Class name>
...
QuotaPeriod 604800
</Class>
```

Description

The QuotaPeriod directive defines the value of the job-quota-period attribute. This directive must appear inside a Class or DefaultClass definition.

State

Examples

```
<Class foo>
...
State idle
</Class>

<Class bar>
...
State stopped
</Class>
```

Description

The State directive defines the initial value of the printer-state attribute. The strings idle and stopped correspond to the IPP enumeration values. This directive must appear inside a Class or DefaultClass definition.

StateMessage

Examples

```
<Class name>
...
StateMessage Ready to print.
</Class>
```

Description

The StateMessage directive defines the initial string for the printer-state-message attribute. This directive must appear inside a Class or DefaultClass definition.

client.conf

The CUPS client applications (lp, lpr, and so forth) use the client.conf file for default settings. The client applications also look in the user's home directory for a file called .cupsrc.

Encryption

Examples

```
Encryption Never
Encryption IfRequested
Encryption Required
Encryption Always
```

Description

The Encryption directive specifies the default encryption settings for the client. The default setting is IfRequested.

ServerName

Examples

```
ServerName foo.bar.com
ServerName 11.22.33.44
```

Description

The ServerName directive sets the remote server that is to be used for all client operations. That is, it redirects all client requests to the remote server.

The default is to use the local server ("localhost").

cupsd.conf

The CUPS scheduler (cupsd) uses the cupsd.conf file to define all the networking, security, and resource settings. This file must be present for the scheduler to function.

AccessLog

Examples

```
AccessLog /var/log/cups/access_log
AccessLog /var/log/cups/access_log-%s
AccessLog syslog
```

Description

The AccessLog directive sets the name of the access log file. If the filename is not absolute then it is assumed to be relative to the ServerRoot directory. The access log file is stored in "common log format" and any Web access reporting tool can use it to generate a report on CUPS server activity.

To include the server name in the filename, use %s in the name.

The special name syslog can be used to send the access information to the system log rather than to a plain file.

The default access log file is /var/log/cups/access_log.

Allow

Examples

```
Allow from All
Allow from None
Allow from *.domain.com
Allow from .domain.com
Allow from host.domain.com
Allow from nnn.*
Allow from nnn.nnn.*
Allow from nnn.nnn.nnn.*
Allow from nnn.nnn.nnn.nnn
Allow from nnn.nnn.nnn.nnn/mm
Allow from nnn.nnn.nnn.nnn/mmm.mmm.mmm.mmm
```

Description

The Allow directive specifies a hostname, IP address, or network that is allowed access to the server. Allow directives are cumulative, so multiple Allow directives can be used to allow access for multiple hosts or networks.

The /mm notation specifies a classless inter-domain routing (CIDR) netmask as shown in Table A.1

TABLE A.1   CIDR netmasks

mm	netmask	mm	netmask
0	0.0.0.0	8	255.0.0.0
1	128.0.0.0	16	255.255.0.0
2	192.0.0.0	24	255.255.255.0
...	...	32	255.255.255.255

The `Allow` directive must appear inside a `Location` directive.

AuthClass

Examples

```
AuthClass Anonymous
AuthClass User
AuthClass System
AuthClass Group
```

Description

The `AuthClass` directive defines what level of authentication is required. The following values are recognized:

- `Anonymous`. No authentication should be performed (default).
- `User`. A valid username and password is required.
- `System`. A valid username and password is required, and the username must belong to the "sys" group; the `SystemGroup` directive can be used to change the required group name.
- `Group`. A valid username and password is required, and the username must belong to the group named by the `AuthGroupName` directive.

The `AuthClass` directive must appear inside a `Location` directive.

NOTE:

The `AuthClass` directive is obsolete. Consider using the Apache-compatible `Require` directive instead, which provides better functionality.

AuthGroupName

Examples

```
AuthGroupName mygroup
AuthGroupName lp
```

Description

The `AuthGroupName` directive sets the group that is to be used for `Group` authentication.

The `AuthGroupName` directive must appear inside a `Location` directive.

> **NOTE:**
>
> The `AuthGroup` directive is obsolete. Consider using the Apache-compatible `Require` directive instead, which provides better functionality.

AuthType

Examples

```
AuthType None
AuthType Basic
AuthType Digest
```

Description

The `AuthType` directive defines the type of authentication to perform, and recognizes the following values:

- `None`. No authentication should be performed (default).
- `Basic`. The Unix password and group files should be used to perform basic authentication.
- `Digest`. The `/etc/cups/passwd.md5` file should be used to perform digest authentication.

When using `Basic` or `Digest` authentication, clients connecting through the localhost interface can also use certificates to authenticate.

The `AuthType` directive must appear inside a `Location` directive.

AutoPurgeJobs

Examples

```
AutoPurgeJobs Yes
AutoPurgeJobs No
```

Description

The AutoPurgeJobs directive specifies whether to purge completed jobs when they are no longer required for quotas.

This option has no effect if quotas are not enabled. The default setting is No.

BrowseAddress

Examples

```
BrowseAddress 255.255.255.255:631
BrowseAddress 192.0.2.255:631
BrowseAddress host.domain.com:631
```

Description

The BrowseAddress directive specifies an address to which browsing information should be sent. Multiple BrowseAddress directives can be specified to send browsing information to different networks or systems.

The default configuration provides no broadcast addresses.

NOTE:

If you are using HP-UX and a subnet that is not 24, 16, or 8 bits, printer browsing (and in fact all broadcast reception) does not work.

BrowseAllow

Examples

```
BrowseAllow from all
BrowseAllow from none
BrowseAllow from 192.0.2
```

```
BrowseAllow from 192.0.2.0/24
BrowseAllow from 192.0.2.0/255.255.255.0
BrowseAllow from *.domain.com
```

Description

The `BrowseAllow` directive specifies a system or network from which to accept browse packets. The default is to accept browse packets from all hosts.

Host and domain name matching require that you enable the `HostNameLookups` directive.

IP address matching supports exact matches, partial addresses that match networks using netmasks of 255.0.0.0, 255.255.0.0, and 255.255.255.0, and network addresses with a specific netmask or bit count.

BrowseDeny

Examples

```
BrowseDeny from all
BrowseDeny from none
BrowseDeny from 192.0.2
BrowseDeny from 192.0.2.0/24
BrowseDeny from 192.0.2.0/255.255.255.0
BrowseDeny from *.domain.com
```

Description

The `BrowseDeny` directive specifies a system or network from which to reject browse packets. The default is to deny browse packets from no hosts.

Host and domain name matching require that you enable the `HostNameLookups` directive.

IP address matching supports exact matches, partial addresses that match networks using netmasks of 255.0.0.0, 255.255.0.0, and 255.255.255.0, and network addresses with a specific netmask or bit count.

BrowseOrder

Examples

```
BrowseOrder allow,deny
BrowseOrder deny,allow
```

Description

The BrowseOrder directive specifies the order of allow/deny processing. The following settings are recognized; the default order is deny,allow:

- allow,deny. Browse packets are accepted unless specifically denied.
- deny,allow. Browse packets are rejected unless specifically allowed.

BrowseInterval

Examples

```
BrowseInterval 0
BrowseInterval 30
```

Description

The BrowseInterval directive specifies the maximum amount of time that is to elapse between browsing updates. Specifying a value of 0 seconds disables outgoing browse updates but enables a server to receive printer information from other hosts.

NOTE:

The BrowseInterval value should always be less than the BrowseTimeout value; otherwise printers and classes disappear from client systems between updates.

BrowsePoll

Examples

```
BrowsePoll 192.0.2.2:631
BrowsePoll host.domain.com:631
```

Description

The BrowsePoll directive polls a server for available printers once every BrowseInterval seconds. Multiple BrowsePoll directives can be specified to poll multiple servers.

If BrowseInterval is set to 0 then the server is polled once every 30 seconds.

BrowsePort

Examples

```
BrowsePort 631
BrowsePort 9999
```

Description

The BrowsePort directive specifies the UDP port number used for browse packets. The default port number is 631.

NOTE:

You must set the BrowsePort to the same value on all the systems that you want to see.

BrowseRelay

Examples

```
BrowseRelay 193.0.2.1 192.0.2.255
BrowseRelay 193.0.2.0/255.255.255.0 192.0.2.255
BrowseRelay 193.0.2.0/24 192.0.2.255
BrowseRelay *.domain.com 192.0.2.255
BrowseRelay host.domain.com 192.0.2.255
```

Description

The BrowseRelay directive specifies source and destination addresses for relaying browsing information from one host or network to another. Multiple BrowseRelay directives can be specified as needed.

BrowseRelay is typically used on systems that use one or more network interfaces to bridge multiple subnets. It can also be used to relay printer information from polled servers with the following line:

```
BrowseRelay 127.0.0.1 255.255.255.255
```

This effectively provides access to printers on a WAN for all clients on the LAN(s).

BrowseShortNames

Examples

```
BrowseShortNames Yes
BrowseShortNames No
```

Description

The BrowseShortNames directive specifies whether short names are used for remote print-ers when possible. A short name is just the remote printer name, without the server ("printer"). If more than one remote printer is detected with the same name, the long names ("printer@server1", "printer@server2") are used instead.

The default value for this option is Yes.

BrowseTimeout

Examples

```
BrowseTimeout 300
BrowseTimeout 60
```

Description

The BrowseTimeout directive sets the timeout for printer or class information that is received in browse packets. After a printer or class times out it is removed from the list of available destinations.

NOTE:

The BrowseTimeout value should always be greater than the BrowseInterval value. If it isn't, print-ers and classes disappear from client systems between updates.

Browsing

Examples

```
Browsing On
Browsing Off
```

Description

The Browsing directive controls whether network printer browsing is enabled. The default setting is On.

NOTE:

If you are using HP-UX and a subnet that is not 24, 16, or 8 bits, printer browsing (and in fact all broadcast reception) does not work.

Classification

Examples

```
Classification
Classification classified
Classification confidential
Classification secret
Classification topsecret
Classification unclassified
```

Description

The Classification directive sets the classification level on the server. When this option is set, at least one of the banner pages is forced to the classification level, and the classification is placed on each page of output. The default is no classification level.

DataDir

Examples

```
DataDir /usr/share/cups
```

Description

The DataDir directive sets the directory that is to be used for data files. The default directory is /usr/share/cups.

DefaultCharset

Examples

```
DefaultCharset utf-8
DefaultCharset iso-8859-1
DefaultCharset windows-1251
```

Description

The DefaultCharset directive sets the default character set that is to be used for client connections. The default character set is utf-8, but is overridden by the character set for the language specified by the client or the DefaultLanguage directive.

DefaultLanguage

Examples

```
DefaultLanguage de
DefaultLanguage en
DefaultLanguage es
DefaultLanguage fr
DefaultLanguage it
```

Description

The DefaultLanguage directive specifies the default language that is to be used for client connections. Setting the default language also sets the default character set if a language localization file exists for it. The default language is en for English.

Deny

Examples

```
Deny from All
Deny from None
Deny from *.domain.com
Deny from .domain.com
Deny from host.domain.com
Deny from nnn.*
Deny from nnn.nnn.*
Deny from nnn.nnn.nnn.*
```

```
Deny from nnn.nnn.nnn.nnn
Deny from nnn.nnn.nnn.nnn/mm
Deny from nnn.nnn.nnn.nnn/mmm.mmm.mmm.mmm
```

Description

The Deny directive specifies a hostname, IP address, or network that is allowed access to the server. Deny directives are cumulative, so multiple Deny directives can be used to allow access for multiple hosts or networks. The /mm notation specifies a CIDR netmask, as shown earlier in Table A.1.

The Deny directive must appear inside a Location directive.

DocumentRoot

Examples

```
DocumentRoot /usr/share/doc/cups
DocumentRoot /foo/bar/doc/cups
```

Description

The DocumentRoot directive specifies the location of Web content for the HTTP server in CUPS. If an absolute path is not specified then it is assumed to be relative to the ServerRoot directory. The default directory is /usr/share/doc/cups.

Documents are first looked up in a sub-directory for the primary language requested by the client (for example, /usr/share/doc/cups/fr/... for French) and then directly under the DocumentRoot directory (for example, /usr/share/doc/cups/...), so it is possible to localize the Web content by providing subdirectories for each language needed.

Encryption

Examples

```
Encryption Never
Encryption IfRequested
Encryption Required
Encryption Always
```

Description

The Encryption directive must appear inside a Location section and specifies the encryption settings for that location. The default setting is IfRequested for all locations.

> **NOTE:**
>
> Because location-based encryption requires support for the HTTP Upgrade protocol, you must use the `SSLPort` directive to use encryption with most Web browsers.

ErrorLog

Examples

```
ErrorLog /var/log/cups/error_log
ErrorLog /var/log/cups/error_log-%s
ErrorLog syslog
```

Description

The `ErrorLog` directive sets the name of the error log file. If the filename is not absolute then it is assumed to be relative to the `ServerRoot` directory. The default error log file is `/var/log/cups/error_log`.

To include the server name in the filename, use `%s` in the name.

The special name `syslog` can be used to send the error information to the system log rather than to a plain file.

FilterLimit

Examples

```
FilterLimit 0
FilterLimit 200
FilterLimit 1000
```

Description

The `FilterLimit` directive sets the maximum cost of all running job filters. It can be used to limit the number of filter programs that are run on a server and thereby minimize disk, memory, and CPU resource problems. A limit of 0 disables filter limiting.

An average print to a non–PostScript printer needs a filter limit of about 200. A PostScript printer needs about half that (100).

Setting the limit below these thresholds effectively limits the scheduler to printing a single job at any time.

The default limit is 0.

FontPath

Examples

```
FontPath /foo/bar/fonts
FontPath /usr/share/cups/fonts:/foo/bar/fonts
```

Description

The FontPath directive specifies the font path that is to be used in searches for fonts. Multiple directories are separated by the colon (:) character. The default font path is /usr/share/cups/fonts.

Group

Examples

```
Group sys
Group system
Group root
```

Description

The Group directive specifies the Unix group for filter and CGI programs. The default group is sys, system, or root, depending on the operating system.

HostNameLookups

Examples

```
HostNameLookups On
HostNameLookups Off
HostNameLookups Double
```

Description

The HostNameLookups directive controls whether CUPS looks up the hostname for connecting clients. The Double setting causes CUPS to verify that the hostname resolved from the address matches one of the addresses returned for that hostname. Double lookups also prevent clients with unregistered addresses from connecting to your server. The default is Off.

NOTE:

Hostname lookups delay the processing of new connections from client machines. If your clients and name server are on a small local network, this delay is likely to be small.

For larger networks or when you are allowing access to systems on the Internet, the name lookup time can become a serious performance issue.

The default is Off to avoid the potential server performance problems that accompany hostname lookups. Set this option to On or Double only if absolutely required.

ImplicitClasses

Examples

```
ImplicitClasses On
ImplicitClasses Off
```

Description

The ImplicitClasses directive controls whether implicit classes are created based upon the available network printers and classes. The default setting is On but is automatically turned Off if Browsing is turned Off.

KeepAlive

Examples

```
KeepAlive On
KeepAlive Off
```

Description

The KeepAlive directive controls whether to support persistent HTTP connections. The default is On.

NOTE:

HTTP/1.1 clients automatically support persistent connections, whereas HTTP/1.0 clients must specifically request them using the Keep-Alive attribute in the Connection: field of each request.

KeepAliveTimeout

Examples

```
KeepAliveTimeout 60
KeepAliveTimeout 30
```

Description

The KeepAliveTimeout directive controls how long a persistent HTTP connection remains open after the last request. The default is 60 seconds.

Limit

Examples

```
<Limit GET POST>
...
</Limit>

<Limit ALL>
...
</Limit>
```

Description

The Limit directive groups access control directives for specific types of HTTP requests and must appear inside a Location section. Access can be limited for individual request types (DELETE, GET, HEAD, OPTIONS, POST, PUT, and TRACE) or for all request types (ALL). The request type names are case sensitive for compatibility with Apache.

LimitExcept

Examples

```
<LimitExcept GET POST>
...
</LimitExcept>
```

Description

The LimitExcept directive groups access control directives for specific types of HTTP requests and must appear inside a Location section. Unlike the Limit directive, LimitExcept restricts access for all requests *except* those listed on the LimitExcept line.

LimitRequestBody

Examples

```
LimitRequestBody 10485760
LimitRequestBody 10m
LimitRequestBody 0
```

Description

The LimitRequestBody directive controls the maximum size of print files, IPP requests, and HTML form data in HTTP POST requests. The default limit is 0, which disables the limit check.

Also see the identical MaxRequestSize directive.

Listen

Examples

```
Listen 127.0.0.1:631
Listen 192.0.2.1:80
Listen foo.bar.com:631
```

Description

The Listen directive specifies a network address and port to listen to for connections. Multiple Listen directives can be provided to enable listening on multiple addresses.

The Listen directive is similar to the Port directive, but enables you to listen to only specific interfaces or networks.

Location

Examples

```
<Location />
...
</Location>

<Location /admin>
...
</Location>
```

```
<Location /printers/name>
...
</Location>
```

Description

The `Location` directive specifies access control and authentication options for the specified HTTP resource or path. The `Allow`, `AuthClass`, `AuthGroupName`, `AuthType`, `Deny`, `Encryption`, `Limit`, `LimitExcept`, `Order`, `Require`, and `Satisfy` directives may all appear inside a location.

LogLevel

Examples

```
LogLevel none
LogLevel emerg
LogLevel alert
LogLevel crit
LogLevel error
LogLevel warn
LogLevel notice
LogLevel info
LogLevel debug
LogLevel debug2
```

Description

The `LogLevel` directive specifies the level of logging for the `ErrorLog` file. Each level logs everything under the preceding levels. The following values are recognized:

- `none`. Log nothing.
- `emerg`. Log emergency conditions that prevent the server from running.
- `alert`. Log alerts that must be handled immediately.
- `crit`. Log critical errors that don't prevent the server from running.
- `error`. Log general errors.
- `warn`. Log errors and warnings.
- `notice`. Log temporary error conditions.
- `info`. Log all requests and state changes (default).
- `debug`. Log basic debugging information.
- `debug2`. Log all debugging information.

MaxClients

Examples

```
MaxClients 100
MaxClients 1024
```

Description

The MaxClients directive controls the maximum number of simultaneous clients allowed by the server. The default is 100 clients.

> **NOTE:**
>
> Because each print job requires a file descriptor for the status pipe, the CUPS server internally limits the MaxClients value to 1/3 of the available file descriptors to avoid possible problems when large numbers of jobs are printing.

MaxJobs

Examples

```
MaxJobs 100
MaxJobs 9999
MaxJobs 0
```

Description

The MaxJobs directive controls the maximum number of jobs that are kept in memory. When the number of jobs reaches the limit, the oldest completed job is automatically purged from the system to make room for the new one. If all the known jobs are still pending or active then the new job is rejected.

Setting the maximum to 0 disables this functionality. The default setting is 0.

MaxJobsPerPrinter

Examples

```
MaxJobsPerPrinter 100
MaxJobsPerPrinter 9999
MaxJobsPerPrinter 0
```

Description

The MaxJobsPerPrinter directive controls the maximum number of active jobs allowed for each printer or class. When a printer or class reaches the limit, new jobs are rejected until one of the active jobs is completed, stopped, aborted, or cancelled.

Setting the maximum to 0 disables this functionality. The default setting is 0.

MaxJobsPerUser

Examples

```
MaxJobsPerUser 100
MaxJobsPerUser 9999
MaxJobsPerUser 0
```

Description

The MaxJobsPerUser directive controls the maximum number of active jobs each user is allowed. When a user reaches the limit, new jobs are rejected until one of the active jobs is completed, stopped, aborted, or cancelled.

Setting the maximum to 0 disables this functionality. The default setting is 0.

MaxLogSize

Examples

```
MaxLogSize 1048576
MaxLogSize 1m
MaxLogSize 0
```

Description

The MaxLogSize directive controls the maximum size of each log file. When a log file reaches or exceeds the maximum size it is closed and renamed to filename.0. This enables you to rotate the logs automatically. The default size is 1048576 bytes (1MB).

Setting the maximum size to 0 disables log rotation.

MaxRequestSize

Examples

```
MaxRequestSize 10485760
MaxRequestSize 10m
MaxRequestSize 0
```

Description

The MaxRequestSize directive controls the maximum size of print files, IPP requests, and HTML form data in HTTP POST requests. The default limit is 0, which disables the limit check.

> **NOTE:**
>
> The MaxRequestSize directive is obsolete and has been replaced by the identical LimitRequestBody directive for Apache compatibility.

Order

Examples

```
Order Allow,Deny
Order Deny,Allow
```

Description

The Order directive defines the default access control. The following values are supported:

- Allow,Deny. Allow requests from all systems except for those listed in a Deny directive.
- Deny,Allow. Allow requests from only those systems listed in an Allow directive.

The Order directive must appear inside a Location directive.

PageLog

Examples

```
PageLog /var/log/cups/page_log
PageLog /var/log/cups/page_log-%s
PageLog syslog
```

Description

The PageLog directive sets the name of the page log file. If the filename is not absolute then it is assumed to be relative to the ServerRoot directory. The default page log file is /var/log/cups/page_log.

To include the server name in the filename, use %s in the name.

The special name syslog can be used to send the page information to the system log rather than to a plain file.

Port

Examples

Port 631
Port 80

Description

The Port directive specifies a port on which to listen. Multiple Port lines can be directed to listen on multiple ports. The default port is 631.

PreserveJobHistory

Examples

PreserveJobHistory On
PreserveJobHistory Off

Description

The PreserveJobHistory directive controls whether the history of completed, cancelled, or aborted print jobs is stored on disk.

A value of On (the default) preserves job information until the administrator purges it with the cancel command.

A value of Off removes the job information as soon as each job is completed, cancelled, or aborted.

NOTE:

Job history information is kept in memory. For servers with many queues or clients, this information can use up a lot of memory on the server and slow the startup of the scheduler. Consider using the MaxJobs or AutoPurgeJobs directives to limit the number of old jobs that are kept in memory.

PreserveJobFiles

Examples

```
PreserveJobFiles On
PreserveJobFiles Off
```

Description

The `PreserveJobFiles` directive controls whether the document files of completed, cancelled, or aborted print jobs are stored on disk.

A value of `On` preserves job files until the administrator purges them with the `cancel` command. Jobs can be restarted (and reprinted) as desired until they are purged.

A value of `Off` (the default) removes the job files as soon as each job is completed, cancelled, or aborted.

This directive is ignored if the `PreserveJobHistory` directive is set to `Off`.

Printcap

Examples

```
Printcap
Printcap /etc/printcap
Printcap /etc/printers.conf
```

Description

The `Printcap` directive controls whether a printcap file is automatically generated and updated with a list of available printers. If specified with no value, then no printcap file is generated. The default is to generate a file named `/etc/printcap`.

When a filename is specified (for example, `/etc/printcap`), the printcap file is written whenever a printer is added or removed. The printcap file can then be used by applications that are hardcoded to look at the printcap file for the available printers.

PrintcapFormat

Examples

```
PrintcapFormat BSD
PrintcapFormat Solaris
```

Description

The PrintcapFormat directive controls the output format of the printcap file. The default is to generate a BSD printcap file.

RemoteRoot

Examples

```
RemoteRoot remroot
RemoteRoot root
```

Description

The RemoteRoot directive sets the username for unauthenticated requests from remote hosts that use the name root. The default username is remroot. Setting RemoteRoot to root effectively disables this security mechanism.

RequestRoot

Examples

```
RequestRoot /var/spool/cups
RequestRoot /foo/bar/spool/cups
```

Description

The RequestRoot directive sets the directory for incoming IPP requests and HTML forms. If an absolute path is not provided then it is assumed to be relative to the ServerRoot directory. The default request directory is /var/spool/cups.

NOTE:

The scheduler changes the ownership and permissions of the RequestRoot directory on startup to limit access to only the user specified by the User directive.

RIPCache

Examples

```
RIPCache 8m
RIPCache 1g
RIPCache 2048k
```

Description

The RIPCache directive sets the size of the memory cache used by Raster Image Processor ("RIP") filters such as imagetoraster and pstoraster. The size can be suffixed with a "k" for kilobytes, "m" for megabytes, or "g" for gigabytes.

The default cache size is "8m," or 8 megabytes.

RunAsUser

Examples

RunAsUser Yes
RunAsUser No

Description

The RunAsUser directive controls whether the scheduler runs as the unprivileged user account (usually lp). The default is No, which leaves the scheduler running as the root user.

> **NOTE:**
>
> Running as a non-privileged user may prevent LPD and locally connected printers from working because of permission problems.
>
> The lpd backend automatically uses a non-privileged mode that is not 100% compliant with RFC 1179. This non-privileged mode may not work with all printers or print servers.
>
> The parallel, serial, and usb backends need write access to the corresponding device files.

Satisfy

Examples

Satisfy All
Satisfy Any

Description

The Satisfy directive specifies whether all Allow/Deny, Encryption, and Require conditions must be satisfied to allow access. The default value of All requires all conditions to be satisfied, whereas a value of Any allows access if any of the Allow/Deny, Encryption, or Require conditions are met.

ServerAdmin

Examples

```
ServerAdmin user@host
ServerAdmin root@foo.bar.com
```

Description

The `ServerAdmin` directive identifies the e-mail address for the administrator on the system. By default the administrator e-mail address is `root@server`, where `server` is the server name.

ServerBin

Examples

```
ServerBin /usr/lib/cups
ServerBin /foo/bar/lib/cups
```

Description

The `ServerBin` directive sets the directory for server-run executables. If an absolute path is not provided then it is assumed to be relative to the `ServerRoot` directory. The default executable directory is `/usr/lib/cups`.

ServerCertificate

Examples

```
ServerCertificate /etc/cups/ssl/server.crt
```

Description

The `ServerCertificate` directive specifies the location of the SSL certificate file the server uses when negotiating encrypted connections. The certificate must not be encrypted (password protected) because the scheduler normally runs in the background and is unable to ask for a password. The default certificate file is `/etc/cups/ssl/server.crt`.

ServerKey

Examples

ServerKey /etc/cups/ssl/server.key

Description

The ServerKey directive specifies the location of the SSL private key file the server uses when negotiating encrypted connections. The default key file is /etc/cups/ssl/server.key.

ServerName

Examples

ServerName foo.domain.com
ServerName myserver.domain.com
ServerName 11.22.33.44

Description

The ServerName directive specifies the hostname or IP address that is reported to clients. By default the server name is the hostname of the system.

ServerRoot

Examples

ServerRoot /etc/cups
ServerRoot /foo/bar/cups

Description

The ServerRoot directive specifies the absolute path to the server configuration and state files. It is also used to resolve relative paths in the cupsd.conf file. The default server directory is /etc/cups.

SSLListen

Examples

```
SSLListen 127.0.0.1:443
SSLListen 192.0.2.1:443
SSLListen foo.bar.com:443
```

Description

The SSLListen directive specifies a network address and port to listen on for secure (HTTPS) connections. Multiple SSLListen directives can be provided to enable listening on multiple addresses.

The SSLListen directive is similar to the SSLPort directive but enables you to listen on specific interfaces or networks.

SSLPort

Examples

```
SSLPort 443
```

Description

The SSLPort directive specifies a port to listen on for secure connections. Multiple SSLPort lines can be specified to enable listening on multiple ports.

SystemGroup

Examples

```
SystemGroup sys
SystemGroup system
SystemGroup root
```

Description

The SystemGroup directive specifies the system administration group for System authentication and for validating the administrative privileges of a user. The default system group is sys, system, or root, depending on the operating system.

TempDir

Examples

```
TempDir /var/spool/cups/tmp
TempDir /foo/bar/tmp
```

Description

The TempDir directive specifies an absolute directory path to use for temporary files. The default directory is /var/spool/cups/tmp.

> **NOTE:**
>
> Temporary directories must have the "sticky" permission bit enabled so that other users cannot delete temporary files. Although a world-writable temporary directory may be used, I recommend that a private temporary directory owned by the user specified by the User directive be used instead.
>
> The following commands create an appropriate temporary directory called /foo/bar/tmp:
>
> ```
> mkdir /foo/bar/tmp ENTER
> chown lp /foo/bar/tmp ENTER
> chmod u+rwxt,go-rwx /foo/bar/tmp ENTER
> ```
>
> If the temporary directory is a subdirectory of the RequestRoot directory, then the ownership and permissions are automatically applied to the temporary directory when the scheduler starts.

Timeout

Examples

```
Timeout 300
Timeout 90
```

Description

The Timeout directive controls the amount of time to wait before an active HTTP or IPP request times out. The default timeout is 300 seconds.

User

Examples

```
User lp
User guest
```

Description

The User directive specifies the Unix user account for filter and CGI programs. The default user is lp.

NOTE:

Do not set the User directive to root. If a remote user discovers a vulnerability in one of the file filters or printer drivers, he could execute arbitrary commands or alter files on your system as the root user. Always use an unprivileged account.

---

mailto.conf

The mailto.conf file provides configuration options for the mailto notifier.

Cc

Examples

```
Cc root
Cc foo@bar.com
```

Description

The Cc directive defines an additional address that is to receive a carbon copy of all notification messages. Multiple Cc directives can be specified so that copies are sent to multiple addresses.

From

Examples

```
From lp
From foo@bar.com
```

Description

The From directive defines the "from" address in the mail message. The default value is "lp".

MailCommand

Examples

```
MailCommand /usr/lib/sendmail
MailCommand /usr/bin/mail
```

Description

The MailCommand directive defines the mail command that is to be executed when mail messages are sent. The default value is /usr/lib/sendmail.

This directive is incompatible with the SMTPServer directive.

ReplyTo

Examples

```
ReplyTo foo@bar.com
```

Description

The ReplyTo directive defines the "reply to" address in the mail message. The default value is undefined.

SMTPServer

Examples

```
SMTPServer localhost
SMTPServer foo.bar.com
```

Description

The SMTPServer directive defines the mail server that is to be contacted when mail messages are sent. The default value is undefined.

This directive is incompatible with the MailCommand directive.

pdftops.conf

The pdftops.conf file provides configuration options for the pdftops filter.

fontmap

Examples

```
fontmap pdffont PostScriptFont
fontmap Arial Helvetica
fontmap Arial-Bold Helvetica-Bold
```

Description

The fontmap directive defines an equivalent PostScript font for the specified font in a PDF file. Multiple fontmap lines can be specified for multiple fonts.

fontpath

Examples

```
fontpath /usr/share/cups/fonts
fontpath /foo/bar/fonts
```

Description

The fontpath directive adds a directory to the font search path.

printers.conf

The CUPS scheduler (cupsd) uses the printers.conf file to store the list of available printers. This file contains only locally defined printers, but not remote printers that are created automatically.

Accepting

Examples

```
<Printer foo>
...
Accepting yes
</Printer>

<Printer bar>
...
Accepting no
</Printer>
```

Description

The Accepting directive defines the initial Boolean value for the printer-is-accepting-jobs attribute. This directive must appear inside a Printer or DefaultPrinter definition.

AllowUser

Examples

```
<Printer name>
...
AllowUser foo
AllowUser bar
</Printer>
```

Description

The AllowUser directive adds a username to the requesting-user-name-allowed attribute. This directive must appear inside a Printer or DefaultPrinter definition.

DefaultPrinter

Examples

```
<DefaultPrinter name>
...
</Printer>
```

Description

The DefaultPrinter directive begins a printer definition for the default server destination.

DenyUser

Examples

```
<Printer name>
...
DenyUser foo
DenyUser bar
</Printer>
```

Description

The DenyUser directive adds a username to the requesting-user-name-denied attribute. This directive must appear inside a Printer or DefaultPrinter definition.

DeviceURI

Examples

```
<Printer name>
...
DeviceURI socket://foo.bar.com:9100
</Printer>
```

Description

The DeviceURI directive defines the value of the device-uri attribute. This directive must appear inside a Printer or DefaultPrinter definition.

Info

Examples

```
<Printer name>
...
Info My Printer
</Printer>
```

Description

The Info directive defines the string for the printer-info attribute. This directive must appear inside a Printer or DefaultPrinter definition.

JobSheets

Examples

```
<Printer name>
...
JobSheets none,standard
</Printer>
```

Description

The JobSheets directive specifies the default banner pages to print before and after a print job. This directive must appear inside a Printer or DefaultPrinter definition.

KLimit

Examples

```
<Printer name>
...
KLimit 1234
</Printer>
```

Description

The KLimit directive defines the value of the job-k-limit attribute. This directive must appear inside a Printer or DefaultPrinter definition.

Location

Examples

```
<Printer name>
...
Location Building 1234
</Printer>
```

Description

The Location directive defines the string for the printer-location attribute. This directive must appear inside a Printer or DefaultPrinter definition.

PageLimit

Examples

```
<Printer name>
...
PageLimit 1234
</Printer>
```

Description

The `PageLimit` directive defines the value of the `job-page-limit` attribute. This directive must appear inside a `Printer` or `DefaultPrinter` definition.

Printer

Examples

```
<Printer name>
...
</Printer>
```

Description

The `Printer` directive begins a printer definition.

QuotaPeriod

Examples

```
<Printer name>
...
QuotaPeriod 604800
</Printer>
```

Description

The `QuotaPeriod` directive defines the value of the `job-quota-period` attribute. This directive must appear inside a `Printer` or `DefaultPrinter` definition.

State

Examples

```
<Printer foo>
...
State idle
</Printer>

<Printer bar>
...
State stopped
</Printer>
```

Description

The State directive defines the initial value of the printer-state attribute. The strings idle and stopped correspond to the IPP enumeration values. This directive must appear inside a Printer or DefaultPrinter definition.

StateMessage

Examples

```
<Printer name>
...
StateMessage Ready to print.
</Printer>
```

Description

The StateMessage directive defines the initial string for the printer-state-message attribute. This directive must appear inside a Printer or DefaultPrinter definition.

IPP Reference

This appendix lists the IPP operations and enumerations with the corresponding CUPS constants.

IPP Finishings

The IPP finishings constants are used for the `finishings`, `finishings-default`, and `finishings-supported` attributes. Table B.1 lists the finishings constants.

TABLE B.1   IPP finishings constants provided by CUPS

Name	Value	CUPS Constant
none	3	IPP_FINISHINGS_NONE
staple	4	IPP_FINISHINGS_STAPLE
punch	5	IPP_FINISHINGS_PUNCH
cover	6	IPP_FINISHINGS_COVER
bind	7	IPP_FINISHINGS_BIND
saddle-stitch	8	IPP_FINISHINGS_SADDLE_STITCH
edge-stitch	9	IPP_FINISHINGS_EDGE_STITCH
fold	10	IPP_FINISHINGS_FOLD
trim	11	IPP_FINISHINGS_TRIM
bale	12	IPP_FINISHINGS_BALE
booklet-maker	13	IPP_FINISHINGS_BOOKLET_MAKER
job-offset	14	IPP_FINISHINGS_JOB_OFFSET
staple-top-left	20	IPP_FINISHINGS_STAPLE_TOP_LEFT
staple-bottom-left	21	IPP_FINISHINGS_STAPLE_BOTTOM_LEFT
staple-top-right	22	IPP_FINISHINGS_STAPLE_TOP_RIGHT
staple-bottom-right	23	IPP_FINISHINGS_STAPLE_BOTTOM_RIGHT
edge-stitch-left	24	IPP_FINISHINGS_EDGE_STITCH_LEFT
edge-stitch-top	25	IPP_FINISHINGS_EDGE_STITCH_TOP
edge-stitch-right	26	IPP_FINISHINGS_EDGE_STITCH_RIGHT
edge-stitch-bottom	27	IPP_FINISHINGS_EDGE_STITCH_BOTTOM
staple-dual-left	28	IPP_FINISHINGS_STAPLE_DUAL_LEFT
staple-dual-top	29	IPP_FINISHINGS_STAPLE_DUAL_TOP
staple-dual-right	30	IPP_FINISHINGS_STAPLE_DUAL_RIGHT
staple-dual-bottom	31	IPP_FINISHINGS_STAPLE_DUAL_BOTTOM
bind-left	50	IPP_FINISHINGS_BIND_LEFT
bind-top	51	IPP_FINISHINGS_BIND_TOP
bind-right	52	IPP_FINISHINGS_BIND_RIGHT
bind-bottom	53	IPP_FINISHINGS_BIND_BOTTOM

IPP Job States

The IPP job state constants are used for the job-state attribute. Table B.2 lists the CUPS constants.

TABLE B.2   IPP job state constants provided by CUPS

Name	Value	CUPS Constant
pending	3	IPP_JOB_PENDING
pending-held	4	IPP_JOB_HELD
processing	5	IPP_JOB_PROCESSING
stopped	6	IPP_JOB_STOPPED
canceled	7	IPP_JOB_CANCELLED
aborted	8	IPP_JOB_ABORTED
completed	9	IPP_JOB_COMPLETED

IPP Operations

The IPP operation constants are used for the operation ID in an IPP request. Table B.3 lists the CUPS constants.

TABLE B.3   IPP operation constants provided by CUPS

Name	Value	CUPS Constant
Print-Job	0x0002	IPP_PRINT_JOB
Print-URI	0x0003	IPP_PRINT_URI
Validate-Job	0x0004	IPP_VALIDATE_JOB
Create-Job	0x0005	IPP_CREATE_JOB
Send-Document	0x0006	IPP_SEND_DOCUMENT
Send-URI	0x0007	IPP_SEND_URI
Cancel-Job	0x0008	IPP_CANCEL_JOB
Get-Job-Attributes	0x0009	IPP_GET_JOB_ATTRIBUTES
Get-Jobs	0x000A	IPP_GET_JOBS
Get-Printer-Attributes	0x000B	IPP_GET_PRINTER_ATTRIBUTES
Hold-Job	0x000C	IPP_HOLD_JOB
Release-Job	0x000D	IPP_RELEASE_JOB
Restart-Job	0x000E	IPP_RESTART_JOB
Pause-Printer	0x0010	IPP_PAUSE_PRINTER
Resume-Printer	0x0011	IPP_RESUME_PRINTER
Purge-Jobs	0x0012	IPP_PURGE_JOBS

TABLE B.3   Continued

Name	Value	CUPS Constant
Set-Printer-Attributes	0x0013	IPP_SET_PRINTER_ATTRIBUTES
Set-Job-Attributes	0x0014	IPP_SET_JOB_ATTRIBUTES
Get-Printer-Supported-Values	0x0015	IPP_GET_PRINTER_SUPPORTED_VALUES
Create-Printer-Subscription	0x0016	IPP_CREATE_PRINTER_SUBSCRIPTION
Create-Job-Subscription	0x0017	IPP_CREATE_JOB_SUBSCRIPTION
Get-Subscription-Attributes	0x0018	IPP_GET_SUBSCRIPTION_ATTRIBUTES
Get-Subscriptions	0x0019	IPP_GET_SUBSCRIPTIONS
Renew-Subscription	0x001A	IPP_RENEW_SUBSCRIPTION
Cancel-Subscription	0x001B	IPP_CANCEL_SUBSCRIPTION
Get-Notifications	0x001C	IPP_GET_NOTIFICATIONS
Send-Notifications	0x001D	IPP_SEND_NOTIFICATIONS
Get-Print-Support-Files	0x0021	IPP_GET_PRINT_SUPPORT_FILES
Enable-Printer	0x0022	IPP_ENABLE_PRINTER
Disable-Printer	0x0023	IPP_DISABLE_PRINTER
Pause-Printer-After-Current-Job	0x0024	IPP_PAUSE_PRINTER_AFTER_CURRENT_JOB
Hold-New-Jobs	0x0025	IPP_HOLD_NEW_JOBS
Release-Held-New-Jobs	0x0026	IPP_RELEASE_HELD_NEW_JOBS
Deactivate-Printer	0x0027	IPP_DEACTIVATE_PRINTER
Activate-Printer	0x0028	IPP_ACTIVATE_PRINTER
Restart-Printer	0x0029	IPP_RESTART_PRINTER
Shutdown-Printer	0x002A	IPP_SHUTDOWN_PRINTER
Startup-Printer	0x002B	IPP_STARTUP_PRINTER
Reprocess-Job	0x002C	IPP_REPROCESS_JOB
Cancel-Current-Job	0x002D	IPP_CANCEL_CURRENT_JOB
Suspend-Current-Job	0x002E	IPP_SUSPEND_CURRENT_JOB
Resume-Job	0x002F	IPP_RESUME_JOB
Promote-Job	0x0030	IPP_PROMOTE_JOB
Schedule-Job-After	0x0031	IPP_SCHEDULE_JOB_AFTER
CUPS-Get-Default	0x4001	CUPS_GET_DEFAULT
CUPS-Get-Printers	0x4002	CUPS_GET_PRINTERS
CUPS-Add-Printer	0x4003	CUPS_ADD_PRINTER
CUPS-Delete-Printer	0x4004	CUPS_DELETE_PRINTER
CUPS-Get-Classes	0x4005	CUPS_GET_CLASSES
CUPS-Add-Class	0x4006	CUPS_ADD_CLASS
CUPS-Delete-Class	0x4007	CUPS_DELETE_CLASS
CUPS-Accept-Jobs	0x4008	CUPS_ACCEPT_JOBS
CUPS-Reject-Jobs	0x4009	CUPS_REJECT_JOBS

TABLE B.3   Continued

Name	Value	CUPS Constant
CUPS-Set-Default	0x400A	CUPS_SET_DEFAULT
CUPS-Get-Devices	0x400B	CUPS_GET_DEVICES
CUPS-Get-PPDs	0x400C	CUPS_GET_PPDS
CUPS-Move-Job	0x400D	CUPS_MOVE_JOB
CUPS-Add-Device	0x400E	CUPS_ADD_DEVICE
CUPS-Delete-Device	0x400F	CUPS_DELETE_DEVICE

IPP Orientations

The IPP orientation constants are used for the orientation-requested, orientation-default, and orientation-supported attributes. Table B.4 lists the CUPS constants.

TABLE B.4   IPP orientation constants provided by CUPS

Name	Value	CUPS Constant
portrait	3	IPP_PORTRAIT
landscape	4	IPP_LANDSCAPE
reverse-landscape	5	IPP_REVERSE_LANDSCAPE
reverse-portrait	6	IPP_REVERSE_PORTRAIT

IPP Printer States

The IPP printer state constants are used for the printer-state attribute. Table B.5 lists the CUPS constants.

TABLE B.5   IPP printer state constants provided by CUPS

Name	Value	CUPS Constant
idle	3	IPP_PRINTER_IDLE
processing	4	IPP_PRINTER_PROCESSING
stopped	5	IPP_PRINTER_STOPPED

IPP Qualities

The IPP orientation constants are used for the quality, quality-default, and quality-supported attributes. Table B.6 lists the CUPS constants.

TABLE B.6   IPP quality constants provided by CUPS

Name	Value	CUPS Constant
draft	3	IPP_QUALITY_DRAFT
normal	4	IPP_QUALITY_NORMAL
high	5	IPP_QUALITY_HIGH

IPP Resolution Units

The IPP resolution constants are used for the units member of all resolution attributes. Table B.7 lists the CUPS constants.

TABLE B.7   IPP resolution unit constants provided by CUPS

Name	Value	CUPS Constant
dots-per-inch	3	IPP_RES_PER_INCH
dots-per-centimeter	4	IPP_RES_PER_CM

IPP Status Codes

The IPP status code constants are used for the status code in an IPP response. Table B.8 lists the CUPS constants.

TABLE B.8   IPP status code constants provided by CUPS

Name	Value	CUPS Constant
successful-ok	0x0000	IPP_OK
successful-ok-ignored-or-substituted-attributes	0x0001	IPP_OK_SUBST
successful-ok-conflicting-attributes	0x0002	IPP_OK_CONFLICT
successful-ok-ignored-subscriptions	0x0003	IPP_OK_IGNORED_SUBSCRIPTIONS
successful-ok-ignored-notifications	0x0004	IPP_OK_IGNORED_NOTIFICATIONS
successful-ok-too-many-events	0x0005	IPP_OK_TOO_MANY_EVENTS
successful-ok-but-cancel-subscription	0x0006	IPP_OK_BUT_CANCEL_SUBSCRIPTION
redirection-other-site	0x0300	IPP_REDIRECTION_OTHER_SITE
client-error-bad-request	0x0400	IPP_BAD_REQUEST
client-error-forbidden	0x0401	IPP_FORBIDDEN
client-error-not-authenticated	0x0402	IPP_NOT_AUTHENTICATED
client-error-not-authorized	0x0403	IPP_NOT_AUTHORIZED

TABLE B.8   Continued

Name	Value	CUPS Constant
client-error-not-possible	0x0404	IPP_NOT_POSSIBLE
client-error-timeout	0x0405	IPP_TIMEOUT
client-error-not-found	0x0406	IPP_NOT_FOUND
client-error-gone	0x0407	IPP_GONE
client-error-request-entity-too-large	0x0408	IPP_REQUEST_ENTITY
client-error-request-value-too-large	0x0409	IPP_REQUEST_VALUE
client-error-document-format-not-supported	0x040A	IPP_DOCUMENT_FORMAT
client-error-attributes-or-values-not-supported	0x040B	IPP_ATTRIBUTES
client-error-uri-scheme-not-supported	0x040C	IPP_URI_SCHEME
client-error-charset-not-supported	0x040D	IPP_CHARSET
client-error-conflicting-attributes	0x040E	IPP_CONFLICT
client-error-compression-not-supported	0x040F	IPP_COMPRESSION_NOT_SUPPORTED
client-error-compression-error	0x0410	IPP_COMPRESSION_ERROR
client-error-document-format-error	0x0411	IPP_DOCUMENT_FORMAT_ERROR
client-error-document-access-error	0x0412	IPP_DOCUMENT_ACCESS_ERROR
client-error-attributes-not-settable	0x0413	IPP_ATTRIBUTES_NOT_SETTABLE
client-error-ignored-all-subscriptions	0x0414	IPP_IGNORED_ALL_SUBSCRIPTIONS
client-error-too-many-subscriptions	0x0415	IPP_TOO_MANY_SUBSCRIPTIONS
client-error-ignored-all-notifications	0x0416	IPP_IGNORED_ALL_NOTIFICATIONS
client-error-print-support-file-not-found	0x0417	IPP_PRINT_SUPPORT_FILE_NOT_FOUND
server-error-internal-error	0x0500	IPP_INTERNAL_ERROR
server-error-operation-not-supported	0x0501	IPP_OPERATION_NOT_SUPPORTED
server-error-service-unavailable	0x0502	IPP_SERVICE_UNAVAILABLE
server-error-version-not-supported	0x0503	IPP_VERSION_NOT_SUPPORTED
server-error-device-error	0x0504	IPP_DEVICE_ERROR
server-error-temporary-error	0x0505	IPP_TEMPORARY_ERROR
server-error-not-accepting-jobs	0x0506	IPP_NOT_ACCEPTING
server-error-busy	0x0507	IPP_PRINTER_BUSY
server-error-job-canceled	0x0508	IPP_ERROR_JOB_CANCELLED
server-error-multiple-jobs-not-supported	0x0509	IPP_MULTIPLE_JOBS_NOT_SUPPORTED
server-error-printer-is-deactivated	0x050A	IPP_PRINTER_IS_DEACTIVATED

IPP Tags

The IPP tag constants are used for the group and value tags in IPP requests, responses, and notifications. Table B.9 lists the CUPS constants.

TABLE B.9   IPP tag constants provided by CUPS

Name	Value	CUPS Constant
-	0x00	IPP_TAG_ZERO
operation-attributes-tag	0x01	IPP_TAG_OPERATION
job-attributes-tag	0x02	IPP_TAG_JOB
end-of-attributes-tag	0x03	IPP_TAG_END
printer-attributes-tag	0x04	IPP_TAG_PRINTER
unsupported-attributes-tag	0x05	IPP_TAG_UNSUPPORTED_GROUP
subscription-attributes-tag	0x06	IPP_TAG_SUBSCRIPTION
event-notification-attributes-tag	0x07	IPP_TAG_EVENT_NOTIFICATION
unsupported	0x10	IPP_TAG_UNSUPPORTED_VALUE
default	0x11	IPP_TAG_DEFAULT
unknown	0x12	IPP_TAG_UNKNOWN
no-value	0x13	IPP_TAG_NOVALUE
not-settable	0x15	IPP_TAG_NOTSETTABLE
delete-attribute	0x16	IPP_TAG_DELETEATTR
admin-define	0x17	IPP_TAG_ADMINDEFINE
integer	0x21	IPP_TAG_INTEGER
boolean	0x22	IPP_TAG_BOOLEAN
enum	0x23	IPP_TAG_ENUM
octetString	0x30	IPP_TAG_STRING
dateTime	0x31	IPP_TAG_DATE
resolution	0x32	IPP_TAG_RESOLUTION
rangeOfInteger	0x33	IPP_TAG_RANGE
begCollection	0x34	IPP_TAG_BEGIN_COLLECTION
textWithLanguage	0x35	IPP_TAG_TEXTLANG
nameWithLanguage	0x36	IPP_TAG_NAMELANG
endCollection	0x37	IPP_TAG_END_COLLECTION
textWithoutLanguage	0x41	IPP_TAG_TEXT
nameWithoutLanguage	0x42	IPP_TAG_NAME
keyword	0x44	IPP_TAG_KEYWORD
uri	0x45	IPP_TAG_URI
uriScheme	0x46	IPP_TAG_URISCHEME
charset	0x47	IPP_TAG_CHARSET
naturalLanguage	0x48	IPP_TAG_LANGUAGE
mimeMediaType	0x49	IPP_TAG_MIMETYPE
memberAttrName	0x4A	IPP_TAG_MEMBERNAME

APPENDIX C

CUPS Constants

This appendix lists the constants provided in the CUPS header files.

Character Encoding Constants

The character encoding constants are used by the CUPS API localization functions. The character encoding is read from the message file and stored as a constant of type cups_encoding_t in the cups_lang_t structure. Table C.1 lists the available character encodings.

TABLE C.1   CUPS character encoding constants

Name	Value	Description
CUPS_US_ASCII	0	US ASCII character encoding
CUPS_ISO8859_1	1	ISO-8859-1 character encoding
CUPS_ISO8859_2	2	ISO-8859-2 character encoding
CUPS_ISO8859_3	3	ISO-8859-3 character encoding
CUPS_ISO8859_4	4	ISO-8859-4 character encoding
CUPS_ISO8859_5	5	ISO-8859-5 character encoding
CUPS_ISO8859_6	6	ISO-8859-6 character encoding
CUPS_ISO8859_7	7	ISO-8859-7 character encoding
CUPS_ISO8859_8	8	ISO-8859-8 character encoding
CUPS_ISO8859_9	9	ISO-8859-9 character encoding
CUPS_ISO8859_10	10	ISO-8859-10 character encoding
CUPS_UTF8	11	UTF-8 (Unicode) character encoding
CUPS_ISO8859_13	12	ISO-8859-13 character encoding
CUPS_ISO8859_14	13	ISO-8859-14 character encoding
CUPS_ISO8859_15	14	ISO-8859-15 character encoding
CUPS_WINDOWS_874	15	Windows code page 874 character encoding
CUPS_WINDOWS_1250	16	Windows code page 1250 character encoding
CUPS_WINDOWS_1251	17	Windows code page 1251 character encoding
CUPS_WINDOWS_1252	18	Windows code page 1252 character encoding
CUPS_WINDOWS_1253	19	Windows code page 1253 character encoding
CUPS_WINDOWS_1254	20	Windows code page 1254 character encoding
CUPS_WINDOWS_1255	21	Windows code page 1255 character encoding
CUPS_WINDOWS_1256	22	Windows code page 1256 character encoding
CUPS_WINDOWS_1257	23	Windows code page 1257 character encoding
CUPS_WINDOWS_1258	24	Windows code page 1258 character encoding

CUPS API Version

The CUPS_VERSION constant defines the CUPS API version number as a floating point number:

MM.mmpp

CUPS version 1.1.8 is defined as 1.0108.

HTTP Constants

The HTTP constants are defined in the <cups/http.h> header file and are used for sending and processing HTTP requests.

Authentication

The http_auth_t enumeration defines several constants that are used to identify the type of authentication that is required in the auth_type member of the http_t structure. Table C.2 lists the values.

TABLE C.2   HTTP authentication constants

Name	Value	Description
HTTP_AUTH_NONE	0	No authentication in use
HTTP_AUTH_BASIC	1	Basic authentication in use
HTTP_AUTH_MD5	2	Digest authentication in use
HTTP_AUTH_MD5_SESS	3	MD5-session authentication in use
HTTP_AUTH_MD5_INT	4	Digest authentication in use for body
HTTP_AUTH_MD5_SESS_INT	5	MD5-session authentication in use for body

Encodings

The HTTP Content-Length and Transfer-Encoding fields are used to specify the length of data sent to and from a server. The data_encoding field of the http_t structure specifies which type of encoding is used when sending a request or receiving a response. Table C.3 lists the supported values of the http_encoding_t enumeration.

TABLE C.3   Data encoding constants

Name	Value	Description
HTTP_ENCODE_LENGTH	0	Data is sent with a Content-Length.
HTTP_ENCODE_CHUNKED	1	Data is chunked via Transfer-Encoding.

Encryption

The `encryption` member of the `http_t` structure defines the current level of encryption to use for the connection. Table C.4 lists the `http_encryption_t` enumeration values that are supported.

TABLE C.4   Encryption constants

Name	Value	Description
HTTP_ENCRYPT_IF_REQUESTED	0	Encrypt if requested by the server via HTTP Upgrade protocol.
HTTP_ENCRYPT_NEVER	1	Never do encryption.
HTTP_ENCRYPT_REQUIRED	2	Encryption is required—upgrade to encryption immediately via HTTP Upgrade protocol.
HTTP_ENCRYPT_ALWAYS	3	Always do encryption.

Field Names

HTTP `request` and `response` fields are stored in the `fields` member of the `http_t` structure. This array of strings contains only the values for each field. The fields themselves are indexed by the `http_field_t` enumeration to more efficiently store the values for each standard HTTP field name. Table C.5 lists the HTTP field names.

TABLE C.5   HTTP field name constants

Name	Value	Description
HTTP_FIELD_UNKNOWN	-1	Used internally to indicate an unknown field name
HTTP_FIELD_ACCEPT_LANGUAGE	0	Accept-Language
HTTP_FIELD_ACCEPT_RANGES	1	Accept-Ranges
HTTP_FIELD_AUTHORIZATION	2	Authorization
HTTP_FIELD_CONNECTION	3	Connection
HTTP_FIELD_CONTENT_ENCODING	4	Content-Encoding
HTTP_FIELD_CONTENT_LANGUAGE	5	Content-Language
HTTP_FIELD_CONTENT_LENGTH	6	Content-Length
HTTP_FIELD_CONTENT_LOCATION	7	Content-Location
HTTP_FIELD_CONTENT_MD5	8	Content-MD5
HTTP_FIELD_CONTENT_RANGE	9	Content-Range
HTTP_FIELD_CONTENT_TYPE	10	Content-Type
HTTP_FIELD_CONTENT_VERSION	11	Content-Version
HTTP_FIELD_DATE	12	Date

TABLE C.5   Continued

Name	Value	Description
HTTP_FIELD_HOST	13	Host
HTTP_FIELD_IF_MODIFIED_SINCE	14	If-Modified-Since
HTTP_FIELD_IF_UNMODIFIED_SINCE	15	If-Unmodified-Since
HTTP_FIELD_KEEP_ALIVE	16	Keep-Alive
HTTP_FIELD_LAST_MODIFIED	17	Last-Modified
HTTP_FIELD_LINK	18	Link
HTTP_FIELD_LOCATION	19	Location
HTTP_FIELD_RANGE	20	Range
HTTP_FIELD_REFERER	21	Referer
HTTP_FIELD_RETRY_AFTER	22	Retry-After
HTTP_FIELD_TRANSFER_ENCODING	23	Transfer-Encoding
HTTP_FIELD_UPGRADE	24	Upgrade
HTTP_FIELD_USER_AGENT	25	User-Agent
HTTP_FIELD_WWW_AUTHENTICATE	26	WWW-Authenticate
HTTP_FIELD_MAX	27	The maximum number of field strings in the http_t structure

Keep-Alive Values

The HTTP Keep-Alive field specifies whether an HTTP/1.0 client supports persistent connections. The keep_alive member of the http_t structure specifies whether Keep-Alive should be used. Table C.6 lists the http_keepalive_t enumeration values.

TABLE C.6   HTTP Keep-Alive constants

Name	Value	Description
HTTP_KEEPALIVE_OFF	0	Don't use HTTP Keep-Alive for the connection.
HTTP_KEEPALIVE_ON	1	Use HTTP Keep-Alive for the connection.

Limits

The HTTP specification and CUPS API enforce several limits on the sizes of URIs, field values, and buffers. Table C.7 lists these limits.

TABLE C.7   CUPS API limits for HTTP functions

Name	Value	Description
HTTP_MAX_URI	1024	Max length of URI string
HTTP_MAX_HOST	256	Max length of hostname string
HTTP_MAX_BUFFER	2048	Max length of data buffer
HTTP_MAX_VALUE	256	Max header field value length

States

The http_t structure maintains several states, depending on the request being performed. The current state is stored in the state member and is defined in the http_state_t enumeration. State values are server-centric but are used for both HTTP client and server applications. Table C.8 lists the state values.

TABLE C.8   HTTP state constants

Name	Value	Description
HTTP_WAITING	0	Waiting for command
HTTP_OPTIONS	1	OPTIONS command waiting for blank line
HTTP_GET	2	GET command waiting for blank line
HTTP_GET_SEND	3	GET command sending data
HTTP_HEAD	4	HEAD command waiting for blank line
HTTP_POST	5	POST command waiting for blank line
HTTP_POST_RECV	6	POST command receiving data
HTTP_POST_SEND	7	POST command sending data
HTTP_PUT	8	PUT command waiting for blank line
HTTP_PUT_RECV	9	PUT command receiving data
HTTP_DELETE	10	DELETE command waiting for blank line
HTTP_TRACE	11	TRACE command waiting for blank line
HTTP_CLOSE	12	Closing connection
HTTP_STATUS	13	Command complete sending status

Status Codes

The httpUpdate() function can return an HTTP response code or an operating system error. The http_status_t enumeration provides all the standard HTTP status codes and an operating system error code. Table C.9 lists the enumeration values.

TABLE C.9 HTTP status code values

Name	Value	Description
HTTP_ERROR	-1	An operating system error occurred
HTTP_CONTINUE	100	Continue processing
HTTP_SWITCHING_PROTOCOLS	101	HTTP upgrade to TLS/SSL
HTTP_OK	200	Command was successful
HTTP_CREATED	201	PUT command was successful
HTTP_ACCEPTED	202	DELETE command was successful
HTTP_NOT_AUTHORITATIVE	203	Information isn't authoritative
HTTP_NO_CONTENT	204	Successful command no new data
HTTP_RESET_CONTENT	205	Content was reset/recreated
HTTP_PARTIAL_CONTENT	206	Only a partial file was received/sent
HTTP_MULTIPLE_CHOICES	300	Multiple files match request
HTTP_MOVED_PERMANENTLY	301	Document has moved permanently
HTTP_MOVED_TEMPORARILY	302	Document has moved temporarily
HTTP_SEE_OTHER	303	See this other link...
HTTP_NOT_MODIFIED	304	File not modified
HTTP_USE_PROXY	305	Must use a proxy to access this URI
HTTP_BAD_REQUEST	400	Bad request
HTTP_UNAUTHORIZED	401	Unauthorized to access host
HTTP_PAYMENT_REQUIRED	402	Payment required
HTTP_FORBIDDEN	403	Forbidden to access this URI
HTTP_NOT_FOUND	404	URI was not found
HTTP_METHOD_NOT_ALLOWED	405	Method is not allowed
HTTP_NOT_ACCEPTABLE	406	Not acceptable
HTTP_PROXY_AUTHENTICATION	407	Proxy authentication is required
HTTP_REQUEST_TIMEOUT	408	Request timed out
HTTP_CONFLICT	409	Request is self-conflicting
HTTP_GONE	410	Server has gone away
HTTP_LENGTH_REQUIRED	411	A content length or an encoding is required
HTTP_PRECONDITION	412	Precondition failed
HTTP_REQUEST_TOO_LARGE	413	Request entity too large
HTTP_URI_TOO_LONG	414	URI too long
HTTP_UNSUPPORTED_MEDIATYPE	415	The requested media type is unsupported
HTTP_UPGRADE_REQUIRED	426	Upgrade to SSL/TLS required
HTTP_SERVER_ERROR	500	Internal server error
HTTP_NOT_IMPLEMENTED	501	Feature not implemented
HTTP_BAD_GATEWAY	502	Bad gateway

TABLE C.9   Continued

Name	Value	Description
HTTP_SERVICE_UNAVAILABLE	503	Service is unavailable
HTTP_GATEWAY_TIMEOUT	504	Gateway connection timed out
HTTP_NOT_SUPPORTED	505	HTTP version not supported

Version Numbers

Every HTTP/1.0 and HTTP/1.1 request includes a version number. The version member of the http_t structure defines the HTTP protocol version to use when sending and receiving data. This version number is stored as an enumeration value of type http_version_t to avoid floating-point precision issues. Table C.10 lists the supported versions.

TABLE C.10   HTTP protocol version number constants

Name	Value	Description
HTTP_0_9	9	HTTP/0.9
HTTP_1_0	100	HTTP/1.0
HTTP_1_1	101	HTTP/1.1

IPP Constants

Most of the IPP constants are defined in Appendix A, IPP Constants. This appendix contains only those constants that are used solely for the CUPS implementation of IPP.

Printer Types

The printer-type and printer-type-mask attributes utilize bitwise values that define the type and capabilities of each printer or class. The cups_ptype_t enumeration defines these bits. Table C.11 lists the printer type constants.

TABLE C.11   Printer type bit constants

Name	Value	Description
CUPS_PRINTER_LOCAL	0x0000	Local printer or class
CUPS_PRINTER_CLASS	0x0001	Printer class
CUPS_PRINTER_REMOTE	0x0002	Remote printer or class
CUPS_PRINTER_BW	0x0004	Can do B&W printing

TABLE C.11   Continued

Name	Value	Description
CUPS_PRINTER_COLOR	0x0008	Can do color printing
CUPS_PRINTER_DUPLEX	0x0010	Can do duplexing
CUPS_PRINTER_STAPLE	0x0020	Can staple output
CUPS_PRINTER_COPIES	0x0040	Can do copies
CUPS_PRINTER_COLLATE	0x0080	Can collate copies
CUPS_PRINTER_PUNCH	0x0100	Can punch output
CUPS_PRINTER_COVER	0x0200	Can cover output
CUPS_PRINTER_BIND	0x0400	Can bind output
CUPS_PRINTER_SORT	0x0800	Can sort output
CUPS_PRINTER_SMALL	0x1000	Can do Letter/Legal/A4
CUPS_PRINTER_MEDIUM	0x2000	Can do Tabloid/B/C/A3/A2
CUPS_PRINTER_LARGE	0x4000	Can do D/E/A1/A0
CUPS_PRINTER_VARIABLE	0x8000	Can do variable sizes
CUPS_PRINTER_IMPLICIT	0x10000	Implicit class
CUPS_PRINTER_DEFAULT	0x20000	Default printer on network
CUPS_PRINTER_OPTIONS	0xfffc	All bits except CLASS, REMOTE, IMPLICIT, and DEFAULT

States

Each ipp_t structure maintains an internal state. The state member of the ipp_t structure contains the current state as described by the ipp_state_t enumeration. Table C.12 lists the IPP state values.

TABLE C.12   IPP state constants

Name	Value	Description
IPP_ERROR	–1	An error occurred.
IPP_IDLE	0	Nothing is happening/request completed.
IPP_HEADER	1	The request header needs to be sent/received.
IPP_ATTRIBUTE	2	One or more attributes need to be sent/received.
IPP_DATA	3	IPP request data needs to be sent/received.

Message Constants

The CUPS message catalog contains localized strings for most of the text that is presented to the user. The cups_msg_t enumeration is used to access most of the messages, whereas HTTP status messages are mapped with the HTTP status constants described earlier. Table C.13 lists the `cups_msg_t` enumeration values.

NOTE:

Many of these constants will change in CUPS 1.2. Although printer drivers, filters, and backends should use the CUPS message catalogs when possible, do not depend on the CUPS message catalogs to localize your applications.

TABLE C.13   CUPS message constant values

Name	Value	English string
CUPS_MSG_OK	0	OK
CUPS_MSG_CANCEL	1	Cancel
CUPS_MSG_HELP	2	Help
CUPS_MSG_QUIT	3	Quit
CUPS_MSG_CLOSE	4	Close
CUPS_MSG_YES	5	Yes
CUPS_MSG_NO	6	No
CUPS_MSG_ON	7	On
CUPS_MSG_OFF	8	Off
CUPS_MSG_SAVE	9	Save
CUPS_MSG_DISCARD	10	Discard
CUPS_MSG_DEFAULT	11	Default
CUPS_MSG_OPTIONS	12	Options
CUPS_MSG_MORE_INFO	13	More Info
CUPS_MSG_BLACK	14	Black
CUPS_MSG_COLOR	15	Color
CUPS_MSG_CYAN	16	Cyan
CUPS_MSG_MAGENTA	17	Magenta
CUPS_MSG_YELLOW	18	Yellow
CUPS_MSG_COPYRIGHT	19	Copyright 1997–2001 by Easy Software Products
CUPS_MSG_GENERAL	20	General
CUPS_MSG_PRINTER	21	Printer
CUPS_MSG_IMAGE	22	Image
CUPS_MSG_HPGL2	23	HP-GL/2
CUPS_MSG_EXTRA	24	Extra
CUPS_MSG_DOCUMENT	25	Document

TABLE C.13   Continued

Name	Value	English string
CUPS_MSG_OTHER	26	Other
CUPS_MSG_PRINT_PAGES	27	Print Pages
CUPS_MSG_ENTIRE_DOCUMENT	28	Entire Document
CUPS_MSG_PAGE_RANGE	29	Page Range
CUPS_MSG_REVERSE_ORDER	30	Reverse Order
CUPS_MSG_PAGE_FORMAT	31	Page Format
CUPS_MSG_1_UP	32	1-Up
CUPS_MSG_2_UP	33	2-Up
CUPS_MSG_4_UP	34	4-Up
CUPS_MSG_IMAGE_SCALING	35	Image Scaling
CUPS_MSG_USE_NATURAL_IMAGE_SIZE	36	Use Natural Image Size
CUPS_MSG_ZOOM_BY_PERCENT	37	Zoom by Percent
CUPS_MSG_ZOOM_BY_PPI	38	Zoom by PPI
CUPS_MSG_MIRROR_IMAGE	39	Mirror Image
CUPS_MSG_COLOR_SATURATION	40	Color Saturation
CUPS_MSG_COLOR_HUE	41	Color Hue
CUPS_MSG_FIT_TO_PAGE	42	Fit to Page
CUPS_MSG_SHADING	43	Shading
CUPS_MSG_DEFAULT_PEN_WIDTH	44	Default Pen Width
CUPS_MSG_GAMMA_CORRECTION	45	Gamma Correction
CUPS_MSG_BRIGHTNESS	46	Brightness
CUPS_MSG_ADD	47	Add
CUPS_MSG_DELETE	48	Delete
CUPS_MSG_MODIFY	49	Modify
CUPS_MSG_PRINTER_URI	50	Printer URI
CUPS_MSG_PRINTER_NAME	51	Printer Name
CUPS_MSG_PRINTER_LOCATION	52	Printer Location
CUPS_MSG_PRINTER_INFO	53	Printer Info
CUPS_MSG_PRINTER_MAKE_AND_MODEL	54	Printer Make and Model
CUPS_MSG_DEVICE_URI	55	Device URI
CUPS_MSG_FORMATTING_PAGE	56	Formatting Page
CUPS_MSG_PRINTING_PAGE	57	Printing Page
CUPS_MSG_INITIALIZING_PRINTER	58	Initializing Printer
CUPS_MSG_PRINTER_STATE	59	Printer State
CUPS_MSG_ACCEPTING_JOBS	60	Accepting Jobs
CUPS_MSG_NOT_ACCEPTING_JOBS	61	Not Accepting Jobs
CUPS_MSG_PRINT_JOBS	62	Print Jobs

TABLE C.13   Continued

Name	Value	English string
CUPS_MSG_CLASS	63	Class
CUPS_MSG_LOCAL	64	Local
CUPS_MSG_REMOTE	65	Remote
CUPS_MSG_DUPLEXING	66	Duplexing
CUPS_MSG_STAPLING	67	Stapling
CUPS_MSG_FAST_COPIES	68	Fast Copies
CUPS_MSG_COLLATED_COPIES	69	Collated Copies
CUPS_MSG_PUNCHING	70	Punching
CUPS_MSG_COVERING	71	Covering
CUPS_MSG_BINDING	72	Binding
CUPS_MSG_SORTING	73	Sorting
CUPS_MSG_SMALL	74	Small
CUPS_MSG_MEDIUM	75	Medium
CUPS_MSG_LARGE	76	Large
CUPS_MSG_VARIABLE	77	Variable
CUPS_MSG_IDLE	78	Idle
CUPS_MSG_PROCESSING	79	Processing
CUPS_MSG_STOPPED	80	Stopped
CUPS_MSG_ALL	81	All
CUPS_MSG_ODD	82	Odd
CUPS_MSG_EVEN_PAGES	83	Even Pages
CUPS_MSG_DARKER_LIGHTER	84	Darker ... Lighter
CUPS_MSG_MEDIA_SIZE	85	Media Size
CUPS_MSG_MEDIA_TYPE	86	Media Type
CUPS_MSG_MEDIA_SOURCE	87	Media Source
CUPS_MSG_ORIENTATION	88	Orientation
CUPS_MSG_PORTRAIT	89	Portrait
CUPS_MSG_LANDSCAPE	90	Landscape
CUPS_MSG_JOB_STATE	91	Job State
CUPS_MSG_JOB_NAME	92	Job Name
CUPS_MSG_USER_NAME	93	User Name
CUPS_MSG_PRIORITY	94	Priority
CUPS_MSG_COPIES	95	Copies
CUPS_MSG_FILE_SIZE	96	File Size
CUPS_MSG_PENDING	97	Pending
CUPS_MSG_OUTPUT_MODE	98	Output Mode
CUPS_MSG_RESOLUTION	99	Resolution

TABLE C.13   Continued

Name	Value	English string
CUPS_MSG_TEXT	100	Text
CUPS_MSG_PRETTYPRINT	101	Pretty Print
CUPS_MSG_MARGINS	102	Margins
CUPS_MSG_LEFT	103	Left
CUPS_MSG_RIGHT	104	Right
CUPS_MSG_BOTTOM	105	Bottom
CUPS_MSG_TOP	106	Top
CUPS_MSG_FILENAME	107	Filename
CUPS_MSG_PRINT	108	Print
CUPS_MSG_HTTP_BASE	200	(Start of HTTP messages)
CUPS_MSG_HTTP_END	505	(End of HTTP messages)
CUPS_MSG_MAX	506	Maximum Number of Messages in Catalog

PPD Constants

The PPD functions provided by the CUPS API make use of many constants.

Colorspaces

The PPD `ColorSpace` attribute is stored in the colorspace member of the `ppd_file_t` structure and defines the default colorspace of the printers. Table C.14 lists the values supported by the `ppd_cs_t` enumeration.

TABLE C.14   PPD colorspace values

Name	Value	Description
PPD_CS_CMYK	–4	CMYK colorspace
PPD_CS_CMY	–3	CMY colorspace
PPD_CS_GRAY	1	Grayscale colorspace
PPD_CS_RGB	3	RGB colorspace
PPD_CS_RGBK	4	RGBK (K = gray) colorspace
PPD_CS_N	5	DeviceN colorspace

Limits

The PPD specification enforces specific limits on the size of option names, option text, and the length of each line in the file. Table C.15 lists these limits.

TABLE C.15   PPD file limits

Name	Value	Description
PPD_MAX_NAME	41	Maximum size of name + 1 for nul
PPD_MAX_TEXT	81	Maximum size of text + 1 for nul
PPD_MAX_LINE	256	Maximum size of line + 1 for nul

Order Dependency Values

Every option in a PPD file has an OrderDependency attribute associated with it. The section member of the ppd_option_t structure contains the required section for the option code. Table C.16 lists the constants defined by the ppd_section_t enumeration.

TABLE C.16   PPD order dependency section values

Name	Value	Description
PPD_ORDER_ANY	0	Option code can be anywhere in the file.
PPD_ORDER_DOCUMENT	1	Option code must be in the DocumentSetup section.
PPD_ORDER_EXIT	2	Option code must be sent before the document.
PPD_ORDER_JCL	3	Option code must be sent as a JCL command.
PPD_ORDER_PAGE	4	Option code must be in the PageSetup section.
PPD_ORDER_PROLOG	5	Option code must be in the Prolog section.

User-Interface Types

Every option in a PPD file has an associate option type attribute that defines the type of user interface the application is to provide to the user. The ui member of the ppd_option_t structure contains the user interface type. Table C.17 lists the constants defined by the ppd_ui_t enumeration.

TABLE C.17   PPD user-interface type values

Name	Value	Description
PPD_UI_BOOLEAN	0	True or False option
PPD_UI_PICKONE	1	Pick one from a list
PPD_UI_PICKMANY	2	Pick zero or more from a list

Version

The PPD_VERSION constant defines the newest version of the Adobe PPD specification that the CUPS API supports. The current version number is 4.3.

Raster Constants

Drivers and filters use raster constants when reading or writing CUPS raster data. Most of these constants are used in the page header structure (cups_page_header_t).

Boolean Values

The cups_bool_t enumeration is used to represent Boolean values. The CUPS_FALSE and CUPS_TRUE constants correspond to false (0) and true (1), respectively.

Color Order Values

Color data is stored in one of three organizations: chunked (CMYK CMYK CMYK), banded (CCC MMM YYY KKK), or planar (CCC ... MMM ... YYY ... KKK ...), depending on the requirements of the printer and driver.

The cups_order_t enumeration defines the constants CUPS_ORDER_CHUNKED, CUPS_ORDER_BANDED, and CUPS_ORDER_PLANAR for these configurations.

Colorspaces

The cupsColorSpace member of the cups_page_header_t structure defines the colorspace associated with the colors in a page. Table C.18 lists the colorspaces in the cups_cspace_t enumeration.

TABLE C.18 Colorspace constants

Name	Value	Description
CUPS_CSPACE_W	0	Luminance
CUPS_CSPACE_RGB	1	Red green blue
CUPS_CSPACE_RGBA	2	Red green blue alpha
CUPS_CSPACE_K	3	Black
CUPS_CSPACE_CMY	4	Cyan magenta yellow
CUPS_CSPACE_YMC	5	Yellow magenta cyan
CUPS_CSPACE_CMYK	6	Cyan magenta yellow black
CUPS_CSPACE_YMCK	7	Yellow magenta cyan black
CUPS_CSPACE_KCMY	8	Black cyan magenta yellow
CUPS_CSPACE_KCMYcm	9	Black cyan magenta yellow light-cyan light-magenta
CUPS_CSPACE_GMCK	10	Gold magenta cyan black
CUPS_CSPACE_GMCS	11	Gold magenta cyan silver
CUPS_CSPACE_WHITE	12	White ink (as black)
CUPS_CSPACE_GOLD	13	Gold foil

TABLE C.18   Continued

Name	Value	Description
CUPS_CSPACE_SILVER	14	Silver foil
CUPS_CSPACE_ICC1	32	1 channel of ICC color data (CUPS 1.2 only)
CUPS_CSPACE_ICC2	33	2 channels of ICC color data (CUPS 1.2 only)
CUPS_CSPACE_ICC3	34	3 channels of ICC color data (CUPS 1.2 only)
CUPS_CSPACE_ICC4	35	4 channels of ICC color data (CUPS 1.2 only)
CUPS_CSPACE_ICC5	36	5 channels of ICC color data (CUPS 1.2 only)
CUPS_CSPACE_ICC6	37	6 channels of ICC color data (CUPS 1.2 only)
CUPS_CSPACE_ICC7	38	7 channels of ICC color data (CUPS 1.2 only)
CUPS_CSPACE_ICC8	39	8 channels of ICC color data (CUPS 1.2 only)

Sync Words

Every CUPS raster file begins with a 4-byte sync word that determines the byte ordering of the rest of the file. CUPS defines two constants: CUPS_RASTER_SYNC and CUPS_RASTER_REVSYNC, or the native and reversed byte order cases.

The sync word is stored in the cups_raster_t structure to enable automatic byte-swapping when raster streams are read from systems with a different default byte order.

Open Modes

The second argument of the cupsRasterOpen() function is the open mode. CUPS supports two open modes: CUPS_RASTER_READ and CUPS_RASTER_WRITE, for reading and writing raster streams.

Jog Values

The Jog member of the cups_page_header_t structure defines what to do with pages that are printed. It corresponds directly to the Jog attribute in the PostScript page device dictionary. Table C.19 lists the constants defined by the cups_jog_t enumeration.

TABLE C.19   Jog value constants

Name	Value	Description
CUPS_JOG_NONE	0	Never move pages
CUPS_JOG_FILE	1	Move pages after this file
CUPS_JOG_JOB	2	Move pages after this job
CUPS_JOG_SET	3	Move pages after this set

Orientation Values

The `Orientation` member of the `cups_page_header_t` structure defines the orientation of pages that are printed. It corresponds directly to the `Orientation` attribute in the PostScript page device dictionary. Table C.20 lists the constants defined by the `cups_orient_t` enumeration.

TABLE C.20   Orientation value constants

Name	Value	Description
CUPS_ORIENT_0	0	Don't rotate the page.
CUPS_ORIENT_90	1	Rotate the page counter-clockwise.
CUPS_ORIENT_180	2	Turn the page upside down.
CUPS_ORIENT_270	3	Rotate the page clockwise.

Cutter Values

The `CutMedia` member of the `cups_page_header_t` structure defines when to cut pages that are printed. It corresponds directly to the `CutMedia` attribute in the PostScript page device dictionary. Table C.21 lists the constants defined by the `cups_cut_t` enumeration.

TABLE C.21   CutMedia value constants

Name	Value	Description
CUPS_CUT_NONE	0	Never cut the roll.
CUPS_CUT_FILE	1	Cut the roll after this file.
CUPS_CUT_JOB	2	Cut the roll after this job.
CUPS_CUT_SET	3	Cut the roll after this set.
CUPS_CUT_PAGE	4	Cut the roll after this page.

Advance Values

The `AdvanceMedia` member of the `cups_page_header_t` structure defines when to advance the media. It corresponds directly to the `AdvanceMedia` attribute in the PostScript page device dictionary. Table C.22 lists the constants defined by the `cups_adv_t` enumeration.

TABLE C.22   Advance value constants

Name	Value	Description
CUPS_ADVANCE_NONE	0	Never advance the roll.
CUPS_ADVANCE_FILE	1	Advance the roll after this file.
CUPS_ADVANCE_JOB	2	Advance the roll after this job.
CUPS_ADVANCE_SET	3	Advance the roll after this set.
CUPS_ADVANCE_PAGE	4	Advance the roll after this page.

Leading Edge Values

The LeadingEdge member of the cups_page_header_t structure defines which side of the media is being fed first. It corresponds directly to the LeadingEdge attribute in the PostScript page device dictionary. Table C.23 lists the constants defined by the cups_edge_t enumeration.

TABLE C.23   Leading edge value constants

Name	Value	Description
CUPS_EDGE_TOP	0	Leading edge is the top of the page.
CUPS_EDGE_RIGHT	1	Leading edge is the right of the page.
CUPS_EDGE_BOTTOM	2	Leading edge is the bottom of the page.
CUPS_EDGE_LEFT	3	Leading edge is the left of the page.

APPENDIX D

CUPS Structures

This appendix provides a detailed description of all the data structures provided by the CUPS software. Please refer to Appendices B and C for a description of the constants used in these data structures.

CUPS API Structures

The CUPS API uses the following structures for basic printing services.

cups_dest_t

The `cups_dest_t` structure describes a single printer or instance and the associated options.

```
typedef struct              /**** Destination ****/
{
  char          *name,      /* Printer or class name */
                *instance;  /* Local instance name or NULL */
  int           is_default; /* Is this printer the default? */
  int           num_options; /* Number of options */
  cups_option_t *options;    /* Options */
} cups_dest_t;
```

cups_job_t

The `cups_job_t` structure describes a single print job.

```
typedef struct              /**** Job ****/
{
  int           id;         /* The job ID */
  char          *dest,      /* Printer or class name */
                *title,     /* Title/job name */
                *user,      /* User that submitted the job */
                *format;    /* Document format */
  ipp_jstate_t  state;      /* Job state */
  int           size,       /* Size in kilobytes */
                priority;   /* Priority (1-100) */
  time_t        completed_time,  /* Time the job was completed */
                creation_time,   /* Time the job was created */
                processing_time; /* Time the job was processed */
} cups_job_t;
```

cups_lang_t

The `cups_lang_t` structure contains localized messages for CUPS programs.

```
typedef struct cups_lang_str            /**** Language Cache ****/
{
  struct cups_lang_str *next;           /* Next language in cache */
  int                  used;            /* Use count */
  cups_encoding_t      encoding;        /* Text encoding */
  char                 language[16];    /* Language/locale name */
  char                 *messages[CUPS_MSG_MAX]; /* Message array */
} cups_lang_t;
```

cups_option_t

The `cups_option_t` structure contains a single option.

```
typedef struct /**** Printer Options ****/
{
  char *name;   /* Name of option */
  char *value;  /* Value of option */
} cups_option_t;
```

HTTP Structures

The HTTP functions utilize a single data structure that contains the current HTTP state information.

http_t

The `http_t` structure contains the HTTP state information.

```
typedef struct
{
  int               fd;             /* File descriptor for this socket */
  int               blocking;       /* To block or not to block */
  int               error;          /* Last error on read */
  time_t            activity;       /* Time since last read/write */
  http_state_t      state;          /* State of client */
  http_status_t     status;         /* Status of last request */
  http_version_t    version;        /* Protocol version */
  http_keepalive_t  keep_alive;     /* Keep-alive supported? */
  struct sockaddr_in hostaddr;      /* Address of connected host */
  char              hostname[HTTP_MAX_HOST],
                                    /* Name of connected host */
                    fields[HTTP_FIELD_MAX][HTTP_MAX_VALUE];
                                    /* Field values */
```

```
char                *data;          /* Pointer to data buffer */
http_encoding_t     data_encoding;  /* Chunked or not */
int                 data_remaining; /* Number of bytes left */
int                 used;           /* Number of bytes used in buffer */
char                buffer[HTTP_MAX_BUFFER];
                                    /* Buffer for messages */
int                 auth_type;      /* Authentication in use */
md5_state_t         md5_state;      /* MD5 state */
char                nonce[HTTP_MAX_VALUE];
                                    /* Nonce value */
int                 nonce_count;    /* Nonce count */
void                *tls;           /* TLS state information */
http_encryption_t   encryption;     /* Encryption requirements */
} http_t;
```

IPP Structures

The IPP functions make use of several data structures and types that are used by the IPP state structure in all function calls.

ipp_t

The ipp_t structure contains the request/response header, attributes, and state information for the current IPP request or response.

```
typedef struct             /**** Request State ****/
{
  ipp_state_t     state;     /* State of request */
  ipp_request_t   request;   /* Request header */
  ipp_attribute_t *attrs,    /* Attributes */
                  *last,     /* Last attribute in list */
                  *current;  /* Current attribute (for read/write) */
  ipp_tag_t       curtag;    /* Current attribute group tag */
} ipp_t;
```

ipp_attribute_t

The ipp_attribute_t structure contains the values for a single attribute.

```
typedef struct ipp_attribute_s     /**** Attribute ****/
{
  struct ipp_attribute_s *next;      /* Next atrtribute in list */
  ipp_tag_t               group_tag, /* Job/Printer/Operation group tag */
                          value_tag; /* What type of value is it? */
```

```
  char                 *name;      /* Name of attribute */
  int                  num_values; /* Number of values */
  ipp_value_t          values[1];  /* Values */
} ipp_attribute_t;
```

ipp_request_t

The ipp_request_t structure contains the IPP request or response header.

```
typedef union                 /**** Request Header ****/
{
  struct                      /* Any Header */
  {
    ipp_uchar_t  version[2];    /* Protocol version number */
    int          op_status;     /* Operation ID or status code*/
    int          request_id;    /* Request ID */
  } any;

  struct                      /* Operation Header */
  {
    ipp_uchar_t  version[2];    /* Protocol version number */
    ipp_op_t     operation_id;  /* Operation ID */
    int          request_id;    /* Request ID */
  } op;

  struct                      /* Status Header */
  {
    ipp_uchar_t  version[2];    /* Protocol version number */
    ipp_status_t status_code;   /* Status code */
    int          request_id;    /* Request ID */
  } status;
} ipp_request_t;
```

ipp_uchar_t

The ipp_uchar_t type is an unsigned 8-bit integer/character.

ipp_value_t

The ipp_value_t union contains members for each IPP value type.

```
typedef union                 /**** Attribute Value ****/
{
  int          integer;    /* Integer/enumerated value */
```

```
char          boolean;     /* Boolean value */

ipp_uchar_t date[11];      /* Date/time value */

struct
{
  int          xres,       /* Horizontal resolution */
               yres;       /* Vertical resolution */
  ipp_res_t   units;       /* Resolution units */
}            resolution;   /* Resolution value */

struct
{
  int          lower,      /* Lower value */
               upper;      /* Upper value */
}            range;        /* Range of integers value */

struct
{
  char         *charset;   /* Character set */
  char         *text;      /* String */
}            string;       /* String with language value */

struct
{
  int          length;     /* Length of attribute */
  void         *data;      /* Data in attribute */
}            unknown;      /* Unknown attribute type */
} ipp_value_t;
```

PPD Structures

The PPD functions utilize several data structures to represent the contents of a PPD file.

ppd_choice_t

The ppd_choice_t structure contains the information for a single option choice.

```
typedef struct              /**** Option choices ****/
{
  char marked,              /* 0 if not selected, 1 otherwise */
       choice[PPD_MAX_NAME], /* Computer-readable option name */
       text[PPD_MAX_TEXT],  /* Human-readable option name */
```

```
         *code;                    /* Code to send for this option */
    void *option;                  /* Pointer to parent option structure */
} ppd_choice_t;
```

ppd_const_t

The `ppd_const_t` structure describes a constraint condition between two options.

```
typedef struct                 /**** Constraints ****/
{
  char option1[PPD_MAX_NAME], /* First keyword */
       choice1[PPD_MAX_NAME], /* First option/choice (blank for all) */
       option2[PPD_MAX_NAME], /* Second keyword */
       choice2[PPD_MAX_NAME]; /* Second option/choice (blank for all) */
} ppd_const_t;
```

ppd_emul_t

The `ppd_emul_t` structure describes a single emulation that is supported by the printer.

```
typedef struct                 /**** Emulators ****/
{
  char name[PPD_MAX_NAME], /* Emulator name */
       *start,                  /* Code to switch to this emulation */
       *stop;                   /* Code to stop this emulation */
} ppd_emul_t;
```

ppd_file_t

The `ppd_file_t` describes an entire PPD file.

```
typedef struct                     /**** Files ****/
{
  int         language_level,  /* Language level of device */
              color_device,    /* 1 = color device */
              variable_sizes,  /* 1 = supports variable sizes */
              accurate_screens, /* 1 = supports accurate screens */
              contone_only,    /* 1 = continuous tone only */
              landscape,       /* -90 or 90 */
              model_number,    /* Device-specific model number */
              manual_copies,   /* 1 = Copies done manually */
              throughput;      /* Pages per minute */
  ppd_cs_t    colorspace;      /* Default colorspace */
  char        *patches;        /* Patch commands to be sent to printer */
```

```
   int          num_emulations;         /* Number of emulations supported */
   ppd_emul_t   *emulations;            /* Emulations and the code to invoke them */
   char         *jcl_begin,             /* Start JCL commands */
                *jcl_ps,                /* Enter PostScript interpreter */
                *jcl_end,               /* End JCL commands */
                *lang_encoding,         /* Language encoding */
                *lang_version,          /* Language (English, Spanish, etc.) */
                *modelname,             /* Model name (general) */
                *ttrasterizer,          /* Truetype rasterizer */
                *manufacturer,          /* Manufacturer name */
                *product,               /* Product name (from PS RIP/interpreter) */
                *nickname,              /* Nickname (specific) */
                *shortnickname;         /* Short version of nickname */
   int          num_groups;             /* Number of UI groups */
   ppd_group_t  *groups;                /* UI groups */
   int          num_sizes;              /* Number of page sizes */
   ppd_size_t   *sizes;                 /* Page sizes */
   float        custom_min[2],          /* Minimum variable page size */
                custom_max[2],          /* Maximum variable page size */
                custom_margins[4];      /* Margins around page */
   int          num_consts;             /* Number of UI/Non-UI constraints */
   ppd_const_t  *consts;                /* UI/Non-UI constraints */
   int          num_fonts;              /* Number of pre-loaded fonts */
   char         **fonts;                /* Pre-loaded fonts */
   int          num_profiles;           /* Number of sRGB color profiles */
   ppd_profile_t *profiles;             /* sRGB color profiles */
   int          num_filters;            /* Number of filters */
   char         **filters;              /* Filter strings... */
   int          flip_duplex;            /* 1 = Flip page for back sides */
} ppd_file_t;
```

ppd_group_t

The ppd_group_t structure contains the options and information for a single group.

```
typedef struct ppd_group_str               /**** Groups ****/
{
   char                 text[PPD_MAX_TEXT]; /* Human-readable group name */
   int                  num_options;        /* Number of options */
   ppd_option_t         *options;           /* Options */
   int                  num_subgroups;      /* Number of sub-groups */
   struct ppd_group_str *subgroups;         /* Sub-groups (max depth = 1) */
} ppd_group_t;
```

ppd_option_t

The ppd_option_t structure contains the choices and information for a single option.

```
typedef struct                          /**** Options ****/
{
  char          conflicted,            /* 1 if conflicts exist */
                keyword[PPD_MAX_NAME],   /* Option keyword name */
                defchoice[PPD_MAX_NAME], /* Default option choice */
                text[PPD_MAX_TEXT];      /* Human-readable text */
  ppd_ui_t      ui;                      /* Type of UI option */
  ppd_section_t section;                 /* Section for command */
  float         order;                   /* Order number */
  int           num_choices;             /* Number of option choices */
  ppd_choice_t  *choices;                /* Option choices */
} ppd_option_t;
```

ppd_profile_t

The ppd_profile_t structure describes a single color profile.

```
typedef struct                     /**** sRGB Color Profiles ****/
{
  char  resolution[PPD_MAX_NAME], /* Resolution or "-" */
        media_type[PPD_MAX_NAME]; /* Media type or "-" */
  float density,                  /* Ink density to use */
        gamma,                    /* Gamma correction to use */
        matrix[3][3];             /* Transform matrix */
} ppd_profile_t;
```

ppd_size_t

The ppd_size_t structure describes a single page size.

```
typedef struct              /**** Page Sizes ****/
{
  int   marked;             /* Page size selected? */
  char  name[PPD_MAX_NAME]; /* Media size option */
  float width,              /* Width of media in points */
        length,             /* Length of media in points */
        left,               /* Left printable margin in points */
        bottom,             /* Bottom printable margin in points */
        right,              /* Right printable margin in points */
        top;                /* Top printable margin in points */
} ppd_size_t;
```

APPENDIX E

CUPS Functions

This appendix describes the functions that are provided in the CUPS API and CUPS Imaging libraries. For a reference on the constants and structures these functions use, please consult Appendices B, C, and D.

cupsAddDest()

Usage

```
int
cupsAddDest(const char  *name,
            const char  *instance,
            int         num_dests,
            cups_dest_t **dests);
```

Arguments

Argument	Type	Description
name	const char *	The name of the destination
instance	const char *	The instance name or NULL
num_dests	int	The number of destinations
dests	cups_dest_t **	The destinations

Returns

The new number of destinations.

Description

The cupsAddDest() function adds a destination to the destinations array. If the destination already exists, then it is not added.

Example

```
#include <cups/cups.h>

...

int         num_dests;
cups_dest_t *dests;

...

num_dests = cupsAddDest("myprinter", "myinstance", num_dests, &dests);
```

See Also

cupsFreeDests(), cupsGetDest(), cupsGetDests(), cupsSetDests()

cupsAddOption()

Usage

```
int
cupsAddOption(const char     *name,
              const char     *value,
              int            num_options,
              cups_option_t **options);
```

Arguments

Argument	Type	Description
name	const char *	The name of the option
value	const char *	The value of the option
num_options	int	The number of options in the options array
options	cups_option_t **	A pointer to the options array

Returns

The new number of options.

Description

The cupsAddOption() function adds an option to the specified array.

Example

```
#include <cups.h>

...

/* Declare the options array */
int            num_options;
cups_option_t *options;

/* Initialize the options array */
num_options = 0;
options     = (cups_option_t *)0;
```

```
/* Add options using cupsAddOption() */
num_options = cupsAddOption("media", "letter", num_options, &options);
num_options = cupsAddOption("resolution", "300dpi", num_options, &options);
```

See Also

cupsFreeOptions(), cupsGetOption(), cupsParseOptions()

cupsCancelJob()

Usage

```
int
cupsCancelJob(const char *dest,
              int         job);
```

Arguments

Argument	Type	Description
dest	const char *	Printer or class name
job	int	The Job ID

Returns

1 on success, 0 on failure. On failure the error can be found by calling cupsLastError().

Description

The cupsCancelJob() function cancels the specified job.

Example

```
#include <cups.h>

cupsCancelJob("LaserJet", 1);
```

See Also

cupsLastError(), cupsPrintFile()

cupsDoFileRequest()

Usage

```
ipp_t *
cupsDoFileRequest(http_t    *http,
                  ipp_t     *request,
                  const char *resource,
                  const char *filename);
```

Arguments

Argument	Type	Description
http	http_t *	HTTP connection to the server
request	ipp_t *	IPP request data
resource	const char *	HTTP resource name for POST
filename	const char *	File that is to be sent with POST request (NULL pointer if none)

Returns

IPP response data or NULL if the request fails. On failure the error can be found by calling cupsLastError().

Description

The cupsDoFileRequest() function does an HTTP POST request and provides the IPP request and optionally the contents of a file to the IPP server. It also handles resubmitting the request and performing password authentication as needed.

Example

```
#include <cups.h>

http_t      *http;
cups_lang_t *language;
ipp_t       *request;
ipp_t       *response;

...

/* Get the default language */
language = cupsLangDefault();

/* Create a new IPP request */
```

```
request  = ippNew();

request->request.op.operation_id = IPP_PRINT_FILE;
request->request.op.request_id   = 1;

/* Add required attributes */
ippAddString(request, IPP_TAG_OPERATION, IPP_TAG_CHARSET,
             "attributes-charset", NULL, cupsLangEncoding(language));

ippAddString(request, IPP_TAG_OPERATION, IPP_TAG_LANGUAGE,
             "attributes-natural-language", NULL,
             language != NULL ? language->language : "C");

ippAddString(request, IPP_TAG_OPERATION, IPP_TAG_URI, "printer-uri",
             NULL, "ipp://hostname/resource");

ippAddString(request, IPP_TAG_OPERATION, IPP_TAG_NAME, "requesting-user-name",
             NULL, cupsUser());

/* Do the request... */
response = cupsDoFileRequest(http, request, "/resource", "filename.txt");
```

See Also

cupsLangDefault(), cupsLangEncoding(), cupsUser(), httpConnect(), ippAddString(),
ippNew()

cupsDoRequest()

Usage

```
ipp_t *
cupsDoRequest(http_t     *http,
              ipp_t      *request,
              const char *resource);
```

Arguments

Argument	Type	Description
http	http_t *	HTTP connection to server
request	ipp_t *	IPP request data
resource	const char *	HTTP resource name for POST

Returns

IPP response data or NULL if the request fails. On failure the error can be found by calling `cupsLastError()`.

Description

The `cupsDoRequest()` function sends an HTTP POST request and provides the IPP request to the IPP server. It also handles resubmitting the request and performing password authentication as needed.

Example

```
#include <cups.h>

http_t      *http;
cups_lang_t *language;
ipp_t       *request;
ipp_t       *response;

...

/* Get the default language */
language = cupsLangDefault();

/* Create a new IPP request */
request  = ippNew();

request->request.op.operation_id = IPP_GET_PRINTER_ATTRIBUTES;
request->request.op.request_id   = 1;

/* Add required attributes */
ippAddString(request, IPP_TAG_OPERATION, IPP_TAG_CHARSET,
             "attributes-charset", NULL, cupsLangEncoding(language));

ippAddString(request, IPP_TAG_OPERATION, IPP_TAG_LANGUAGE,
             "attributes-natural-language", NULL,
             language != NULL ? language->language : "C");

ippAddString(request, IPP_TAG_OPERATION, IPP_TAG_URI, "printer-uri",
             NULL, "ipp://hostname/resource");

/* Do the request... */
response = cupsDoRequest(http, request, "/resource");
```

See Also

cupsLangDefault(), cupsLangEncoding(), cupsUser(), httpConnect(), ippAddString(),
ippNew()

cupsEncodeOptions()

Usage

```
void
cupsEncodeOptions(ipp_t          *request,
                  int            num_options,
                  cups_option_t *options);
```

Arguments

Argument	Type	Description
request	ipp_t *	The IPP request
num_options	int	Number of options in array
options	cups_option_t *	Pointer to options array

Description

The cupsEncodeOptions() function adds options in the options array to the specified IPP request.

Example

```
#include <cups/cups.h>

...

ipp_t          *request;
int            num_options;
cups_option_t *options;

...

cupsEncodeOptions(request, num_options, options);
```

See Also

cupsAddOption(), cupsGetOption(), cupsMarkOptions(), cupsParseOptions()

cupsEncryption()

Usage

```
http_encryption_t
cupsEncryption(void);
```

Description

The cupsEncryption() function returns the current default encryption mode.

Example

```
#include <cups/cups.h>

printf("Default encryption = %d\n", cupsEncryption());
```

See Also

cupsSetEncryption(), httpConnectEncrypt(), httpEncryption()

cupsFreeDests()

Usage

```
void
cupsFreeDests(int          num_dests,
              cups_dest_t *dests);
```

Arguments

Argument	Type	Description
num_dests	int	Number of destinations in array
dests	cups_dest_t *	Pointer to destinations array

Description

The `cupsFreeDests()` function frees all memory associated with the destination array specified.

Example

```
#include <cups/cups.h>

int        num_dests;
cups_dest_t *dests;

...

cupsFreeDests(num_dests, dests);
```

See Also

cupsAddDest(), cupsGetDest(), cupsGetDests(), cupsSetDests()

cupsFreeJobs()

Usage

```
void
cupsFreeJobs(int        num_jobs,
             cups_job_t *jobs);
```

Arguments

Argument	Type	Description
num_jobs	int	Number of jobs in array
jobs	cups_job_t *	Pointer to jobs array

Description

The `cupsFreeJobs()` function frees all memory associated with the job array specified.

Example

```
#include <cups/cups.h>

int        num_jobs;
```

```
cups_job_t *jobs;

...

cupsFreeJobs(num_jobs, jobs);
```

See Also

cupsGetJobs()

cupsFreeOptions()

Usage

```
void
cupsFreeOptions(int            num_options,
                cups_option_t *options);
```

Arguments

Argument	Type	Description
num_options	int	Number of options in array
options	cups_option_t *	Pointer to options array

Description

The cupsFreeOptions() function frees all memory associated with the option array specified.

Example

```
#include <cups/cups.h>

int            num_options;
cups_option_t *options;

...

cupsFreeOptions(num_options, options);
```

See Also

cupsAddOption(), cupsGetOption(), cupsMarkOptions(), cupsParseOptions()

cupsGetClasses()

Usage

```
int
cupsGetClasses(char ***classes);
```

Arguments

Argument	Type	Description
classes	char ***	Pointer to char pointer array pointer

Returns

The number of printer classes available.

Description

The cupsGetClasses() function gets a list of the available printer classes. The free() function should be used to free the returned array when it is no longer needed.

Example

```
#include <cups/cups.h>

int  i;
int  num_classes;
char **classes;

...

num_classes = cupsGetClasses(

...

if (num_classes > 0)
{
  for (i = 0; i <num_classes; i ++)
```

```
    free(classes[i]);

  free(classes);
}
```

See Also

```
    cupsGetDefault(), cupsGetPrinters()
```

cupsGetDefault()

Usage

```
const char *
cupsGetDefault(void);
```

Returns

A pointer to the default destination.

Description

The cupsGetDefault() function gets the default destination printer or class. The default destination is stored in a static string and is overwritten (usually with the same value) after each call.

Example

```
#include <cups/cups.h>

printf("The default destination is %s\n", cupsGetDefault());
```

See Also

```
    cupsGetClasses(), cupsGetPrinters()
```

cupsGetDest()

Usage

```
cups_dest_t *
cupsGetDest(const char  *name,
```

```
                const char  *instance,
                int         num_dests,
                cups_dest_t *dests);
```

Arguments

Argument	Type	Description
name	const char *	The name of the destination or NULL for the default destination
instance	const char *	The instance name or NULL
num_dests	int	The number of destinations in the array
dests	cups_dest_t *	The destinations array

Returns

A pointer to the destination or NULL if the destination is not defined.

Description

The cupsGetDest() function returns the named destination. The destination name can be a NULL pointer to get the default destination. The instance name can be a NULL pointer to get the base destination.

Example

```
#include <cups/cups.h>

int         num_dests;
cups_dest_t *dests;
cups_dest_t *dest;

...

dest = cupsGetDest(NULL, NULL, num_dests, dests);

if (dest)
  printf("Default destination is %s%s%s.\n", dest->name,
         dest->instance ? "/" : "", dest->instance ? dest->instance : "");
```

See Also

cupsAddDest(), cupsFreeDests(), cupsGetDests()

cupsGetDests()

Usage

```
int
cupsGetDests(cups_dest_t **dests);
```

Arguments

Argument	Type	Description
dests	cups_dest_t **	The destinations array

Returns

The number of destinations found.

Description

The cupsGetDests() function returns the number of destinations that were found.

Example

```
#include <cups/cups.h>

int         num_dests;
cups_dest_t *dests;

...

num_dests = cupsGetDests(&dests);
```

See Also

cupsAddDest(), cupsFreeDests(), cupsGetDest()

cupsGetJobs()

Usage

```
int
cupsGetOption(cups_job_t **jobs,
            const char *dest,
```

```
int        myjobs,
int        completed);
```

Arguments

Argument	Type	Description
jobs	cups_job_t **	The jobs array
dest	const char *	The destination or NULL
myjobs	int	1 = show my jobs only
completed	int	1 = show completed jobs

Returns

The number of jobs found.

Description

The cupsGetJobs() function returns a list of jobs (if any) on the specified destination. If the destination name is NULL then jobs on all destinations are listed.

Example

```
#include <cups/cups.h>

int        num_jobs;
cups_job_t *jobs;

...

num_jobs = cupsGetJobs(&jobs, NULL, 0, 0);
```

See Also

cupsFreeJobs()

cupsGetOption()

Usage

```
const char *
cupsGetOption(const char    *name,
```

```
int            num_options,
cups_option_t *options);
```

Arguments

Argument	Type	Description
name	const char *	The name of the option
num_options	int	The number of options in the array
options	cups_option_t *	The options array

Returns

A pointer to the option values or NULL if the option is not defined.

Description

The cupsGetOption() function returns the first occurrence of the named option. If the option is not included in the options array then a NULL pointer is returned.

Example

```
#include <cups/cups.h>

int            num_options;
cups_option_t *options;
const char    *media;

...

media = cupsGetOption("media", num_options, options);
```

See Also

cupsAddOption(), cupsFreeOptions(), cupsMarkOptions(), cupsParseOptions()

cupsGetPassword()

Usage

```
const char *
cupsGetPassword(const char *prompt);
```

Arguments

Argument	Type	Description
prompt	const char *	The prompt that is to be displayed to the user

Returns

A pointer to the password that was entered or NULL if no password was entered.

Description

The cupsGetPassword() function displays the prompt string and asks the user for a password. The password text is not echoed to the user.

Example

```
#include <cups/cups.h>

char *password;

...

password = cupsGetPassword("Please enter a password:");
```

See Also

cupsServer(), cupsSetPasswordCB(), cupsSetServer(), cupsSetUser(), cupsUser()

cupsGetPPD()

Usage

```
const char *
cupsGetPPD(const char *printer);
```

Arguments

Argument	Type	Description
printer	const char *	The name of the printer

Returns

The name of a temporary file containing the PPD file or NULL if the printer cannot be located or does not have a PPD file.

Description

The cupsGetPPD() function gets a copy of the PPD file for the named printer. The printer name can be of the form "printer" or "printer@hostname."

You should remove (unlink) the PPD file after you finish using it. The filename is stored in a static buffer and is overwritten with each call to cupsGetPPD().

Example

```
#include <cups/cups.h>

char *ppd;

...

ppd = cupsGetPPD("printer@hostname");

...

unlink(ppd);
```

cupsGetPrinters()

Usage

```
int
cupsGetPrinters(char ***printers);
```

Arguments

Argument	Type	Description
printers	char ***	Pointer to the char pointer array pointer

Returns

The number of printers available.

Description

The `cupsGetPrinters()` function gets a list of the available printers. The `free()` function should be used to free the returned array when it is no longer needed.

Example

```
#include <cups/cups.h>

int   i;
int   num_printers;
char **printers;


...


num_printers = cupsGetPrinters(


...


if (num_printers > 0)
{
  for (i = 0; i <num_printers; i ++)
    free(printers[i]);

  free(printers);
}
```

See Also

`cupsGetClasses()`, `cupsGetDefault()`

cupsLangDefault()

Usage

```
const char *
cupsLangDefault(void);
```

Returns

A pointer to the default language structure.

Description

The cupsLangDefault() function returns a language structure for the default language. The default language is defined by the LANG environment variable. If the specified language cannot be located, then the POSIX (English) locale is used.

Call cupsLangFree() to free any memory associated with the language structure when you are finished.

Example

```
#include <cups/language.h>

cups_lang_t *language;
...

language = cupsLangDefault();

...

cupsLangFree(language);
```

See Also

cupsLangEncoding(), cupsLangFlush(), cupsLangFree(), cupsLangGet(), cupsLangString()

cupsLangEncoding()

Usage

```
char *
cupsLangEncoding(cups_lang_t *language);
```

Arguments

Argument	Type	Description
language	cups_lang_t *	The language structure

Returns

A pointer to the encoding string.

Description

The cupsLangEncoding() function returns the language encoding used for the specified language, for example "iso-8859-1," "utf-8," and so on.

Example

```
#include <cups/language.h>

cups_lang_t *language;
char        *encoding;
...

language = cupsLangDefault();
encoding = cupsLangEncoding(language);
...

cupsLangFree(language);
```

See Also

cupsLangDefault(), cupsLangFlush(), cupsLangFree(), cupsLangGet(), cupsLangString()

cupsLangFlush()

Usage

```
void
cupsLangFlush(void);
```

Description

The cupsLangFlush() function frees all language structures that have been allocated.

Example

```
#include <cups/language.h>

...

cupsLangFlush();
```

See Also

cupsLangDefault(), cupsLangEncoding(), cupsLangFree(), cupsLangGet(), cupsLangString()

cupsLangFree()

Usage

```
void
cupsLangFree(cups_lang_t *language);
```

Arguments

Argument	Type	Description
language	cups_lang_t *	The language structure that is to be freed

Description

The cupsLangFree() function frees the specified language structure.

Example

```
#include <cups/language.h>

cups_lang_t *language;
...

cupsLangFree(language);
```

See Also

cupsLangDefault(), cupsLangEncoding(), cupsLangFlush(), cupsLangGet(), cupsLangString()

cupsLangGet()

Usage

```
cups_lang_t *
cupsLangGet(const char *name);
```

Arguments

Argument	Type	Description
name	const char *	The name of the locale

Returns

A pointer to a language structure.

Description

The cupsLangGet() function returns a language structure for the specified locale. If the locale is not defined then the POSIX (English) locale is substituted.

Example

```
#include <cups/language.h>

cups_lang_t *language;

...

language = cupsLangGet("fr");

...

cupsLangFree(language);
```

See Also

cupsLangDefault(), cupsLangEncoding(), cupsLangFlush(), cupsLangFree(), cupsLangString()

cupsLangString()

Usage

```
char *
cupsLangString(cups_lang_t *language,
               cups_msg_t  message);
```

Arguments

Argument	Type	Description
language	cups_lang_t *	The language to query
message	cups_msg_t	The message number

Returns

A pointer to the message string or NULL if the message is not defined.

Description

The cupsLangString() function returns a pointer to the specified message string in the specified language.

Example

```
#include <cups/language.h>

cups_lang_t *language;
char        *s;
...

language = cupsLangGet("fr");

s = cupsLangString(language, CUPS_MSG_YES);

...

cupsLangFree(language);
```

See Also

cupsLangDefault(), cupsLangEncoding(), cupsLangFlush(), cupsLangFree(), cupsLangGet()

cupsLastError()

Usage

```
ipp_status_t
cupsLastError(void);
```

Returns

An enumeration containing the last IPP error.

Description

The cupsLastError() function returns the last IPP error that occurred. If no error occurred then it returns IPP_OK or IPP_OK_CONFLICT.

Example

```
#include <cups/cups.h>

ipp_status_t status;

...

status = cupsLastError();
```

See Also

cupsCancelJob(), cupsPrintFile()

cupsMarkOptions()

Usage

```
int
cupsMarkOptions(ppd_file_t    *ppd,
                int           num_options,
                cups_option_t *options);
```

Arguments

Argument	Type	Description
ppd	ppd_file_t *	The PPD file to mark
num_options	int	The number of options in the options array
options	cups_option_t *	The options array

Returns

The number of conflicts found.

Description

The `cupsMarkOptions()` function marks options in the PPD file. It also handles mapping of IPP option names and values to PPD option names.

Example

```
#include <cups/cups.h>

int         num_options;
cups_option_t *options;
ppd_file_t    *ppd;


...


cupsMarkOptions(ppd, num_options, options);
```

See Also

`cupsAddOption()`, `cupsFreeOptions()`, `cupsGetOption()`, `cupsParseOptions()`

cupsParseOptions()

Usage

```
int
cupsParseOptions(const char    *arg,
                 int           num_options,
                 cups_option_t **options);
```

Arguments

Argument	Type	Description
arg	const char *	The string containing one or more options
num_options	int	The number of options in the options array
options	cups_option_t *	The options array

Returns

The new number of options in the array.

Description

The cupsParseOptions() function parses the specified string for one or more options of the form "name=value," "name," or "noname." It can be called multiple times to combine the options from several strings.

Example

```
#include <cups/cups.h>

int           num_options;
cups_option_t *options;


...


num_options = 0;
options     = (cups_option_t *)0;
num_options = cupsParseOptions(argv[5], num_options, &options);
```

See Also

cupsAddOption(), cupsFreeOptions(), cupsGetOption(), cupsMarkOptions()

cupsPrintFile()

Usage

```
int
cupsPrintFile(const char    *printer,
              const char    *filename,
              const char    *title,
              int           num_options,
              cups_option_t *options);
```

Arguments

Argument	Type	Description
printer	const char *	The printer or class to print to
filename	const char *	The file to print
title	const char *	The job title
num_options	int	The number of options in the options array
options	cups_option_t *	The options array

Returns

The new job ID number or 0 on error.

Description

The cupsPrintFile() function sends a file to the specified printer or class for printing. If the job cannot be printed the error code can be found by calling cupsLastError().

Example

```
#include <cups/cups.h>

int         num_options;
cups_option_t *options;
int         jobid;

...

jobid = cupsPrintFile("printer@hostname", "filename.ps", "Job Title",
                      num_options, options);
```

See Also

cupsCancelJob(), cupsLastError(), cupsPrintFiles()

cupsPrintFiles()

Usage

```
int
cupsPrintFiles(const char    *printer,
               int           num_files,
               const char    **files,
               const char    *title,
               int           num_options,
               cups_option_t *options);
```

Arguments

Argument	Type	Description
printer	const char *	The printer or class to print to
num_files	int	The number of files to print
files	const char **	The files to print

Argument	Type	Description
title	const char *	The job title
num_options	int	The number of options in the options array
options	cups_option_t *	The options array

Returns

The new job ID number or 0 on error.

Description

The cupsPrintFiles() function sends multiple files to the specified printer or class for printing. If the job cannot be printed the error code can be found by calling cupsLastError().

Example

```
#include <cups/cups.h>

int         num_files;
const char  *files[100];
int         num_options;
cups_option_t *options;
int         jobid;


...


jobid = cupsPrintFiles("printer@hostname", num_files, files,
                       "Job Title", num_options, options);
```

See Also

cupsCancelJob(), cupsLastError(), cupsPrintFile()

cupsRasterClose()

Usage

```
void
cupsRasterClose(cups_raster_t *ras);
```

Arguments

Argument	Type	Description
ras	cups_raster_t *	The raster stream to close

Description

The cupsRasterClose() function closes the specified raster stream.

Example

```
#include <cups/raster.h>

cups_raster_t *ras;

...

cupsRasterClose(ras);
```

See Also

cupsRasterOpen(), cupsRasterReadHeader(), cupsRasterReadPixels(),
cupsRasterWriteHeader(), cupsRasterWritePixels()

cupsRasterOpen()

Usage

```
cups_raster_t *
cupsRasterOpen(int       fd,
          cups_mode_t mode);
```

Arguments

Argument	Type	Description
fd	int	The file descriptor that is to be used
mode	cups_mode_t	The mode that is to be used: CUPS_RASTER_READ or CUPS_RASTER_WRITE

Returns

A pointer to a raster stream or NULL if there was an error.

Description

The cupsRasterOpen() function opens a raster stream for reading or writing.

Example

```
#include <cups/raster.h>

cups_raster_t *ras;

...

ras = cupsRasterOpen(0, CUPS_RASTER_READ);
```

See Also

cupsRasterClose(), cupsRasterReadHeader(), cupsRasterReadPixels(),
cupsRasterWriteHeader(), cupsRasterWritePixels()

cupsRasterReadHeader()

Usage

```
unsigned
cupsRasterReadHeader(cups_raster_t      *ras,
                     cups_page_header_t *header);
```

Arguments

Argument	Type	Description
ras	cups_raster_t *	The raster stream to read from
header	cups_page_header_t *	A pointer to a page header structure to read into

Returns

1 on success, 0 on EOF or error.

Description

The `cupsRasterReadHeader()` function reads a page header from the specified raster stream.

Example

```
#include <cups/raster.h>

int                 line;
cups_raster_t       *ras;
cups_raster_header_t header;
unsigned char       pixels[8192];
...

while (cupsRasterReadHeader(ras, &header))
{
  ...

  for (line = 0; line < header.cupsHeight; line ++)
  {
    cupsRasterReadPixels(ras, pixels, header.cupsBytesPerLine);

    ...
  }
}
```

See Also

`cupsRasterClose()`, `cupsRasterOpen()`, `cupsRasterReadPixels()`, `cupsRasterWriteHeader()`, `cupsRasterWritePixels()`

cupsRasterReadPixels()

Usage

```
unsigned
cupsRasterReadPixels(cups_raster_t *ras,
                     unsigned char *pixels,
                     unsigned       length);
```

Arguments

Argument	Type	Description
ras	cups_raster_t *	The raster stream from which to read
pixels	unsigned char *	The pointer to a pixel buffer
length	unsigned	The number of bytes of pixel data to read

Returns

The number of bytes read or 0 on EOF or error.

Description

The cupsRasterReadPixels() function reads pixel data from the specified raster stream.

Example

```
#include <cups/raster.h>

int                 line;
cups_raster_t       *ras;
cups_raster_header_t header;
unsigned char       pixels[8192];
...

while (cupsRasterReadHeader(ras, &header))
{
  ...

  for (line = 0; line < header.cupsHeight; line ++)
  {
    cupsRasterReadPixels(ras, pixels, header.cupsBytesPerLine);

    ...
  }
}
```

See Also

cupsRasterClose(), cupsRasterOpen(), cupsRasterReadHeader(), cupsRasterWriteHeader(), cupsRasterWritePixels()

cupsRasterWriteHeader()

Usage

```
unsigned
cupsRasterWriteHeader(cups_raster_t      *ras,
                      cups_page_header_t *header);
```

Arguments

Argument	Type	Description
ras	cups_raster_t *	The raster stream to write to
header	cups_page_header_t *	The page header structure to write

Returns

1 on success, 0 on error.

Description

The cupsRasterWriteHeader() function writes the specified page header to a raster stream.

Example

```
#include <cups/raster.h>

int                line;
cups_raster_t      *ras;
cups_raster_header_t header;
unsigned char      pixels[8192];
...

cupsRasterWriteHeader(ras, &header);

for (line = 0; line < header.cupsHeight; line ++)
{
  ...

  cupsRasterWritePixels(ras, pixels, header.cupsBytesPerLine);
}
```

See Also

cupsRasterClose(), cupsRasterOpen(), cupsRasterReadHeader(), cupsRasterReadPixels(), cupsRasterWritePixels()

cupsRasterWritePixels()

Usage

```
unsigned
cupsRasterWritePixels(cups_raster_t *ras,
                      unsigned char *pixels,
                      unsigned       length);
```

Arguments

Argument	Type	Description
ras	cups_raster_t *	The raster stream to write to
pixels	unsigned char *	The pointer to a pixel buffer
length	unsigned	The number of bytes of pixel data to write

Returns

The number of bytes written.

Description

The cupsRasterWritePixels() function writes the specified pixel data to a raster stream.

Example

```
#include <cups/raster.h>

int                line;
cups_raster_t      *ras;
cups_raster_header_t header;
unsigned char      pixels[8192];
...


cupsRasterWriteHeader(ras, &header);
```

```
for (line = 0; line < header.cupsHeight; line ++)
{
  ...

  cupsRasterWritePixels(ras, pixels, header.cupsBytesPerLine);
}
```

See Also

cupsRasterClose(), cupsRasterOpen(), cupsRasterReadHeader(), cupsRasterReadPixels(),
cupsRasterWriteHeader()

cupsServer()

Usage

```
const char *
cupsServer(void);
```

Returns

A pointer to the default server name.

Description

The cupsServer() function returns a pointer to the default server name. The server name is stored in a static location and will be overwritten with every call to cupsServer().

The default server is determined from the following locations:

1. The CUPS_SERVER environment variable,

2. The ServerName directive in the client.conf file,

3. The default host, "localhost."

Example

```
#include <cups/cups.h>

const char *server;

server = cupsServer();
```

See Also

cupsGetPassword(), cupsSetPasswordCB(), cupsSetServer(), cupsSetUser(), cupsUser()

cupsSetDests()

Usage

```
void
cupsSetDests(int          num_dests,
             cups_dest_t *dests);
```

Arguments

Argument	Type	Description
num_dests	int	The number of destinations in the array
dests	cups_dest_t *	The destinations array

Description

The cupsSetDests() function saves the destinations array to the system-wide lpoptions file (if the current user is the super-user) or the user .lpoptions file.

Example

```
#include <cups/cups.h>

...

int          num_dests;
cups_dest_t *dests;

...

cupsSetDests(num_dests, dests);
```

See Also

cupsAddDest(), cupsFreeDests(), cupsGetDest(), cupsGetDests()

cupsSetEncryption()

Usage

```
void
cupsSetEncryption(http_encryption_t encryption);
```

Arguments

Argument	Type	Description
encryption	http_encryption_t	The type of encryption that is to be used.

Description

The cupsSetEncryption() function sets the default encryption method that is to be used for IPP requests.

Example

```
#include <cups/cups.h>

...

cupsSetEncryption(HTTP_ENCRYPT_REQUIRED);
```

See Also

cupsEncryption()

cupsSetPasswordCB()

Usage

```
void
cupsSetPasswordCB(const char *(*cb)(const char *prompt));
```

Arguments

Argument	Type	Description
cb	const char *(*)(const char *)	The password callback function

Description

The cupsSetPasswordCB() function sets the callback function that is to be used when asking the user for a password. The callback function must accept a single character string pointer (the prompt string) and return NULL if the user did not enter a password string or a pointer to the password string.

Example

```
#include <cups/cups.h>

const char *
my_password_cb(const char *prompt)
{
  return (getpass(prompt));
}

...

char *password;

...

cupsSetPasswordCB(my_password_cb);
password = cupsGetPassword("Please enter a password:");
```

See Also

cupsServer(), cupsSetServer(), cupsSetUser(), cupsUser()

cupsSetServer()

Usage

```
void
cupsSetServer(const char *server);
```

Arguments

Argument	Type	Description
server	const char *	The default server that is to be used

Description

The cupsSetServer() function sets the default server that is to be used for the CUPS API. If the server argument is NULL, the default server is used.

Example

```
#include <cups/cups.h>

cupsSetServer("foo.bar.com");
```

See Also

cupsServer(), cupsSetPasswordCB(), cupsSetUser(), cupsUser()

cupsSetUser()

Usage

```
void
cupsSetUser(const char *user);
```

Arguments

Argument	Type	Description
user	const char *	The user name string that is to be used.

Description

The cupsSetUser() function sets the default user name for authentication. If the user argument is NULL then the current login user is used.

Example

```
#include <cups/cups.h>

...

cupsSetUser("root");
```

See Also

cupsServer(), cupsSetPasswordCB(), cupsSetServer(), cupsUser()

cupsTempFd()

Usage

```
int
cupsTempFd(char *filename,
           int  length);
```

Arguments

Argument	Type	Description
filename	char *	The temporary filename buffer
length	int	The size of the filename buffer in bytes

Returns

A file descriptor opened for the temporary file in exclusive read-write mode. If cupsTempFd() is unable to create a temporary file, -1 is returned.

Description

The cupsTempFd() function safely creates a temporary file in the /var/tmp directory or the directory specified by the TMPDIR environment variable.

Example

```
#include <cups/cups.h>

char filename[256];
int  fd;

fd = cupsTempFd(filename, sizeof(filename));
```

cupsTempFile()

Usage

```
char *
cupsTempFile(char *filename,
             int  length);
```

Arguments

Argument	Type	Description
filename	char *	The temporary filename buffer
length	int	The size of the filename buffer in bytes

Returns

A pointer to `filename` or `NULL` if a temporary file cannot be created.

Description

The `cupsTempFile()` function safely creates a temporary file in the `/var/tmp` directory or the directory specified by the `TMPDIR` environment variable. It then closes the file so it may be opened at a later time.

This function is vulnerable to certain types of "same user" symlink attacks, so whenever possible the `cupsTempFd()` function should be used instead.

Example

```
#include <cups/cups.h>

char filename[256];

cupsTempFile(filename, sizeof(filename));
```

cupsUser()

Usage

```
const char *
cupsUser(void);
```

Returns

A pointer to the current username or NULL if the user ID is undefined.

Description

The cupsUser() function returns the current user name. Initially this is the name associated with the current user ID as reported by the getuid() system call; however, the cupsSetUser() function can be used to change this.

Example

```
#include <cups/cups.h>

const char *user;

user = cupsUser();
```

See Also

cupsGetPassword(), cupsServer(), cupsSetUser()

httpBlocking()

Usage

```
void
httpBlocking(http_t *http,
             int    blocking)
```

Arguments

Argument	Type	Description
http	http_t *	The HTTP connection
blocking	int	0 if the connection should be non-blocking, 1 if it should be blocking

Description

The httpBlocking() function sets the blocking mode for the HTTP connection. By default HTTP connections block (stop) the client program until data is available or can be sent to the server.

Example

```
#include <cups/http.h>

http_t *http;

http = httpConnect("server", port);
httpBlocking(http, 0);
```

See Also

httpCheck(), httpConnect()

httpCheck()

Usage

```
int httpCheck(http_t *http);
```

Arguments

Argument	Type	Description
http	http_t *	The HTTP connection

Returns

0 if there is no data pending, 1 otherwise.

Description

The httpCheck() function checks to see whether any data is pending on an HTTP connection.

Example

```
#include <cups/http.h>

http_t *http;

if (httpCheck(http))
{
   ... do something ...
}
```

See Also

httpBlocking(), httpConnect(), httpGets() , httpRead()

httpCheck()

Usage

```
int
httpCheck(http_t *http)
```

Arguments

Argument	Type	Description
http	http_t *	The HTTP connection

Returns

1 if input from the HTTP server is pending, and 0 if not.

Description

The httpCheck() function checks to see whether input from the HTTP server is pending.

Example

```
#include <cups/http.h>

...

http_t *http;

...

if (httpCheck(http))
  puts("Server has something to say!");
```

See Also

httpConnect()

httpClearFields()

Usage

```
void
httpClearFields(http_t *http)
```

Arguments

Argument	Type	Description
http	http_t *	The HTTP connection

Description

The httpClearFields() function clears all HTTP request fields for the HTTP connection.

Example

```
#include <cups/http.h>

http_t *http;

httpClearFields(http);
```

See Also

httpConnect(), httpGetField(), httpSetField()

httpClose()

Usage

```
void
httpClose(http_t *http);
```

Arguments

Argument	Type	Description
http	http_t *	The HTTP connection

Description

The httpClose() function closes an active HTTP connection.

Example

```
#include <cups/http.h>

http_t *http;

httpClose(http);
```

See Also

httpConnect()

httpConnect()

Usage

```
http_t *
httpConnect(const char *hostname,
            int        port);
```

Arguments

Argument	Type	Description
hostname	const char *	The hostname or IP address of the server that is to be contacted
port	int	The port number that is to be used

Returns

A pointer to an HTTP connection structure or NULL if the connection could not be made.

Description

The httpConnect() function opens an HTTP connection to the specified server and port.

Example

```
#include <cups/http.h>
```

```
http_t *http;

http = httpConnect(cupsServer(), ippPort());
```

See Also

httpClose(), httpConnectEncrypt(), httpGet(), httpGets(), httpPost(), httpRead(), httpWrite()

httpConnectEncrypt()

Usage

```
http_t *
httpConnectEncrypt(const char       *hostname,
                   int              port,
                   http_encryption_t encryption);
```

Arguments

Argument	Type	Description
hostname	const char *	The hostname or IP address of the server that is to be contacted
port	int	The port number that is to be used
encryption	http_encryption_t	The type of encryption that is to be used

Returns

A pointer to an HTTP connection structure or NULL if the connection could not be made.

Description

The httpConnectEncrypt() function opens an HTTP connection to the specified server and port using the specified encryption mode.

Example

```
#include <cups/http.h>

http_t *http;

http = httpConnectEncrypt(cupsServer(), ippPort(), HTTP_ENCRYPT_REQUIRED);
```

See Also

httpClose(), httpConnect(), httpGet(), httpGets(), httpPost(), httpRead(), httpWrite()

httpDecode64()

Usage

```
char *
httpDecode64(char       *out,
             const char *in);
```

Arguments

Argument	Type	Description
out	char *	The output string
in	const char *	The input string

Returns

A pointer to the decoded string.

Description

The httpDecode64() function decodes a base-64 encoded string to the original string.

Example

```
#include <cups/http.h>

char encoded_string[255];
char original_string[255];

httpDecode64(original_string, encoded_string);
```

See Also

httpEncode64()

httpDelete()

Usage

```
int
httpDelete(http_t     *http,
           const char *uri);
```

Arguments

Argument	Type	Description
http	http_t *	The HTTP connection
uri	const char *	The URI that is to be deleted

Returns

0 on success, non-zero on failure.

Description

The httpDelete() function sends an HTTP DELETE request to the server.

Example

```
#include <cups/http.h>

http_t *http;

httpDelete(http, "/some/uri");
```

See Also

httpConnect(), httpSetField(), httpUpdate()

httpEncode64()

Usage

```
char *
httpEncode64(char       *out,
             const char *in);
```

Arguments

Argument	Type	Description
out	char *	The output string
in	const char *	The input string

Returns

A pointer to the encoded string.

Description

The httpEncode64() function decodes a base-64 encoded string to the original string.

Example

```
#include <cups/http.h>

char encoded_string[255];
char original_string[255];

httpEncode64(encoded_string, original_string);
```

See Also

httpDecode64()

httpEncryption()

Usage

```
void
httpEncryption(http_t          *http,
               http_encryption_t encryption);
```

Arguments

Argument	Type	Description
http	http_t *	The HTTP connection
encryption	http_encryption_t	The type of encryption that is to be used

Description

The httpEncryption() function sets the type of encryption that is to be used on the connection to the HTTP server. This function may close and reconnect to the server to establish the new type of encryption.

Example

```
#include <cups/http.h>

http_t *http;

httpEncryption(http, HTTP_ENCRYPT_REQUIRED);
```

See Also

```
httpConnectEncrypt()
```

httpError()

Usage

```
int
httpError(http_t *http);
```

Arguments

Argument	Type	Description
http	http_t *	The HTTP connection

Returns

The last error that occurred or 0 if no error has occurred.

Description

The httpError() function returns the last error that occurred on the HTTP connection.

Example

```
#include <cups/http.h>

http_t *http;
```

```
if (httpError(http))
{
  ... show an error message ...
}
```

See Also

httpConnect()

httpFlush()

Usage

```
void
httpFlush(http_t *http);
```

Arguments

Argument	Type	Description
http	http_t *	The HTTP connection

Description

The httpFlush() function flushes any remaining data left from a GET or POST operation.

Example

```
#include <cups/http.h>

http_t *http;

httpFlush(http);
```

See Also

httpConnect()

httpGet()

Usage

```
int
httpGet(http_t    *http,
        const char *uri);
```

Arguments

Argument	Type	Description
http	http_t *	The HTTP connection
uri	const char *	The URI to GET

Returns

0 on success, non-zero on failure.

Description

The httpGet() function sends an HTTP GET request to the server.

Example

```
#include <cups/http.h>

http_t *http;

httpGet(http, "/some/uri");
```

See Also

httpConnect(), httpSetField(), httpUpdate()

httpGetDateString()

Usage

```
const char *
httpGetDateString(time_t time);
```

Arguments

Argument	Type	Description
time	time_t	The Unix date/time value

Returns

A pointer to a static string containing the HTTP date/time string for the specified Unix time value.

Description

The httpGetDateString() function generates a date/time string suitable for HTTP requests from a Unix time value. The date/time string is overwritten with each call.

Example

```
#include <cups/http.h>

puts(httpGetDateString(time(NULL)));
```

See Also

httpGetDateTime()

httpGetDateTime()

Usage

```
time_t
httpGetDateTime(const char *date);
```

Arguments

Argument	Type	Description
date	const char *	The HTTP date/time string

Returns

A Unix time value.

Description

The `httpGetDateTime()` function converts an HTTP date/time string to a Unix time value.

Example

```
#include <cups/http.h>

printf("%d\n", httpGetDateTime("Fri, 30 June 2000 12:34:56 GMT"));
```

See Also

```
httpGetDateString()
```

httpGetField()

Usage

```
const char *
httpGetField(http_t      *http,
             http_field_t field);
```

Arguments

Argument	Type	Description
http	http_t *	The HTTP connection
field	http_field_t	The HTTP field

Returns

A pointer to the field value string.

Description

The `httpGetField()` function returns the current value for the specified HTTP field. An empty field is represented by a string of 0 length.

Example

```
#include <cups/http.h>

http_t *http;
```

```
httpGet(http, "/some/uri");
while (httpUpdate(http) == HTTP_CONTINUE);

puts(httpGetField(http, HTTP_FIELD_CONTENT_TYPE));
```

See Also

httpGetSubField(), httpSetField()

httpGetLength()

Usage

```
int
httpGetLength(http_t *http);
```

Arguments

Argument	Type	Description
http	http_t *	The HTTP connection

Returns

The content length of the GET or POST data.

Description

The httpGetLength() function returns the number of bytes returned by a GET or POST request.

Example

```
#include <cups/http.h>

http_t *http;

httpGet(http, "/some/uri");
while (httpUpdate(http) == HTTP_CONTINUE);

printf("Content length = %d\n", httpGetLength(http));
```

See Also

```
httpConnect()
```

httpGets()

Usage

```
char *
httpGets(char    *line,
         int     length,
         http_t *http)
```

Arguments

Argument	Type	Description
line	char *	The line buffer
length	int	The size of the line buffer in bytes
http	http_t *	The HTTP connection

Returns

A pointer to the string or NULL if no line could be retrieved.

Description

The httpGets() function is used to read a request line from the HTTP connection. It is not normally used by a client program.

Example

```
#include <cups/http.h>

http_t *http;
char line[1024];

if (httpGets(line, sizeof(line), http))
{
  ... process the line ...
}
```

See Also

httpConnect(), httpUpdate()

httpGetSubField()

Usage

```
const char *
httpGetSubField(http_t        *http,
                http_field_t  field,
                const char    *name,
                char          *value);
```

Arguments

Argument	Type	Description
http	http_t *	The HTTP connection
field	http_field_t	The HTTP field
name	const char *	The sub-field name
value	char [HTTP_MAX_NAME]	The sub-field value

Returns

A pointer to the sub-field value string or NULL if the field is not defined.

Description

The httpGetSubField() function returns a sub-value from the specified HTTP field. If the sub-field is not present, the value string is cleared and NULL is returned.

Example

```
#include <cups/http.h>

...

http_t *http;
char    value[HTTP_MAX_VALUE];

...
```

```
httpGet(http, "/some/uri");
while (httpUpdate(http) == HTTP_CONTINUE);

if (httpGetSubField(http, HTTP_FIELD_WWW_AUTHENTICATE, "realm", value))
  printf("Please enter password for %s:", value);
```

See Also

```
httpGetField()
```

httpHead()

Usage

```
int
httpHead(http_t    *http,
         const char *uri);
```

Arguments

Argument	Type	Description
http	http_t *	The HTTP connection
uri	const char *	The URI to HEAD

Returns

0 on success, non-zero on failure.

Description

The httpHead() function sends an HTTP HEAD request to the server.

Example

```
#include <cups/http.h>

http_t *http;

httpHead(http, "/some/uri");
```

See Also

httpConnect(), httpSetField(), httpUpdate()

httpInitialize()

Usage

```
void
httpInitialize(void);
```

Description

The httpInitialize() function initializes the networking code as needed by the underlying platform. It is called automatically by the httpConnect() and httpConnectEncrypt() functions.

Example

```
#include <cups/http.h>

httpInitialize();
```

See Also

httpConnect(), httpConnectEncrypt()

httpMD5()

Usage

```
char *
httpMD5(const char *username,
        const char *realm,
        const char *passwd,
        char       md5[33]);
```

Arguments

Argument	Type	Description
username	const char *	The username for the MD5 sum
realm	const char *	The realm for the MD5 sum

Argument	Type	Description
passwd	const char *	The password for the MD5 sum
md5	char [33]	The MD5 sum in hexadecimal

Returns

A pointer to the MD5 sum string.

Description

The httpMD5() function computes the MD5 sum of the username, realm, and password separated by colons (:).

Example

```
#include <cups/http.h>

...

char md5[33];

...

puts(httpMD5("username", "realm", "password", md5));
```

See Also

httpMD5Final(), httpMD5String()

httpMD5Final()

Usage

```
char *
httpMD5Final(const char *nonce,
             const char *method,
             const char *resource,
             char        md5[33])
```

Arguments

Argument	Type	Description
nonce	const char *	The server-supplied nonce string
method	const char *	The request method string
resource	const char *	The resource path in the request
md5	char [33]	The MD5 sum in hexadecimal

Returns

The MD5 sum string.

Description

The httpMD5Final() function updates the MD5 sum computed by httpMD5() to include the server-supplied nonce value, the method string ("GET", "POST", and so forth), and the resource path. The output is the final MD5 sum used for authentication.

Example

```
#include <cups/http.h>

...

char md5[33];

...

httpMD5Final("nonce", "GET", "/", md5);
```

See Also

httpMD5(), httpMD5String()

httpMD5String()

Usage

```
char *
httpMD5String(const md5_byte_t *sum,
              char             md5[33])
```

Arguments

Argument	Type	Description
sum	const md5_byte_t *	The raw MD5 sum
md5	char [33]	The MD5 sum in hexadecimal

Returns

The MD5 string.

Description

The httpMD5String() function converts a 16-byte raw MD5 sum to a 32-byte hexadecimal string.

Example

```
#include <cups/http.h>

...

md5_byte_t digest[16];
char       md5[33];

...

puts(httpMD5String(digest, md5));
```

See Also

httpMD5(), httpMD5Final()

httpOptions()

Usage

```
int
httpOptions(http_t    *http,
            const char *uri);
```

Arguments

Argument	Type	Description
http	http_t *	The HTTP connection
uri	const char *	The URI to check for options

Returns

0 on success, non-zero on failure.

Description

The httpOptions() function sends an HTTP OPTIONS request to the server.

Example

```
#include <cups/http.h>

http_t *http;

httpOptions(http, "/some/uri");
```

See Also

httpConnect(), httpSetField(), httpUpdate()

httpPost()

Usage

```
int
httpPost(http_t     *http,
         const char *uri);
```

Arguments

Argument	Type	Description
http	http_t *	The HTTP connection
uri	const char *	The URI to POST to

Returns

0 on success, non-zero on failure.

Description

The `httpPost()` function sends an HTTP POST request to the server.

Example

```
#include <cups/http.h>

http_t *http;

httpPost(http, "/some/uri");
```

See Also

`httpConnect()`, `httpSetField()`, `httpUpdate()`

httpPrintf()

Usage

```
int
httpPrintf(http_t     *http,
           const char *format,
           ...);
```

Arguments

Argument	Type	Description
http	http_t *	The HTTP connection
format	const char *	A printf-style format string
...	varies	Additional arguments as needed

Returns

The number of bytes written.

Description

The httpPrintf() function sends a formatted string to the HTTP connection. Normally, only the CUPS API and scheduler use it.

Example

```
#include <cups/http.h>

http_t *http;

httpPrintf(http, "GET / HTTP/1.1 \r\n");
```

See Also

httpConnect()

httpPut()

Usage

```
int
httpPut(http_t    *http,
        const char *uri);
```

Arguments

Argument	Type	Description
http	http_t *	The HTTP connection
uri	const char *	The URI to PUT to

Returns

0 on success, non-zero on failure.

Description

The httpPut() function sends an HTTP PUT request to the server.

Example

```
#include <cups/http.h>
```

```
http_t *http;

httpPut(http, "/some/uri");
```

See Also

httpConnect(), httpSetField(), httpUpdate()

httpRead()

Usage

```
int
httpRead(http_t *http,
         char   *buffer,
         int    length);
```

Arguments

Argument	Type	Description
http	http_t *	The HTTP connection
buffer	char *	The buffer to read into
length	int	The maximum number of bytes to read

Returns

The number of bytes read or –1 on error.

Description

The httpRead() function reads data from the HTTP connection, possibly the result of a
GET or POST request.

Example

```
#include <cups/http.h>

http_t *http;
char buffer[1024];
int  bytes;
```

```
httpGet(http, "/");
while (httpUpdate(http) != HTTP_CONTINUE);
while ((bytes = httpRead(http, buffer, sizeof(buffer) - 1)) > 0)
{
  buffer[bytes] = '\0';
  fputs(buffer, stdout);
}
```

See Also

httpConnect(), httpWrite()

httpReconnect()

Usage

```
int
httpReconnect(http_t *http);
```

Arguments

Argument	Type	Description
http	http_t *	The HTTP connection

Returns

0 on success, non-zero on failure.

Description

The httpReconnect() function reconnects to the HTTP server. This is usually done automatically if the HTTP functions detect that the server connection has terminated.

Example

```
#include <cups/http.h>

http_t *http;

httpReconnect(http);
```

See Also

httpConnect(), httpConnectEncrypt()

httpSeparate()

Usage

```
void
httpSeparate(const char *uri,
            char       *method,
            char       *username,
            char       *host,
            int        *port,
            char       *resource);
```

Arguments

Argument	Type	Description
uri	const char *	The URI that is to be separated
method	char [HTTP_MAX_URI]	The method (scheme) of the URI
username	char [HTTP_MAX_URI]	The username (and password) portion of the URI, if any
host	char [HTTP_MAX_URI]	The hostname portion of the URI, if any
port	int *	The port number for the URI, either as specified or as default for the method/scheme
resource	char [HTTP_MAX_URI]	The resource string, usually a filename on the server

Description

The httpSeparate() function separates the specified URI into its component parts. The method, username, hostname, and resource strings should be at least HTTP_MAX_URI characters long to avoid potential buffer overflow problems.

New programs should use the httpSeparateLen() function instead.

Example

```
char uri[HTTP_MAX_URI];
char method[HTTP_MAX_URI];
char username[HTTP_MAX_URI];
char host[HTTP_MAX_URI];
char resource[HTTP_MAX_URI];
```

```
int  port;

httpSeparate(uri, method, username, host, &port, resource);
```

See Also

```
httpConnect(), httpConnectEncrypt()
```

httpSetField()

Usage

```
void
httpSetField(http_t      *http,
             http_field_t field,
             const char   *value);
```

Arguments

Argument	Type	Description
http	http_t *	The HTTP connection
field	http_field_t	The HTTP field
value	const char *	The string value for the field

Description

The httpSetField() function sets the current value for the specified HTTP field.

Example

```
#include <cups/http.h>

http_t *http;

httpSetField(http, HTTP_FIELD_AUTHORIZATION, "Basic dfdr34453454325"));
httpGet(http, "/some/uri");
while (httpUpdate(http) == HTTP_CONTINUE);
```

See Also

```
httpConnect(), httpGetField()
```

httpTrace()

Usage

```
int
httpTrace(http_t      *http,
          const char *uri);
```

Arguments

Argument	Type	Description
http	http_t *	The HTTP connection
uri	const char *	The URI to be traced

Returns

0 on success, non-zero on failure.

Description

The httpTrace() function sends an HTTP TRACE request to the server.

Example

```
#include <cups/http.h>

http_t *http;

httpTrace(http, "/some/uri");
```

See Also

httpConnect(), httpSetField(), httpUpdate()

httpUpdate()

Usage

```
http_status_t
httpUpdate(http_t *http);
```

Arguments

Argument	Type	Description
http	http_t *	The HTTP connection

Returns

The HTTP status of the current request.

Description

The httpUpdate() function updates the current request status. It is used after any DELETE, GET, HEAD, OPTIONS, POST, PUT, or TRACE request to finalize the HTTP request and retrieve the request status.

Because proxies and the current blocking mode can cause the request to take longer, programs should continue calling httpUpdate() until the return status is not the constant value HTTP_CONTINUE .

Example

```
#include <cups/http.h>

http_t *http;
http_status_t status;

httpGet(http, "/some/uri");
while ((status = httpUpdate(http)) == HTTP_CONTINUE);
printf("Request status is %d\n", status);
```

See Also

httpConnect(), httpDelete(), httpGet() , httpHead(), httpOptions(), httpPost() , httpPut(), httpTrace()

httpWrite()

Usage

```
int
httpWrite(http_t *http,
          char   *buffer,
          int    length);
```

Arguments

Argument	Type	Description
http	http_t *	The HTTP connection
buffer	char *	The buffer from which to write from
length	int	The number of bytes to write

Returns

The number of bytes written or –1 on error.

Description

The httpWrite() function writes data to the HTTP connection, usually as part of a POST or PUT request.

Example

```
#include <cups/http.h>

http_t *http;
FILE *fp;
char buffer[1024];
int  bytes;

httpPost(http, "/");

while ((bytes = fread(buffer, 1, sizeof(buffer), fp)) > 0)
  httpWrite(http, buffer, bytes);

while (httpUpdate(http) != HTTP_CONTINUE);

while ((bytes = httpRead(http, buffer, sizeof(buffer) - 1)) > 0)
{
  buffer[bytes] = '\0';
  fputs(buffer, stdout);
}
```

See Also

httpConnect(), httpRead()

ippAddBoolean()

Usage

```
ipp_attribute_t *
ippAddBoolean(ipp_t     *ipp,
              ipp_tag_t group,
              const char *name,
              char      value);
```

Arguments

Argument	Type	Description
ipp	ipp_t *	The IPP request
group	ipp_tag_t	The IPP group
name	const char *	The name of the attribute
value	char	The Boolean value

Returns

A pointer to the new attribute or NULL if the attribute could not be created.

Description

The ippAddBoolean() function adds a single Boolean attribute value to the specified IPP request.

Example

```
#include <cups/ipp.h>

ipp_t *ipp;

ippAddBoolean(ipp, IPP_TAG_OPERATION, "my-jobs", 1);
```

See Also

ippAddBooleans(), ippAddDate(), ippAddInteger(), ippAddIntegers(), ippAddRange() ,
ippAddRanges(), ippAddResolution(), ippAddResolutions(), ippAddSeparator(),
ippAddString(), ippAddStrings()

ippAddBooleans()

Usage

```
ipp_attribute_t *
ippAddBooleans(ipp_t    *ipp,
               ipp_tag_t group,
               const char *name,
               int       num_values,
               const char *values);
```

Arguments

Argument	Type	Description
ipp	ipp_t *	The IPP request
group	ipp_tag_t	The IPP group
name	const char *	The name of the attribute
num_values	int	The number of Boolean values
values	const char *	The Boolean values

Returns

A pointer to the new attribute or NULL if the attribute could not be created.

Description

The ippAddBooleans() function adds one or more Boolean attribute values to the specified IPP request. If the values pointer is NULL then an array of num_values false values is created.

Example

```
#include <cups/ipp.h>

ipp_t *ipp;
char values[10];

ippAddBooleans(ipp, IPP_TAG_OPERATION, "some-attribute", 10, values);
```

See Also

ippAddBoolean(), ippAddDate(), ippAddInteger(), ippAddIntegers(), ippAddRange() , ippAddRanges(), ippAddResolution(), ippAddResolutions(), ippAddSeparator(), ippAddString(), ippAddStrings()

ippAddDate()

Usage

```
ipp_attribute_t *
ippAddDate(ipp_t      *ipp,
           ipp_tag_t   group,
           const char *name,
           ipp_uchar_t *value);
```

Arguments

Argument	Type	Description
ipp	ipp_t *	The IPP request
group	ipp_tag_t	The IPP group
name	const char *	The name of the attribute
value	ipp_uchar_t *	The date value

Returns

A pointer to the new attribute or NULL if the attribute could not be created.

Description

The ippAddDate() function adds a single date-time attribute value to the specified IPP request.

Example

```
#include <cups/ipp.h>

ipp_t *ipp;

ippAddDate(ipp, IPP_TAG_OPERATION, "some-attribute",
           ippTimeToDate(time(NULL)));
```

See Also

ippAddBoolean(), ippAddBooleans(), ippAddInteger(), ippAddIntegers(), ippAddRange() , ippAddRanges(), ippAddResolution(), ippAddResolutions(), ippAddSeparator(), ippAddString(), ippAddStrings(), ippTimeToDate()

ippAddInteger()

Usage

```
ipp_attribute_t *
ippAddInteger(ipp_t      *ipp,
              ipp_tag_t  group,
              ipp_tag_t  tag,
              const char *name,
              int        value);
```

Arguments

Argument	Type	Description
ipp	ipp_t *	The IPP request
group	ipp_tag_t	The IPP group
tag	ipp_tag_t	The IPP value tag
name	const char *	The name of the attribute
value	int	The integer value

Returns

A pointer to the new attribute or NULL if the attribute could not be created.

Description

The ippAddInteger() function adds a single integer attribute value to the specified IPP request.

Example

```
#include <cups/ipp.h>

ipp_t *ipp;

ippAddInteger(ipp, IPP_TAG_OPERATION, "limit", 100);
```

See Also

ippAddBoolean(), ippAddBooleans(), ippAddDate(), ippAddIntegers(), ippAddRange() ,
ippAddRanges(), ippAddResolution(), ippAddResolutions(), ippAddSeparator(),
ippAddString(), ippAddStrings()

ippAddIntegers()

Usage

```
ipp_attribute_t *
ippAddIntegers(ipp_t     *ipp,
               ipp_tag_t group,
               ipp_tag_t tag,
               const char *name,
               int        num_values,
               const int  *values);
```

Arguments

Argument	Type	Description
ipp	ipp_t *	The IPP request
group	ipp_tag_t	The IPP group
tag	ipp_tag_t	The IPP value tag
name	const char *	The name of the attribute
num_values	int	The number of integer values
values	const int *	The integer values

Returns

A pointer to the new attribute or NULL if the attribute could not be created.

Description

The ippAddIntegers() function adds one or more integer attribute values to the specified
IPP request. If the values pointer is NULL then an array of 0 values is created.

Example

```
#include <cups/ipp.h>

ipp_t *ipp;
int values[100];

ippAddIntegers(ipp, IPP_TAG_OPERATION, "some-attribute", 100, values);
```

See Also

ippAddBoolean(), ippAddBooleans(), ippAddDate(), ippAddInteger(), ippAddRange(),
ippAddRanges(), ippAddResolution(), ippAddResolutions(), ippAddSeparator(),
ippAddString(), ippAddStrings()

ippAddRange()

Usage

```
ipp_attribute_t *
ippAddRange(ipp_t     *ipp,
            ipp_tag_t  group,
            const char *name,
            int        low,
            int        high);
```

Arguments

Argument	Type	Description
ipp	ipp_t *	The IPP request
group	ipp_tag_t	The IPP group
name	const char *	The name of the attribute
low	int	The lower range value
high	int	The upper range value

Returns

A pointer to the new attribute or NULL if the attribute could not be created.

Description

The ippAddRange() function adds a single range attribute value to the specified IPP request.

Example

```
#include <cups/ipp.h>

ipp_t *ipp;

ippAddRange(ipp, IPP_TAG_OPERATION, "page-ranges", 1, 10);
```

See Also

ippAddBoolean(), ippAddBooleans(), ippAddDate(), ippAddInteger(), ippAddIntegers(),
ippAddRanges(), ippAddResolution(), ippAddResolutions(), ippAddSeparator(),
ippAddString(), ippAddStrings()

ippAddRanges()

Usage

```
ipp_attribute_t *
ippAddRanges(ipp_t      *ipp,
             ipp_tag_t  group,
             const char *name,
             int        num_values,
             const int  *lows,
             const int  *highs);
```

Arguments

Argument	Type	Description
ipp	ipp_t *	The IPP request
group	ipp_tag_t	The IPP group
name	const char *	The name of the attribute
num_values	int	The number of range values
lows	const int *	The lower range values
highs	const int *	The upper range values

Returns

A pointer to the new attribute or NULL if the attribute could not be created.

Description

The ippAddRanges() function adds one or more range attribute values to the specified IPP request. If the values pointer is NULL then an array of 0 to 0 ranges is created.

Example

```
#include <cups/ipp.h>

ipp_t *ipp;
```

```
int lows[2];
int highs[2];

ippAddRanges(ipp, IPP_TAG_OPERATION, "page-ranges", 2, lows, highs);
```

See Also

ippAddBoolean(), ippAddBooleans(), ippAddDate(), ippAddInteger(), ippAddIntegers(),
ippAddRange(), ippAddResolution(), ippAddResolutions(), ippAddSeparator(),
ippAddString(), ippAddStrings()

ippAddResolution()

Usage

```
ipp_attribute_t *
ippAddResolution(ipp_t        *ipp,
                 ipp_tag_t    group,
                 const char   *name,
                 int        .  xres,
                 int           yres,
                 ipp_res_t     units);
```

Arguments

Argument	Type	Description
ipp	ipp_t *	The IPP request
group	ipp_tag_t	The IPP group
name	const char *	The name of the attribute
xres	int	The horizontal resolution value
yres	int	The vertical resolution value
units	ipp_res_t	The resolution units value

Returns

A pointer to the new attribute or NULL if the attribute could not be created.

Description

The ippAddResolution() function adds a single resolution attribute value to the specified
IPP request.

Example

```
#include <cups/ipp.h>

ipp_t *ipp;

ippAddBoolean(ipp, IPP_TAG_OPERATION, "printer-resolution",
              720, 720, IPP_RES_PER_INCH);
```

See Also

ippAddBoolean(), ippAddBooleans(), ippAddDate(), ippAddInteger(), ippAddIntegers(), ippAddRange(), ippAddRanges(), ippAddResolutions(), ippAddSeparator(), ippAddString(), ippAddStrings()

ippAddResolutions()

Usage

```
ipp_attribute_t *
ippAddResolutions(ipp_t          *ipp,
                  ipp_tag_t      group,
                  const char     *name,
                  int            num_values,
                  const int      *xres,
                  const int      *yres,
                  const ipp_res_t *units);
```

Arguments

Argument	Type	Description
ipp	ipp_t *	The IPP request
group	ipp_tag_t	The IPP group
name	const char *	The name of the attribute
num_values	int	The number of resolution values
xres	const int *	The horizontal resolution values
yres	const int *	The vertical resolution values
units	const ipp_res_t *	The resolution units values

Returns

A pointer to the new attribute or NULL if the attribute could not be created.

Description

The ippAddResolutions() function adds one or more resolution attribute values to the specified IPP request. If the values pointer is NULL then an array of 0x0 resolutions is created.

Example

```
#include <cups/ipp.h>

ipp_t *ipp;
int xres[5];
int yres[5];
ipp_res_t units[5];

ippAddBoolean(ipp, IPP_TAG_OPERATION, "printer-resolutions-supported",
              5, xres, yres, units);
```

See Also

ippAddBoolean(), ippAddBooleans(), ippAddDate(), ippAddInteger(), ippAddIntegers(),
ippAddRange(), ippAddRanges(), ippAddResolution(), ippAddSeparator(), ippAddString(),
ippAddStrings()

ippAddSeparator()

Usage

```
ipp_attribute_t *
ippAddSeparator(ipp_t *ipp);
```

Arguments

Argument	Type	Description
ipp	ipp_t *	The IPP request

Returns

A pointer to the new separator or NULL if the separator could not be created.

Description

The ippAddSeparator() function adds a group separator to the specified IPP request.

Example

```
#include <cups/ipp.h>

ipp_t *ipp;

ippAddSeparator(ipp);
```

See Also

ippAddBoolean(), ippAddBooleans(), ippAddDate(), ippAddInteger(), ippAddIntegers(),
ippAddRange(), ippAddRanges(), ippAddResolution(), ippAddResolutions(), ippAddString(),
ippAddStrings()

ippAddString()

Usage

```
ipp_attribute_t *
ippAddString(ipp_t      *ipp,
             ipp_tag_t  group,
             ipp_tag_t  tag,
             const char *name,
             const char *charset,
             const char *value);
```

Arguments

Argument	Type	Description
ipp	ipp_t *	The IPP request
group	ipp_tag_t	The IPP group
tag	ipp_tag_t	The IPP value tag
name	const char *	The name of the attribute
charset	const char *	The character set for the string
value	const char *	The string value

Returns

A pointer to the new attribute or NULL if the attribute could not be created.

Description

The ippAddString() function adds a single string attribute value to the specified IPP request. For IPP_TAG_NAMELANG and IPP_TAG_TEXTLANG strings, the charset value is provided with the string to identify the string encoding used. Otherwise the charset value is ignored.

Example

```
#include <cups/ipp.h>

ipp_t *ipp;

ippAddString(ipp, IPP_TAG_OPERATION, IPP_TAG_NAME, "job-name",
            NULL, "abc123");
```

See Also

ippAddBoolean(), ippAddBooleans(), ippAddDate(), ippAddInteger(), ippAddIntegers(), ippAddRange(), ippAddRanges(), ippAddResolution(), ippAddResolutions(), ippAddSeparator(), ippAddStrings()

ippAddStrings()

Usage

```
ipp_attribute_t *
ippAddStrings(ipp_t      *ipp,
            ipp_tag_t  group,
            ipp_tag_t  tag,
            const char *name,
            int        num_values,
            const char *charset,
            const char **values);
```

Arguments

Argument	Type	Description
ipp	ipp_t *	The IPP request
group	ipp_tag_t	The IPP group
tag	ipp_tag_t	The IPP value tag
name	const char *	The name of the attribute
num_values	int	The number of string values

Argument	Type	Description
charset	const char *	The character set for the strings
values	const char **	The string values

Returns

A pointer to the new attribute or NULL if the attribute could not be created.

Description

The ippAddStrings() function adds one or more string attribute values to the specified IPP request. For IPP_TAG_NAMELANG and IPP_TAG_TEXTLANG strings, the charset value is provided with the strings to identify the string encoding used. Otherwise the charset value is ignored. If the values pointer is NULL then an array of NULL strings is created.

Example

```
#include <cups/ipp.h>

ipp_t *ipp;
char *values[2] = { "one", "two" };

ippAddStrings(ipp, IPP_TAG_OPERATION, IPP_TAG_KEYWORD, "attr-name",
          2, NULL, values);
```

See Also

ippAddBoolean(), ippAddBooleans(), ippAddDate(), ippAddInteger(), ippAddIntegers(), ippAddRange(), ippAddRanges(), ippAddResolution(), ippAddResolutions(), ippAddSeparator(), ippAddString()

ippDateToTime()

Usage

```
time_t
ippDateToTime(const ipp_uchar_t date[11]);
```

Arguments

Argument	Type	Description
date	const ipp_uchar_t [11]	The IPP date-time value

Returns

A Unix time value.

Description

The `ippDateToTime()` function converts an IPP date-time value to a Unix time value.

Example

```
#include <cups/ipp.h>

ipp_uchar_t date[11];

printf("UNIX time is %d\n", ippDateToTime(date));
```

See Also

```
ippTimeToDate()
```

ippDelete()

Usage

```
void
ippDelete(ipp_t *ipp);
```

Arguments

Argument	Type	Description
ipp	ipp_t *	The IPP request

Description

The `ippDelete()` function deletes all memory used by an IPP request or response.

Example

```
#include <cups/ipp.h>

ipp_t *ipp;

ippDelete(ipp);
```

See Also

ippNew()

ippFindAttribute()

Usage

```
ipp_attribute_t *
ippFindAttribute(ipp_t      *ipp,
                 const char *name,
                 ipp_tag_t  tag);
```

Arguments

Argument	Type	Description
ipp	ipp_t *	The IPP request
name	const char *	The IPP attribute name
tag	ipp_tag_t	The IPP value tag or IPP_TAG_ZERO for any type of value

Returns

A pointer to the first occurrence of the requested attribute, or NULL if it was not found.

Description

The ippFindAttribute() function finds the first occurrence of the named attribute. The tag parameter restricts the search to a specific value type. Use IPP_TAG_ZERO to find any value with the name.

The value tags IPP_TAG_NAME and IPP_TAG_TEXT match the values with or without a language component.

Example

```
ipp_attribute_t *attr;

attr = ippFindAttribute(response, "printer-state-message", IPP_TAG_TEXT);
```

See Also

cupsDoFileRequest(), cupsDoRequest(), ippDelete(), ippFindNextAttribute(), ippNew()

ippFindNextAttribute()

Usage

```
ipp_attribute_t *
ippFindNextAttribute(ipp_t       *ipp,
                     const char *name,
                     ipp_tag_t  tag);
```

Arguments

Argument	Type	Description
ipp	ipp_t *	The IPP request
name	const char *	The IPP attribute name
tag	ipp_tag_t	The IPP value tag or IPP_TAG_ZERO for any type of value

Returns

A pointer to the next occurrence of the requested attribute, or NULL if it was not found.

Description

The ippFindNextAttribute() function finds the next occurrence of the named attribute. The tag parameter restricts the search to a specific value type. Use IPP_TAG_ZERO to find any value with the name.

The value tags IPP_TAG_NAME and IPP_TAG_TEXT match the values with or without a language component.

Example

```
ipp_attribute_t *attr;

attr = ippFindNextAttribute(response, "printer-state-message", IPP_TAG_TEXT);
```

See Also

cupsDoFileRequest(), cupsDoRequest(), ippDelete(), ippFindAttribute(), ippNew()

ippLength()

Usage

```
int
ippLength(ipp_t *ipp);
```

Arguments

Argument	Type	Description
ipp	ipp_t *	The IPP request

Returns

The total encoded length of the IPP request or response in bytes.

Description

The ippLength() function returns the length of the IPP request or response in bytes.

Example

```
printf("The length of the response is %d bytes.\n", ippLength(response));
```

See Also

ippDelete(), ippNew()

ippNew()

Usage

```
ipp_t *
ippNew(void);
```

Returns

A pointer to a new IPP request or response.

Description

The ippNew() function creates a new IPP request or response.

Example

```
#include <cups/ipp.h>

ipp_t *ipp;

ipp = ippNew();
```

See Also

```
ippDelete()
```

ippPort()

Usage

```
int
ippPort(void);
```

Returns

The default TCP/IP port number for IPP requests.

Description

The ippPort() function returns the default IPP port number for requests.

Example

```
#include <cups/http.h>
#include <cups/ipp.h>

http_t *http;

http = httpConnect(cupsServer(), ippPort());
```

See Also

```
cupsServer(), ippSetPort()
```

ippRead()

Usage

```
ipp_state_t
ippRead(http_t *http,
        ipp_t   *ipp);
```

Arguments

Argument	Type	Description
http	http_t *	The HTTP connection
ipp	ipp_t *	The IPP request

Returns

The current read state.

Description

The ippRead() function reads IPP attributes from the specified HTTP connection. Programs should continue calling ippRead() until IPP_ERROR or IPP_DATA is returned.

Example

```
#include <cups/http.h>
#include <cups/ipp.h>

http_t *http;
ipp_t *ipp;
ipp_state_t status;

ipp = ippNew();

while ((status = ippRead(http, ipp)) != IPP_ERROR)
  if (status == IPP_DATA)
    break;

if (status == IPP_DATA)
{
  ... read additional non-IPP data using httpRead() ...
}
```

See Also

```
ippWrite()
```

ippSetPort()

Usage

```
void
ippSetPort(int port);
```

Arguments

Argument	Type	Description
port	int	The port number that is to be used

Description

The ippSetPort() function sets the default IPP port number for requests.

Example

```
#include <cups/http.h>
#include <cups/ipp.h>

...

ippSetPort(8631);
```

See Also

```
ippPort()
```

ippTimeToDate()

Usage

```
ipp_uchar_t *
ippTimeToDate(time_t time);
```

Arguments

Argument	Type	Description
time	time_t	The Unix time value

Returns

A static pointer to an IPP date-time value.

Description

The ippTimeToDate() function converts a Unix time to an IPP date-time value. The date value is overwritten by each call.

Example

```
#include <cups/ipp.h>

ipp_uchar_t *date;

date = ippTimeToDate(time(NULL));
```

See Also

ippDateToTime()

ippWrite()

Usage

```
ipp_state_t
ippWrite(http_t *http,
         ipp_t  *ipp);
```

Arguments

Argument	Type	Description
http	http_t *	The HTTP connection
ipp	ipp_t *	The IPP request

Returns

The current write state.

Description

The ippWrite() function writes IPP attributes to the specified HTTP connection.
Programs should continue calling ippWrite() until IPP_ERROR or IPP_DATA is returned.

Example

```
#include <cups/http.h>
#include <cups/ipp.h>

http_t *http;
ipp_t *ipp;
ipp_state_t status;

ipp = ippNew();
... add attributes ...

while ((status = ippWrite(http, ipp)) != IPP_ERROR)
  if (status == IPP_DATA)
    break;

if (status == IPP_DATA)
{
  ... read additional non-IPP data using httpWrite() ...
}
```

See Also

ippRead()

ppdClose()

Usage

```
void
ppdClose(ppd_file_t *ppd);
```

Arguments

Argument	Type	Description
ppd	ppd_file_t *	The PPD file

Description

The ppdClose() function frees all memory associated with the PPD file.

Example

```
#include <cups/ppd.h>

ppd_file_t *ppd;

ppdClose(ppd);
```

See Also

ppdOpen(), ppdOpenFd(), ppdOpenFile()

ppdConflicts()

Usage

```
int
ppdConflicts(ppd_file_t *ppd);
```

Arguments

Argument	Type	Description
ppd	ppd_file_t *	The PPD file

Returns

The number of option conflicts in the file.

Description

The ppdConflicts() function returns the number of conflicts with the currently selected (marked) options.

Example

```
#include <cups/ppd.h>

ppd_file_t *ppd;

printf("%d conflicts\n", ppdConflicts(ppd));
```

See Also

cupsMarkOptions(), ppdIsMarked(), ppdMarkDefaults(), ppdMarkOption()

ppdEmit()

Usage

```
int
ppdEmit(ppd_file_t    *ppd,
        FILE          *file,
        ppd_section_t section);
```

Arguments

Argument	Type	Description
ppd	ppd_file_t *	The PPD file
file	FILE *	The file to write to
section	ppd_section_t	The option section that is to be written

Returns

0 on success, -1 on error.

Description

The ppdEmit() function sends printer-specific option commands to the specified file.

Example

```
#include <cups/ppd.h>

ppd_file_t *ppd;

ppdEmit(ppd, stdout, PPD_ORDER_PAGE);
```

See Also

ppdEmitJCL(), ppdEmitFd()

ppdEmitFd()

Usage

```
int
ppdEmitFd(ppd_file_t    *ppd,
          int           fd,
          ppd_section_t section);
```

Arguments

Argument	Type	Description
ppd	ppd_file_t *	The PPD file
fd	int	The file descriptor that is to be written to
section	ppd_section_t	The option section that is to be written

Returns

0 on success, –1 on error.

Description

The ppdEmitFd() function sends printer-specific option commands to the specified file descriptor.

Example

```
#include <cups/ppd.h>

ppd_file_t *ppd;

ppdEmitFd(ppd, 1, PPD_ORDER_PAGE);
```

See Also

ppdEmit(), ppdEmitJCL()

ppdEmitJCL()

Usage

```
int
ppdEmitJCL(ppd_file_t    *ppd,
           FILE          *file,
           int           job_id,
           const char    *user,
           const char    *title);
```

Arguments

Argument	Type	Description
ppd	ppd_file_t *	The PPD file
file	FILE *	The file that is to be written to.
job_id	int	The job ID
user	const char *	The owner of the job
title	const char *	The title of the job

Returns

0 on success, –1 on error.

Description

The ppdEmitJCL() function sends printer-specific job control commands to the specified file. When a known JCL language is used by the PPD file, the job ID, username, and title of the job are included in the JCL commands.

Example

```
#include <cups/ppd.h>

...

ppd_file_t *ppd;

...

ppdEmitJCL(ppd, stdout, 123, "user", "title");
```

See Also

ppdEmit(), ppdEmitFd()

ppdFindChoice()

Usage

```
ppd_choice_t *
ppdFindChoice(ppd_option_t *option,
              const char   *choice);
```

Arguments

Argument	Type	Description
option	ppd_option_t *	A pointer to the option
choice	const char *	The name of the choice

Returns

A pointer to the choice data or NULL if the choice does not exist.

Description

The ppdFindChoice() function returns a pointer to the choice data for the specified option.

Example

```
#include <cups/ppd.h>

ppd_file_t *ppd;
ppd_option_t *option;
ppd_choice_t *choice;

option = ppdFindOption(ppd, "PageSize");
choice = ppdFindChoice(option, "Letter");
```

See Also

ppdFindMarkedChoice(), ppdFindOption()

ppdFindMarkedChoice()

Usage

```
ppd_choice_t *
ppdFindMarkedChoice(ppd_file_t *ppd,
                    const char *keyword);
```

Arguments

Argument	Type	Description
ppd	ppd_file_t *	The PPD file
keyword	const char *	The name of the option

Returns

A pointer to the choice data or NULL if the option does not exist or is not marked.

Description

The ppdFindMarkedChoice() function returns a pointer to the marked choice data for the specified option.

Example

```
#include <cups/ppd.h>

ppd_file_t *ppd;
ppd_choice_t *choice;

choice = ppdFindMarkedChoice(ppd, "PageSize");
```

See Also

ppdFindChoice(), ppdFindOption()

ppdFindOption()

Usage

```
ppd_option_t *
ppdFindOption(ppd_file_t *ppd,
              const char *keyword);
```

Arguments

Argument	Type	Description
ppd	ppd_file_t *	The PPD file
keyword	const char *	The name of the option

Returns

A pointer to the option data or NULL if the option does not exist.

Description

The ppdFindOption() function returns a pointer to the option data for the specified option.

Example

```
#include <cups/ppd.h>

ppd_file_t *ppd;
ppd_option_t *option;

option = ppdFindOption(ppd, "PageSize");
```

See Also

ppdFindChoice(), ppdFindMarkedChoice()

ppdIsMarked()

Usage

```
int
ppdIsMarked(ppd_file_t *ppd,
            const char *keyword,
            const char *choice);
```

Arguments

Argument	Type	Description
ppd	ppd_file_t *	The PPD file
keyword	const char *	The name of the option
choice	const char *	The name of the choice

Returns

1 if the choice is marked, 0 otherwise.

Description

The `ppdIsMarked()` function returns whether the specified option choice is marked.

Example

```
#include <cups/ppd.h>

ppd_file_t *ppd;

printf("Letter size %s selected.\n",
       ppdIsMarked(ppd, "PageSize", "Letter") ? "is" : "is not");
```

See Also

cupsMarkOptions(), ppdConflicts(), ppdIsMarked(), ppdMarkDefaults(), ppdMarkOption()

ppdMarkDefaults()

Usage

```
void
ppdMarkDefaults(ppd_file_t *ppd);
```

Arguments

Argument	Type	Description
ppd	ppd_file_t *	The PPD file

Description

The `ppdMarkDefaults()` function marks all of the default choices in the PPD file.

Example

```
#include <cups/ppd.h>

ppd_file_t *ppd;

ppdMarkDefaults(ppd);
```

See Also

cupsMarkOptions(), ppdConflicts(), ppdIsMarked(), ppdMarkDefaults(), ppdMarkOption()

ppdMarkOption()

Usage

```
int
ppdMarkOption(ppd_file_t *ppd,
              const char *keyword,
              const char *choice);
```

Arguments

Argument	Type	Description
ppd	ppd_file_t *	The PPD file
keyword	const char *	The name of the option
choice	const char *	The name of the choice

Returns

The number of conflicts in the PPD file.

Description

The ppdMarkOption() function marks the specified option choice.

Example

```
#include <cups/ppd.h>

ppd_file_t *ppd;

ppdMarkOption(ppd, "PageSize", "Letter");
```

See Also

cupsMarkOptions(), ppdConflicts(), ppdIsMarked(), ppdMarkDefaults(), ppdMarkOption()

ppdOpen()

Usage

```
ppd_file_t *
ppdOpen(FILE *file);
```

Arguments

Argument	Type	Description
file	FILE *	The file from which to read

Returns

A pointer to a PPD file structure or NULL if the PPD file could not be read.

Description

The ppdOpen() function reads a PPD file from the specified file into memory.

Example

```
#include <cups/ppd.h>

ppd_file_t *ppd;
FILE *file;

file = fopen("filename.ppd", "rb");
ppd = ppdOpen(file);
fclose(file);
```

See Also

ppdClose(), ppdOpenFd(), ppdOpenFile()

ppdOpenFd()

Usage

```
ppd_file_t *
ppdOpenFd(int fd);
```

Arguments

Argument	Type	Description
fd	int	The file descriptor from which to read

Returns

A pointer to a PPD file structure or NULL if the PPD file could not be read.

Description

The ppdOpenFd() function reads a PPD file from the specified file descriptor into memory.

Example

```
#include <cups/ppd.h>

ppd_file_t *ppd;
int        fd;

fd = open("filename.ppd", O_RDONLY);
ppd = ppdOpenFd(fd);
close(fd);
```

See Also

ppdClose(), ppdOpen(), ppdOpenFile()

ppdOpenFile()

Usage

```
ppd_file_t *
ppdOpenFile(const char *filename);
```

Arguments

Argument	Type	Description
filename	const char *	The file from which to read

Returns

A pointer to a PPD file structure or NULL if the PPD file could not be read.

Description

The ppdOpenFile() function reads a PPD file from the named file into memory.

Example

```
#include <cups/ppd.h>

ppd_file_t *ppd;

ppd = ppdOpenFile("filename.ppd");
```

See Also

ppdClose(), ppdOpen(), ppdOpenFd()

ppdPageLength()

Usage

```
float
ppdPageLength(ppd_file_t *ppd,
              const char *name);
```

Arguments

Argument	Type	Description
ppd	ppd_file_t *	The PPD file
name	const char *	The name of the media size

Returns

The length of the specified page size in points or 0 if the page size does not exist.

Description

The ppdPageLength() function returns the page length of the specified page size.

Example

```
#include <cups/ppd.h>

ppd_file_t *ppd;

printf("Length = %.0f\n", ppdPageLength(ppd, "Letter"));
```

See Also

ppdPageLength(), ppdPageSize(), ppdPageWidth()

ppdPageSize()

Usage

```
ppd_size_t *
ppdPageSize(ppd_file_t *ppd,
            const char *name);
```

Arguments

Argument	Type	Description
ppd	ppd_file_t *	The PPD file
name	const char *	The name of the media size

Returns

A pointer to the page size record of the specified page size in points or NULL if the page size does not exist.

Description

The ppdPageSize() function returns the page size record for the specified page size.

Example

```
#include <cups/ppd.h>

ppd_file_t *ppd;
ppd_size_t *size;
```

```
size = ppdPageSize(ppd, "Letter");
if (size != NULL)
{
  printf(" Width = %.0f\n", size->width);
  printf("Length = %.0f\n", size->length);
  printf("  Left = %.0f\n", size->left);
  printf(" Right = %.0f\n", size->right);
  printf("Bottom = %.0f\n", size->bottom);
  printf("   Top = %.0f\n", size->top);
}
```

See Also

ppdPageLength(), ppdPageWidth()

ppdPageWidth()

Usage

```
float
ppdPageWidth(ppd_file_t *ppd,
             const char *name);
```

Arguments

Argument	Type	Description
ppd	ppd_file_t *	The PPD file
name	const char *	The name of the media size

Returns

The width of the specified page size in points or 0 if the page size does not exist.

Description

The ppdPageWidth() function returns the page width of the specified page size.

Example

```
#include <cups/ppd.h>

ppd_file_t *ppd;

printf("Width = %.0f\n", ppdPageWidth(ppd, "Letter"));
```

See Also

ppdPageLength(), ppdPageSize()

**Common UNIX
Printing System
License Agreement**

Introduction

The Common UNIX Printing System™, ("CUPS™"), is provided under the GNU General Public License ("GPL") and GNU Library General Public License ("LGPL"), Version 2. A copy of these licenses follows this introduction.

The GNU LGPL applies to the CUPS API library, located in the cups subdirectory of the CUPS source distribution and in the /usr/include/cups directory and libcups.a, libcups.sl, or libcups.so files in the binary distributions.

The GNU GPL applies to the remainder of the CUPS distribution, including the pstoraster filter, which is based upon GNU Ghostscript 5.50, and the pdftops filter, which is based upon Xpdf 0.92.

For those not familiar with the GNU GPL, the license basically allows you to:

- Use the CUPS software at no charge.
- Distribute verbatim copies of the software in source or binary form.
- Sell verbatim copies of the software for a media fee, or sell support for the software.
- Distribute or sell printer drivers and filters that use CUPS so long as source code is made available under the GPL.

What this license *does not* allow you to do is make changes or add features to CUPS and then sell a binary distribution without source code. You must provide source code for any new drivers, changes, or additions to the software, and all code must be provided under the GPL or LGPL as appropriate.

The GNU LGPL relaxes the "link-to" restriction, allowing you to develop applications that use the CUPS API library under other licenses and/or conditions as appropriate for your application.

Trademarks

Easy Software Products has trademarked the Common UNIX Printing System, CUPS, and CUPS logo. These names and logos may be used freely in any direct port or binary distribution of CUPS. To use them in derivative products, please contract Easy Software Products for written permission. Our intention is to protect the value of these trademarks and ensure that any derivative product meets the same high-quality standards as the original.

Binary Distribution Rights

Easy Software Products also sells rights to the CUPS source code under a binary distribution license for vendors that are unable to release source code for their drivers, additions, and modifications to CUPS under the GNU GPL and LGPL. For information please contact us at the address shown earlier.

The Common UNIX Printing System provides a `pstoraster` filter that utilizes the GNU GhostScript 5.50 core to convert PostScript files into a stream of raster images. For binary distribution licensing of this software, please contact:

```
Miles Jones
Director of Marketing
Artifex Software Inc.
454 Las Gallinas Ave., Suite 108
San Rafael, CA 94903 USA
Voice: +1.415.492.9861
Fax: +1.415.492.9862
E-mail: info@arsoft.com
```

The `pdftops` filter is based on the Xpdf 0.92 software. For binary distribution licensing of this software, please contact:

```
Derek B. Noonburg
E-mail: derekn@foolabs.com
WWW: http://www.foolabs.com/xpdf/
```

Support

Easy Software Products sells software support for CUPS as well as a commercial printing product based on CUPS called ESP Print Pro. You can find out more at our Web site:

```
http://www.easysw.com
```

GNU GENERAL PUBLIC LICENSE

Version 2, June 1991

Copyright 1989, 1991 Free Software Foundation, Inc.

59 Temple Place, Suite 330, Boston, MA 02111-1307 USA

Everyone is permitted to copy and distribute verbatim copies of this license document, but changing it is not allowed.

Preamble

The licenses for most software are designed to take away your freedom to share and change it. By contrast, the GNU General Public License is intended to guarantee your freedom to share and change free software—to make sure the software is free for all its users. This General Public License applies to most of the Free Software Foundation's software and to any other program whose authors commit to using it. (Some other Free Software Foundation software is covered by the GNU Library General Public License instead.) You can apply it to your programs, too.

When we speak of free software, we are referring to freedom, not price. Our General Public Licenses are designed to make sure that you have the freedom to distribute copies of free software (and charge for this service if you wish), that you receive source code or can get it if you want it, that you can change the software or use pieces of it in new free programs, and that you know you can do these things.

To protect your rights, we need to make restrictions that forbid anyone to deny you these rights or ask you to surrender the rights. These restrictions translate to certain responsibilities for you if you distribute copies of the software, or if you modify it.

For example, if you distribute copies of such a program, whether gratis or for a fee, you must give the recipients all the rights that you have. You must make sure that they, too, receive or can get the source code. And you must show them these terms so they know their rights.

We protect your rights with two steps: (1) copyright the software, and (2) offer you this license which gives you legal permission to copy, distribute and/or modify the software.

Also, for each author's protection and ours, we want to make certain that everyone understands that there is no warranty for this free software. If the software is modified by someone else and passed on, we want its recipients to know that what they have is not the original, so that any problems introduced by others will not reflect on the original authors' reputations.

Finally, any free program is threatened constantly by software patents. We wish to avoid the danger that redistributors of a free program will individually obtain patent licenses, in effect making the program proprietary. To prevent this, we have made it clear that any patent must be licensed for everyone's free use or not licensed at all.

The precise terms and conditions for copying, distribution and modification follow.

GNU GENERAL PUBLIC LICENSE—TERMS AND CONDITIONS FOR COPYING, DISTRIBUTION, AND MODIFICATION

1. This License applies to any program or other work which contains a notice placed by the copyright holder saying it may be distributed under the terms of this General Public

License. The "Program," below, refers to any such program or work, and a "work based on the Program" means either the Program or any derivative work under copyright law: that is to say, a work containing the Program or a portion of it, either verbatim or with modifications and/or translated into another language. (Hereinafter, translation is included without limitation in the term "modification.") Each licensee is addressed as "you."

Activities other than copying, distribution, and modification are not covered by this License; they are outside its scope. The act of running the Program is not restricted, and the output from the Program is covered only if its contents constitute a work based on the Program (independent of having been made by running the Program). Whether that is true depends on what the Program does.

2. You may copy and distribute verbatim copies of the Program's source code as you receive it, in any medium, provided that you conspicuously and appropriately publish on each copy an appropriate copyright notice and disclaimer of warranty, keep intact all the notices that refer to this License and to the absence of any warranty, and give any other recipients of the Program a copy of this License along with the Program.

You may charge a fee for the physical act of transferring a copy, and you may at your option offer warranty protection in exchange for a fee.

3. You may modify your copy or copies of the Program or any portion of it, thus forming a work based on the Program, and copy and distribute such modifications or work under the terms of Section 1 above, provided that you also meet all these conditions:

  a. You must cause the modified files to carry prominent notices stating that you changed the files and the date of any change.

  b. You must cause any work that you distribute or publish, that in whole or in part contains or is derived from the Program or any part thereof, to be licensed as a whole at no charge to all third parties under the terms of this License.

  c. If the modified program normally reads commands interactively when run, you must cause it, when started running for such interactive use in the most ordinary way, to print or display an announcement including an appropriate copyright notice and a notice that there is no warranty (or else, saying that you provide a warranty) and that users may redistribute the program under these conditions, and telling the user how to view a copy of this License. (Exception: If the Program itself is interactive but does not normally print such an announcement, your work based on the Program is not required to print an announcement.)

These requirements apply to the modified work as a whole. If identifiable sections of that work are not derived from the Program, and can be reasonably considered independent and separate works in themselves, then this License, and its terms, do not apply to those sections when you distribute them as separate works. But when you distribute the same sections as part of a whole which is a work based on the Program, the distribution of the whole must be on the terms of this License, whose permissions for other licensees extend to the entire whole, and thus to each and every part regardless of who wrote it.

Thus, it is not the intent of this section to claim rights or contest your rights to work written entirely by you; rather, the intent is to exercise the right to control the distribution of derivative or collective works based on the Program.

In addition, mere aggregation of another work not based on the Program with the Program (or with a work based on the Program) on a volume of a storage or distribution medium does not bring the other work under the scope of this License.

4. You may copy and distribute the Program (or a work based on it, under Section 2) in object code or executable form under the terms of Sections 1 and 2 above provided that you also do one of the following:

    a. Accompany it with the complete corresponding machine-readable source code, which must be distributed under the terms of Sections 1 and 2 above on a medium customarily used for software interchange; or,

    b. Accompany it with a written offer, valid for at least three years, to give any third party, for a charge no more than your cost of physically performing source distribution, a complete machine-readable copy of the corresponding source code, to be distributed under the terms of Sections 1 and 2 above on a medium customarily used for software interchange; or,

    c. Accompany it with the information you received as to the offer to distribute corresponding source code. (This alternative is allowed only for noncommercial distribution and only if you received the program in object code or executable form with such an offer, in accord with Subsection b above.)

The source code for a work means the preferred form of the work for making modifications to it. For an executable work, complete source code means all the source code for all modules it contains, plus any associated interface definition files, plus the scripts used to control compilation and installation of the executable. However, as a special exception, the source code distributed need not include anything that is normally distributed (in either source or binary form) with the major components (compiler, kernel, and so on) of the operating system on which the executable runs, unless that component itself accompanies the executable.

If distribution of executable or object code is made by offering access to copy from a designated place, then offering equivalent access to copy the source code from the same place counts as distribution of the source code, even though third parties are not compelled to copy the source along with the object code.

5. You may not copy, modify, sublicense, or distribute the Program except as expressly provided under this License. Any attempt otherwise to copy, modify, sublicense or distribute the Program is void, and will automatically terminate your rights under this License. However, parties who have received copies, or rights, from you under this License will not have their licenses terminated so long as such parties remain in full compliance.

6. You are not required to accept this License, since you have not signed it. However, nothing else grants you permission to modify or distribute the Program or its derivative works. These actions are prohibited by law if you do not accept this License. Therefore, by modifying or distributing the Program (or any work based on the Program), you indicate your acceptance of this License to do so, and all its terms and conditions for copying, distributing or modifying the Program or works based on it.

7. Each time you redistribute the Program (or any work based on the Program), the recipient automatically receives a license from the original licensor to copy, distribute or modify the Program subject to these terms and conditions. You may not impose any further restrictions on the recipients' exercise of the rights granted herein. You are not responsible for enforcing compliance by third parties to this License.

8. If, as a consequence of a court judgment or allegation of patent infringement or for any other reason (not limited to patent issues), conditions are imposed on you (whether by court order, agreement or otherwise) that contradict the conditions of this License, they do not excuse you from the conditions of this License. If you cannot distribute so as to satisfy simultaneously your obligations under this License and any other pertinent obligations, then as a consequence you may not distribute the Program at all. For example, if a patent license would not permit royalty-free redistribution of the Program by all those who receive copies directly or indirectly through you, then the only way you could satisfy both it and this License would be to refrain entirely from distribution of the Program.

If any portion of this section is held invalid or unenforceable under any particular circumstance, the balance of the section is intended to apply and the section as a whole is intended to apply in other circumstances.

It is not the purpose of this section to induce you to infringe any patents or other property right claims or to contest validity of any such claims; this section has the sole purpose of protecting the integrity of the free software distribution system, which is implemented by public license practices. Many people have made generous contributions to the wide range of software distributed through that system in reliance on consistent application of that system; it is up to the author/donor to decide if he or she is willing to distribute software through any other system and a licensee cannot impose that choice.

This section is intended to make thoroughly clear what is believed to be a consequence of the rest of this License.

9. If the distribution and/or use of the Program is restricted in certain countries either by patents or by copyrighted interfaces, the original copyright holder who places the Program under this License may add an explicit geographical distribution limitation excluding those countries, so that distribution is permitted only in or among countries not thus excluded. In such case, this License incorporates the limitation as if written in the body of this License.

10. The Free Software Foundation may publish revised and/or new versions of the General Public License from time to time. Such new versions will be similar in spirit to the present version, but may differ in detail to address new problems or concerns.

Each version is given a distinguishing version number. If the Program specifies a version number of this License which applies to it and "any later version," you have the option of following the terms and conditions either of that version or of any later version published by the Free Software Foundation. If the Program does not specify a version number of this License, you may choose any version ever published by the Free Software Foundation.

11. If you wish to incorporate parts of the Program into other free programs whose distribution conditions are different, write to the author to ask for permission. For software which is copyrighted by the Free Software Foundation, write to the Free Software Foundation; we sometimes make exceptions for this. Our decision will be guided by the two goals of preserving the free status of all derivatives of our free software and of promoting the sharing and reuse of software generally.

NO WARRANTY

11. BECAUSE THE PROGRAM IS LICENSED FREE OF CHARGE, THERE IS NO WARRANTY FOR THE PROGRAM, TO THE EXTENT PERMITTED BY APPLICABLE LAW. EXCEPT WHEN OTHERWISE STATED IN WRITING THE COPYRIGHT HOLDERS AND/OR OTHER PARTIES PROVIDE THE PROGRAM "AS IS" WITHOUT WARRANTY OF ANY KIND, EITHER EXPRESSED OR IMPLIED, INCLUDING, BUT NOT LIMITED TO, THE IMPLIED WARRANTIES OF MERCHANTABILITY AND FITNESS FOR A PARTICULAR PURPOSE. THE ENTIRE RISK AS TO THE QUALITY AND PERFORMANCE OF THE PROGRAM IS WITH YOU. SHOULD THE PROGRAM PROVE DEFECTIVE, YOU ASSUME THE COST OF ALL NECESSARY SERVICING, REPAIR OR CORRECTION.

12. IN NO EVENT UNLESS REQUIRED BY APPLICABLE LAW OR AGREED TO IN WRITING WILL ANY COPYRIGHT HOLDER, OR ANY OTHER PARTY WHO MAY MODIFY AND/OR REDISTRIBUTE THE PROGRAM AS PERMITTED ABOVE, BE LIABLE TO YOU FOR DAMAGES, INCLUDING ANY GENERAL, SPECIAL, INCIDENTAL OR CONSEQUENTIAL DAMAGES ARISING OUT OF THE USE OR INABILITY TO USE THE PROGRAM (INCLUDING BUT NOT LIMITED TO LOSS OF DATA OR DATA BEING RENDERED INACCURATE OR LOSSES SUSTAINED BY YOU OR THIRD PARTIES OR A FAILURE OF THE PROGRAM TO OPERATE WITH ANY OTHER PROGRAMS), EVEN IF SUCH HOLDER OR OTHER PARTY HAS BEEN ADVISED OF THE POSSIBILITY OF SUCH DAMAGES.

END OF TERMS AND CONDITIONS

GNU LIBRARY GENERAL PUBLIC LICENSE

Version 2, June 1991

Copyright (C) 1991 Free Software Foundation, Inc.

59 Temple Place, Suite 330, Boston, MA 02111-1307, USA

Everyone is permitted to copy and distribute verbatim copies of this license document, but changing it is not allowed.

[This is the first released version of the library GPL. It is numbered 2 because it goes with version 2 of the ordinary GPL.]

Preamble

The licenses for most software are designed to take away your freedom to share and change it. By contrast, the GNU General Public Licenses are intended to guarantee your freedom to share and change free software—to make sure the software is free for all its users.

This license, the Library General Public License, applies to some specially designated Free Software Foundation software, and to any other libraries whose authors decide to use it. You can use it for your libraries, too.

When we speak of free software, we are referring to freedom, not price. Our General Public Licenses are designed to make sure that you have the freedom to distribute copies of free software (and charge for this service if you wish), that you receive source code or can get it if you want it, that you can change the software or use pieces of it in new free programs; and that you know you can do these things.

To protect your rights, we need to make restrictions that forbid anyone to deny you these rights or to ask you to surrender the rights. These restrictions translate to certain responsibilities for you if you distribute copies of the library, or if you modify it.

For example, if you distribute copies of the library, whether gratis or for a fee, you must give the recipients all the rights that we gave you. You must make sure that they, too, receive or can get the source code. If you link a program with the library, you must provide complete object files to the recipients so that they can relink them with the library, after making changes to the library and recompiling it. And you must show them these terms so they know their rights.

Our method of protecting your rights has two steps: (1) copyright the library, and (2) offer you this license which gives you legal permission to copy, distribute and/or modify the library.

Also, for each distributor's protection, we want to make certain that everyone understands that there is no warranty for this free library. If the library is modified by someone else and passed on, we want its recipients to know that what they have is not the original version, so that any problems introduced by others will not reflect on the original authors' reputations.

Finally, any free program is threatened constantly by software patents. We wish to avoid the danger that companies distributing free software will individually obtain patent licenses, thus in effect transforming the program into proprietary software. To prevent this, we have made it clear that any patent must be licensed for everyone's free use or not licensed at all.

Most GNU software, including some libraries, is covered by the ordinary GNU General Public License, which was designed for utility programs. This license, the GNU Library General Public License, applies to certain designated libraries. This license is quite different from the ordinary one; be sure to read it in full, and don't assume that anything in it is the same as in the ordinary license.

The reason we have a separate public license for some libraries is that they blur the distinction we usually make between modifying or adding to a program and simply using it. Linking a program with a library, without changing the library, is in some sense simply using the library, and is analogous to running a utility program or application program. However, in a textual and legal sense, the linked executable is a combined work, a derivative of the original library, and the ordinary General Public License treats it as such.

Because of this blurred distinction, using the ordinary General Public License for libraries did not effectively promote software sharing, because most developers did not use the libraries. We concluded that weaker conditions might promote sharing better.

However, unrestricted linking of non-free programs would deprive the users of those programs of all benefit from the free status of the libraries themselves. This Library General Public License is intended to permit developers of non-free programs to use free libraries, while preserving your freedom as a user of such programs to change the free libraries that are incorporated in them. (We have not seen how to achieve this as regards changes in header files, but we have achieved it as regards changes in the actual functions of the Library.) The hope is that this will lead to faster development of free libraries.

The precise terms and conditions for copying, distribution and modification follow. Pay close attention to the difference between a "work based on the library" and a "work that uses the library". The former contains code derived from the library, while the latter only works together with the library.

Note that it is possible for a library to be covered by the ordinary General Public License rather than by this special one.

TERMS AND CONDITIONS FOR COPYING, DISTRIBUTION AND MODIFICATION

0. This License Agreement applies to any software library which contains a notice placed by the copyright holder or other authorized party saying it may be distributed under the terms of this Library General Public License (also called "this License"). Each licensee is addressed as "you".

A "library" means a collection of software functions and/or data prepared so as to be conveniently linked with application programs (which use some of those functions and data) to form executables.

The "Library," below, refers to any such software library or work which has been distributed under these terms. A "work based on the Library" means either the Library or any derivative work under copyright law: that is to say, a work containing the Library or a portion of it, either verbatim or with modifications and/or translated straightforwardly into another language. (Hereinafter, translation is included without limitation in the term "modification.")

"Source code" for a work means the preferred form of the work for making modifications to it. For a library, complete source code means all the source code for all modules it contains, plus any associated interface definition files, plus the scripts used to control compilation and installation of the library.

Activities other than copying, distribution and modification are not covered by this License; they are outside its scope. The act of running a program using the Library is not restricted, and output from such a program is covered only if its contents constitute a work based on the Library (independent of the use of the Library in a tool for writing it). Whether that is true depends on what the Library does and what the program that uses the Library does.

1. You may copy and distribute verbatim copies of the Library's complete source code as you receive it, in any medium, provided that you conspicuously and appropriately publish on each copy an appropriate copyright notice and disclaimer of warranty, keep intact all the notices that refer to this License and to the absence of any warranty, and distribute a copy of this License along with the Library.

You may charge a fee for the physical act of transferring a copy, and you may at your option offer warranty protection in exchange for a fee.

2. You may modify your copy or copies of the Library or any portion of it, thus forming a work based on the Library, and copy and distribute such modifications or work under the terms of Section 1 above, provided that you also meet all of these conditions:

    a. The modified work must itself be a software library.

    b. You must cause the files modified to carry prominent notices stating that you changed the files and the date of any change.

c. You must cause the whole of the work to be licensed at no charge to all third parties under the terms of this License.

d. If a facility in the modified Library refers to a function or a table of data to be supplied by an application program that uses the facility, other than as an argument passed when the facility is invoked, then you must make a good faith effort to ensure that, in the event an application does not supply such function or table, the facility still operates, and performs whatever part of its purpose remains meaningful.

(For example, a function in a library to compute square roots has a purpose that is entirely well-defined independent of the application. Therefore, Subsection 2d requires that any application-supplied function or table used by this function must be optional: if the application does not supply it, the square root function must still compute square roots.)

These requirements apply to the modified work as a whole. If identifiable sections of that work are not derived from the Library, and can be reasonably considered independent and separate works in themselves, then this License, and its terms, do not apply to those sections when you distribute them as separate works. But when you distribute the same sections as part of a whole which is a work based on the Library, the distribution of the whole must be on the terms of this License, whose permissions for other licensees extend to the entire whole, and thus to each and every part regardless of who wrote it.

Thus, it is not the intent of this section to claim rights or contest your rights to work written entirely by you; rather, the intent is to exercise the right to control the distribution of derivative or collective works based on the Library.

In addition, mere aggregation of another work not based on the Library with the Library (or with a work based on the Library) on a volume of a storage or distribution medium does not bring the other work under the scope of this License.

3. You may opt to apply the terms of the ordinary GNU General Public License instead of this License to a given copy of the Library. To do this, you must alter all the notices that refer to this License, so that they refer to the ordinary GNU General Public License, version 2, instead of to this License. (If a newer version than version 2 of the ordinary GNU General Public License has appeared, then you can specify that version instead if you wish.) Do not make any other change in these notices.

Once this change is made in a given copy, it is irreversible for that copy, so the ordinary GNU General Public License applies to all subsequent copies and derivative works made from that copy.

This option is useful when you wish to copy part of the code of the Library into a program that is not a library.

4. You may copy and distribute the Library (or a portion or derivative of it, under Section 2) in object code or executable form under the terms of Sections 1 and 2 above provided that you accompany it with the complete corresponding machine-readable source code, which must be distributed under the terms of Sections 1 and 2 above on a medium customarily used for software interchange.

If distribution of object code is made by offering access to copy from a designated place, then offering equivalent access to copy the source code from the same place satisfies the requirement to distribute the source code, even though third parties are not compelled to copy the source along with the object code.

5. A program that contains no derivative of any portion of the Library, but is designed to work with the Library by being compiled or linked with it, is called a "work that uses the Library." Such a work, in isolation, is not a derivative work of the Library, and therefore falls outside the scope of this License.

However, linking a "work that uses the Library" with the Library creates an executable that is a derivative of the Library (because it contains portions of the Library), rather than a "work that uses the library." The executable is therefore covered by this License. Section 6 states terms for distribution of such executables.

When a "work that uses the Library" uses material from a header file that is part of the Library, the object code for the work may be a derivative work of the Library even though the source code is not. Whether this is true is especially significant if the work can be linked without the Library, or if the work is itself a library. The threshold for this to be true is not precisely defined by law.

If such an object file uses only numerical parameters, data structure layouts and accessors, and small macros and small inline functions (ten lines or less in length), then the use of the object file is unrestricted, regardless of whether it is legally a derivative work. (Executables containing this object code plus portions of the Library will still fall under Section 6.)

Otherwise, if the work is a derivative of the Library, you may distribute the object code for the work under the terms of Section 6. Any executables containing that work also fall under Section 6, whether or not they are linked directly with the Library itself.

6. As an exception to the Sections above, you may also compile or link a "work that uses the Library" with the Library to produce a work containing portions of the Library, and distribute that work under terms of your choice, provided that the terms permit modification of the work for the customer's own use and reverse engineering for debugging such modifications.

You must give prominent notice with each copy of the work that the Library is used in it and that the Library and its use are covered by this License. You must supply a copy of this License. If the work during execution displays copyright notices, you must include the copyright notice for the Library among them, as well as a reference directing the user to the copy of this License. Also, you must do one of these things:

a. Accompany the work with the complete corresponding machine-readable source code for the Library including whatever changes were used in the work (which must be distributed under Sections 1 and 2 above); and, if the work is an executable linked with the Library, with the complete machine-readable "work that uses the Library," as object code and/or source code, so that the user can modify the Library and then relink to produce a modified executable containing the modified Library. (It is understood that the user who changes the contents of definitions files in the Library will not necessarily be able to recompile the application to use the modified definitions.)

b. Accompany the work with a written offer, valid for at least three years, to give the same user the materials specified in Subsection 6a, above, for a charge no more than the cost of performing this distribution.

c. If distribution of the work is made by offering access to copy from a designated place, offer equivalent access to copy the above-specified materials from the same place.

d. Verify that the user has already received a copy of these materials or that you have already sent this user a copy.

For an executable, the required form of the "work that uses the Library" must include any data and utility programs needed for reproducing the executable from it. However, as a special exception, the source code distributed need not include anything that is normally distributed (in either source or binary form) with the major components (compiler, kernel, and so on) of the operating system on which the executable runs, unless that component itself accompanies the executable.

It may happen that this requirement contradicts the license restrictions of other proprietary libraries that do not normally accompany the operating system. Such a contradiction means you cannot use both them and the Library together in an executable that you distribute.

7. You may place library facilities that are a work based on the Library side by side in a single library together with other library facilities not covered by this License, and distribute such a combined library, provided that the separate distribution of the work based on the Library and of the other library facilities is otherwise permitted, and provided that you do these two things:

a. Accompany the combined library with a copy of the same work based on the Library, uncombined with any other library facilities. This must be distributed under the terms of the Sections above.

b. Give prominent notice with the combined library of the fact that part of it is a work based on the Library, and explaining where to find the accompanying uncombined form of the same work.

8. You may not copy, modify, sublicense, link with, or distribute the Library except as expressly provided under this License. Any attempt otherwise to copy, modify, sublicense, link with, or distribute the Library is void, and will automatically terminate your rights under this License. However, parties who have received copies, or rights, from you under this License will not have their licenses terminated so long as such parties remain in full compliance.

9. You are not required to accept this License, since you have not signed it. However, nothing else grants you permission to modify or distribute the Library or its derivative works. These actions are prohibited by law if you do not accept this License. Therefore, by modifying or distributing the Library (or any work based on the Library), you indicate your acceptance of this License to do so, and all its terms and conditions for copying, distributing or modifying the Library or works based on it.

10. Each time you redistribute the Library (or any work based on the Library), the recipient automatically receives a license from the original licensor to copy, distribute, link with or modify the Library subject to these terms and conditions. You may not impose any further restrictions on the recipients' exercise of the rights granted herein. You are not responsible for enforcing compliance by third parties to this License.

11. If, as a consequence of a court judgment or allegation of patent infringement or for any other reason (not limited to patent issues), conditions are imposed on you (whether by court order, agreement or otherwise) that contradict the conditions of this License, they do not excuse you from the conditions of this License. If you cannot distribute so as to satisfy simultaneously your obligations under this License and any other pertinent obligations, then as a consequence you may not distribute the Library at all. For example, if a patent license would not permit royalty-free redistribution of the Library by all those who receive copies directly or indirectly through you, then the only way you could satisfy both it and this License would be to refrain entirely from distribution of the Library.

If any portion of this section is held invalid or unenforceable under any particular circumstance, the balance of the section is intended to apply, and the section as a whole is intended to apply in other circumstances.

It is not the purpose of this section to induce you to infringe any patents or other property right claims or to contest validity of any such claims; this section has the sole purpose of protecting the integrity of the free software distribution system which is implemented by public license practices. Many people have made generous contributions to the wide range of software distributed through that system in reliance on consistent application of that system; it is up to the author/donor to decide if he or she is willing to distribute software through any other system and a licensee cannot impose that choice.

This section is intended to make thoroughly clear what is believed to be a consequence of the rest of this License.

12. If the distribution and/or use of the Library is restricted in certain countries either by patents or by copyrighted interfaces, the original copyright holder who places the Library under this License may add an explicit geographical distribution limitation excluding those

countries, so that distribution is permitted only in or among countries not thus excluded. In such case, this License incorporates the limitation as if written in the body of this License.

13. The Free Software Foundation may publish revised and/or new versions of the Library General Public License from time to time. Such new versions will be similar in spirit to the present version, but may differ in detail to address new problems or concerns.

Each version is given a distinguishing version number. If the Library specifies a version number of this License which applies to it and "any later version", you have the option of following the terms and conditions either of that version or of any later version published by the Free Software Foundation. If the Library does not specify a license version number, you may choose any version ever published by the Free Software Foundation.

14. If you wish to incorporate parts of the Library into other free programs whose distribution conditions are incompatible with these, write to the author to ask for permission. For software which is copyrighted by the Free Software Foundation, write to the Free Software Foundation; we sometimes make exceptions for this. Our decision will be guided by the two goals of preserving the free status of all derivatives of our free software and of promoting the sharing and reuse of software generally.

NO WARRANTY

15. BECAUSE THE LIBRARY IS LICENSED FREE OF CHARGE, THERE IS NO WARRANTY FOR THE LIBRARY, TO THE EXTENT PERMITTED BY APPLICABLE LAW. EXCEPT WHEN OTHERWISE STATED IN WRITING THE COPYRIGHT HOLDERS AND/OR OTHER PARTIES PROVIDE THE LIBRARY "AS IS" WITHOUT WARRANTY OF ANY KIND, EITHER EXPRESSED OR IMPLIED, INCLUDING, BUT NOT LIMITED TO, THE IMPLIED WARRANTIES OF MERCHANTABILITY AND FITNESS FOR A PARTICULAR PURPOSE. THE ENTIRE RISK AS TO THE QUALITY AND PERFORMANCE OF THE LIBRARY IS WITH YOU. SHOULD THE LIBRARY PROVE DEFECTIVE, YOU ASSUME THE COST OF ALL NECESSARY SERVICING, REPAIR OR CORRECTION.

16. IN NO EVENT UNLESS REQUIRED BY APPLICABLE LAW OR AGREED TO IN WRITING WILL ANY COPYRIGHT HOLDER, OR ANY OTHER PARTY WHO MAY MODIFY AND/OR REDISTRIBUTE THE LIBRARY AS PERMITTED ABOVE, BE LIABLE TO YOU FOR DAMAGES, INCLUDING ANY GENERAL, SPECIAL, INCIDENTAL OR CONSEQUENTIAL DAMAGES ARISING OUT OF THE USE OR INABILITY TO USE THE LIBRARY (INCLUDING BUT NOT LIMITED TO LOSS OF DATA OR DATA BEING RENDERED INACCURATE OR LOSSES SUSTAINED BY YOU OR THIRD PARTIES OR A FAILURE OF THE LIBRARY TO OPERATE WITH ANY OTHER SOFTWARE), EVEN IF SUCH HOLDER OR OTHER PARTY HAS BEEN ADVISED OF THE POSSIBILITY OF SUCH DAMAGES.

END OF TERMS AND CONDITIONS

Index

O